RACISM ON CAMPUS

Drawing on content from yearbooks published by prominent colleges in Virginia, this book explores changes in race relations that have occurred at universities in the United States since the late 19th century. It juxtaposes the content published in predominantly White university yearbooks to that published by Howard University, a historically Black college. The study is a work of visual sociology, with photographs, line drawings and historical prints that provide a visual account of the institutional racism that existed at these colleges over time. It employs Bonilla-Silva's concept of structural racism to shed light on how race ordered all aspects of social life on campuses from the period of post–Civil War Reconstruction to the present. It examines the lives of the Black men and women who worked at these schools and the racial attitudes of the White men and women who attended them. As such, *Racism on Campus* will appeal to scholars of sociology, history and anthropology with interests in race, racism and visual methods.

Stephen C. Poulson is Professor of Sociology at James Madison University, USA. He is the author of *Why Would Anyone Do That? Lifestyle Sport in the Twenty-First Century* and *Social Movements in Twentieth-Century Iran: Culture, Ideology and Mobilizing Frameworks.*

D1206649

RACISM ON CAMPUS

A Visual History of Prominent Virginia Colleges and Howard University

Stephen C. Poulson

Routledge
Taylor & Francis Group

LONDON AND NEW YORK

First published 2022
by Routledge
2 Park Square, Milton Park, Abingdon, Oxon OX14 4RN

and by Routledge
605 Third Avenue, New York, NY 10158

Routledge is an imprint of the Taylor & Francis Group, an informa business

British Library Cataloguing-in-Publication Data
A catalogue record for this book is available from the British Library

Library of Congress Cataloging-in-Publication Data
Names: Poulson, Stephen C., 1966- author.
Title: Racism on campus : a visual history of prominent Virginia
colleges and Howard University / Stephen C. Poulson.
Description: Abingdon, Oxon ; New York, NY : Routledge, 2021. |
Includes bibliographical references and index.
Identifiers: LCCN 2021013336 (print) | LCCN 2021013337 (ebook) |
ISBN 9780367681579 (hardback) | ISBN 9780367681562 (paperback) |
ISBN 9781003134480 (ebook)
Subjects: LCSH: Howard University. | Racism in higher education—
Virginia. | Racism in higher education—Washington (D.C.) | College
integration—Virginia. | College integration—Washington (D.C.) |
Universities and colleges—Virginia. | Visual sociology—United States. |
Educational sociology—United States. | Virginia—Race
relations—History. | Washington (D.C.)—Race relations—History.
Classification: LCC LC212.422.V57 P68 2021 (print) |
LCC LC212.422.V57 (ebook) | DDC 379.2/609755—dc23
LC record available at https://lccn.loc.gov/2021013336
LC ebook record available at https://lccn.loc.gov/2021013337

ISBN: 978-0-367-68157-9 (hbk)
ISBN: 978-0-367-68156-2 (pbk)
ISBN: 978-1-003-13448-0 (ebk)

DOI: 10.4324/9781003134480

Typeset in Bembo Std
by KnowledgeWorks Global Ltd.

For

John Lewis, Congressman and Civil Rights activist who passed away in 2020

&

With appreciation for the university librarians, archivists and support staff who made this study possible

CONTENTS

COLOR PLATES

FIGURES

ACKNOWLEDGMENTS

The Sociology and Anthropology Department and College of Arts and Letters at James Madison University offered financial support used to secure the high-quality copies of the Howard University yearbook material. Also, three particularly diligent James Madison University students—Tyler Wolfe, Hailey McGee and Kira Lambert—did much, most, or all of the coding of the James Madison University, Washington and Lee University and Virginia Military Institute yearbooks. Another James Madison University colleague, Matt Ezzell, provided valuable feedback on the opening chapters. Christine Poulson gave the text a thorough reading and offered many insightful comments.

This study was made possible by a small army of librarians, archivists and library staff—there are too many to name all of them—who have created and now maintain the online digital archives of university yearbooks, photographs and advertising that were vital to undertaking this study. While all the visual material in this text is available online, many of these professionals further assisted me by making high-quality copies from their physical yearbook archives that were reproduced in this text. All the previous was done during the Covid-19 pandemic that often made access to library material sometimes more difficult, at times when there were fewer student and graduate assistants available.

The institutions and collections that provided the archived pictures, paintings and drawings for this study are listed below.

The Boston Public Library, through Digital Commonwealth, provided the material used in Figures 1.2, 1.3, 1.4 and 2.1. A few of these are from a very interesting trading card collection.

The United States Library of Congress, Prints and Photographs Division, provided the image of *The Battle of Chancellorsville* print in Color Plate 1 and the picture of Peter Briggs, later rendered into a postcard, on the UVA campus in Figure 2.22.

The George Mason University Library Special Collections Research Center maintains the *Advocate* yearbook digital archive. Material in Figures 4.12 and 5.8 were provided by the library as a courtesy.

The Hampden-Sydney College Bortz Library provides online access to the *Kaleidoscope* yearbooks. Figures 4.7, 4.18, 4.23, 4.24 and Color Plate 8 were provided as a courtesy from the library.

The Howard University Library and Moorland-Spingarn Research Center maintains *The Bison, The Mirror, The Howard University Yearbook* and the *NIKH* in their digital yearbook archive. Figures 3.2, 3.4, 3.5, 3.6, 3.7, 5.1, 5.2, 5.3, 5.4, 5.5 and 5.6 were provided courtesy of the Manuscript Division of the Moorland-Spingarn Research Center.

James Madison University Library and Educational Technologies maintains the *Schoolma'am* and *The Bluestone* yearbook digital archive. The library provided material used in this study as a courtesy, and it appears in Figures 2.27, 2.29, 4.11, 4.16, 5.9, 5.13, 5.15.

Old Dominion University Library, though a Digital Commons, maintains the *Troubadour, The Laureate* and *The Chieftain* yearbooks archive. The library provided material used in this study as a courtesy and is included in Figures 4.20 and 5.14 and Color Plate 6.

The University of Richmond Scholarship Repository maintains *The Spider* and *The Web* yearbook archives. The UR Library provided material used in this study as a courtesy that is included in Figures 2.5, 2.16, and 4.22.

The University of Virginia Special Collections Library maintains the *Corks the Curls* yearbook digital archive. Material in this study provided courtesy of the library includes Color Plates 2 and 3 and Figures 2.2, 2.3, 2.4, 2.8, 2.13, 2.14, 2.20, 2.21, 2.25, 2.26, 4.8, 4.19, 5.11 and 5.12. The UVA Albert and Shirley Small Special Collections Library maintains the Holsinger Studio Collection and provided the picture used in Figure 2.24. The Visual History Collection from the UVA library provided the picture used in Figure 2.23.

The Virginia Commonwealth University Library, Digital Collections, maintains the online archive of *The X-Ray* yearbooks, which were originally issued by the Medical College of Virginia (MCV). Material in this study provided as a courtesy of the library is included in Figures 2.9, 2.10, 2.11, 2.12, 2.15, 2.18, and 2.19

The Virginia Commonwealth University Library also maintains a digital archive of pictures from the 1963 Farmville, Virginia, Civil Rights protest that were provided courtesy of the library and are included in Figures 4.1 and 4.2.

The Virginia Military Institute Library and Archives maintains *The Bomb* yearbook digital archive. Material in this study provided courtesy of the library is included in Figures 4.5, 4.6, 4.9, 4.10, 4.13, 4.14, an 4.17 and Color Plates 5 and 7.

The Virginia Tech Library archives maintains *The Bugle* yearbook digital archive. Material in this study provided courtesy of the library is included in Figure 5.7.

The Washington and Lee University Library Special Collection and Archives maintains *The Calyx* yearbook digital archive. Material in this study was provided courtesy of the W&L library and archives and is included in Figures 2.6, 2.7, 2.17, 2.28, 2.30, 4.15 4.21, and 5.10 and Color Plate 4.

1

USING VISUAL SOCIOLOGY TO STUDY INSTITUTIONAL RACISM AT VIRGINIA UNIVERSITIES

This inquiry was inspired by a scandal in 2019 when it was discovered that Virginia Governor Ralph Northam's Eastern Virginia Medical School yearbook page featured a man represented in blackface standing beside another costumed as a member of the Ku Klux Klan—the KKK (see Figure 1.1). After this picture was discovered there was a rush of ad hoc investigations by news organizations that examined university yearbooks throughout the United States (Murphy 2019). It was quickly found that blackface, and other racialized imagery, was common. Along the way, pictures of prominent public officials in blackface— Prime Minister of Canada Justin Trudeau, for example—were also discovered (Carlisle and Kambhampaty 2019).

During this period I decided a more systematic exploration of annual yearbooks could be extraordinary useful in capturing institutional norms and changes associated with race relation at universities throughout the country. Given this potential, it was remarkable so few studies had previously investigated yearbook content (Panayotidis and Stortz 2008; Caudill 2007; Nehls 2002). As a result, with a group of James Madison University (JMU) students, I began content-analyzing yearbooks published by 11 prominent Virginia schools: The University of Virginia (UVA), Virginia Commonwealth University (VCU), Old Dominion University (ODU), Washington and Lee University (W&L), Longwood College, Hampden-Sydney College, The University of Richmond (UR), Virginia Military Institute (VMI), George Mason University (GMU), James Madison University (JMU) and Virginia Tech (VPI). Most of these schools began publishing annual yearbooks in the 1880s and 1890s.

The work later became related to the Black Lives Matter protest that occurred in the United States during the following summer of 2020. While those protests began as demonstrations against police brutality, in Virginia, they precipitated

DOI: 10.4324/9781003134480-1

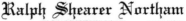

Alma Mater: Virginia Military Institute
Interest: Pediatrics
Quote: There are more old drunks than old
doctors in this world so I think I'll have
another beer.

105

FIGURE 1.1 Virginia Governor Ralph Northam's personal page in the 1984 edition of the Eastern Virginia Medical School yearbook. The discovery of these pictures caused a scandal in Virginia (in 2019) in which many called for Northam to resign. Similar content was published in other annual yearbooks until the current president of the university, Dr. Homan, ended the "tradition" in 2014.

a broader discussion about systemic racism in the state. While this is an academic inquiry, I became far more motivated to produce this text because of its direct relevance to ongoing debates taking place at public and private colleges in Virginia. The yearbooks examined in this study were first issued in the 1880s and 1890s, and they document the preoccupation that White Virginians at elite schools had with ordering race relations. They also indicate continuing racism and resistance to desegregation well into the 1960s.

The schools in this study include prominent public universities (such as UVA and VPI) and well-regarded private colleges (W&L, Longwood College and Hampden-Sydney College). Most of these schools began as same-sex institutions—JMU, for example, was initially founded as a state Normal School for women—that later transitioned into coeducational institutions. Originally, the intention was to also include the historically Black colleges and universities (HBCUs) in Virginia, but none had digitalized their yearbook collections for easy online access. But Howard University, considered a flagship HBCU located in nearby Washington, DC, does have a reasonably complete digital archive of its yearbooks, so this content was added in order to make a comparison between the White Virginia colleges and a prominent HBCU.

This study shows how academic life in Virginia—particularly the period in the late 19th century when these yearbooks were first issued—was intimately associated with a strict ordering of race relations between White and Black society. It documents how issues of race were often a preoccupation among the administrators, faculty, staff and students who matriculated at these schools. This ordering of race relations was reflected in the most mundane interactions of people on college campuses—most often when the almost entirely Black staff literally served and supported an entirely White student body and faculty. But even more so, race rules and racial caricature saturated all the routine acts associated with college life—from campus entertainment (during minstrel productions, when choral groups routinely performed in blackface, when the Robert E. Lee Literary Society sponsored public readings etc.) to campus sporting events (when the Virginia schools refused to compete against teams with Black players). Further, many of the prominent alumni of these schools—the men these yearbooks were often dedicated too—were often proponents, known nationwide, for maintaining racial segregation in the so-called New South (see chapter 2).

This study also chronicles the degree to which these institutions were culpable in incubating and maintaining racial norms in the South and nationwide. Often, institutions of higher learning are regarded as places where enlightened ideals are introduced and earnestly discussed among faculty and students. These institutions are thought of as places where social injustices are examined and then addressed—within the institution—with the goal of creating a more just and equitable society. While this was clearly the case at Howard University, there is really no indication that any Virginia institutions played this role associated with improving race relations until the 1970s. Of course, there were lonely voices on many of these campuses that pushed against the most egregious forms of racial hatred and bigotry, but what these yearbooks indicate is a deep and intransigent ordering of race relations that was actively maintained by faculty and students and then actively disseminated into wider society for most of these institutions' histories. This was particularly the case for institutions with law schools, such as the University of Virginia (UVA) and Washington and Lee College (W&L).

Put simply, these institutions—with the exception of Howard University— were not usually vehicles of positive social change associated with race relations. They were, in fact, among the staunchest advocates for maintaining the status quo. They did not often institute racial reforms from within—they desegregated largely when forced by federal authorities, federal courts and professional associations in law and medicine. And even then, they did so grudgingly. In short, these institutions were, when compared to many of their peers nationwide, among the last to eliminate the most egregious forms of racism that existed on these campuses until well into the 1960s. And even when changes in policy were finally implemented—when a few Black students were admitted to these colleges (beginning in the 1950s)—there was still considerable resistance to challenging the informal race norms (e.g. desegregating fraternities) that remained on these campuses.

The importance of Virginia politics in American racial history

Virginia is an ideal state in terms of examining the broader racial history of the United States. Prominent Virginians such as George Washington, Thomas Jefferson and James Madison are often credited with shaping a uniquely American system of democratic governance. One school in this study is named after James Madison. Another, the University of Virginia, was founded by Thomas Jefferson. Undoubtedly, events of national significance occurred in the state. Jamestown, Virginia, for example, is the site of the first successful American colony—and also where the first enslaved workers were brought into the region. Not far from there is the Yorktown Battlefield, where George Washington's improbable victory over General Cornwallis essentially ended the Revolutionary War. Afterward, beginning with George Washington and ending with Zachery Taylor, seven of the first 11 US presidents were Virginians.

But if the state has had an outsize influence on the early political events of the country, surely this influence extends to the problematic area of race relations too. For example, all seven of the early Virginia Presidents—from George Washington to Zachery Taylor—owned slaves too. Indeed, electing slave-holding Virginians has sometimes been characterized as strategy to help politicians in the slave-holding Southern states better accept allegiance to the national union. The last US president born in Virginia was Woodrow Wilson. During his lifetime Wilson was considered a progressive reformer despite the fact that he was also, as many White Virginians were during this period, an admirer of the Ku Klux Klan (KKK). During his presidency his progressive politics did not extend to race relations, as he worked diligently to purge the federal government of Black public officials and Black professional staff (Yellen 2013).

Probably most associated with the creation of America's racial politics is the central role of Virginia politics before, during and after the Civil War. Indeed, Virginia has long been considered the demarcation point between the slave-holding and non-slave-holding states. It is the state where, in the cultural and political memory of Americans, "the South" begins. Richmond, Virginia—currently the state capital—was the capital of the Confederate states during the American Civil War. More Civil War battles were fought in Virginia than in any other state. Currently, Virginia has the most edifices—schools, buildings, courthouses, monuments, statues and the like—dedicated to leaders of the failed Confederacy ("Whose Heritage?" 2019).

The early yearbooks examined in this study were produced when historical narratives associated with the "Lost Cause of the Confederacy" were particularly resonant throughout the entire United States (see chapter 2). This mythology later became explicitly linked to a political drive to legislate racial purity in Virginia. During this period the University of Virginia became a national center for the pseudo-scientific study of eugenics (Dorr 2008). This scholarship later became integral to the passing of Virginia's infamous 1924 Racial Integrity Act enacted to prevent miscegenation, more commonly referred to as "race mixing" (see chapter 2). Meant to preserve White racial integrity, it made inter-racial marriage illegal in Virginia until the US Supreme Court, in the 1967 *Loving v. Virginia* case, ruled it unconstitutional.

The other problematic racial history closely associated with Virginia was its response to the 1954 *Brown v. Board of Education of Topeka* decision that deseg-regated American public schools. Two colleges in this study are located in, and a couple miles from, the community of Farmville, Virginia, whose segregated public schools were directly addressed in the *Brown* decision. Notably, rather than accept the Supreme Court decision the state of Virginia instead engaged in a campaign of "massive resistance" to school desegregation. In the case of Farmville and surrounding Prince Edward County, officials actually closed its public schools rather than comply with the court order to desegregate (see chapter 4). Some Virginia colleges in this study did not accept a Black student until 1968.

A brief note on yearbook portrayal of other ethnic groups

Other racial and ethnic groups are negatively portrayed in yearbooks, but space here does not permit a thorough examination of this content. This is particularly the case as relates to the portrayal of Native American and East Asian (mostly Chinese) peoples. And unlike Black Americans, the construction of Native American and Asian ethnic identity was done almost entirely in the absence of any meaningful contact with these peoples, as neither Native Americans nor Asian Americans have worked at or attended these schools in large numbers during most of the period examined. Despite this, there were periods when yearbook content did reflect a greater preoccupation with defining and charac-terizing these groups too. This was more so the case at the few colleges located in areas that once had prominent Native American tribal groups such as in the Tidewater region—an area of eastern Virginia proximate to the James River and Chesapeake Bay. While most tribes from this region had long been dispersed, it was clear that past history made the ongoing construction of Native American identity a more likely enterprise at many of these schools. Indeed, the expropri-ation of Native American culture by elite White students—done in the absence of any meaningful knowledge of the history and culture of these tribes—allowed them extraordinary latitude in quite literally making up imaginary "Indians." Often, this was accomplished through the adoption of Native American mascots. Here, William and Mary University, the oldest college in the country, is exem-plary in that the school mascot transitioned from a slew of "Indian" names (e.g. the Braves) and mascots (including an "Indian Pony") that sometimes referred to different sporting teams until the more generic "Indians" was adopted for all teams. Eventually, the school settled on "The Tribe" for its sporting nick-name, which remains to this day. Another example is that there were periods when the yearbooks issued by Old Dominion University (*The Pow Wow* and *The*

Chieftain) and Virginia Commonwealth University (*The Wigwam*) directly referenced Native American culture.

Literature review

The primary anchor for this inquiry is Eduardo Bonilla-Silva's (1997) concept of structural racism. Here, "the social relations between the races become institutionalized (forming a structure as well as a culture)" that affects and orders the social life of all people within a society. This is true irrespective of the "personal feelings" people have toward those of different races (473). Here, race clearly structured the lives of the Black men and women who worked at these schools and the White men and women who attended them. Obviously, schools represent a social structure, among the most influential, that teaches citizens how they should interpret events in the wider world. And clearly university life reflects cultural norms expressed by elite interests at the time. But these institutions should also be regarded as "incubators" and "hubs" of racial meaning and racial policy (Stevens, Armstrong and Arum 2008, 140)—places where White students literally learned how to further align the meaning of race during their formal studies and during routine interactions with Black staff on campus.

Scholars of education have investigated the extent to which universities can act as incubators (of social ties), temples (to legitimate knowledge), sieves (as related to social stratification) and hubs (places were various social sectors interact) (127–151). This inquiry explores racial stratification at universities in Virginia, but it also examines the fact that these institutions often acted as incubators, temples and hubs for the dissemination of "race rules" and "race facts" that ordered relations throughout Virginia. For example, during much of the early period investigated these universities were clearly sieves—places where the Southern White elite sent mostly men to be educated. Some may insist that these institutions are largely reflections of dominant intellectual and cultural norms associated with race relations at the time, but this text presents evidence that faculty and students at these institutions actively shaped these norms as experts in their fields and as current and future community leaders. As such, identifying cultural tropes associated with race on university campuses provides evidence of how these norms were maintained by elite interests within the wider society.

Sociological studies of higher education during this early period have largely been neglected. Further, inquiries into racial policy have been somewhat obscured by recent modest increases associated with class mobility and access to higher education. For example, in Steven, Armstrong and Arum's (2008) widely cited review of studies of higher education there is no mention of periods when Black men and women were most often excluded (as students) from most universities in the country. But the authors do assert that "historically, U.S. elites have been unable to agree fully on the proper relationship between higher education and class exclusion" (140). Here, with respect to racial exclusion of Black men and women, there was no ambiguity in the South among elite interests as to their proper relationship within institutions of higher education. In fact, the relationship was quite clear: Black labor was essential for the maintenance of institutions where an elite White student body was groomed and taught how to wield financial and political power throughout the South. Here, these institutions acted as more than just sieves that sorted people and helped maintain social distinctions; they also, at times, incubated destructive normative beliefs associated with race that were then disseminated by students throughout society.

The yearbook content presented in this inquiry provides greater insight into a wide variety of very specific social structural conditions that Black men and women encountered when they worked on, and later were students at, these Virginia campuses. These annuals also provide greater insight into the symbolic constructions of a racial hierarchy that elite White interests maintained as a means of normalizing their position of dominance throughout the South. These institutions were also clearly active in creating and maintaining ideas that acted not just as social barriers related to access to higher education but also as means by which to terrorize Black men and women and keep them from exercising their rights as American citizens (see McInnis and Nelson 2019).

Importantly, the institutional histories of schools examined in this study differ significantly—some schools are among the most prominent in the country, whereas others are considered more parochial and geared toward women's education. Some were founded before the Civil War and others founded after—and these differing histories affected these institutions' orientation toward many of the pressing social issues of the day. For example, the future James Madison University (JMU) was initially founded, well after the US Civil War, as a progressive institution designed to help remedy a lack of opportunities for women to attend college ("Historical Timeline" 2020). Here, including schools with all-women student bodies and no direct or obvious history associated with slavery or the Civil War is useful for making comparisons to schools founded before the Civil War that had entirely male student bodies.

A few schools in this study have a direct martial history of student and alumni involvement in the American Civil War. Perhaps the best-known example is a long march undertaken by students at the Virginia Military Institute (VMI) through the Shenandoah Valley in order to reinforce Confederate troops during the Battle of New Market, an event that is memorialized to this day. Further, Thomas "Stonewall" Jackson, a prominent Confederate general, is the most memorialized past professor at VMI. For example, the VMI museum on campus displays the raincoat that Jackson was wearing when he was mortally wounded (accidentally shot by his own troops) during the Civil War ("VMI Museum" VMI). Within a mile of the VMI museum is Robert E. Lee's mausoleum, located on the Washington and Lee (W&L) campus, where he served as the president of Washington College for five years until his death in 1870. The college was renamed Washington and Lee College shortly after. During his presidency, in 1867, Lee requested that a chapel be built on campus. Completed in 1868, the chapel became the centerpiece for the many important institutional rituals (e.g. the graduation ceremony in 1868) closely associated with the college.

After his death Lee was buried beneath the chapel. His body was later moved to an adjacent addition (constructed in 1883) that also serves as the Lee family crypt ("History – About the Chapel" W&L).

Visual sociology

Another purpose of this study is to demonstrate how methods within the field of visual sociology can provide a thorough account of what life at these universities was like as it relates to race relations over time. The analysis of visual materials issued periodically has particular promise for future visual studies. Probably yearbooks and other periodicals offer the most complete accounts available of past student life as it relates to institutional rituals, discipline, gender relations, the portrayal of disability and LGBTQ+ relations—all topics of inquiry that have long preoccupied sociologists.

The broadest definition of *visual sociology* is that it "uses images to study society." More specifically, "visual sociology and visual anthropology are grounded in the idea that valid scientific insight in society can be acquired by observing, analyzing, and theorizing its visual manifestations" (Pauwels 2010, 545). The field includes methods in which researchers make visual products, but it has more often focused on analysis of historical artifacts, often photographs, drawings and art. Sometimes the visual data are at the forefront of the project and other times they might be supplemental (e.g. pictures that accompany a study). For example, creating a visual record to accompany a study was a technique used by ethnographer Mitchell Duneier (1999), who in his study of Black men who sold used books on the sidewalks of Greenwich Village decided to produce a documentary that captured these men's daily routines.

Another common approach is to investigate how photographic images were constructed within different social contexts. For example, as photographic technology became more widespread, Pierre Bourdieu (Bourdieu and Boltanski [1965] 1996) became interested in what kinds of photographs were being created by amateur photographers. In this case, the photographs themselves were not particularly interesting; rather, it was the routine and often mundane constructions of content (e.g. family pictures) that he examined as it relates to "middle-brow art." Indeed, in Bourdieu's influential edited volume there are hardly any pictures at all—instead there are in-depth descriptions of people's relationship to the act of picture making and how these photographs are judged by viewers (see Castel and Schnapper [1965] 1996).

Perhaps the most well-known sociological inquiry that deconstructed the composition and meaning of photographs and pictures is Erving Goffman's (1979) study of gender display in advertising. In this case, these drawings and photographs are not designed to capture the natural world but are sociologically interesting because of how they constructed gender meaning for those consuming the pictures (see Figure 1.2). Indeed, approaches similar to Goffman's—and the study of advertising—are probably the most well-known within the field of visual sociology.

FIGURE 1.2 An early example of gender display in an advertisement for coffee. In this case, the advertising represents gender norms before the turn of the century, where idealized women were (as they are today) routinely displayed to sell products ("Mountain Coffee," Boston Public Library, Digital Commonwealth).

Other visual studies have focused on the construction of photographic content that appears in public and private spheres. In these cases, researchers might explore why participants choose to photograph certain subjects or how photographs are judged by observers. In the previous cases, the inquiry examines photographic evidence with the intention of learning how the makers of pictures symbolically create and stage content so that it is meaningful to themselves and others (see Pauwels 2010; Harper 1998; Grady 1996) In effect, analyzing pictures is an opportunity to see what is most meaningful in people's lives. With respect to pictures designed to document institutional histories (such as school yearbooks), it is assumed that photographs are attempts to distill and document the normative ideas and logics of these organizations (see Margolis and Rowe 2004; Margolis 1988). Of course, there are also important insights to be gained from looking at photographic evidence when the subjects are unsuspecting participants. Here, pictures that reveal more routine acts (e.g. of work) can provide just as much analytic value as photographs that have been more thoroughly constructed and curated (see Margolis and Rowe 2011).

Racism in popular art and memorabilia

In this study, a significant number of the pictures analyzed are not photographs but instead line drawings and caricatures. Notably, other studies have investigated the construction of ethnic identity by analyzing turn-of-the-century popular art. One excellent example is Metrick-Chen's (2007) study of Chinese images represented on trading cards that were routinely included with popular items (e.g. baking soda, washing detergent) sold at the turn of the century (see Figure 1.3). Generally, the popularity of these sometime fantastical images reflected White America's growing interest with the increasing number of Chinese who were immigrating to the United States. The pictures provide a visual representation of all the contradictions associated with Chinese American ethnic identity. For example, White Americans could sometimes consider Asians as clean, industrious and wise, but in other cases as dirty and superstitious.

Here, it should not be surprising that Black men and women were also routinely portrayed on trading cards and popular art at the turn of the century too (see Figure 1.4).

The remarkable work of David Pilgrim (2015), an applied sociologist, is also relevant to this study. Pilgrim, an avid collector of racist memorabilia created during the Jim Crow period, is best known for establishing and curating the Jim Crow Museum at Ferris State University. Of particular note is his text *Understanding Jim Crow: Using Racist Memorabilia to Teach Tolerance and Promote Social Justice*, which presents pictures of some of these artifacts in order to explain the perniciousness of Jim Crow racism and also teach racial tolerance. Here, one of the purposes of this work is to use yearbook pictures and texts to demonstrate past periods of racial discrimination, which might also be used as a teaching tool for current students and faculty at these schools and, hopefully, might also inspire them to actively

FIGURE 1.3 A soap trading card depicting an Asian American near the turn of the twentieth century ("Me Wash-ee," Boston Public Library Soap Trade Card Collection).

FIGURE 1.4 A soap trading card depicting an African American near the turn of the twentieth century ("Monday," Boston Public Library Soap Trade Card Collection).

support and work toward creating programs of redress that address the harm these institutions did to communities of color during much of their histories.

The study of public art is also useful for understanding social norms as they existed in the past. Indeed, much public art is designed to create popular narratives as frames for understanding past historical events. Specifically related to this inquiry is a study, *The Confederate Image*, that examined popular prints depicting events that took place during the Civil War. Mostly, these prints helped institutionalize a civil religion that scholars have labeled "The Lost Cause of the Confederacy" (Neely, Holzer and Boritt 2000). In this case, the Civil War was reimagined as a chivalrous endeavor undertaken against extraordinary odds with the intention of maintaining a "natural" and virtuous way of life. Importantly, Lost Cause iconography was routinely found in all the yearbooks examined, even though many of these schools were established well after the period of Southern Reconstruction.

BATTLE OF CHANCELLORSVILLE.

COLOR PLATE 1 *The Battle of Chancellorsville* print depicting Thomas "Stonewall" Jackson being mortally wounded during the decisive day of fighting. The picture is not accurate, as Jackson was wounded on May 2, a day before the decisive engagement, when accidentally shot by Confederate troops while returning from a scouting trip. Similar apocryphal accounts of Jackson's conduct during the war remain an integral part of the culture at VMI, where he was a former member of the faculty. Recently, as a result of a state government investigation into allegations of racism on the VMI campus, some have begun to re-examine Jackson's prominent role in the campus culture (Kurz and Allison, *The Battle of Chancellorsville*, print provided by the Library of Congress).

In Color Plate 1 there is an example of a popular Lost Cause print of this period, *The Battle of Chancellorsville*, which is useful for understanding the mythology associated with Thomas "Stonewall" Jackson, who is discussed later (in chapter 4) concerning the institutional logics of the Virginia Military Institute (VMI). In the print, Jackson is portrayed as being mortally wounded during the decisive day of fighting at Chancellorsville, Virginia. Supposedly, the day before the battle, as he observed the number of VMI-trained officers in the field, he is said to have commented: "The Institute will be heard from today." The print provided in Color Plate 1 is not historically accurate. In fact, Jackson was mortally wounded—accidentally shot by Confederate troops—the day before the decisive engagement. Despite a recent ongoing examination Jackson's prominence on the VMI campus—the result of a state government inquiry into charges of widespread racism on campus—these types of apocryphal accounts of Jackson's conduct remain an integral part of the culture at VMI. For example, while a statue of Jackson was recently removed from campus, at this writing (on May 27, 2021) some of the popular mythology remains evident on the campus website (see "Stonewall Jackson FAQ" VMI).

Past studies of schools using visual methods

Many public schools were established close to the turn of the century as photography became more widespread and affordable. Often, those working at these educational institutions were preoccupied with documenting institutional histories and increasingly used photography. One early pioneer in the use of visual methods, Eric Margolis, was among the first to examine historical photographs of schools, documenting how these institutions shaped ethnic and racial identities during this period. Perhaps his best-known work used institutional photographs taken by those documenting Indian Schools in order to explore propaganda associated with Native American assimilation into American society (see Figure 1.5 below).

Eric Margolis also explored representations of discipline and labor at these schools and others, and he has conducted comparative work with a focus on how schools ordered social class. With colleagues he has also investigated school rituals, school surveillance and school discipline (see Margolis, 2005; 2004; Margolis and Fram, 2007; Chappell, Chappell and Margolis 2011). Along the way, Margolis developed many of the theoretical and methodological approaches that are now routinely associated with the field of visual sociology. For example, he sometimes stressed understanding the symbolic content of highly staged photographic images (Margolis 2004). He mostly employed visual methods to demonstrate how these ostensibly progressive schools were actually the means through which the ethnocide of many indigenous Native American cultures was perpetuated by the US government. Of course, others have explored the role of Indian Schools (see Woods 2016)—it is now commonly accepted that these institutions were designed, in part, to eliminate indigenous culture—but the pictures

ALEX. GARDNER, Photographer,   311 Seventh Street, Washington

ACROSS THE CONTINENT ON THE KANSAS PACIFIC RAILROAD.

(ROUTE OF THE 35TH PARALLEL.)

St. Mary's Mission, Kansas, Pottawattamie Indian School,
90 MILES WEST OF MISSOURI RIVER

FIGURE 1.5 An Indian School picture taken in Kansas (1886). The picture shows the boys who attend the school, all wearing European clothing, assembled in front of the school with their teachers (Photographer Alexander Gardner, picture provided by the Digital Commonwealth).

Margolis examined help provide a depth of understanding that would be hard to convey through words alone (see Margolis 2004; Margolis and Rowe 2004).

Research methods

This study draws on now well-established methods in visual sociology that have been refined over the past few decades. The study should also be categorized as historically comparative in its outlook (Kiser and Hechter 1991). Ultimately, historical knowledge—usually gained through some sleuthing concerning the people represented in these yearbooks and the people who created yearbook content—was necessary to characterize what the yearbook material meant both for those creating and those consuming its content. Often, it was common for a modern observer encountering past pictures and texts to sometimes be flummoxed by some yearbook content, but inevitably the meaning became clearer with the help of primary source material. For example, a close reading of memoirs and political commentary written by notable alumni mentioned in yearbooks was often extraordinarily useful in understanding past yearbook content.

The use of visual methods has certainly expanded and advanced over time, but it is still somewhat on the margins within the larger field of sociology. This is curious, given the extraordinary amount of visual data people in modern societies now encounter, combined with the fact that access to historical visual data has dramatically increased following the digitalization of important archives (see Margolis and Rowe 2004). For example, this study was made possible by the digitalization of primary source material—in this case yearbooks. Importantly, while the pictures and texts analyzed in this study remain accessible to everyone, recent scandals associated with yearbook content have caused some universities to remove or obscure their digital yearbook archives (see Troung 2019).

Methodological concerns in visual methods

One conundrum associated with visual sociology is how to determine which images matter. In effect, what type of selection process is best used when determining how images get collected, coded, organized and sorted? This might be associated with where the images are stored (e.g. a specific photographic database, a visual record within a periodical etc.) and the methods used to find and then either lump or split the images into distinct categories of analysis. Given the vast amounts of photographic data available, picking which images count can be a somewhat subjective enterprise even when researchers find inventive ways to systematically capture and cull visual representations of specific social phenomena (see Margolis 2004; Margolis and Rowe 2004).

In general, coding photographs and pictures for content is not too different than using established methods for analyzing text, except that those who routinely work with visual materials are usually impressed, and sometimes overwhelmed, by the richness of photographic evidence. Further, it is common to find that while pictures and their content can be placed in the same analytical boxes, they are often clearly not equal in terms of their impact on viewers. In effect, a single picture really can be worth a thousand words in terms of the information it conveys to an observer. This can make coding pictures difficult, particularly in accounting for the often rich symbolic content—both intended and unintended—that they convey.

The previous questions also concern how the meaning and value of visual artifacts should be evaluated by modern viewers. Related is how much specificity sociologists should invest in their analysis of these images. Here, because some images are clearly more remarkable than others, there is a tendency to present the extraordinary images, first and foremost, as evidence. But is it really the case that the most remarkable images actually tell us more than other, less remarkable images? In fact, might it make more sense to assume that the prevalence of certain types of mundane images is an indication of greater resonance among the public viewing these pictures?

All the foregoing issues were considered in developing the methodological approach used in this study. Practically, many of the pictures presented in this study are somewhat mundane, such as those showing routine acts of labor. At the same time, there are some photographs presented in the study that will likely be judged as extraordinary by modern viewers—the pictures of the KKK committing acts of violence, for example—although these pictures were, at the time published, probably not considered particularly provocative.

I believe the basic strategy (outlined further below) developed in this study could be a useful template in future inquiries that analyze periodic publications issued by institutions. In particular, coding annual editions goes some way toward addressing selection concerns common in visual methods. Yearbooks are, after all, dense historical documents, issued annually, that are explicitly designed to characterize life at these institutions. Further, while yearbook content does change over time, the format is somewhat stable from year to year. Importantly, much of the categorization of content has already been undertaken by stakeholders at these institutions who have conveniently organized and then compiled pictures and texts designed to represent the most important aspects of university life (e.g. annual dances, school rituals, popular clubs). In effect, the pictures and the categories in which they were placed within these yearbooks are designed—by virtue of the genre itself—to characterize what is important and what is shared by the stakeholders within the institution.

Given the previous advantages, it is notable how few studies have coded yearbooks for content. Here, there appear to be only three academic studies in the social sciences and humanities that have systematically coded yearbooks for content over time. For example, one study investigated changes in humor (Panayotidis and Stortz 2008). Another study made the case for treating yearbooks as a category of genre (Caudill 2007). Of course, there are a few historical studies that have used yearbook pictures as supplemental data. The most relevant to this study is an exploration of how the Confederate battle flag was adopted by University of Virginia students to support the football team from 1941 to 1951 (Nehls 2002).

Strategy for gathering material and analytical process

With the previous concerns in mind, I began this ongoing study with the intention to collect and inventory the universe of photographic and written texts published in yearbooks by 11 colleges in Virginia and Howard University as associated within a broadly defined category of "race relations on campus." As noted earlier, the Virginia institutions examined are The University of Virginia, Virginia Commonwealth University, Old Dominion University, Washington and Lee University, Longwood College, Hampden-Sydney College, The University of Richmond, Virginia Military Institute, George Mason University,

James Madison University and Virginia Tech. Howard University, the only HBCU in the study, was included to provide a contrast with the Virginia colleges. Although not all the school yearbook content has been coded for some of these schools, the ongoing goal is to collect all the visual content (pictures or drawings) and texts (captions, accounts written by students etc.) in which race relations were characterized or expressed within these yearbooks. In each case these pictures and texts are copied (with a screen shot) and then stored in a Google Drive account. It usually takes roughly one to two hours for someone to do the initial coding of a single yearbook for the relevant content.

One methodological concern is that while yearbooks are often variations on a common theme, there are enough differences—the size of the student body, the amount that individual students are allowed to editorialize etc.—to ensure that yearbook content across institutions is not strictly a comparison of the same units of analysis. Despite the previous, the incidences of certain types of pictures and other content presented in different university yearbooks over time probably indicate important institutional differences related to race relations at these institutions.

Once the material is documented, both manifest and latent coding is used to capture a few basic variables (e.g. type of picture, where published, and the race, gender, ethnicity of those in the picture) associated with the content that provides a summary description of the picture and text. Dummy variables are also used to summarize picture content and then entered into an Excel spreadsheet to provide a database for each school. Symbolic representations (e.g. drawings and pictures of the Confederate battle flag, representation of Lost Cause memorialization) that are important markers of a larger racial ideology were also captured and coded. Most images in yearbooks represent staged symbolic content, but there are also a considerable number of images and texts that captured more routine and natural interactions.

This initial "grab everything" strategy freed coders from trying to make on-the-spot judgments as to which images mattered the most and which were best suited for later analysis. Practically, the coding strategy was designed to create a database that made finding specific content (e.g. pictures of Black university workers) easier when doing an analysis. In cases where the coding of all school yearbooks has been completed, it is possible to run summary reports concerning what type of content was most prevalent at certain institutions during certain periods of time—for example, which schools routinely represented the Confederate battle flag in their yearbooks, or which schools most often employed racial caricature in yearbooks.

Notwithstanding the previous sorting of images, the methods of analysis used in this study are qualitative. Here, when confronted with thousands of images, I and my assistants used both inductive and deductive reasoning to create the analytic categories that are explored throughout the text. Usually, these categories were easy to identify—they were often already organized by yearbook editors—as there were clearly standard types of pictures (e.g. racial caricatures) often being issued by the same groups (e.g. the state clubs) during certain periods (e.g. before World War II) that revisited the same or similar themes year after year. These pictures and accounts—and sometimes even specific people and caricatures (e.g. the school mascot)—were an integral part of a university tradition. It was usually quite clear what these images meant to observers, to the extent that it was often easy to identify very specific narrative tropes (inside jokes, for example) that were used to convey shared meaning concerning race relations at specific institutions.

While many categories of analysis were determined when there was a high incidence of certain types of content, this was not the only determining factor for all the content categories explored in this text. Specifically, Black university staff are sometimes—but comparatively not as often as White students and White faculty—photographed in university yearbooks. In some cases, they were inadvertently captured when they appeared in the background of a formally staged photograph (e.g. as servers behind a more formally assembled group). Obviously, the Black staff at colleges are not usually the focus of yearbook content—although sometimes Black staff were actually showcased—but the available pictures and descriptions of laborers did provide remarkable insights into the jobs and conditions that Black men, and later an increasing number of Black women, encountered at these institutions. Combined with personal accounts offered by students who characterized these workers, this content offered a very full picture of what the Black staff at these colleges encountered when working on campus.

Content categories and the organization of the text

The remaining chapters of the text are devoted to exploring race relations—specifically the relationship between White and Black Americans—that existed at campuses in Virginia in the period before World War II (chapter 2) and at Howard University during the same period (chapter 3). Then follows an investigation of Virginia campuses after World War II and during the civil rights period (chapter 4). The last chapter explores social movement activism at Howard University and the Virginia colleges, largely from the civil rights period to the present (chapter 5). The analytical categories shift somewhat during each chapter but consistently look at *popular caricatures* (pictures and texts) of Black men and women that routinely appeared in yearbooks. This content provides highly developed examples of racial "humor" (both pictures and stories) often constructed by students. The text also investigates, over time, the *service roles African Americans played at these institutions*. This latter category includes pictures of Black laborers and accounts as to how this labor was evaluated by White students and faculty. Another category provides examples of racialized content that occurred during *routine extracurricular campus events*—sporting events, musical productions, plays, literary events and so on—that students participated in. A final category investigates images and texts related to *Civil War memorialization and Lost Cause iconography*.

The last chapter, on social movement activism, does not use the previous categories of analysis. Instead, it looks at well-known periods of social activism in the country—associated with the civil rights campaigns—and then investigates how yearbook content characterizes these periods. Notably, some campuses did have periods of widespread student activism—a nationwide anti–Vietnam War strike in May 1970, for example—and these periods are examined specifically in terms of how they advanced race relations on campus. This final chapter includes a brief analysis of the increasing amounts of pro-social racial imagery that began to appear on Virginia campuses, for the most part, in the 1970s.

Conclusion

Currently, there are nascent movements on college campuses involving students, faculty and administrators that are attempting to confront periods of past institutional racism with an idea of creating programs for redress and reparation for past injustices (see Coates 2014; Hassan 2019). This study is meant to be a part of this debate. I assume that if people at colleges throughout the South are serious about redress, then administrators, faculty, staff and students need to confront just how pernicious institutional racism was and how destructive it continues to be. Much of the material presented in this study will likely make people who study and work at these institutions uneasy. This is probably not how they imagined, if they imagined at all, their institution's racial history. But it is important to understand that the material presented in this study was not exceptional during the period it was published. Nor does it represent a brief period of time, perhaps a period that was a historical aberration—a time, so to speak, when "God was asleep at the switch." Rather, the material presented in this study was carefully selected and scrutinized by both students and faculty—and selected to represent the accepted social history that ordered race relations throughout the South, in Virginia, and at these schools specifically. It is not a pretty picture.

Ideally, this study will help people better contemplate in a clear-eyed manner the exact roles that educational institutions played in creating and then maintaining ideals that continue to fuel racial hatred at the present time. For example, this study began during a period when acts of racism were increasing throughout the United States and often on college campuses too. Particularly, it began shortly after a White supremacist Unite the Right march took place on the University of Virginia (UVA) campus and in the community of Charlottesville, Virginia. The event ended in violence when Heather Heyer was killed after being run over by a car driven by James Alex Fields, a self-identified White supremacist (Heim 2017). Many found these events remarkable—Charlottesville, Virginia, is now considered a liberal university community—but a White supremacist organizer of the march, Richard Spencer (a UVA graduate) apparently believed the community's history made it an ideal place to hold this protest (Heim 2018). Here, the pictures presented in this text will help explain why it should not be surprising that a "modern-day" White supremacist is also a UVA graduate, and why he also regarded Charlottesville, Virginia, as a place where his ideals would find support.

References

Battle of Chancellorsville. 1890. Kurz & Allison Art Publishers. LC-DIG-pga-01844 (Digital file from original print). Library of Congress Prints and Photographs Division.

Bonilla-Silva, Eduardo. 1997. "Rethinking Racism: Toward a Structural Interpretation," *American Sociological Review* 62 (3): 465–480.

Bourdieu, Pierre, and Luc Boltanski, eds. [1965] 1996. *Photography: A Middle-Brow Art*. Translated by Shaun Whiteside. Cambridge: Polity Press.

Carlisle, Madeline, and Anna Purna Kambhampaty. 2019. "Justin Trudeau Says He Didn't Remember Blackface and Brownface Photos and Admits There Could Be More." *Time Magazine*, September 19.

Castel, Robert, and Dominique Schnapper. [1965] 1996. "Aesthetic Ambitions and Social Aspirations: The Camera Club as a Secondary-Group." Translated by Shaun Whiteside. In *Photography: A Middle-Brow Art*, edited by Pierre Bourdieu and Luc Boltanski, 73–98. Cambridge: Polity Press.

Caudill, Melissa. 2007. *"Yearbooks as a Genre: A Case Study."* Master's thesis, Clemson University, https://tigerprints.clemson.edu/all _theses/281.

Chappell, Drew, Sharon Chappell and Eric Margolis. 2011. "School as Ceremony and Ritual: How Photography Illuminates Performances of Ideological Transfer." *Qualitative Inquiry* 17 (1): 56–73.

Coates, Ta-Nehisi. 2014. "The Case for Reparations." *The Atlantic* 313 (5): 54–71.

Dorr, Gregory M. 2008. *Segregation's Science: Eugenics and Society in Virginia*. Charlottesville, VA: University of Virginia Press.

Duneier, Mitchell. 1999. *Sidewalk*. Photographs by Ovie Carter. New York: Farrar, Straus & Giroux.

Eastern Virginia Medical School. 1984. "Ralph Northam Yearbook Page."

Gardner, Alexander. 1867. "St. Mary's Mission, Kansas, Pottawattamie Indian School, 90 miles west of Missouri River." Photograph. *Digital Commonwealth*, https://ark.digital commonwealth.org/ark:/50959/70796d495 (Accessed September 25, 2020).

Goffman, Erving. 1979. *Gender Advertisements*. New York: Macmillan International Higher Education.

Grady, John. 1996. "The Scope of Visual Sociology." *Visual Studies* 1 (2): 10–24.

Harper, Douglas. 1998. "An Argument for Visual Sociology." In *Image-Based Research: A Sourcebook for Qualitative Researchers*, edited by Jon Prosser, 24–41. New York: Psychology Press.

Hassan, Adeel. 2019. "Georgetown Students Agree to Create Reparations Fund," *New York Times*, August 12. LexisNexis Academic.

Heim, Joe. 2017. "Recounting a Day of Rage, Hate, Violence and Death." *Washington Post*. August 14. LexisNexis Academic.

Heim, Joe. 2018. "University of Virginia Bans Richard Spencer and Others from Campus." *Washington Post*, October 26. LexisNexis Academic.

"Historical Timeline: JMU Centennial Celebration." 2006. James Madison University. https://www.jmu.edu/centennialcelebration/timeline.html.

"History – About the Chapel." Washington & Lee University. https://my.wlu.edu/lee-chapel-and-museum/about-the-chapel/history (Accessed May 27, 2021).

Kiser, Edgar, and Michael Hechter 1991. "The Role of General Theory in Comparative-Historical Sociology." *American Journal of Sociology* 97 (1): 1–30.

Margolis, Eric. 1988. "Mining Photographs: Unearthing the Meaning of Historical Photos." *Radical History Review* 40: 32–48.

Margolis, Eric. 2004. "Looking at Discipline, Looking at Labour: Photographic Representations of Indian Boarding Schools." *Visual Studies* 19 (1): 72–96.

Margolis, Eric. 2005. "Liberal Documentary Goes to School: Farm Security Administration Photographs of Students, Teachers and Schools." In *American Visual Cultures*, edited by D. Holloway and J. Beck, 107–115. London: Continuum.

Margolis, Eric, and Jeremy Rowe. 2004. "Images of Assimilation: Photographs of Indian Schools in Arizona." *History of Education* 33 (2): 199–230.

Margolis, Eric, and Jeremy Rowe. 2011. "Methodological Approaches to Disclosing Historic Photographs." In *The Sage Handbook of Visual of Research Methods*, edited by Eric Margolis and Luc Pauwels, 337–358. New York: Sage Publishing.

Margolis, Eric, and S. Fram. 2007. "Caught Napping: Images of Surveillance, Discipline and Punishment on the Body of the Schoolchild." *History of Education* 36 (2): 191–211.

Metrick-Chen, Lenore. 2007. "The Chinese of the American Imagination: 19th Century Trade Card Images." *Visual Anthropology Review* 23 (2): 115–136.

McInnis, Maurie D., and Louis P. Nelson, eds. 2019. *Educated in Tyranny: Slavery at Thomas Jefferson's University.* Charlottesville, VA: University of Virginia Press.

"'Me wash-ee all clean-ee, me use-ee Soapine-ee.'" 1870. Trading Card. *Digital Commonwealth*, https://ark.digitalcommonwealth.org/ark:/50959/7m01bs470 (Accessed September 25, 2020).

"'Monday—Monday is de wash day, and I neber sulk or mope, because de close am nice and clean, by using Higgins' Soap.'" 1870. Trading Card. Boston: Forbes Company. *Digital Commonwealth*, https://ark.digitalcommonwealth.org/ark:/50959/7 m01bq17v (Accessed September 25, 2020).

"Mountain Coffee, Reeves, Parvin & Company." 1870. Card. New York: Samuel Crump Label Co. *Digital Commonwealth*, https://ark.digitalcommonwealth.org/ark:/50959/3b591d58m (Accessed September 25, 2020).

Murphy, Brett. 2019. "Blackface, KKK Hoods and Mock Lynchings: Review of 900 Yearbooks Finds Blatant Racism." *USA Today*, February 21. https://www.usatoday.com/in-depth/news/investigations/2019/02/20/Blackface-racist-photos-yearbooks-colleges-kkk-lynching-mockery-fraternities-Black-70-s-80-s/2858921002/.

Neely, Mark E., Harold Holzer and Gabor S. Boritt. 2000. *The Confederate Image: Prints of the Lost Cause.* Chapel Hill, NC: UNC Press Books.

Nehls, Christopher C. 2002. "Flag-Waving Wahoos: Confederate Symbols at the University of Virginia, 1941–51." *Virginia Magazine of History and Biography* 110 (4): 461–848.

Panayotidis, E. Lisa, and Paul Stortz. 2008. "Visual Interpretations, Cartoons, and Caricatures of Student and Youth Cultures in University Yearbooks, 1898–1930." *Journal of the Canadian Historical Association* 19 (1): 195–227.

Pauwels, Luc. 2010. "Visual Sociology Reframed: An Analytical Synthesis and Discussion of Visual Methods in Social and Cultural Research." *Sociological Methods & Research* 38 (4): 545–581.

Pilgrim, David. 2015. *Understanding Jim Crow: Using Racist Memorabilia to Teach Tolerance and Promote Social Justice.* Oakland, CA: PM Press.

The Pow Wow. Old Dominion University. https://digitalcommons.odu.edu/scua_yearbooks/.

Stevens, Mitchell L., Elizabeth A. Armstrong and Richard Arum. 2008. "Sieve, Incubator, Temple, Hub: Empirical and Theoretical Advances in the Sociology of Higher Education." *Annual Review of Sociology* 34 (1): 127–151.

"Stonewall Jackson FAQ." VMI website. https://www.vmi.edu/archives/stonewall-jackson-resources/stonewall-jackson-faq/. (Accessed May 27, 2020)

The Chieftain. Old Dominion University. https://digitalcommons.odu.edu/scua_yearbooks/.

The Wigwam. Virginia Commonwealth University. https://digitalarchive.wm.edu/ handle/ 10288/2112.

Troung, Debbie. 2019. "A Va. University Temporarily Removes Yearbooks with Blackface from Digital Archives." *Washington Post*, April 3. LexisNexis Academic.

"VMI Museum." Virginia Military Institute. https://www.vmi.edu/museums-and-archives/vmi-museum/. (Accessed May 27, 2020)

"Whose Heritage? Public Symbols of the Confederacy." 2019. *Southern Poverty Law Center.* https://www.splcenter.org/20190201/whose-heritage-public-symbols-Confederacy.

Woods, Eric Taylor. 2016. *A Cultural Sociology of Anglican Mission and the Indian Residential Schools in Canada: The Long Road to Apology.* New York: Springer Publishing, 2016.

Yellin, Eric S. 2013. *Racism in the Nation's Service: Government Workers and the Color Line in Woodrow Wilson's America.* Chapel Hill, NC: UNC Press Books.

2

JIM CROW RACISM ON CAMPUS

Post–Civil War Reconstruction to
World War II (1890–1942)

Historians have often argued that the low point of race relations in the United States occurred directly following the end of post–Civil War Reconstruction (1865–1878) (see Logan [1965] 1997). During this time, so-called Jim Crow laws became the popular shorthand reference for state and local laws in the South that separated Black and White people in public and private life. These laws became institutionalized following the *Plessy v. Ferguson* Supreme Court decision in 1896, which ruled that the separation of Black and White public facilities was legal if they were "equal" in quality. Shortly after, the Virginia state government, using the logic of *Plessy v. Ferguson*, began to pass laws designed to deny Black Virginians their basic rights, particularly as related to the acquisition of property and voting. During this period the state also institutionalized a written bar exam for admittance to the legal profession. The Virginia bar exam effectively created the first professional law schools, and soon those at the University of Virginia (UVA), Washington and Lee (W&L) and the University of Richmond (UR) became among the most prominent. Practically, nearly all Black men and women were barred from practicing law in Virginia because they could not attain a law degree at any Virginia universities. The exceptions were two Black men, trained at Howard University, who passed the Virginia bar exam (Matthew 2019).

The previous history helps inform the meaning of many pictures presented in this chapter, but is also useful in understanding the myriad ways in which prominent colleges—particularly those with law schools—became directly culpable in creating and maintaining the laws that were formally established during this period. Here, it is not surprising that Charlottesville, Virginia, home to the University of Virginia, quickly enacted pernicious local laws that forcefully segregated the races within the city. These laws limited where Blacks could live,

DOI: 10.4324/9781003134480-2

own property, run a business and attend school. For example, the last inter-racial neighborhoods in the city were outlawed by the Charlottesville City Council in 1912 when it unanimously adopted an ordinance: "To Secure for White and Colored People a Separate Location of Residence for Each Race" (Matthew 2019, 301).

This study begins with the Jim Crow period because this is when the first annual yearbooks were published by Virginia colleges. While the study sample includes a few schools that were established in the 20th century—James Madison University (JMU), Old Dominion University (ODU) and George Mason University (GMU)—nearly all the other schools began their yearbook publications in the 1880s and 1890s. For example, the University of Virginia (UVA) began publishing *Corks and Curls* in 1888 and Washington and Lee (W&L) followed shortly after when it began publishing *The Calyx* in 1895. Hampden-Sydney College (*Kaleidoscope* in 1893), Longwood College (*The Normal Light* in 1898), the University of Richmond (UR) (*The Web* in 1897), Virginia Military Institute (VMI) (*The Bomb*, continuously from 1895) and Virginia Tech (VT) (*The Bugle* in 1895) also began publishing yearbooks during this period. The Medical College of Virginia (later Virginia Commonwealth University [VCU]) issued its first yearbook (*The X-Ray*) in 1913.

Black stereotypes from 1880 to 1941: minstrelsy and the "Lost Cause of the Confederacy"

During the period examined Jim Crow became the shorthand moniker for legalized racial segregation. Notably, the Jim Crow character was directly associated with the minstrel tradition—along with many other stock Black characters—all of whom routinely appeared in many of the college yearbooks investigated. The Jim Crow character was first widely introduced to Americans in the middle 19th century by a Northerner, Thomas B. Rice, who was among the first to appear in blackface during theatrical productions. Later, and directly corresponding with the period investigated in this chapter, minstrel shows became one of the first widespread popular forms of entertainment in the United States (see Lemons 1977; Toll 1974). In fact, there is considerable anecdotal evidence that the name of the UVA yearbook, *Corks and Curls*, is a direct reference to the burnt cork that performers often used to blacken their faces in minstrel shows ("History," Backstory 2019). Not surprising, yearbook content indicates these productions were commonplace on campuses at this time. Blackface performances (e.g. choral groups that performed in blackface) were evident on some of these campuses well into the 1960s (see *The Bomb* 1962, 275).

Often, the Jim Crow character who appeared in early minstrel shows dressed in tattered and patched clothing with a battered hat and well-worn shoes (see Figure 2.1). Notwithstanding his appearance, Jim Crow was also something of a charlatan and dandy—not particularly inclined toward hard work—he "skates

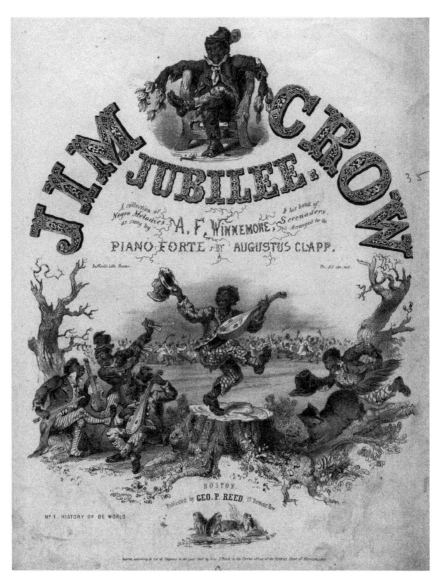

FIGURE 2.1 The Jim Crow figure was first performed by Thomas B. "Daddy" Rice in one of the earliest blackface performances. He became a popular nationwide performer in the 1830s–50s. Other performers reprised the act. The sheet music of the "Jim Crow Jubilee" was published in Boston, Massachusetts, in 1847. Provided by the *Digital Commonwealth, Boston Public Library* (Lith 1847).

by" using his wit and buffoonish charm. William T. Lhamon (2003), who has read and commented on many of the Thomas Rice productions, regards the early Jim Crow character as the classic "trickster." He also argues that the original character—one that likely had its origins within the African American community—was far different than that which later became closely associated with the Jim Crow South. He indicates that the early figure represented the opposite of Jim Crow segregation and was, rather, a symbol of the "dizzy" freedom briefly enjoyed by runaway or newly freed Blacks in the middle 19th century (Lhamon 2003).

During the period examined in this chapter, minstrel shows—usually performed by White actors in blackface—moved negative characterizations of Black men and women to the forefront of American popular culture. Toll (1974) indicates that at the center of these shows were two Black stereotypes: Zip Coon (a "preposterous black dandy") and the later Jim Crow, who was now often portrayed as a "slow-witted plantation darky" (see also Lemons 1977, 102). Other common tropes portrayed Black men as comical "chicken stealers" or, conversely, as dangerous bestial men who routinely wielded razors (105–110). Other Black stereotypes became widely used in popular advertising, often on trading cards distributed with common household products. These figures included "Old Uncle Tom or Uncle Remus, Aunt Jemima or Mandy the maid, Preacher Brown and Deacon Jones, Rastus and Sambo, and the ol' mammy" (102). Some of these figures were closely associated with popular products such as Cream O' Wheat and Uncle Ben's Rice. Likewise, in the late 1890s, Tin Pan Alley song writers created the genre of "Coon Songs" with over 600 popular songs and "shouts" being produced during this period. The titles included "Coon, Coon, (How I Wish My Color Would Fade)," "If the Man in the Moon Were a Coon," "Saint Patrick Day Is a Bad Day for Coons" and "All Coons Look Alike to Me" (105–107).

The Lost Cause of the Confederacy

The period when these yearbooks were first issued also corresponds with the creation of a mythical social history that has been broadly characterized as the "Lost Cause of the Confederacy." The Lost Cause has its origins in revisionists' texts—often written by leaders of the Confederacy—that appeared shortly after the Civil War and provided idealized accounts of the Southern war effort (see Page [1887] 1991; 1898; 1904a; 1905; 1911). Importantly, the Lost Cause narrative was often reinforced by both popular (see Page 1911) and academic histories (see Freeman 1934)—often written from the "Great Man" perspective. The period examined also corresponds with a very successful campaign by the Daughters of the Confederacy to increase the memorialization of Southern Civil War heroes in public spaces. Here, the organization commissioned statues and also successfully advocated for the renaming of public institutions—particularly public schools—after Confederate leaders ("Whose Heritage," 2019). The creation of public art honoring the Southern war heroes was also part of this effort (see Neely, Holzer and Boritt 2000).

The Lost Cause perspective promoted the idea that the Southern states fought valiantly during a "War of Northern Aggression" to preserve a virtuous and chivalrous society and that the conflict primarily concerned the preservation of states' rights as opposed to slavery. But it was also argued that Northerners did not really understand the benefits, for all involved, concerning the institution of slavery. That Black slaves benefited from their oversight by "kindly" masters, particularly as compared to conditions they would have faced in Africa (see Gallagher and Nolan 2000). Like many of the stereotypes associated with minstrelsy and popular songs of the period, it was argued that enslaved people came from primitive societies and that after slavery was abolished, without the guidance of White masters, many would revert to a primitive social condition. The entire Lost Cause mythology is far more detailed, but the foregoing themes are most directly related to understanding imagery discussed in this chapter.

The work of Thomas Nelson Page—both his popular stories (see [1887] 1991) and social commentary (particularly *The Negro: The Southerner's Problem* [1904a])—are excellent examples of the genre. Importantly, while Page was among the most prolific and popular of Lost Cause authors during this period, he was also among the most prominent alumnus routinely mentioned in the UVA and W&L yearbooks examined during this time. Here, Thomas Nelson Page was an undergraduate at W&L who later studied law as a student at UVA (see *Corks and Curls* 1907, 3–7).

During the latter period explored in this chapter, Katz & Braly (1933) investigated common racial and ethnic stereotypes held by students at Princeton University, which although located in New Jersey had a disproportionately large Southern student body (about 40%). Here, the specific characterizations of African Americans as "highly superstitious, lazy, happy-go-lucky, ignorant, musical, and ostentatious" largely reflected the dominant cultural tropes popular at that time. Notably, Katz and Braly (1933) wanted to understand the relationship between "private" and "public" social selves. In some respects, this is an early precursor of Bonilla-Silva's (1997) concept of structural racism in that they argued that irrespective of the private feelings of students, the decisions they made were still ordered by normative public characterizations of race and ethnicity. For example, in the Katz and Braly (1933) study students sometimes claimed to have "nothing against" members of an ethnic, religious or racial minority group but still felt it necessary to exclude members of these groups from school organizations such as their fraternities (231).

Categories of images and text in university yearbooks

In this chapter, the yearbook pictures and text are organized into four content categories. The first are *popular caricatures* of Black men and women that routinely appeared in yearbooks. This content is highly developed examples of racial "humor" (both pictures and stories) often constructed by students. The second is content that provides indications of the *service roles African Americans played at these institutions*. This includes pictures of Black laborers and accounts as to how this labor was evaluated by White students. The third category provides examples of racialized content that occurred as *routine extracurricular campus events*—sporting events, musical productions, plays, literary events etc.—that students participated in. The final category investigates images and text related to *Civil War memorialization and Lost Cause iconography*. Collectively, these pictures and texts provide examples of Bonilla-Silva's (1997) assertion that race (like social class)—particularly during the period (1890–1930) investigated—is best conceived as a social structural condition. This structure was maintained, by cultural norms that ordered people's interactions with one another irrespective of the personal beliefs they held associated with race relations. Further, this culture was actively constructed and disseminated by people associated with the university who were often prominent figures locally and nationally.

Racial and institutional history of a few colleges in the study

While this chapter offers a range of visual material published by institutions located throughout Virginia, it focuses on the histories and corresponding yearbook content of three colleges in particular: Washington and Lee University (W&L), The University of Virginia (UVA) and James Madison University (JMU). The decision to focus on these schools was made for practical reasons. First, it is important to provide a limited institutional history of the colleges included in this study in order to effectively compare and contrasts their yearbook content, but space constraints make it difficult to provide all these histories. In the following chapters other schools will feature more prominently and their institutional histories will likewise be provided. Second, these institutions are all proximate to one another, located about 60 miles from each other in the Shenandoah Valley and Piedmont regions of Virginia, and they are somewhat representative of the different institutions of higher learning that existed in the Commonwealth at the time. During the period investigated, UVA and W&L accepted men, whereas the State Normal and Industrial School for Woman at Harrisonburg (later James Madison University) was established in 1908 as a college to educate women. At the time, UVA was among the most prominent public colleges in the country, while W&L was considered an excellent private college where men from affluent Southern families often matriculated. Finally, while there are ample Lost Cause representations in all the yearbooks studied, W&L College is clearly an exceptional case in this regard. Here, as outlined in greater detail below, the college was quite literally built upon a Civil War mythology directly associated with a past president of the college, the foremost military hero of the Confederate army, former General Robert E. Lee.

Washington and Lee University

Washington and Lee University is located in Lexington, Virginia, and is the ninth oldest institution of higher education in the United States. It was originally founded in 1749 as the Augusta Academy for men. The school became larger and more prominent following a gift of capital stock, in 1796, from George Washington that prevented its financial failure ("University Chronology" 2020). With the exception of one man, John Chavis, a freed Black man enrolled during this early period of the college, no Black students were admitted until 1966 when Dennis Haston and Leslie Smith entered the undergraduate college and law school respectively (Hill et al. 2020). Women were admitted to the law school in 1972 and to the undergraduate school in 1985.

The institution benefited directly and indirectly from enslaved labor. For example, in 1826 the school was granted the entire estate of "Jockey" Robinson, which included 70 to 84 enslaved men and women. Between the period of 1826 and 1852 these men and women were used as a labor force for construction of multiple university buildings, hired out to local citizens in the town, and eventually sold for the university's profit (Hill et al. 2020). During the Civil War era, the school's faculty and student body strongly supported the Confederate cause. In one case they sent students—in tandem with their peers from the neighboring Virginia Military Institute (VMI)—to join the ranks of General "Stonewall" Jackson's Brigade during the Battle of New Market, Virginia ("University Chronology" 2020).

Following the defeat of the Confederacy, former General Robert E. Lee became the president of the institution for five years until his death in 1870. During this time the school expanded its curriculum to include journalism, law and engineering. There have been historical accounts of hate crimes directed toward Black citizens by students during Lee's presidency that were largely unpunished. One Lee biographer, Elizabeth Pryor (2007), investigating his correspondence, reports that during his tenure students from the college formed their own branch of the Ku Klux Klan (KKK) and repeatedly attempted to rape Black girls living in Lexington. There were also at least two attempted lynchings carried out by students during his tenure (Serwer 2017). Almost immediately following Lee's death, Washington College was renamed Washington and Lee University ("University Chronology" 2020).

Beginning in 1905, increasingly large endowments allowed the school to create a School of Commerce and a new library. Well after the Civil War the school still attracted members of the Southern planter class, and administrators fashioned the institution as the embodiment of an agrarian and aristocratic Southern ideal. For example, in 1920 the W&L yearbook (*The Calyx,* 49) includes a letter that reports on the first million-dollar capital campaign and makes the following pitch to possible donors:

> In their public conventions over the South, the Confederate Veterans and the Daughters of the Confederacy are publicly accepting Washington and Lee as the typical all Southern University, and commending the patronage and liberality of all who value the ideas of the Old South.

Throughout the period examined in this study W&L was considered an excellent regional college and drew much of its enrollment from prominent families located throughout the South. It continues to attract a well-heeled student body. Using data gathered by Raj Chetty and his colleagues (2017), the *New York Times* ("Some Colleges" 2017) reported that in 2013 (in 2015 dollars) it was one of 38 schools in the United States that had more students from families in the top 1% of income earners (19.1%) as compared to the bottom 60% of income earners (8.4%). Generally, the school continues to enjoy an excellent reputation as a small liberal arts college and law school. Its 2018 enrollment (excluding the law school) totaled just 1,822 students. The student body is now evenly split in terms of gender (920 men and 902 women in 2018). Currently, a little less than 15% of the student body self-reports as being a member of a minority group. About 2.7% of the student population during this period was Black ("Facts and Stats" 2020)

James Madison University history

James Madison University is located in Harrisonburg, Virginia. It was founded as an all-women's school in 1908, originally the State Normal and Industrial School for Woman at Harrisonburg. The school was largely created because of an increasing need for classroom teachers, but it was also associated with the idea that opportunities for the higher education of women had been neglected. As such, the Normal School was seen as a progressive landmark in Virginia's education history. The population of students admitted in its first year of 1908 was "more than two hundred" women (*Schoolma'am* 1910, 23–27). In 1924, the school became known as the State Teachers College at Harrisonburg. In 1938 the school was renamed Madison College in honor of former President James Madison. This same year enrollment surpassed 1,000 students ("Historical Timeline" 2020).

In 1966, the Virginia General Assembly approved full coeducational status for the institution, which led to the first enrollments of men with residency on campus. That same year, Sheary Darcus became the first African American woman to be enrolled into the institution. In March of 1977, a bill was passed to rename the institution James Madison University. A decade later, the total enrollment had passed 10,000 students ("Historical Timeline" 2020). As of 2019, enrollment had increased to 21,763 students on a campus that is nearly 800 acres. That year the student body was 58% women and 42% men. By race/ethnicity the student population was 75% White, 6.5% Hispanic, 4.8% Black and 4.4% Asian ("Fact Book" 2019).

The school attracts a relatively affluent student body, although comparatively not as affluent as W&L or UVA. Using data gathered by Raj Chetty and his colleagues (2017), the *New York Times* ("Some Colleges" 2017) found that the 2013 freshman class at JMU ranked third in median family income ($147,000 in 2015 dollars) among its peer institutions in the United States. About 70% of the student population comes from families in the top 20% of income earners in the United States.

University of Virginia

Thomas Jefferson established this public university in 1819 in Charlottesville, Virginia. Much of the building of the university was done by enslaved Black laborers who were leased by the university. In 1825 the first classes were held with about 40–100 students enrolled. Between 1830 and 1860 there were an estimated 108–182 enslaved people serving the university. During this period, several university professors made academic arguments for the maintenance of slavery (see Holcombe 1858; Bledsoe 1856). By 1857 enrollment had increased to 645 students. During the Civil War roughly 3,500 alumni, students and faculty served in the war on the Confederate side; about 50 served in the Union army. The University of Virginia served as a hospital during the war and was occupied by the Union army in 1865. Between 1865 and 1888, the schools of industrial chemistry (1867) and agriculture (1869) were created. In 1888 the first edition of the *Corks and Curls* yearbook was published. In 1893 the granddaughter of a professor earned a math certificate, but not a degree because she was a woman. The following year the Board of Visitors decided there would be no women admitted to the university (see Gates 2018).

By 1929 student enrollment increased to 2,200, and the faculty increased to 290. In 1935 an African American woman, Alice Jackson, who graduated from Virginia Union, was denied admission to the university. In June of 1953 the first African American man was awarded a doctorate degree in education. Two months later the first African American woman, E. Louis Stokes Hunter, was awarded a doctorate degree in education. In 1969 a Black admissions officer was appointed, in part, to address the university's poor treatment of African Americans in the past. This same year the Board of Visitors proposed the limited admission of woman over 10 years. Officially, in 1972, women were admitted to the university on the same basis as men. In 1971 nearly 2,500 women applied to the university and represented 39% of the class that enrolled in Fall 1972. The following year saw the first African American fraternity and sorority on campus. In 1980 the number of women enrolled in the entering class surpassed the number of men. In the following decades there were efforts to modernize and update the university. In 2017 the Freedom Ring was built to honor the enslaved laborers that built the university (Gates 2018).

Currently, UVA is considered one of the best public universities in the United States, with a total enrollment of about 23,800 students and 3,200 full-time faculty. The undergraduate student body at UVA in 2018 was 6.7% African American, 14.6% Asian American, 6.4% Hispanic American, 56.8% White, and the remaining 15.5% from mixed ethnic and racial backgrounds ("Demographics" UVA). Using data gathered by Raj Chetty and his colleagues (2017), the *New*

York Times ("Some Colleges" 2017) found that the 2013 freshman class at UVA ranked 44th in median family income ($155,500 in 2015 dollars) as compared to its elite peer institutions in the United States. Close to 70% of the student population comes from families within the top 20% of income earners in the United States. Less than 20% come from the bottom 60% of income earners.

Visual representations of racial caricature

By far the most common representations of Black Americans in yearbooks during this period were caricatures that reflect stereotypes common in minstrel shows, popular songs and advertising at the time. For example, in *Corks and Curls* (UVA) there were well over 100 of these pictures and in *The Calyx* (W&L) there were close to 50 pictures. Comparatively, even though there were 12–17 fewer JMU yearbooks during the period examined, it was relatively rare to encounter these types of pictures in *Schoolma'am* yearbooks (seven pictures total). Moreover, the caricatures in *Schoolma'am*, except for one picture, were small background figures—as opposed to often front-and-center caricatures presented in the men's school yearbooks. Here, in three instances there was a relatively small caricature, an identical image that appears in three different yearbooks that all reference visiting minstrel shows (see *Schoolma'am* 1922, 64; 1923, 177). While there is other evidence (discussed below) that demonstrates race relations still largely ordered life among college women at the Normal School, the comparatively small amount of racial caricature in the *Schoolma'am* yearbooks is perhaps an indication that the active construction of racial meaning during these periods was often gendered. Mostly, it appears that White men during this period more actively participated in the construction and dissemination of the most malicious racial tropes and often presented material that referenced violence being committed toward Black men and women.

In terms of specific caricatures encountered, they represent all the dominant racial tropes of the period. For example, as shown in Figure 2.2, there are pictures of Black men stealing chickens (*Corks and Curls* 1913, 296); gambling (1920, 376); in trouble with police (1903, 61; 1920, 376); and eating watermelon (*The Calyx* 1904, 66). There are quite a few (n = 34) pictures depicting small Black children, or "pickaninnies" (see Figure 2.3), and also Black "Mammy" figures (n = 15) (see *The Calyx* 1908, 256). Sometimes, on the Florida and Louisiana State pages, the Black children are being chased by alligators (*Corks and Curls* 1906, 218; 1915, 385 and see Figure 2.6). The previous is far from an exhaustive list. Most of these pictures are ink-and-pencil drawings, but sometimes the caricatures are presented as staged photographs or more elaborate sketches as in Figures 2.2 and 2.3.

Figure 2.4 is an example of another reoccurring racial trope in which Black men, women and children are characterized as savages. Here, and in similar pictures, the setting often appears to be a tropical area where these men and women

FIGURE 2.2 Police officer with "Chicken Stealer" in *Corks and Curls* (1903, 61). Pictures of Black men stealing chickens and in trouble with police were common racial tropes portrayed in the yearbooks of the period.

Two Little **V**irginia Niggers.

1 (FLIM) : If y'r don't gimme piece that ar bixit I'll shove y'r ober.

2 (DAVE) : O, Lordy ! Now see what y'r done !

3 (DAVE, after recovering himself) : If y'r eber fools wid me agin I'll —— (Loses his balance).

4 (FLIM) : A-h ! I'm *so* glad !

FIGURE 2.3 Caricature of "Two Little Virginia Niggers" in *Corks and Curls* (1892, 147). Small Black children, or "pickaninnies," were by far the most common caricatures. Nearly all were pencil drawings. This skit was one of the few illustrated with photographs.

FIGURE 2.4 Image on the Golf Club page in *Corks and Curls* (1920, 357). A reoccurring theme in University of Virginina yearbooks involved caricatures that presented Black men, women and children as confounded by common modern objects. Or, they are shown fashioning primitive versions of a modern object, as presented in this picture.

FIGURE 2.5 Typical caricature associated with the introduction of student clubs in yearbooks. Published in the University of Richmond yearbook, *The Spider* (1899, 83).

are confounded by common modern objects (e.g. machines, equipment, instruments, teapots). Or, conversely, they are shown fashioning primitive versions of a modern object, in this case a golf club.

Mostly, these images are presented on the pages that introduced clubs, particularly the "State Clubs" and "Athletics" sections. These usually list student members and sometimes university professors are included as honorary members of these clubs. Figure 2.5 is a fairly typical caricature representation that introduces the university clubs in the University of Richmond (UR) yearbook.

Figure 2.6 is a typical representation of caricature on the Louisiana Club page at W&L. Here, the caricatures almost always appear as a header above (or within) the club name, with the student members (and sometimes faculty members) listed below.

Why do these pictures so routinely appear in the "State Clubs" section of the yearbooks? Probably the racial imagery acted to buttress Lost Cause mythology wherein states' rights—the organization of independent states—was the supposed primary motivation for the establishment of the Confederate States of America. Further, at the time these pictures were published there was a well-developed narrative among popular Southern writers that after the end of slavery Black Americans were increasingly reverting to a primitive state. This is sometimes characterized as comical, other times as a dangerous threat to White society.

J. A. Lee . . . . *President*
J. B. Gladney . . . . *Vice-President*
G. M. Hearne . . . . *Secretary*
A. S. Marx . . . . *Treasurer*

A. M. Cromwell	S. R. Jenkins
M. Frank	G. T. Madison
G. A. Fritchie	T. H. Scovell, Jr.
E. L. Gladney	T. C. Standifer
H. C. Hearne	W. F. Taylor

FIGURE 2.6 Typical state club racial imagery in *The Calyx* (1916, 242). It was routine to see depictions of "comical" violence—in this case an alligator chases a boy—on these pages. Student members of the club are listed, and sometimes faculty members are listed as honorary members.

Thomas Nelson Page (1904a), previously introduced as an alumni of both W&L and UVA, offers a typical Lost Cause perspective on the growing "depravity" and "retrogression" of Blacks in the post-slavery South in his text *The Negro: The Southerner's Problem* (1904a, 81):

> Universally, they [Southern Whites] will tell you that while the old-time Negroes were industrious, saving, and, when not misled, well-behaved, kindly, respectful, and self-respecting, and while the remnant of them who remain still retain generally these characteristics, the "new issue," for the most part, are lazy, thriftless, intemperate, insolent, dishonest, and without the most rudimentary elements of morality

They unite further in the opinion that education such as they receive in the public schools, so far from appearing to uplift them, appears to be without any appreciable beneficial effect upon their morals or their standing as citizens. But more than this; universally, they report *a general depravity and retrogression* of the Negroes at large in sections in which they are left to themselves, closely resembling a reversion to barbarism.

Notably, Thomas Nelson Page wrote the previous when he was a nationally acclaimed author who was largely credited with inventing the "plantation tales" genre. He later became an ambassador to Italy during the Woodrow Wilson administration. He is also typical of the Virginia aristocratic class that commonly matriculated at these schools. Here, both the Nelson and Page families had once owned large plantations around the state—Page County and Nelson County in Virginia are named after these families—and Page's relatives included past congressmen, a past state governor and a signer of the Declaration of Independence (Gross 1966).

Importantly, Thomas Nelson Page was routinely characterized as among the most notable and honorable of alumni in the W&L (where he received a honorary doctorate) and UVA (where he eventually passed his law exam) yearbooks examined during this period. In particular, the 1907 edition of *Corks and Curls* (1907, 3–6) is dedicated to him and opens with a biography of his life and accomplishments. The dedication (1907, xi) is roughly reproduced below:

WITH SENTIMENTS
OF THE HIGHEST ADMIRATION, PRIDE
AND AFFECTION THIS VOLUME OF CORKS AND CURLS
IS DEDICATED TO
THOMAS NELSON PAGE, LL.D.
WHO
WITH GRACEFUL PEN AND BRILLIANT IMAGINATION
HAS IMMORTALIZED
THE TENDER GRACE OF THE OLD SOUTH
GIVEN INSPIRATION TO THE NEW
AND WITH STEADFAST SERVICE AND LOVE
HAS PROVEN HIMSELF
NOT ONLY ONE OF THE MOST DISTINGUISHED
BUT ONE OF THE MOST LOYAL SONS
OF HIS AND OUR
ALMA MATR

It is later commented, "There is probably no writer of today who more thoroughly understands the negro character, and whilst Dr. Page recognizes the so-called negro question is one the future alone can solve, he has contributed to the discussion more than one paper, showing careful thought and wise suggestion" (5).

There are also a few instances in which Page (1904b)—in UVA alumni publications—comments on specific Black staff at UVA (see his references to

Henry Martin below). Importantly, other characterizations of "honorable" Black men who worked at these universities in general, and at UVA in particular, are always described in the manner in which Page characterized "old-time Negroes." Usually this includes an assertion that these old-time Negroes care little for education or other political opportunities (e.g. voting in elections) that they had been afforded directly after the Civil War (see Patton 1915). Taken together, it seems that Page's (1904a; 1904b) characterization of race relations was the normative standard held by most of the students attending UVA and W&L during this period.

The characterization of "Negro barbarism" and "social menace" in academic study at the University of Virginia

Accounts by popular authors like Thomas Page Nelson align completely with the dominant line of academic study—specifically in the field of eugenics— being undertaken at the University of Virginia during this period. Here, the study of racial superiority and inferiority saturated academic departments at the college during this period (see Dorr 2008; Reynolds 2018). At the time some of the more prominent eugenicists included faculty in the medical school, school of education and biology department (including the chair Ivey Lewis) (Reynolds 2020). More than that, as this study helps make clear, this "hierarchy of races" perspective ordered all race relations at the university.

An exemplary case of a faculty member influencing eugenics study at the University of Virginia School of Medicine is the tenure of Dr. Paul B. Barringer. A former UVA graduate who later returned to the school as a professor, Barringer wielded considerable influence as chairman of the faculty at UVA (1895–1903) during this period. He essentially acted as the dean of the medical college when its first modern hospital was being constructed in 1901. He later became the sixth president of Virginia Tech (1907–1913). Throughout his tenure at UVA, Barringer cultivated faculty who studied eugenics (Dorr 2008).

It would be hard to overstate the condescension—and at times vitriol— often directed at Black institutions of higher learning like Howard University (explored in the following chapter) by people associated with the Virginia colleges in this study. For example, Barringer (1901), while a professor at the UVA medical college, characterized institutions like Howard as committing a "crime against nature," as shown in the excerpt below from "The American Negro: His Past and Future," which outlines his views on Black education during this period. A copy of this paper was presented at the Tenth Annual Meeting of the Southern Education Association in Richmond, Virginia (1901), but was originally delivered at the Southern Medical Association Annual Meeting. Because of its popularity, it was being widely distributed to educational and medical associations throughout the South. In it Barringer (1901, 133) claims Black professionals are "an anti-social product, a social menace" and the institutions that train them are committing a "crime" against nature (italics added):

It is claimed that since education has raised up for this people its own leaders, the problem is solved. Far from it. An education that makes leaders at the expense of the led, is a failure. *Every negro doctor, negro lawyer, negro teacher, or other "leader" in excess of the immediate needs of his own people is an anti-social product, a social menace.* Neither in the North, the South, the East, nor the West can such a professional man make a living at his calling through White patronage; and to give him the ambition and the capacity, and then to blast his opportunity through caste prejudice and racial instinct is to commit a *crime against nature.* Nature made the White man and the Black; it made the natural and unalterable prejudice between the two races, and hence *the crime lies at the door of him who knowingly attempts the impossible.*

Notably, Barringer (1901, 134) also disapproved of providing freed Blacks with an industrial education—the more popular position championed by Booker T. Washington—which he argued would create political and economic "menace" (each use of this word is italicized below).

It is now suggested that the hope of the negro is industrial education. It is hailed as a discovery, and it is shrewdly claimed that this education will check political antagonism. This is a mistake. Any education will be used by the negro politically, for politics, once successful, is now an instinctive form of warfare. The question, then, plainly put, is simply this: Shall we, having by great effort gotten rid of the negro as a *political menace,* deliberately proceed to equip the negro of the future as an *economic menace?* Shall we, knowing his primitive racial needs, arm him and pit him against the poor White of the South?

Notable is that the president of Roanoke College, Julias D. Dreher (1901, 133–146) does offer a rebuttal of Barringer's (1901) paper (it was not delivered in person) that specifically calls into question the increasing "criminality" of Black Americans.

But overall, Thomas Nelson Page's (1904) characterization of African American reversion to barbarism after the Civil War—and his assertions that slavery was actually a civilizing institution—was completely in line with the ongoing academic discourse at UVA during this period. Moreover, as his and Barringer's ideas became accepted facts by the public at large, increasing numbers of groups—including prominent UVA alumni—advocated that the state legislature adopt the Racial Integrity Act establishing the so-called one-drop rule of racial categorization, which was passed in 1924 (Preston 2018). The one-drop rule officially designated anyone with a Black ancestor as being officially a member of the Negro race.

Important with respect to information presented in the following chapter concerning yearbook content published at Howard University—a college that also had a university hospital and was actively training Black doctors, nurses and dentists at the time—is Barringer's (1901) characterization of African Americans as "antisocial products, a *social menace*" (134), as well as his assertion that the responsibility for African American education should be taken from Black educators and given to White teachers who would train Blacks to be "law-abiding laborers" (134).

Racial caricature and representations of violence

While the caricatures presented previously represent shared "humor," past studies have indicated that characterizing groups of people as less human—and

FIGURE 2.7 "Yells" in *The Calyx* (1903, 141). Here, a man makes a small Black boy "dance" by pointing a shotgun at him. A Washington and Lee school cheer is shown beside this picture. Portraying people as less than human is often a precursor to legitimating violence against them. It was common to find caricatures in which violence is directed at Black men, women and children.

certainly as a social menace—is a common precursor toward legitimating violence toward these groups (see Hagan and Rymond-Richmond 2008). In particular, Roediger (1991) has documented incidences of violence in Northern cities directed toward African Americans during and after minstrel shows and blackface performances. To this end, it was not hard to find—in UVA and W&L yearbooks—caricatures in which violence is being directed at Black men, women and children. For example, there were depictions of KKK figures, a few of which were extraordinarily menacing and include hangings (see *The Calyx* 1928, 115 picture presented at the end of this chapter). Other pictures are presented as humor, usually depicting characters or animals chasing Black men and children (see Louisiana State Club picture, Figure 2.6). Figures 2.7 and 2.8 are a few examples of pictures that depict assault as humor. The first appeared in the W&L *Calyx* and shows a man who appears to be making a small Black boy "dance" by pointing a shotgun at him. A school cheer is presented beside this picture.

In the next example, Figure 2.8, the casualness and specificity of the assault—combined with its portrayal as comedy—may be an indication that this type of assault was fairly common on campus.

The following excerpt is an example of humor in the W&L *Calyx* (1902, 172) that includes a common racial trope of the period—that Black men sexually desire White women—which is then followed by backhanded praise for the intellect of Black activist Booker T. Washington. This also includes an example of another common narrative trope in which White students mock the pretensions of educated Black men. In this case, the reference is to the "brainy" Booker T. Washington, who actually had deeply conservative views on race relations and education, believing that Blacks should be pursuing vocational education designed to make them a productive labor force within White society.

> What's the name of that callow youth who always walks in front of the band? E.D. Ott? Well, please tell him that Booker Washington is no relative of mine, and if he is in favor of *my ex slaves* calicoing with Southern girls, he should at least keep his scandals out of the *Southern Collegian*.
>
> I haven't any grudge against Booker Washington; he is a brainy man and deserves credit for raising himself to a level so far beyond his race, but as for coons in general, confound them! Pardon my profanity; I picked that word up from one of your worthy professors.

Of note, Edward Dulaney Ott, referred to above, was a W&L student at the time and apparently had progressive views. He is sometimes referred to as "the idiot" throughout this yearbook (see *The Calyx* 1902, 68).

Finally, the picture in Color Plate 2 is not a caricature—it depicts members of the KKK on horseback at night—but it is included because it was used to introduce the "Clubs and Organizations" section of the 1922 edition of *Corks and*

FIGURE 2.8 The Basketball Club page in the University of Virginia yearbook, *Corks and Curls* (1928, 313), shows two men throwing snowballs at a Black woman carrying a basket of clothes.

Curls. Mostly, the picture helps demonstrate just how accepted the KKK was in Virginia society at this time, and apparently on the UVA campus too. Here, Kirt von Daacke and Ashley Schmidt (2019) have provided a detailed history, using local newspaper accounts, of KKK activity in Charlottesville, Virginia, where

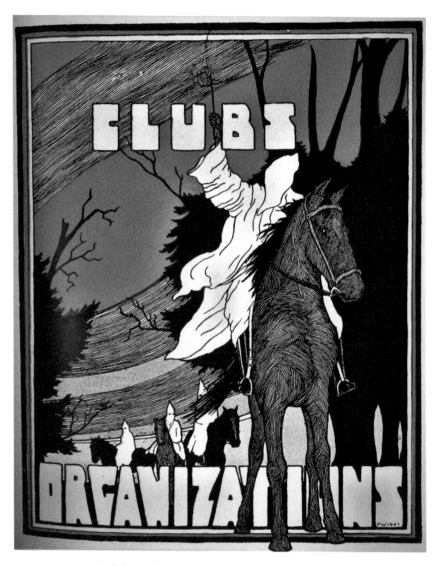

COLOR PLATE 2 "Clubs and Organizations" section in the University of Virginia yearbook with an image depicting the Ku Klux Klan riding horses at night (*Corks and Curls* 1922, 359). There were two Klan chapters in Charlottesville, Virginia, during this period, and one was located on the UVA campus.

there were two chapters in the community during this period, one located at the university. Inspired by the film *Birth of a Nation*, the UVA chapter was established around the time that the image in Color Plate 2 was published. So, while the KKK was not a club officially recognized in the UVA yearbook, the image may be a literal, if veiled reference to the fact that the organization did have a presence on campus.

Racial caricature and representations of medical care

One of the most interesting yearbooks of this period is *The X-Ray*, issued by the Medical College of Virginia (MCV) in Richmond, Virginia. For the most part, this yearbook includes many of the same types of racial caricatures as those presented in the previous section, but it also provides insights into how prejudices affected the delivery of medical care. Recently, there has been increasing focus on the uneven patterns of healthcare that different racial and ethnic communities in the United States receive, and here it is plainly observable as to how this was also the case, even more so, just after the turn of the century (Mays, Cochran and Barnes 2007). Figure 2.9 is an example in which a Black man—in the caricature he is actually chained to the gurney—receives attention from a young medical student who, it appears, is having difficulty giving the man an IV. In the picture the student is portrayed sitting on the man's chest and is clearly discombobulated. The Black patient is also clearly distressed.

In the panel series below (Figure 2.10), the scene describes the harried life of an OB-GYN doctor who is repeatedly getting calls for deliveries—he is actually shown traveling to a patient's house—in the middle of the night. In this case, one patient is an African American woman and he is shown delivering a child early in the morning. The last panel cuts to "four years later" and the same patient is pictured pregnant, waiting outside his office, but with three young children in tow.

The following pictures are presented side by side (Figures 2.11 and 2.12) that show students training to be dentists as they progress through the class ranks. Here, it is implied that the novice dentists, still working on their craft, practice on Black patients while the seniors, now confident in their ability, are given the White patients.

That Black patients, and also Black corpses, were routinely used to train MCV medical students is now well established. In particular, during renovations in 1994 that took place beside the old MCV medical building (the "Egyptian Building"), a repository of human bones was discovered in a well—long covered up—that was once beside the building (Kapsidelis 2011). Forensic study of these bones indicated that nearly all were of African American men and women. Here, it was soon clear that it was routine for MCV medical students during this period to dissect human corpses that had been retrieved from nearby Black cemeteries. Notably, one of the primary grave robbers, or "Resurrectionists," employed by the university to secure these corpses was a Black man, Chris Baker, who actually lived in the basement of the MCV medical building, where he worked "scraping bones" and preparing cadavers for dissection (Kapsidelis 2011; Utsey 2011). "Old Chris" and his work are well chronicled in the MCV yearbooks, where he is sometimes referred to as an Anatomist whose primary responsibilities were to prepare the cadavers and bones of human corpses for medical study (see *The X-Ray* 1913, 180 and discussed further below).

FIGURE 2.9 Racial caricatures that indicate how the quality and types of medical care associated with the White and Black communities was racialized at the Medical College of Virginia. In this picture a Black man, who is chained to a gurney, receives attention from a young medical student who, it appears, is having difficulty giving the man an IV. The student is pictured sitting on the man's chest. The Black patient is also distressed (*The X-Ray* 1921, 49).

FIGURE 2.10 The life of a harried OB-GYN portrayed in the Medical College of Virginia yearbook (*The X-Ray* 1934, 49). The doctor is called to deliver a baby and travels, in the middle of the night, to the house where he has been called. His patient is African American—the doctor is shown delivering a child early in the morning. Four years later the same woman is pictured pregnant and outside his office with three young children in tow.

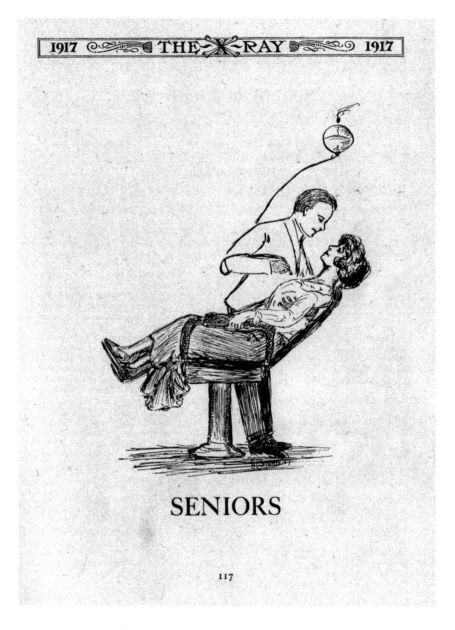

FIGURES 2.11–2.12 These two yearbook pages appeared in the same Medical College of Virginia yearbook and show student dentists progressing through the ranks of their training (*The X-Ray* 1917, 117 & 131). Here, it is implied that the novice dentists, still working on their craft, practice on Black patients, while the seniors, now confident in their craft, are given the sophisticated White patients.

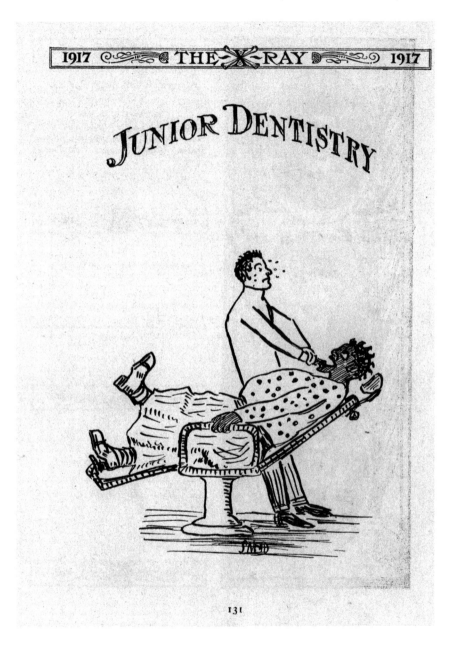

131

FIGURES 2.11–2.12 (*Continued*)

Race relations on campus: representations of university staff

Virginia college yearbooks routinely show black labor on campus. For example, all the wait-staff portrayed in these yearbooks—waiters, janitors, bellboys, groundskeepers, bellhops etc.—are Black men. Often, they appear in the background—literally standing behind the members of a club, for example (see Figure 2.13)—poised to be of service to the club members. Commonly found throughout the yearbooks is the appearance of servants wearing Black pants, a White shirt, a tie (or bowtie) and occasionally a White smock that hangs from the waist. Most of the time—with a few important exceptions discussed below—there is little corresponding text that references the specific roles these men performed.

There are some differences between the men's and women's colleges with respect to references to Black labor at these institutions. The women at the Normal School (later JMU) almost always reference the work that Black men and women do on campus with some appreciation: "Walker—Loyal and intelligent janitor for a score of years" is captioned beside one worker (*Schoolma'am* 1933, 178). In another representation, the caption "Their Patience Beside the Toiler" accompanies a picture of Black agricultural workers reaping hay (*Schoolma'am*

ACADEMIC DEPARTMENT—PARALLEL WORK OF THE CLASS IN THE SCIENCE OF SOCIETY.

FIGURE 2.13 A typical representation of a Black server on campus in *Corks and Curls* (1895, 46). The drawing depicts a Black man serving White men who are mostly seated around a formal dining table while another stands and gives a toast.

1925, 185). Comparatively, while these pictures clearly represent an established social hierarchy based on race, there is very rarely malevolence or humor being directed toward specific Black workers, and this contrast with much of the content in the UVA and W&L yearbooks.

A typical illustration (Figure 2.13 on the previous page) of Black staff in *Corks and Curls* (1895, 46) shows a small dining room wherein men in an academic department sit at a table covered in white tablecloth. In the foreground are a few figures sitting at a table, obviously enjoying themselves. Standing beside the table is an African American wearing the typical server outfit. Here, the man stands with his hands behind his back, but he is clearly ready to be of service to the young White men seated around the table. This illustration covers an entire page, and it was more common to find these types of illustrations that depict servers as compared to photographs.

Similarly, the image in Figure 2.14 is from a fraternity page in which the White members are seated and standing for a picture and the Black servant, employed by the fraternity, is similarly depicted "at the ready." Here, we can draw upon Erving Goffman's (1959) seminal study of everyday life to understand the symbolic meaning of how these African Americans are posed. Goffman

Lawrence, Wiant, C., Yeatts, Williams, L., Smith, Swanson
Gagge, Brydon, Vickers, Williams, R., Paschall, Robey, "Arthur"
Sanders, W., Sampson, Head, Kerr, Stennis, Benckenstein, Parker, Williams, W., O'Keefe, Wiant, A.

FIGURE 2.14 Fraternity photograph in *Corks and Curls* (1927, 222). The Black servant, "Arthur," stands with his hands behind his back while the fraternity members are mostly sitting with hands in their laps. Unlike "Arthur," the fraternity members are listed by last name.

claimed, "If unacquainted with the individual, observers can glean clues from his conduct and appearance which allows them to apply their previous experience with individuals roughly similar to the one before them or, more important, to apply untested stereotypes of him" (120). In the case of these fraternity photos, it is likely that the servers were staged in a way that was outside their own control, that they were instructed how to position themselves in these photographs, which reaffirmed their social hierarchy at these colleges.

The previous picture shows the Sigma Phi Epsilon fraternity photograph members seated in three rows in which nearly all have their hands across their laps. Also in the photograph is an African American who wears the typical server outfit and stands slightly apart from the group. Instead of having his hands or arms crossed, he stands with his arms behind his back, similar to the drawing presented previously. Also, the Black servant's name, "Arthur," is the only first name listed and appears in quotes. This picture is highly staged, probably the photographer or fraternity members told the server how to present himself, and the photograph reflects the regulation of race relations in which Black men at the institution are subservient. These types of fraternity pictures—arranged in roughly the same manner—are represented in UVA yearbooks into the 1970s (see chapter 4).

Notably, including African American staff in fraternity photographs was not a common practice at this time—it would become more common in the future— as no other pictures this year included Black staff standing among the White members. For example, in another fraternity photograph in the same yearbook, the Theta Chi fraternity has a different depiction of these servers. In this image the fraternity members are aligned much as in the previous picture, but their African American server is not pictured next to the group. Instead, he is in the background, seen leaning against a column with his arms crossed (*Corks and Curls* 1927, 226). Considering how staged these images are, it is unlikely that this man just happened to be caught in the picture. Rather, it was decided in this instance to place the servant behind the group.

Another fairly common representation of Black servants in some yearbooks is to present them in a montage, usually a page with several Black men that often indicates they have served the institution for a long period of time. For example, in a picture published in *Corks and Curls* several Black service workers from town and campus (apparently a local barber and a porter at the train station) are presented, often with an indication of their job (e.g. baggage transfer) under the caption "They're Still Here." The caption beneath one man, Charlie Brown, has the quote "I used to know your father" (*Corks and Curls* 1929, 48).

The montage presented In Figure 2.15, "Old-Timers We Have Known," was published in the Medical College of Virginia yearbook (*The X-Ray*), and while the names and specific occupations of the Black staff are not identified, many of the men appear to be servers and one appears to be working as a laboratory technician.

Old Timers We Have Known

55

FIGURE 2.15 Black staff pictured in the yearbook of the Medical College of Virginia (later Virginia Commonwealth University), located in Richmond, Virginia (*The X-Ray* 1921, 55).

On occasion, individual staff members—particularly those who are long serving and characterized as ideal servants—are remembered with affection by White students, university professors and administrators in yearbooks. Often, when these Black men are recognized there is a narrative trope that these men's long service to the university—along with the affection that students and staff have for these men—is an indication that notwithstanding new ideas about race relations, the "old ways" are clearly superior. An example from the University of Richmond (UR) yearbook (*The Web*) is presented in Figure 2.16 in which a *Richmond Times-Dispatch* editorial is reproduced with a quote in which the president of the university praises John Johnson—at the time the longest-serving employee at the college, having worked as a janitor for 43 years. The quote (italics added) from the editorial states:

> When the President of a University of learning steadily increasing in value, remembers a colored servitor in such words as these, *there is no danger that mounting figures of progress will alter the spirit of the institution*—The Richmond Times Dispatch, June 15th 1924. (*The Web* 1925, 437)

At the same time, it was also common to find narratives in which Black staff were denigrated and mocked by the very students and professors they were serving. An exemplary passage is offered below in which W&L students, apparently first in the student newspaper and then later when the column was reproduced in the annual yearbook (*The Calyx*), disparage a Black staff member who is portrayed as considering a "better opportunity" at another institution. Here, the satire mocks the idea that the man, as a janitor, is engaged in a profession that is valuable to the institution or that he can find meaning in his work. Further, it takes issue with the idea that there are opportunities for advancement within the context of this man's avocation.

Janitor Receives the Call: Washington and Lee in danger of losing valuable servant

Dick Gooch, our popular janitor, has just received a call from the trustees of the University of Bushwah, near Peoria, Ill. in which he is offered a position like he holds here....

When interviewed by a representative of the *Rank-Bum Fie*, he said, "Ah don' know weathah ah shall recept the offah or not, but it suttingly looks lumpricious to me. If ah does leave heah, hit won't be foh the fouh dollars extry a month which ah will git, but ah shall go foh de opachunity of distructive work which the field affodes."

"Ah was up dere free yeahs ago when ah axdressed the 'Janitors Sociation' of colleges, and lawdy, man, ah never saw sich a place as what needs mo' cleanin in all ma life. Ah shall gib ma answer to de publick as soon as ah can and ah promises ah will except only atter full consideration." (*The Calyx* 1912, 303)

It was also common to find caricatures and drawings in which apparently well-heeled individuals and/or students engaged in often backhanded abuse of the Black staff who are present to serve them. Usually these scenes are likewise

JOHN JOHNSON

"I hope it may not be thought inappropriate for me to mention here the forty-three years of faithful service of our colored janitor, John Johnson, who has been in the employ of Richmond College longer than any other person now living."—*From the twenty-ninth annual report of Dr. F. W. Boatwright, President of the University of Richmond.*

"When the President of a University of learning steadily increasing in value, remembers a colored servitor in such words as these, there is no danger that mounting figures of progress will alter the spirit of the institution."—*Richmond Times Dispatch, June 15, 1924.*

FIGURE 2.16 Yearbook page dedicated to John Johnson, at the time the longest-serving employee (43 years) at the University of Richmond (*The Web* 1925, 437). He was a university janitor, and his commendation by the UR president for his long service is editorialized by the *Richmond Times-Dispatch* as an indication of the "spirit of the institution."

COLOR PLATE 3 Portrayal of Black staff preceding the "Clubs and Organizations" section of the University of Virginia yearbook (*Corks and Curls* 1923, 333).

presented as humor. In the example represented in Color Plate 3 from *Corks and Curls* (1923, 333), a Black waiter, clearly perturbed, holds an ashtray beside a seated White man who is reading the paper and smoking. Figure 2.17 is a depiction of the Black wait-staff depicted in *The Calyx* (1913, 282).

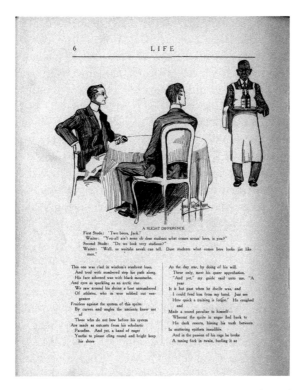

FIGURE 2.17   Black service and student humor appearing in *The Calyx* (1913, 282; insert p. 6).

The division of labor at Medical College of Virginia

In most respects, the Black labor at MCV was employed in many of the same occupations as represented in other Virginia schools. But the yearbook also indicates the division of labor in the medical fields in which Black men were also employed as lab technicians. Probably the most interesting occupation of Black men chronicled over time in *The X-Ray* is related to their jobs in the Dissecting Hall, where many were described as Anatomists (they work in the Anatomy Department). Here, the job is sometimes described as "preparing the bones" for the students and also "pickling cadavers," a description of preparing the bodies for the students to dissect. The Anatomists also constructed skeletons—made from human bones—for study too.

One of the longest-serving men was Chris Baker ("Old Chris"). In one account, Chris and some of his co-workers are described as "bogey men"—a reference to the fact that they routinely work with human corpses and also probably that they were once employed as grave robbers (or Resurrectionists) to secure cadavers for the college. Here, before the use of human cadavers was legal in Virginia, Baker was employed by the university—he received between 10 and

15 dollars a body—to secure cadavers that MCV students could use for study. Most of the cadavers that Baker collected were from a Black cemetery proximate to the college. In fact, shortly after Baker and four White medical students were caught grave robbing in 1882, the governor pardoned everyone involved and soon after the Virginia state legislature passed a bill allowing the college to use unclaimed corpses in the city morgue (see Kapsidelis 2011; Utsey 2011).

Because of his vocation, Baker was well known—and largely reviled—among Richmond's Black community, which was also often deeply suspicious of the Medical College too. In fact, it was routine for members of the community to avoid the areas proximate to the college because they believed that live Black bodies were being snatched and used for medical study (Utsey 2011). Below, the fact that the community (and apparently some students too) regarded Chris as a bogey man is referenced in the MCV yearbook.

Bogey men

> The Southland has given us many men who occupy niches in the Hall of Fame: there is however, a class of celebrities well known in song and story, but whose position is not so high. I speak of the bogey man, or as we always call them "boga man."... Around Richmond they used to tell you that Chris Baker would get you if you did not behave. "Chris" does not know how this started, but he says, "It's all account the fol niggers an de ignany Whites."
>
> Chris was born somewhere in Richmond, "fo de war" on the estate of Mr. Alexander Nott.... When the Retreat for the Sick was founded "Chris" went to work there as a general factotum for Dr. Frank Cunningham.... He went to the Medical College of Virginia then with Dr. Cunningham at the time the Old Dominion Hospital was being erected. (*The X-Ray* 1916, 213)

On the following page is a picture of Chris (Figure 2.18) and a poem that provides medical humor associated with "pickling" bodies in the Dissecting Hall.

"Old Chris" remained employed by the Medical College well after his career as a Resurrectionist—and his knowledge of human anatomy was apparently somewhat legendary among many students and professors at the college. The following poem portrays the work that Chris does as "ghastly and ghoulish" but also necessary for science and was accompanied by a painting that appeared in the *X-Ray* (1926, 72) done by Dr. William Brodnax, who was employed at MCV during this period.

> To Old Chris
> To thee, who mindless of the helpless dead,
> These crude, unpolished lines are for you penned;
> Who'll daily sit in age, with hoary head,

The X-Ray, '13

180

Dissecting Hall

*They did not die that we might learn; but ill's the wind
that blows no man good.*

Freshman—He who dreams by night alone knows no
fear.

Sophomore—I believe I could eat a cadaver.

Lame Duck—A little hard luck.

Dr. Christian—"King."

Poem

We know not of the days of then,
When Brown Sequard was there,
But just a line or two, my pen,
Of the present tell-tale air.

I've heard and told of "Cussing Jones,"
But here the things for now,
A vault of dampened meat and bones,
Text, scalpell and sweating brow.

Vats of human beings pickled,
And some on tables, too,
And solemn Chris, laughing, tickled,
As he shifts the pickled crew.

Hard work, hot scrubs, and then perfume
But the smell is always there,
'Till Dr. Christian plays the tune,
"We have passed the Pickle Chair."

F. H. Lee.

"CHRIS"

FIGURE 2.18 "Chris," along with some other Black men chronicled over time in *The X-Ray*, the Medical College of Virginia yearbook, worked in the Dissecting Hall and is described as an "Anatomist" (*The X-Ray* 1913, 180). These men are described as "preparing the bones" for the students and also "pickling" cadavers for dissection. "Chris" is often the Anatomist shown during this early period. He appears to have done this work at MCV before the civil war for a doctor who eventually took up residency at the college.

And scrape their bones, unthinking of your end.
While you pursue your ghastly, ghoulish trade,
Does no compunction ever come to you?
That as these cadavers, you were made.
And may have to receive this treatment, too.
Yet, let us in good feeling, you protect.
And all have one kind word to say to you;
That the ghouls are the students, who dissect,
And will give you this after task to do.
For science 'tis aimed, yet you get no part
In what is gained, and they the honors bear;
In co-partnership, you share not their art.
But day by day must sit and cut and pare.

Dr. John W. Brodnax

The painting shown in Figure 2.19, also by Dr. Brodnax, represents another Anatomist at MCV, Peyton Johnson—it shows him scraping bones—who worked at the college for 21 years before his death in 1928, and it is also accompanied by a poem. Similar to the portrayal of "Old Chris," the poem describes Peyton as a "Grim Scavenger" working in a "hall so grim and drear." It also indicates, when it describes the body of a "negro homicide" that Peyton is working on, that well after the era of body snatching was ended, most of the bodies that the Anatomists were preparing for students were Black men and women unclaimed at the city morgue.

As stated previously, before the Virginia legislature allowed for the legal trade of corpses for medical use, it was routine for MCV and UVA medical students to secure human corpses for dissection from Black cemeteries in Richmond. Often, black janitors employed at these colleges were paid to secure these bodies. Probably one reason why Chris Baker lived, with his family, in basement floor of the MCV medical building was so that he could take possession of bodies at night when they were delivered to the medical college. Afterward, he would work "scraping bones" and also preparing cadavers—described above as "pickling" the bodies because they were placed in large barrels and then "stirred"—for dissection (Kapsidelis 2011; Utsey 2011). While "Old Chris" was a notorious grave robber, it appears that "Peyton"—described as an elder of his church—was employed after the era of grave robbing had largely ended (see *The X-Ray* 1915, 213).

Black staff at the University of Virginia: Henry Martin ("Uncle Henry") and Peter Briggs ("Uncle Peter")

By far the most chronicled members of Black university staff encountered in the yearbooks were accounts of "Uncle Henry" (Henry Martin) and "Uncle Peter" (Peter Briggs) that occurred over roughly three decades in *Corks and Curls*. These

THE ANATOMIST

Peyton

Grim Scavenger old who still holds sway
In your hall so grim and drear,
I believe you think as you toil away,
Scraping the bones that soon will lay
In the students' boxes for many a day,
Even after you're dead and gone your way—
What those bodies were while here.

You scrape them and boil them long and well
In your hall so grim and drear,
I'm sure you know what tales they tell,
While the cauldron bubbles and vapours smell,
Tales of deeds that were dark and fell,
As the darkest pit in deepest Hell,
Tales you'd do well to fear.

That bag you picked and set aside
In your hall so grim and drear,
Holds the hand of a dainty infanticide,
And you placed it apart with a sense of pride—,
Away from the bones of a suicide,
And the skull of a negro homicide,
Which leered so ghastly it seemed to deride
The Fate that had placed it there.

You've become such a part of this musty room,
Your hall so grim and drear,
That after you've gone to meet your doom
And the twilight shadows, gathering, loom
Deep in this alcove—a potter's tomb—
The skeletons, hanging, will miss their groom,
And rattle and clash in the darkening gloom
—But I think you'll still be near.

"K"—'26.

104

FIGURE 2.19 A painting of Peyton Johnston at work in the Medical College of Virginia Department of Anatomy "preparing bones" for the MCV students. (*The X-Ray* 1926, 104). Two years after this picture appeared he was memorialized following his death in 1928 having worked at the college for 21 years.

began with an in-depth characterization of both men in the 1890 issue that included other university staff as well (128–135). Both these men had previously been enslaved laborers who worked at the university before the Civil War. Henry Martin was subsequently employed at UVA his entire adult life. Martin, usually referred to as "Uncle Henry," was widely known as the campus "Bell-Ringer" and was also employed as a janitor. One account of Henry's life that appears in the *Corks and Curls* (1914, 149–151) as a "Dramatic Monologue"—it was clearly written by a White student—was published four years after his retirement following nearly 60 years of service. In this "dramatic" account, shown in figure 2.20 below, Uncle Henry tells the story concerning his life at UVA as the school's Bell-Ringer.

Importantly, accounts of Uncle Henry in *Corks and Curls* are fictionalized, although almost always presented from his point of view. The following account tells of how Uncle Henry was connected to the university since "before the war" when he was 19 years old. The account also offers a direct association with Thomas Jefferson, stating that Martin was born at Monticello, where his family was enslaved. In this rendition of his life, Uncle Henry states that his mother "belonged to Mr. Jefferson" because she married Jefferson's man-servant. Later, Henry was bought by Colonel William Carr (spelled "Cyarr" in the dramatic account) after Jefferson's home, Monticello, was sold. Here, Henry Martin became associated with UVA by Colonel William Carr's uncle, Dr. Frank Carr, who was a member of the governing board at UVA and personal friend of Jefferson. In fact, Henry Martin was, during his lifetime, owned by several members of the Carr family in Albemarle County and apparently loaned to the university at times both before and during the Civil War ("Henry Martin" 2020).

In the previous idealized passage Uncle Henry recalls how he values "politeness" over "education"—and most other accounts of Henry's worldview usually include that he always voted Democratic (as opposed to Lincoln's Republican Party) (see Patton 1915). In this fictionalized account in *Corks and Curls* (1914, 50) Henry recalls how Colonel Venable characterized his political views by stating, "Uncle Henry, you belong to the Know-nothin' Party, don't you?" Henry agrees, and then he reinforces his place in the social hierarchy by stating:

> A crowd of folks said to me once: "Henry, we're goin' to send a colored man to Congress." I said, "My dog would be recognized as good as any colored man you could send." No, sir, I knew it wouldn't ease my mind to vote for a colored man and I ain't ever done it."

Thomas Nelson Page, a prominent alumnus of UVA and W&L discussed previously, encountered Henry Martin as a student at UVA and later wrote about him. Here, Page (1904b, 118) characterizes Henry in the same manner as the "old-time Negroes" who he considered "well-behaved, kindly, respectful, and

Uncle Henry: Bell-Ringer

A DRAMATIC MONOLOGUE

"As true to that bell as to my God"

"I DUN know why they named me Henry Martin. Ole Missus got it out'n a book. I was born the fo'th day o' July, 1826, the day Mr. Jefferson died. Colonel William Cyarr bought me when Monticello was sold. I was raised on the Benefer [Bentivar] Farm six miles from here. My mother belonged to Mr. Jefferson. She married his body-servant. Cose I don't remember Mr. Jefferson, but I remember my mother and she was a good woman. No, sir, Colonel William Cyarr didn't have nothin' to do with the University, but his uncle, Dr. Frank Cyarr, was a member o' the Boa'd and a pus'nal friend o' Mr. Jefferson. I been connected with the University sence I was nineteen years old, but not 'ficially connected with it till they made me bell-ringer. Yes, sir, I was bell-ringer at this University for fifty-three years and, P'fessor, I been as true to that bell as to my God. Bell-ringin' don't 'mount to much now. I sometimes think the University'd go right on if they didn't have no bell. Pete don't ring it till ha'f pas' seven, but up to the Surrender I rang it at fo' o'clock every mornin'. After the Surrender I rang it at ha'f pas' fo', then at five. P'fessor, it means somethin' for a man to ring a bell continuous at this University for fifty-three years.

"They don't seem to me to pay much 'tention to the bell now, but I had to wake up the cooks and the dormitory students. Now as I come to think on

FIGURE 2.20 A picture and "dramatic account" of the life of "Uncle Henry," the UVA "Bell- Ringer," in *Corks and Curls* (1914, 149–151). Henry Martin was a formerly enslaved man who later worked at UVA for nearly 60 years and is often represented as the "ideal" Black servant. This account was clearly written by a White student, published several years after Martin had retired from the university.

self-respecting" (Page 1904a, 81). In effect, Uncle Henry "knows his place" in the social hierarchy on campus. Indeed, it is possible that Thomas Nelson Page had Henry Martin specifically in mind when he characterized "old-time Negroes." For example, in a UVA alumni publication he characterized Uncle Henry—who brings him supper during his Bachelor of Laws examination—using similar language. He reports that Uncle Henry bolstered his low spirits when he said, "Mr. Page, I'm prayin' for you." Page (1904b, 118) summarizes: "He is a type of what will never be again: a fine old fellow whose life does more to solve the race problem than all the discussions of politicians." Similarly, another university professor, in a memoir of his time at the University of Virginia, stated that Martin "fully recognized that he was neither a professor, or student, nor a White man," but just a Bell-Ringer, and that "to serve was his delight" (Culbreth 1908).

One can only speculate what Henry Martin's real and true feelings were, although they were likely far more nuanced then those attributed to him by White students and faculty. Here, his characterization by White men always reinforces that Henry Martin's renown is associated with his long service—he is often characterized as being quietly diligent—along with the fact that he knew his duty was to serve White men on campus. Or, as John S. Patton (1915, 587) observed in an alumni publication shortly after his death: "To the day of his death he maintained that it was the duty of the Negro to serve the White folks faithfully, to acquire good manners rather than book-learning, and to vote the Democratic ticket."

It is important to recognize that John S. Patton's opinion was the normative account held by those who worked and attended UVA. Further, Patton was also a man of considerable stature in the Charlottesville and university community. For example, during his life he served as the Superintendent of the Charlottesville Public Schools and also as a librarian at the university. Patton (1906; Patton and Doswell 1900) also authored texts about the history of the university and Thomas Jefferson. In short, Patton's view of history—including the history of Henry Martin—was considered the definitive account.

Peter Briggs ("Uncle Peter" and "Buzzard Pete")

In the introduction of this study it was asserted that universities can be conceived as incubators and hubs of racial context that students later applied to ongoing race relations during their lifetime. The intention was to generally characterize the broad effects that a university's race structure had on maintaining negative racial tropes within a society. But here, with respect to the characterization of Peter Briggs, there is an example of how a specific image and racial caricature—crafted and shared by Virginia alumni over what appears to be a period of over 30 years—was fashioned into a grotesque representation of racial stereotype that was then quite literally sold for public consumption.

Along with Henry Martin, the other Black worker featured most prominently in *Corks and Curls* during the period investigated was "Uncle Peter" (Peter Briggs). Often, his temperament was negatively juxtaposed to that of Uncle Henry. Again, the following, written by John S. Patton (1915), appeared in the *Alumni Bulletin* shortly after Martin's death. In the piece Patton directly compares the two men: "Henry Martin represented the best type of the negro of the Old South. He had none of the buffoonery of that almost equally famous University character, 'Uncle Peter,' but was sedate, dignified, and studiously polite" (587).

The most libelous characterization of Peter Briggs was published in *Corks and Curls* (1890, 131–132) and states the following:

> Uncle Peter's accomplishments are comparatively few; his favorite occupations seem to be doffing his hat, requesting a dime and purloining coal. No one could say that Uncle Peter had a fine tenor voice, but he can be induced by the exercise of a little diplomatic coaxing and a portion of "the almighty dollar," to chant a soft melody (hardly of the Italian School) the burden of which song is the unfortunate fate of a young person who was indiscreet enough to appropriate a watermelon from an adjoining neighbor's patch, and whose family amused themselves for a subsequent period in removing a load of birdshot from the aforesaid unlucky individual's back.

And again, nearly two decades later, also in *Corks in Curls* (1909, 305), the following imagined conversation between Uncle Peter and Uncle Henry was published (see also Figure 2.21). Here, there is a fantastical rendering in which the two men are characterized as rivals of each other, and Uncle Peter—in a supposed conversation with Henry Martin—plaintively ask him:

> Lis'en heah, Henry, lis'en heah,
> Why you walk so stiff, foh Gowd,
> Why you no laugh'n scrape erbout,
> Why you swallow dat ramrod?

Importantly, there has been some investigation by historians in Charlottesville, particularly by Brendan Wolfe (2013a; 2013b; 2013c) at the Virginia Humanities Council, that uncovered some of Peter Briggs's biography. What precipitated Wolfe's investigation was a picture of Briggs, characterized as "Buzzard Pete," which was evidently fashioned into a postcard by a Detroit publishing company in 1905. Wolfe encountered the postcard and the original picture on a popular blog, and this led to speculation concerning the identity of the man who was clearly standing on the UVA campus. The original picture is presented in Figure 2.22 and its rendering into a postcard in Figure 2.23.

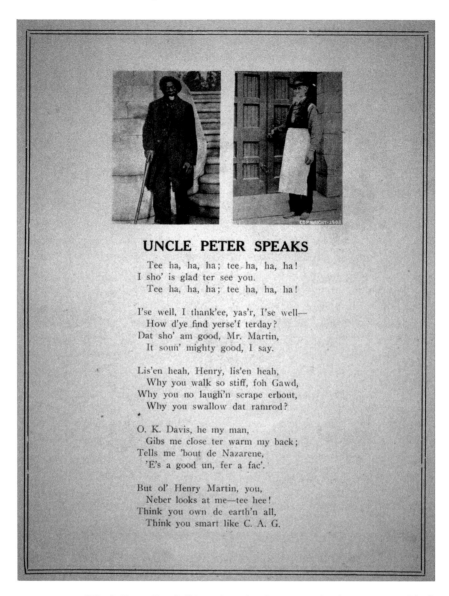

FIGURE 2.21 "Uncle Peter Speaks" is an imagined conversation between two Black University of Virginia employees, "Uncle Peter" and "Uncle Henry," published in the UVA yearbook, *Corks and Curls* (1909, 305). Here, there is a fantastical rendering in which the two men are characterized as rivals.

FIGURE 2.22 Peter Briggs, described as "Buzzard Pete," pictured on the UVA campus, was rendered into a postcard in 1905 by the Detroit Publishing Company. This picture was made available from a collection at the Library of Congress ("Buzzard Pete" Library of Congress).

This is not the only postcard of Peter Briggs in that a very similar composition, titled "Uncle Peter's Laugh," in the UVA Visual History Collection, appears to have been issued around the same period (1905–1920). Brendan Wolfe and others then conducted a quick internet search and found that Peter Briggs

FIGURE 2.23 The tinted postcard rendered from the previous picture (see Figure 2.22) that was produced by the Detroit Publishing Company in 1905. Provided by the University of Virginia Library ("Buzzard Pete" UVA).

FIGURE 2.24 A man who has been identified as likely being Peter Briggs, probably sitting for Rufus Holsinger, a well-known community photographer. ("Uncle Peter" from the *Holsinger Studio Collection, Albert and Shirley Small Special Collections Library, University of Virginia*).

was still being referred to in alumni publications many years after his death. Below is an example from *The Virginia Reel* ("Alumnal Lament" 1921, 23):

> Alumnal Lament
> There's someone ELSE I'd like to greet—
> The Lawn is melancholy; sweet,
> It's true, the Arcades now appear
> In the mellow glow of yeaster year—
> But who is missing?—Uncle Pete—
> Old Buzzard Dancer Uncle Pete!
> A Black old man all filled with glee—
> A grizzled face I'd like to see;
> A cracked old voice I'd like to hear
> (Ah, 'twas music to the ear!)
> "Yassuh! Yassuh! Hee-hee-hee!"
> Old Buzzard Pete I'd like to see—

Given the previous characterizations of Peter Briggs, it is important to present a picture where the composition is different and better captures his humanity. In the UVA library is a picture of a man who is likely Peter Briggs (see Figure 2.24) that was taken by Rufus Holsinger who posed Briggs in a more dignified manner. Holsinger was a well-known community photographer, and the UVA library special collections include many portraits of Black university workers, as well as Black residents who lived in Charlottesville during this period.

Race and extracurricular campus life: sports and entertainment

Sports

Washington and Lee College was among the first colleges to enact the so-called Gentlemen's Agreement in which the college demanded that opposing sports teams "sit" their Black players. Probably this unwritten policy was created during the 1916–17 season when W&L traveled to Rutgers for a game and threatened to forfeit if the Rutgers team did not bench their only Black player, Paul Robeson, who later became a prominent singer and actor. Rutgers agreed to sit Robeson, and the game ended in a tie (Duberman 1996, 107–111).

The local and national press later debated the "color line" in 1923 when Washington and Jefferson College refused to bench the football team's Black quarterback and W&L decided to forfeit rather than play the game. The player who refused to sit, Charlie "Pruner" West, later became the first Black quarterback to play in the Rose Bowl (Pell 2017). Remarkably, following this forfeit *The Calyx* (1924, 188) editors claimed the opposing team had acted with dishonor and marshaled support for their position by citing regional newspapers who supported the decision to forfeit the game.

> Several press opinions are as follows: from a Richmond paper–"Rightfully, the blame belongs to the Institution which so forgets the properties as to decline to yield a point in favor of its competitor's traditions. Washington and Jefferson must have known that no Southern team would meet a negro in sport, and the tacit agreement must have been that West should not play."
>
> *Charleston Gazette*–But the facts are that the *World* does not mention that a gentleman's agreement was broken, if not a verbal contract, and if there was any lack of courage it was manifest when fear of public opinion and anger prevented the pact from being kept.

University of Virginia teams also quickly adopted the Gentlemen's Agreement, which was maintained until after World War II (see chapter 4). Sometimes debate over the color line in sports is alluded to in *Cork and Curls*. Mostly, it is discussed as parody that often mocks Black athletes and suggests that Black sports are farcical. The sketch in Figure 2.25, "Some Color Lines on College Sports" (*Cork and Curls* 1923, 282), employs this strategy by describing a baseball game played by Black teams as absurdity. Here, the author's "hometown darkey friends cavort around the bases" at such a great rate that their "bright red uniforms" eventually enrage a nearby bull, which charges the field after a close call at home plate (282).

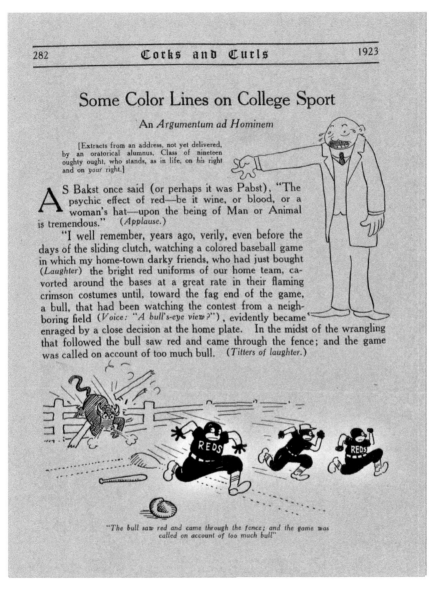

Corks and Curls 1923

Some Color Lines on College Sport

An *Argumentum ad Hominem*

[Extracts from an address, not yet delivered, by an oratorical alumnus, Class of nineteen oughty ought, who stands, as in life, on *his* right and on *your* right.]

AS Bakst once said (or perhaps it was Pabst), "The psychic effect of red—be it wine, or blood, or a woman's hat—upon the being of Man or Animal is tremendous." (*Applause.*)

"I well remember, years ago, verily, even before the days of the sliding clutch, watching a colored baseball game in which my home-town darky friends, who had just bought (*Laughter*) the bright red uniforms of our home team, cavorted around the bases at a great rate in their flaming crimson costumes until, toward the fag end of the game, a bull, that had been watching the contest from a neighboring field (*Voice:* "*A bull's-eye view?*"), evidently became enraged by a close decision at the home plate. In the midst of the wrangling that followed the bull saw red and came through the fence; and the game was called on account of too much bull. (*Titters of laughter.*)

"*The bull saw red and came through the fence; and the game was called on account of too much bull*"

FIGURE 2.25 "Some Color Lines in College Sport" in *Corks and Curls* (1923, 282). Debate over the "color line" and the Gentlemen's Agreement in college sports is alluded to in the yearbooks. Here, Black sports are discussed as parody that suggests they are farcical. This sketch and narrative employ this strategy when describing a baseball game played by Black teams as absurdity.

The caption below states: "The bull saw red and came through the fence; and the game was called on account of too much bull" (282).

While these college teams refused to play against teams with Black players, it appears that many did employ Black porters who were responsible for the

WAMPLER, PHOTO.

UNIVERSITY OF VIRGINIA BASE-BALL TEAM, '93.

R. D. ANDERSON, Manager. SMITH, Captain. ROBERTSON, Pres. G. A. A. GEORGE, the Porter.
RHETT. WATTS. HUME. TURLEY. WORTHINGTON. STONE.
G. NELSON. ROBT. NELSON. McGUIRE. ABBOT. R. E. LEE MARSHALL.

FIGURE 2.26 The baseball team at the University of Virginia, with George, the team porter, in *Corks and Curls* (1894, 133). Players are designated by last names, but George, the team porter, like other Black staff included in photographs, is identified only by his first name.

equipment and other team arrangements. On very few occasions, these men are pictured with the team, such as in the picture presented in Figure 2.26.

Minstrel shows

At all the schools, minstrel shows and choral groups that performed in blackface were common. Notably, while there appear to be some differences between the women and men as related to some racial attitudes, it is clear that the women at the Normal School often watched, and looked forward to, minstrel productions on campus. Sometimes these appear to have been visiting productions, and at other times they appear to have been student productions. For example, *Schoolma'am* yearbooks include repeated references to the visiting VMI minstrels but also reference women who appear to be part of blackface performances (see *Schoolma'am* 1921, 95; 1922, 164; 1922, 169; 1923, 177). On at least one occasion the students themselves staged a production, and that picture is presented in Figure 2.27.

Figure 2.28 shows a similarly composed picture that appeared in the University of Richmond (UR) yearbook (*The Spider* 1897, 68) under the heading

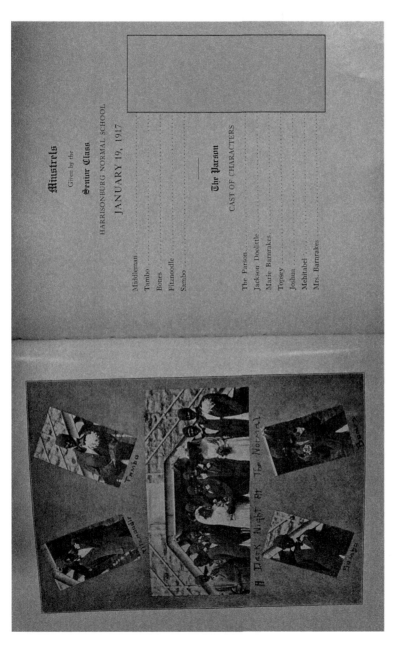

FIGURE 2.27 "A Dark Night at the Normal" minstrel production at the Harrisonburg, Virginia, Normal School in *Schoolma'am* (1917, 38–39). Women at the Harrisonburg Normal School looked forward to attending visiting minstrel productions (often staged by nearby men's colleges) and also staged their own shows. This show was performed on Robert E. Lee's birthday, at the time a state holiday in Virginia.

THESPIANS FROM "DARKEST AFRICA."

Photographed by J. W. Buck.

FIGURE 2.28 "Thespians from 'Darkest Africa'" is a typical minstrel performance staged at the University of Richmond (*The Spider* 1897, 68).

FIGURE 2.29 Campus performances at Washington and Lee College depicted in *The Calyx* (1920, 214).

"Thespians from the Darkest Africa." The next picture, Figure 2.29, is a fairly typical montage photograph from *The Calyx* (1920) of what are likely several performances that took place on the W&L campus during the academic year in which there were often a few figures represented in blackface.

During this period, there were also pictures—particularly in *Corks and Curls*—that showed choral groups performing on campus in blackface. Here, two local Charlottesville historians have detailed the long history of blackface performances by the UVA Glee Club, which traveled to venues throughout the state. These performances were well established before the first UVA yearbooks were published and continued into the 1930s (von Daacke and Schmidt 2019). While there were no pictures of women choral groups at the Normal School in Harrisonburg performing in blackface, Meg Mulrooney (2019), a professor of history at JMU, has investigated scrapbooks and diaries of women students during this period and found that they also routinely dressed and performed skits in blackface. In particular, dressing in blackface and performing skits as minstrel characters appears to have been part of the initiation ceremony into the Lee Literary Society, likely established by a professor of history at the university, John C. Wayland. Notably, the connection between blackface performance and Civil War iconography was often quite explicit at this school. In particular, the minstrel production previously represented, in Figure 2.27, "A Dark Night at the Normal," was staged on Robert E. Lee's birthday, at that time an official state holiday in Virginia.

Lost Cause memorialization

That Robert E. Lee is routinely memorialized in Washington and Lee year-books will not surprise most readers. Moreover, few will be surprised that the content of *The Calyx* yearbooks is sometimes associated with the ongoing creation of General Robert E. Lee as a great American. Importantly, on the W&L campus there is an extraordinary memorial to Robert E. Lee that during its commission, building and inauguration was the epitome of Lost Cause iconography. Here, Lee Chapel—a 600-seat church directly commissioned by Robert E. Lee shortly before his death—inters the body of not only Robert E. Lee but also members of his immediate family. The crypt is located adjacent and below the chapel. In the center of Lee Chapel—the focal point within the building— is a slightly larger than life-size marble statue, often referred to as the "Recumbent Robert E. Lee" in which he is rendered "asleep" on the battlefield (see Figure 2.30). Although Lee is not interred within the sculpture, it has the effect of being a sarcophagus, and it was referred to as such by the sculptor and men who commissioned the work (see Daniel 1883). In all, the chapel and statue are an extraordinary example of a bricks-and-mortar edifice designed to create and then maintain what has been characterized as the "civil religion" of the Lost Cause (see Wilson 1980).

During this period there were efforts—some more successful than others— to expand and incorporate the Lost Cause mythology into the institutional framework of nearly all public and private educational institutions in the region. For example, there was clearly an effort to institutionalize the mythology associated with Lee specifically, and the Lost Cause generally, at the

FIGURE 2.30 "The Spirit of Lee" in *Schoolma'am* (1918, 119), with the recumbent Lee statue in the background. The photograph is accompanied by a poem that characterizes Robert E. Lee's mausoleum on the Washington and Lee campus as "her holiest Mecca."

Normal School in Harrisonburg even though this institution was founded over 40 years after the Civil War.

While there is comparatively much less Civil War iconography and memorialization in the *Schoolma'am* yearbooks, it was notable that around the 50th anniversary of the Civil War there was an increase in material in which pictures of Lee, and a Lee Literary Society, appear more often (see *Schoolma'am* 1914, 101; 1917, 110; 1918, 119). Often, the school calendar indicates events—public readings, for example—that took place on January 19, the date of Robert E. Lee's birthday, which was designated by the Virginia Assembly, in 1889, as an official state holiday. The picture presented in Figure 2.30—the recumbent statue within Lee Chapel—also routinely appears in the W&L yearbook (see *The Calyx* 1926, 280; 1924, 62). In the *Schoolma'am* (1918, 119) yearbook a photograph of the recumbent Lee is accompanied by a poem that characterizes Robert E. Lee's resting on the W&L campus as "her holiest Mecca."

Below is a poem characteristic of content generated and discussed within the Lee Literary Society at the Normal School in Harrisonburg. It was published below a drawing of the Confederate battle flag (*Schoolma'am* 1917, 110):

> *Lee*
>
> Thou who leddest our gray-clad band
> Far beyond Virginia's land—
> Oh, to give a name to thee,
> One that will forever be,
> Builded out of love for thee—
> This Virginia gives to Lee.
> Thou who hold'st the hearts of all—
> Listen and hear Virginia's call:
> "Oh, to weave a wreath for thee,
> One that will forever be
> Woven out of love for thee"—
> This Virginia weaves for Lee.
> Thou who fate could not cast down,
> Thou whose coverage was a crown—
> Oh, to voice a song for thee,
> One that sweeter e'er shall be,
> Spoken from the heart of me—
> This my wish, beloved Lee!

In many respects, this period during, and shortly after, the 50th anniversary of the Civil War (1915) and Lee's death (1920) appears to represent a high-water mark regarding the memorialization of the Civil War in general (and Lee in particular) at the women's college. At the same time, that regional institutions honored Robert E. Lee is an indication of the extent to which Lost Cause mythology was being adopted within the region by all academic institutions.

While all the schools examined memorialized the Civil War, Washington & Lee University is still unique in that Lee's mythology—his supposed exemplary life and superior moral philosophy—is quite literally the ideal upon which the institution was being constructed. Often, this effort is directly connected to memorializing Robert E. Lee as the greatest of all American leaders (see below). In effect, the success of W&L at this time—in terms of its increasingly stellar reputation, in terms of its increasing endowment etc.—was directly related to maintaining and expanding the strength and resonance of the Lost Cause narrative not just for people in Virginia but also throughout the country. Here, administrators at W&L closely associated the institution as one that quite literally embodied Lee's concepts of honor and education.

By way of example, the enthusiastic endorsement by Edward Southy Joynes that appeared in *The Calyx* (1908) is typical. Importantly, Joynes is not a minor figure, as it relates his influence on curriculum decisions at many schools (public and private) throughout the South. Before being hired by Robert E. Lee to teach at Washington and Lee, he was employed at William and Mary University. Later, he worked at Vanderbilt and the University of Tennessee. He had his longest tenure at the University of South Carolina, and he also helped establish the Columbia, South Carolina, public school system. He was later a co-founder of Winthrop University (Hemphill 1907). Below, Joynes offers an endorsement for using Robert E. Lee as inspiration—"an Ideal"—for the "Greater University" that appeared in *The Calyx* (1908, 8):

> **General Lee as an Ideal for the Greater University, Being an Interpretation of the Great Leader's Hopes and Life-Work by One of His Faculty, Professor Edward S. Joynes, now of the University of South Carolina.**
>
> ... But for this "Greater University"—this new Washington and Lee, founded and endowed in memory and in honor of President Lee—the ideal is always set—it is General Lee himself—his life, his deeds, his character. To such a man our ambition should be to build a worthy monument, not in stone or brass, but in living service as he lived to serve his country and fellow-men. That such is the monument which General Lee would have most desired, those who knew him are sure. Let, then, the ideal of your Greater University be to realize in its character and influence the great qualities of its great Exemplar, and so to perpetuate the influence of that great example upon suceeding generations. There could be no higher ideal than this—no nobler inspiration—no greater or more difficult task for those who shall build or administer your "Greater University." That such and less may be their aspiration and effort, and that through the Greater Washington and Lee University General Lee may be made a living presence and power forever, is my earnest hope.

Obviously, in modern times these characterizations of Robert E. Lee appear extraordinary—particulalrly when they are associated, as they often are, with Lee's mausoleum on campus. Indeed, the most comparable contemporary examples may be the "cults of personality" associated with Fascist leaders (e.g. Francisco Franco's crypt at Valle de los Caídos) and Communist leaders (e.g. Lenin's mausoleum on Red Square). Of course, one difference is that Lee's mythology is associated with maintaining a link to a lost civilization (that of the pre–Civil War

He finds his home in ruins, his farm devastated, his slaves free, his people without law...

• Grady

COLOR PLATE 4 Image of the Ku Klux Klan in Washington and Lee College yearbook that shows a man hanged in the background. The quote is from Henry W. Grady's then famous "New South" speech (*The Calyx* 1928, 115).

South), whereas Franco's mausoleum and Lenin's tomb were constructed to help maintain and craft a once ongoing ideal of governance associated with Fascist Spain and Communism in the USSR.

While it might be assumed that this type of idolization had resonance only for people at W&L (or among people in Virginia and the South), it has been shown that memorialization of Lee during this period spread throughout the entire United States, where he was increasingly mentioned along with past leaders like George Washington and Abraham Lincoln as among the great men of America ("Whose Heritage," 2019). By way of example, the following sentimental account

FIGURE 2.31   Image of the Ku Klux Klan in the Washington and Lee yearbook that shows hooded figures terrorizing Black inhabitants of a small cabin, as shown in *The Calyx* (1930, 300–301).

of Robert E. Lee appeared in *The Calyx* (1906, 117–18) and was written by an author who characterizes himself as "Northern born." It described his emotional visit to Lee's mausoleum on campus:

> It is difficult for me to speak now of what was to come. I had paused by the Hall tablet, and it was some time before I felt rather than saw the beauty and wonder of what lay beyond the reading desk—Valentine's superb recumbent statue of Robert E. Lee. I did not know of it, or believed it elsewhere, and certainly had not imagined anything could be so beuatiful…. How beautifully the South remembers her dead! I am Northern born, and my father was a soldier in the Northern army; and yet I am free to say that there is nothing in the National Museum at Washington that is comparable to moving pathos as the relics of Lee, Jackson and "Jeb" Stuart in the Confederate Museum in Richmond.

While much of the memorialization of the Civil War that appears in yearbooks is directly associated with the glories of Lee's life or the honor of the men who fought valiantly in the conflict, there are also times when memorialization is presented alongside pictures of the Ku Klux Klan (KKK) directing violence toward Black men, women and children. Two of the most provocative pictures appeared in the 1928 and 1930 *Calyx*. In Color Plate 4 there is a picture that shows KKK figures. In this case, in the upper right-hand corner of the picture there is the outline of a body that has been hanged behind three robed figures It also includes a direct quote from Henry W. Grady—at the time a noted writer, journalist and Georgia newspaper editor who had attended UVA as a law student—which describes how White Southerners felt when they returned to their farms following the Civil War.

Grady (1910) was also a well-known advocate for maintaining White supremacy in the "New South." Importantly, a student journalist at W&L, Hannah Denham (2019) also found and commented on these pictures during her own investigation of yearbook content she undertook shortly after the Northam scandal. The following figure (Figure 2.31) also shows KKK figures published in the W&L yearbook—they are pictured at night and illuminated by a torch as they terrorize the Black inhabitants of a small cabin.

Conclusion

The pictures and texts are jarring to modern sensibilities. Sometimes the malice depicted in these pictures—the representation of a Black body hanging from a tree, the Black figures cowering in fear at night while being terrorized by the KKK—seem extraordinary, even within the context of the other images presented. But just as important is that the yearbooks paint a picture of how a "hierarchy of races" perspective enabled the more routine degradations of the Black laborers that worked on campus and those who lived in the community. This is true for pictures that demonstrate the offhand cruelty and everyday violence depicted in the caricatures—men throwing snowballs at a Black woman, students mistreating Black staff—that also give insight into the routine degradations that took place on these campuses. Perhaps the most egregious example was the routine use of Black bodies—both dead and alive—by MCV medical students.

But here, the more appropriate and chilling characterization of these pictures is not so much that they are remarkable but rather that they were—for most of the student body at that time—the characterization of a widely shared history. The inclusion of violent pictures in these yearbooks was not happenstance. Before being published, these pictures were scrutinized by students on the yearbook staff, and likely scrutinized by a few faculty members too. These pictures were not considered aberrations during the period they were published—rather, they coincide with the history being taught to students by the faculty at Virginia universities during this time.

References

"Alumnal Lament." 1921. *The Virginia Reel* 1: 23.

Barringer, Paul B. 1901. "The American Negro: His Past and Future." Presented at the *Negro Education in the South* session during the Tenth Annual Meeting of the Southern Education Association Proceedings, 133–146. Richmond, VA: The Education Association. Available at: https://archive.org/details/american negro his00barr/page/6/mode/2up.

Bledsoe, Albert Taylor. 1856. *An Essay on Liberty and Slavery.* New York: J.B. Lippincott & Company.

The Bomb. 1885–2010. Virginia Military Institute Yearbooks. Digital Archive available from the VMI library at: https://www.vmi.edu/archives/digital-collections/vmi-yearbook-digital-archives/.

Bonilla-Silva, Eduardo. 1997. "Rethinking Racism: Toward a Structural Interpretation." *American Sociological Review* 62 (3): 465–480.

"Buzzard Pete." 1905. Charlottesville, VA: University of Virginia Library. https://v3.lib.virginia.edu/catalog/uva-lib:2159714#?c=0&m=0&s=0&cv= 0&xywh=-1401%2C-181%2C4875%2C3614.

"Buzzard Pete." 1905. Library of Congress, LC-D4-33849. https://www.loc.gov/pictures/item/2016795441/.

The Calyx. 1895–2019. Washington and Lee Library Digital Yearbook Archive. https://dspace.wlu.edu/handle/11021/26929.

Chetty, Raj, John N. Friedman, Emmanuel Saez, Nicholas Turner and Danny Yagan. 2017. "Mobility Report Cards: The Role of Colleges in Intergenerational Mobility." National Bureau of Economic Research Working Paper No. 23618, July 2017.

Corks and Curls. 1888–2018. University of Virginia Library Digital Yearbook Archive. https://v3.lib.virginia.edu/catalog/u126747.

Culbreth, David M.R. 1908. "Henry Martin." In *The University of Virginia: Memories of Her Student-Life and Professors,"* 440–442. New York: Neale Publishing. This section on Henry Martin is available from the *Encyclopedia Virginia*, Virginia Humanities Council, https://www.encyclopediavirginia.org/_Henry_Martin _.

Daniel, John W. 1883. "Ceremonies Connected with the Inauguration of the Mausoleum and the Unveiling of the Recumbent Figure of General Robert Edward Lee, at Washington and Lee University, Lexington, Va., June 28. Oration of John W. Daniel, LL.D." *Historical Sketch of the Lee Memorial Association. Vol. 3.* New York: West, Johnston & Company.

"Demographic Report." 2019. The University of Virginia Office of Institutional Research. https://ira.virginia.edu/ university-stats-facts.

Denham, Hannah. 2019. "Washington and Lee Yearbooks Depicted Blackface Too: A Review of Old *Calyx* Yearbooks Archived in Special Collections Showed Racist Photos, Jokes and Drawings, as well as References to Sexual Assault." *Ring-tum Phi* (W&L School Newspaper), February 27.

Dorr, Gregory M. 2008. *Segregation's Science: Eugenics and Society in Virginia.* Charlottesville, VA: University of Virginia Press.

Dreher, Julius D. 1901. "Response to Barringer's American Negro." Presented at the *Negro Education in the South* session during the Tenth Annual Meeting of the Southern Education Association Proceedings, 146–151. Richmond, VA: The Education Association.

Duberman, Martin. 1996. "The Higher Education of Paul Robeson." *Journal of Blacks in Higher Education* 13: 107–111.

"Economic Diversity and Student Outcomes at America's Colleges and Universities: Find Your College." 2017. *New York Times.* https://www. nytimes.com/interactive/ projects/college-mobility/.

"Fact Book." 2019. James Madison University. The 2018–19 report is available at: https:// www.jmu.edu/oir/oir-research/statsum/2018-19/2018-19toc.shtml.

"Facts and Stats." 2020. Washington and Lee University enrollment reports. https://my. wlu.edu/strategic-analysis-and-institutional-research/facts-and-stats.

Freeman, Douglas Southall. 1934. *Robert E. Lee* (4 vols.). New York: Charles Scribner's Sons.

Gallagher, Gary W., and Alan T. Nolan, eds. 2000. *The Myth of the Lost Cause and Civil War History.* Bloomington, IN: Indiana University Press.

Gates, Ernie. 2018. "Serpentine Timeline: Some of the Twists and Turns of UVA History." *Virginia.* Winter 2018. https://uvamagazine.org/articles/serpentine_timeline.

Goffman, Erving. 1959. *The Presentation of Self in Everyday Life.* New York: Doubleday Publishing.

Grady, Henry Woodfin. 1910. *The Complete Orations and Speeches of Henry W. Grady.* New York: Hinds, Noble & Eldredge Publishing.

Gross, Theodore L. 1966. "Thomas Nelson Page: Creator of a Virginia Classic." *Georgia Review* 20 (3): 338–351.

Hagan, John, and Wenona Rymond-Richmond. 2008. "The Collective Dynamics of Racial Dehumanization and Genocidal Victimization in Darfur." *American Sociological Review* 73 (6): 875–902.

Hemphill, James Calvin. 1907. "Edward Southy Jones." In *Men of Mark in South Carolina: Ideals of American Life: A Collection of Biographies of Leading Men of the State*, 96–99. Cleveland, OH: Men of Mark Publishing Company.

"Henry Martin." 2020. President's Commission on Slavery and the University. University of Virginia. https://slavery.virginia.edu/henry-martin/.

Hill, Michael, Rebecca Benefiel, Tom Camden, Ted DeLaney, Donald Gaylord, MaKayla Lorick, Drewry Sackett and Tammi Simpson. 2020. "African Americans at Washington and Lee: A Timeline." https://www.wlu.edu/presidents-office/issues-and-initiatives/institutional-history/working-group-on-african-american-history/timeline-of-african-americans-at-wandl.

"Historical Timeline." 2020. James Madison University. https://www.jmu.edu/centennialcelebration/timeline.shtml.

"History behind the Headlines: *Corks and Curls.*" 2019. Backstory Podcast. February 8. https://backstory.exposure.co/history-behind-the-headlines-corks-curls.

Holcombe, James Philemon. 1858. "Is Slavery Consistent with Natural Law?" *Southern Literary Messenger* 27: 401–421.

Kapsidelis, Karin. 2011. "Confronting the Story of Bones Discarded in an Old MCV Well." *Richmond Times Dispatch*, November 11. https://richmond.com/news/confronting-the-story-of-bones-discarded-in-an-old-mcv-well/article_4a784033-ca30-5a30-be4d-80c7fd9a3783. html.

Katz, Daniel, and Kenneth Braly. 1933. "Racial Stereotypes of One Hundred College Students." *Journal of Abnormal and Social Psychology* 28 (3): 280–290.

Lemons, Stanley J. 1977. "Black Stereotypes as Reflected in Popular Culture, 1880–1920." *American Quarterly* 29 (1): 102–116.

Lhamon, William T. 2003. *Jump Jim Crow: Lost Plays, Lyrics, and Street Prose of the First Atlantic Popular Culture.* Boston: Harvard University Press.

Lith, Bufford. 1847. *Jim Crow Jubilee.* Print. Boston: Published by George P. Reed. *Digital Commonwealth.* https://ark.digitalcommonwealth.org/ark:/50959/08612v170 (Accessed September 25, 2020).

Logan, Rayford Whittingham. [1965] 1997. *The Betrayal of the Negro, from Rutherford B. Hayes to Woodrow Wilson.* New York: Da Capo Press.

Matthew, Dayna Bowen. 2019. "On Charlottesville." *Virginia Law Review* 105: 269–341.

Mays, Vickie, Susan D. Cochran and Namdi W. Barnes. 2007. "Race, Race-Based Discrimination, and Health Outcomes among African Americans." *Annual Review of Psychology* 58: 201–225.

Mulrooney, Megan. 2019. "Confronting Blackface." Civic Learning and Democratic Engagement, February 12. Available at: https://sites.lib. jmu. edu/civic/2019/02/12/dr-meg-mulrooney-on-confronting-Blackface-at-jmu/.

Neely Jr., Mark E., Harold Holzer and Gabor S.Boritt. 2000. *The Confederate Image: Prints of the Lost Cause.* Chapel Hill, NC: UNC Press Books.

Page, Thomas Nelson. [1887] 1991. *In Ole Virginia: Or, Marse Chan and Other Stories.* New York: J.S. Sanders Books.

Page, Thomas Nelson. 1898. *Social Life in Old Virginia before the War.* New York: Charles Scribner's Sons.

Page, Thomas Nelson. 1904a. *The Negro: The Southerner's Problem.* New York: Charles Scribner's Sons.

Page, Thomas Nelson. 1904b. "Letter from Alumni." *UVA Alumni Bulletin* 4 (2): 118.

Page, Thomas Nelson. 1905. *The Old South: Essays Social and Political.* New York: New York: Charles Scribner's Sons.

Page, Thomas Nelson. 1911. *Robert E. Lee: Man and Soldier.* New York: Charles Scribner's Sons.

Patton, John Shelton. 1906. *Jefferson, Cabell and the University of Virginia.* New York: Neale Publishing Company.

Patton, John Shelton. 1915. "Henry Martin 1826–1915." *Alumni Bulletin of the University of Virginia.* https://encyclopediavirginia.org/entries/henry-martin-1826-1915-by-john-s-patton-alumni-bulletin-october-1915/.

Patton, John Shelton, and Sallie J. Doswell. 1900. *The University of Virginia: Glimpses of Its Past and Present.* New York: J.P. Bell Company.

Pell, Samantha. 2017. "Her Dad Was the Rose Bowl's First Black QB in 1922. This Year, He'll Join the Hall of Fame." *Washington Post*, December 28. LexisNexis Academic.

Pryor, Elizabeth Brown. 2007. *Reading the Man: A Portrait of Robert E. Lee through His Private Letters.* New York: Penguin Publishing.

Reynolds, P. Preston. 2020. "UVA and the History of Race: Eugenics, the Racial Integrity Act, Health Disparities." *UVA Today*. https://news.virginia.edu/content/uva-and-history-race-eugenics-racial-integrity-act-health-disparities.

Reynolds. P. Preston. 2018. "Eugenics at the University of Virginia and Its Impact on Health Disparities" *Charlottesville 2017: The Legacy of Race and Inequity*, edited by Claudrena N. Harold and Louis P. Nelson, 118–132. Charlottesville, VA: University of Virginia Press.

Roediger, David. 1991. *The Wages of Whiteness: Race and the Making of the American Working Class*. London: Verso.

Schoolma'am. 1910–1962. James Madison University Library Digital Yearbook Archive. https://commons.lib.jmu.edu/allyearbooks/39/.

"Some Colleges Have More Students from the Top 1 Percent Than the Bottom 60. Find Yours." 2017. *New York Times*, January 18. https://www.nytimes.com/interactive/2017/01/18/upshot/some-colleges-have-more-students-from-the-top-1-percent-than-the-bottom-60.html (Accessed October 20, 2019).

Serwer, Adam. 2017. "The Myth of the Kindly Robert E. Lee: The Legend of the Confederate Leader's Heroism and Decency Is Based in the Fiction of a Person Who Never Existed." *Atlantic Monthly*. June 4. https://www.theatlantic.com/politics/archive/2017/06/the-myth-of-the-kindly-general-lee/529038/.

The Spider. 1897–1921. University of Richmond Library Digital Yearbook Archive. https://scholarship.richmond.edu/the-spider/.

Toll, Robert C. 1974. *Blacking Up: The Minstrel Show in Nineteenth-Century America*. New York: Oxford University Press.

"Uncle Peter." N.D. *Holsinger Studio Collection*. Albert and Shirley Small Special Collections Library, University of Virginia.

"Uncle Peter's Laugh." 1905–1920. University of Virginia Visual History Collection. Charlottesville, VA: University of Virginia Library.

"University Chronology." 2020. Washington and Lee University. https://www.wlu.edu/about-wandl/history-and-traditions/a-brief-history/university-chronology.

Utsey, Shawn, director. 2011. *Until the Well Runs Dry: Medicine and the Exploitation of Black Bodies. Documentary Film. Virginia Commonwealth University. Department of African American Studies and Burn Baby Burn Productions*. Richmond, VA: Privately Published.

von Daacke, Kirt and Ashley Schmidt. 2019. "UVA and the History of Race: When the KKK Flourished in Charlottesville." *UVA Today*, September 25. Available at: https://news.virginia.edu/content/uva-and-history-race-when-kkk-flourished-charlottesville.

The Web. 1922–2002. University of Richmond Library Digital Yearbook Archive. https://scholarship.richmond.edu/the-web/.

The X-Ray. 1913–2010. Medical College of Virginia (MCV) Yearbooks. VCU Library Digital Archive. https://digital.library.vcu.edu/islandora/object/vcu:ybk.

"Whose Heritage? Public Symbols of the Confederacy." 2019. *Southern Poverty Law Center*, https://www.splcenter.org/20190201/whose-heritage-public-symbols-Confederacy.

Wilson, Charles Reagan. 1980. *Baptized in Blood: The Religion of the Lost Cause, 1865–1920*. Atlanta, GA: University of Georgia Press.

Wolfe, Brendan. 2013a. "Who Was Buzzard Pete?" *Encyclopedia Virginia, The Blog*. April 5. https://www.evblog.virginiahumanities.org/2013/04/who-was-buzzard-pete/.

Wolfe, Brendan. 2013b. "Uncle Peter and the Rebel Yell." *Encyclopedia Virginia, The Blog*. April 11. https://www.evblog.virginiahumanities.org/2013/04/uncle-peter-and-the-rebel-yell/.

Wolfe, Brendan. 2013c. "Still More on Peter Briggs." *Encyclopedia Virginia, The Blog*. April 19. https://www.evblog.virginiahumanities.org/2013/04/still-more-on-peter-biggs/.

3

ACADEMIC CULTURE AND RACE PERSPECTIVES AT HOWARD UNIVERSITY BEFORE WORLD WAR II (1914–1942)

Howard University, as compared to the Virginia colleges in this study, is exceptional. The school has always admitted both men and women of all races but was founded to provide educational opportunities to African Americans after the Civil War. As characterized in *The Bison* (1924, 6) yearbook:

> AT THE CLOSE OF THE CIVIL WAR, human slavery in America had been abolished forever, and a new problem in the field of education presented itself—the immortal stroke of Lincoln's pen had liberated about four million slaves. This group accustomed to the crudest tools of industry, an almost inhuman manner of living, the most imperfect use of a modern language could be made citizens only in name. The North and South had exactly opposite views concerning the welfare, the possibilities of the Negro. The one was sympathetic, and believed that educational advantages would be one of the chief factors in solving the problem; the other looked upon the freedmen as a hoard of savages turned loose on the country, and had no more desire to help release them from the chains of intellectual bondage than from physical bondage.

In 1909, Howard University established its first medical hospital although it had long been training medical doctors, dentists and nurses. It also had an early program for the study of law, and the law school became more prominent during the 1930s. Importantly, the institution largely rejected the narrow philosophy of Black education associated with Booker T. Washington—increasingly popular at the time—who advocated training Black men and women in vocational fields (Norell 2009). Instead, Howard University always trained a Black professional class of doctors, lawyers and teachers.

DOI: 10.4324/9781003134480-3

Put simply, Howard University was founded on egalitarian principles, designed explicitly to increase Black social mobility and to also inculcate students with a desire to commit to a lifetime of public service. From the founding of the school to its present day, Howard University created far more social mobility for its graduates as compared to any of the other schools included in this study (see Chetty et al. 2017; "Economic Diversity," *New York Times*). This chapter uses yearbook content from Howard University to explore the differences in the perspectives of students and faculty at this historically Black university (HBCU) concerning race relations as compared to the views held by those attending historically White colleges in Virginia. Notably, it appears that the school's commitment to racial justice and community service made students who attended Howard University—particularly during the period examined in this chapter—much more serious minded as compared to students attending elite White schools in Virginia during the same period.

Using Howard University yearbook content, this chapter will make the argument that its faculty and students had a far more prescient view of race relations than those at the Virginia schools examined previously. This is, admittedly, an easy argument to make. But also important is that Howard University was, at the time, providing a far more cosmopolitan educational experience for its students, with far fewer resources at its deposal than a school like the University of Virginia (UVA)—at the time often considered the flagship university in Virginia. Here, the Howard University students—on balance—appear to have been far more engaging, simply far better students, than most of the students attending the Virginia schools too.

The yearbook content does indicate that there were sometimes conflicts between students and administrators on campus. Often, these are outlined in the "Student Government" sections of the yearbook that detail, usually in forthright terms, student grievances. For example, in 1934 the student editors of *The Hilltop* resisted having the paper's finances overseen by the administration (*The Bison* 1934, 52):

> The Treasurer of the University asserted his right to negotiate contracts for the paper and, later, to supervise the advertising accounts. Believing that students should be allowed the right to exercise full control over student organizations. *The Hilltop* staff resisted this move.... Throughout the year, *The Hilltop* has championed student rights against the encroachments of administrators. It has also backed the projects of the Council and other student organizations and has encouraged the formation of new and more extensive student organizations.

Mostly, the previous represent the inevitable types of debate that take place when the organizing mission of an institution is directly related to student empowerment. At times, though, it became clear that the Howard administration became vexed—particularly during the period of the 1960s explored in chapter 5—when students inevitably interpreted the "Howard Spirit" as meaning they should actively voice concerns over their education at the university too. Notwithstanding the mostly peaceable kingdom presented in the yearbook content below, there were, in fact, aspects of Howard culture during this period that some students and faculty forthrightly criticized. And this high level of student activism was notable in comparison to most of the other universities in this study. As we will see, this activist spirit became a more defining feature of the school over time.

The Howard culture was often conservative concerning interpersonal conduct and morality even though clearly progressive, at times radical, concerning the institutional views on race relations. As a result, the sanctions for minor infractions associated with decorum could be significant. For example, Thomas Montgomery Gregory, one of the most innovative and energetic faculty members discussed further below, was dismissed from the college (and later reinstated) for what appears to have been a relatively modest breach of decorum (see Gregory 2015). Another example was that Alain Leroy Locke, another well-regarded scholar, was likewise dismissed (and also later reinstated), either because of the content he offered in a series of lectures associated with race relations or perhaps after he questioned why the Black faculty was being paid less than the White faculty. Notably, Locke was reinstated by the first Black president of Howard, Mordecai Wyatt Johnson (see Stewart 2018).

Brief history of Howard University

Howard University is a flagship HBCU in Washington, DC. The school was established by the US Congress on March 10, 1867, after being championed by members the First Congregational Society of Washington. The goal was to provide freed slaves and Black Americans with educational opportunities and professional training. Not too soon after its establishment, the school was organized into the College of Liberal Arts and College of Medicine. From the beginning, the college was co-educational and provided both vocational and professional training in the fields of education, ministry, medicine and law. Early in the 20th century a teaching and research hospital was established (Logan 1969). Howard law school graduates later formed the nucleus for the National Association for the Advancement of Colored People (NAACP). The law school's most notable alumnus during this period was Thurgood Marshall, who after graduating would later win more cases argued in front of the US Supreme Court than any other lawyer. He was appointed the first Black member of this court in 1967 (Tushnet 1994).

The institution is named after General Oliver Otis Howard, a Northern Civil War hero and also a founding member of the school. Directly after the Civil War he was appointed as the director of the Bureau of Refugees, Freedmen and Abandoned Lands, commonly known as the Freedmen's Bureau, which provided education and training to freed slaves and poor Whites after the Civil

War. He served as the president of the college from 1869 to 1874. During this early period the faculty was multi-racial and multi-ethnic. During the period examined in this chapter—in direct contrast to the other schools in this study—the college also employed a considerable number of women as instructors and professors (Logan 1969). Importantly, the yearbooks do indicate that much of the instruction was still gendered, with the women on the faculty usually instructing women students in the areas of social work and education. At the same time, women also studied medicine with men at the university after the second year of the school's establishment and entered the law school in the early 1920s. During this period, in 1925, Dr. Sarah W. Brown became the first woman appointed to the Howard University Board (Logan 1969). The first Black president of the college was Mordecai Wyatt Johnson who, to date, also had the longest tenure (1926–1960) in this position (McKinney 1997).

Currently, Howard University is classified as a selective private research-intensive university. It continues to be a top producer of minority medical professionals, lawyers, journalists and students who later earn PhDs in the natural sciences ("Howard at a Glance" Howard). The total enrollment in 2019 was 19,392 students, with 84.6% identifying as Black or African American, 2.91% Asian, 2.91% White and 1.28% Hispanic or Latino. In Raj Chetty et al.'s (2017) study on social mobility at different colleges, it was found that the median family income of students at Howard in 2013 (reported in 2015 dollars) was $68,300 and that 29% of incoming students had family incomes in the top 20% of the United States (see "Economic Diversity," *New York Times*). This median income ranked Howard at 485 out of 614 selective private colleges within its peer group. Comparably, the median family income of Howard students was approximately $70,000–$80,000 less than the median family income of students who attended the three predominantly White colleges—University of Virginia (UVA), James Madison University (JMU) and Washington and Lee (W&L)—featured in chapter 2 this text. The school performs well in Chetty et al.'s (2017) social mobility index—this measures the likelihood that students attending a university will move up two income quintiles during their lifetime—where it was ranked 42 out of 578 selective small colleges (see "Economic Diversity," *New York Times*).

The Howard motto: Truth and Service

The "Howard Spirit" is constantly reinforced throughout all the yearbooks that were examined. A typical example associated with the project of Black uplift is presented here from *The Bison* (1927, 12) yearbook dedication:

> HOWARD UNIVERSITY has a singular task. A pioneer in the field of higher education for the Freedman, in America—she has blazed a trail, that her sons and daughters might scale the heights to Achievement. The purpose of the 1927 Bison is to portray in a small way that progress and Achievement.

Howard was founded with the ideal that a positive Black racial identity and racial politics—including the need to improve race relations in the United States—were at the forefront of the institution's organizing principles. The yearbook content indicates that service was a lived experience—the guiding organizational principle—that ordered day-to-day life for students. For example, the school motto *Veritas et Utilitas* (Truth and Service) is still prominently displayed on Howard University promotional material. Of course, all universities—and particularly the women's Normal Schools in this study—often discuss the importance of community service. But at Howard, more so than any other college examined, service was embedded into the institution. To be a student at Howard was to accept that service to community—specifically the Black community in the United States—was the organizing principle of the student's educational, civic and professional life. Below is a fairly typical representation of how the ethic was reinforced as a moral imperative—characterized within a broader project of racial uplift (italics added)—as described in the "Oath of African-American Youth" (*NIKH Yearbook* 1915, 9):

OATH OF AFRO-AMERICAN YOUTH

> I will never bring disgrace upon my race by any unworthy deed or dishonorable act: I will live a clean, decent, manly life and will ever respect the virtue and honor of womanhood; I will uphold and obey the just laws of my country and of the community in which I live, and will encourage others to do likewise; I will not allow prejudice, injustice, insult or outrage to cower my spirit or sour my soul, but will ever preserve the inner freedom of heart and conscience; I will not allow myself to be overcome of evil, but will overcome evil with good; I will endeavor to exert the best within me for my own personal improvement, and will strive to quicken the sense of racial duty and responsibility; *I will in all these ways aim to uplift my race so that, to everyone bound to it by ties of blood, it shall become a bond of ennoblement, and not a byword of reproach.*

Not surprisingly, much of the artwork and many of the pictures in the Howard University yearbooks associate Black men and women with educational attainment and a cosmopolitan worldview that reinforces the message of service. A typical representation (*The Bison* 1923, 28) is offered in the picture shown in Figure 3.1.

Howard students compared to students at Virginia colleges: meritocracy versus the "Gentleman's C"

To live the Howard ideal seems a daunting undertaking—but the evidence from the Howard University yearbooks is that many worked hard to live up to these ideals as students and later in life too. Here, the Howard yearbooks offer an unusually thorough account of student life and the institutional history of the university. These yearbooks were among the most professionally

FIGURE 3.1 Artwork before introducing the 1923 graduating class at Howard University (*The Bison* 1923, 28).

assembled—they are remarkably polished documents. The content is highly edited, the artwork carefully arranged, the print quality excellent. The overall effect is to present Howard University as a serious place, with serious-minded students, whose alumni were making daily, and direct, impacts on the Black community in the United States and also in the wider world.

The early Howard yearbooks represent the standard style used many years afterward in terms of outlining student backgrounds and their achievements at the school. They indicate the level of commitment that students at Howard had regarding community service—they were clearly joiners in civic clubs. And these students' future plans—outlined when students became seniors—often included professional careers that were civic minded. Many students also pursued post-graduate work—often at Ivy League schools—while others who attended Howard as undergraduates, then migrated into the medical school or law school to pursue professional degrees.

Notably, the Howard students contrast somewhat with how some students at the elite Virginia schools presented themselves. There, unlike at Howard University, were usually a smattering of students who seem to revel in the fact that they were not much concerned with academic achievement during their university careers. For example, the W&L yearbooks during this period tend to be organized in largely the same manner as the Howard yearbooks in which the graduating seniors have their college careers and future plans characterized. And, like some students at Howard, many W&L students appear to have excelled during their school careers. But usually there are also a few students who—in the absence of any noteworthy achievements—are provided with more lyrical summaries of their academic careers that hint they were not much concerned with their studies. An example comes from the W&L yearbook, which informs that a student—his nickname is "Dip"—is appearing in the yearbook for a second time because the previous year it was assumed he would graduate. Instead, he apparently failed one of his last law school classes that year.

> This is Dip's second appearance with the Senior Law Class representation in the CALYX for the book of 1917 will be found to contain an account of the statesman under discussion. It seems that Dip planned to get his L.L.B. last Spring, and that one of the professors had made entirely different arrangements. The result was that Dip summered in Lexington, browsing around in Beal Property for exercise. He discovered a four leaf clover and succeeded in ridding himself of the only detriment to his degree. This June the faculty will present him with it, therefore. (*The Calyx* 1918, 47)

The most obvious difference encountered while surveying the pre–World War II Howard University yearbooks—directly after doing the same concerning the White universities included in this study—was that the Howard University faculty and students were remarkably progressive and even optimistic on the issue of race relations in the United States. This was so even as they confronted increasing racial violence during this historical period. For example, there are insightful interpretations of constitutional law in these yearbooks at a time when law was being used to re-subjugate Blacks in the South, particularly in Virginia (see examples below). Moreover, these interpretations were clearly more informed when compared to content found in the Virginia yearbooks that had law schools. Practically, these perspectives were later foundational to arguments used by the NAACP at the Supreme Court—particularly by Howard graduate Thurgood Marshall—that ended legal segregation in the United States (Carter 1988).

More broadly, Howard is a place where intellectual curiosity—particularly as it relates to events in the wider world—appears part of the institutional DNA. This fact stands out even more so when compared to the sometimes intense parochialism of many of the White students attending Virginia colleges. For example, even the extra-curricular activities at Howard look more erudite, though largely because they take advantage of the school's location in Washington, DC.

Perhaps some readers will regard the previous assertions with incredulity. Were the students at Howard better than the students attending the elite Virginia schools? This assessment is, of course, somewhat subjective—there certainly appear to have been some excellent students at the Virginia colleges too—and there is inevitably also variation within any institution concerning the quality and work ethic of students. Still, in the aggregate, Howard University students appeared, judging from the early yearbook content, far more engaging, more open minded, more serious minded and far more studious than their White peers in Virginia.

Some of these characteristics relate to the fact that many of the elite universities in Virginia during this period were not intended to be meritocracies. And to be clear, Howard University also routinely recruited many students from what would be considered the emerging Black elite. But, on balance, Howard University presents as a meritocracy much more so than the Virginia colleges included this study. Howard also tended to have a monopoly—along with a few other prominent HBCUs—on the best Black students in the country during this period, with Black communities throughout the United States funding scholarships to send their top students to the college.

By way of contrast, the prominence of elite Virginia institutions in this study was often closely associated with their being supported by the Virginia gentry over time. Put simply, a good number of White students considered attendance at these Virginia schools a birthright. For a few, the primary goal appears to have been to achieve the "Gentleman's C" in their academic studies. This overall attitude is nicely expressed in an essay by Michael Weishan (2014), who explored the Gentleman's C as it existed at Harvard. He offers the following poem by Robert Grant, who in 1873 earned a law degree from Harvard University, as an example of this attitude:

> The able-bodied C man! He sails swimmingly along.
> His philosophy is rosy as a skylark's mating song.
> The light of his ambition is respectably to pass,
>
> And to hold a firm position in the middle of his class.

Howard University students, even though many came from prominent Black families—what Howard sociologist E. Franklin Frazier ([1962] 1997) later termed the Black bourgeoisie—do not appear to have felt as entitled as their White counterparts. In all, it seems clear that Howard students were far less inclined to social loafing when compared to their White peers. Probably another reason for the relative seriousness of students at Howard University during this period was the strong pre-professional curriculum that offered degrees in medicine (including dentistry), law, social work and education. There is a similar pre-professional orientation evident at the Virginia women's colleges in this study (James Madison University and Longwood College), where many women were being trained as primary and secondary school teachers. At the same time, these women—and the Howard students too— did sometimes make the point that that they were not always grinds. Indeed, while all the schools in this study have rituals associated with school tradition, this seems particularly the case at Howard University. In particular, the enthusiastic founding and extension of Black fraternities and sororities at Howard is an indication that students were often engaged in social diversions too. But even these social fraternities and sororities appear to have regarded service to community much more seriously than those at historically White Virginia colleges.[1]

Progressive political engagement during the Jim Crow era

The cosmopolitanism of Howard students (1914 to 1942)

Howard University students, as compared to their Virginia peers, appear far more cosmopolitan and worldly. To some extent, this is because Howard is located in Washington, DC, and none of the Virginia schools are located in a city of similar size. Throughout the Howard yearbooks are examples of students and faculty taking advantage of the Washington, DC, location. At the time it was common for visiting dignitaries—ambassadors from countries around the world—to routinely make visits to Howard at the behest of both the faculty and the students. For example, the French Club sometimes invited ambassadors from French-speaking countries, often from the Caribbean, to address the club (Cook 1938). National politicians and prominent statesmen—both Black and White—are also well represented in the yearbooks. For example, President Calvin Coolidge delivered the school's 1924 commencement address (Coolidge 1924). A few years previously, a delegation of Howard students had meet with President Harding (*The Bison* 1923, 148).

Also important to the cosmopolitan worldview of Howard students was the increasingly diverse student body, which included a reasonably large foreign student population. For example, this difference is clearly evident in the representation of the state clubs at the Virginia colleges as compared to Howard. At the Virginia schools, the "State Clubs" pages presented the most derogatory forms of racial caricature encountered in this study. Moreover, these clubs rarely presented information concerning their activities on campus.

At Howard University, there are fewer state clubs represented in the yearbooks as compared to many Virginia schools. But the clubs that are chronicled are clearly active at the university and their pages always offer a list of events and programs that they have sponsored throughout the year. Among the largest during the early period examined was the Florida Club, founded by Zora Neale Hurston, later a renowned writer whose stories were often set in Florida (see *The Bison* 1924, 244). She also co-founded what became an excellent student newspaper, *The Hilltop* (Boyd 2003).

At Howard, while state pride was clearly part of the organizing ideal associated with these state clubs, the clubs were also established to make the transition to college life easier for students who came from these regions. Usually, these clubs raised funds to help incoming students with housing and school materials, and they also offered regional scholarships. Other times, the clubs focused on political and literary issues associated with their regions. Importantly, and indicative of the cosmopolitan feel of the Howard University yearbooks, a few of these clubs were international in scope. For example, the Caribbean Club—consisting of students from the Caribbean region—was one of the regional clubs. Figure 3.2 shows a Howard yearbook page that provides examples of the previous with respect to the South American Club.

While the yearbook content constructed by students at elite White universities was sometimes preoccupied with regional history—particularly as concerns the memorialization of Civil War figures (see chapter 2)—Howard University students more often remained focused on the wider world and the future. The yearbook excerpt presented below describes the founding of the Student Progressive Club under the heading "World Movements." This entry—typically descriptive of those found in the Howard yearbooks—first outlines the club's charter:

> We, the students of Howard University, in order to promote a greater Howard, to advance higher education among Negro youth, and affiliate for mutual helpfulness with national and international student groups for the advancement of civilization and democracy, do hereby ordain and establish our constitution. (*The Bison* 124, 238)

The page then details club activities, indicating that there were weekly discussions on issues such as the ongoing Russian Revolution, Gandhi's national movement in India, student movements throughout Europe and the establishment of the Bok Peace Plan in the United States (238). Notably, Howard University students and faculty often felt a particular kinship with ongoing national liberation movements. Often, they felt these movements mirrored the struggles that Black Americans were confronting in the United States (Aptheker 1969). Further, the yearbooks clearly reflect the ongoing

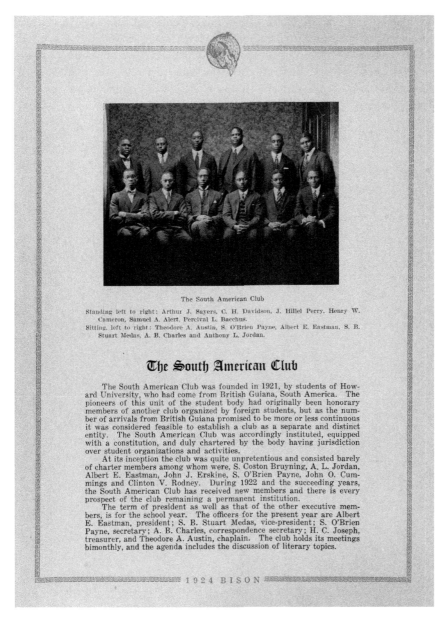

The South American Club

Standing left to right: Arthur J. Sayers, C. H. Davidson, J. Hillel Perry, Henry W. Cameron, Samuel A. Alert, Percival L. Bacchus.
Sitting, left to right: Theodore A. Austin, S. O'Brien Payne, Albert E. Eastman, S. B. Stuart Medas, A. B. Charles and Anthony L. Jordan.

The South American Club

The South American Club was founded in 1921, by students of Howard University, who had come from British Guiana, South America. The pioneers of this unit of the student body had originally been honorary members of another club organized by foreign students, but as the number of arrivals from British Guiana promised to be more or less continuous it was considered feasible to establish a club as a separate and distinct entity. The South American Club was accordingly instituted, equipped with a constitution, and duly chartered by the body having jurisdiction over student organizations and activities.

At its inception the club was quite unpretentious and consisted barely of charter members among whom were, S. Coston Bruyning, A. L. Jordan, Albert E. Eastman, John J. Erskine, S. O'Brien Payne, John O. Cummings and Clinton V. Rodney. During 1922 and the succeeding years, the South American Club has received new members and there is every prospect of the club remaining a permanent institution.

The term of president as well as that of the other executive members, is for the school year. The officers for the present year are Albert E. Eastman, president; S. B. Stuart Medas, vice-president; S. O'Brien Payne, secretary; A. B. Charles, correspondence secretary; H. C. Joseph, treasurer, and Theodore A. Austin, chaplain. The club holds its meetings bimonthly, and the agenda includes the discussion of literary topics.

1924 BISON

FIGURE 3.2 The South American Club as it appeared in *The Bison* (1924, 247) yearbook. The "State Clubs" pages in the Howard University yearbooks were far more detailed when compared to the listings at Virginia colleges. There is usually a formal picture of club members and an iteration of club events and future goals.

development of a Black intellectual movement associated with Pan-Africanism and socialism that was later championed by leaders such as Marcus Garvey and W.E.B. Du Bois (see Du Bois 1995). Throughout the Howard yearbooks there are references to Black intellectuals of the time that reinforce that Howard students are part of this academic tradition. A typical example is presented in Figure 3.3.

FIGURE 3.3 Howard yearbook page (*The Bison* 1925, 9) referencing Black leaders and academic traditions that framed the students' Howard experience.

Finally, both the worldliness and the generosity of Howard students is often reflected in the humor within these yearbooks. As indicated, these yearbooks are remarkably polished—even the low humor (at the expense of other students and the faculty, for example) is remarkably generous, usually delivered with more affection than malice. Of course, there are plenty of middling-to-bad jokes too—a staple in almost all yearbooks. But more so than the other yearbooks reviewed, the Howard yearbooks displayed a contained but expansive wit. A typical example, presented below, is "Epicureanism—Past and Present" (*The Bison* 1925, 206). Here, Epicureanism—often characterized as a restrained hedonism focused on the pleasures of thought—captures much of the humor routinely encountered in Howard yearbooks. Clearly, while these students were often serious, there is a purposefully fashioned levity presented in these yearbooks too.

Epicureanism—Past and Present

A la Omar Khayyam
A Book of Verses underneath the Bough
A Jug of Wine, a loaf of Bread—and Thou
Beside me singing in the Wilderness—
Oh, Wilderness, were Paradise now!
A la 1925—*The Little Brown Jug*
With a bottle or two of rare old wine.
And a maiden of features and from divine;
On a night just made for love and laughter;
Say, who gives a damn for "the morning after!"

One example of humor from this period—actually somewhat at odds with the constrained presentation of yearbook material at the time—was a page in which the Howard Teetotalers artfully send up the ongoing period of Prohibition (see Figure 3.4). They also appear to be taking a jab at the campus club structure (one officer is the "General Exhausted Ruler of the Royal Keg"), administrative authority (they claim the dean threatened them with "annihilation") and some of the more chaste organizations at the university too.

Progressive national politics: women's rights and law

Student engagement with national politics—usually (but not always) associated with ongoing American race relations—is evident in the Howard yearbook content. Notably, the women at Howard seemed far more engaged in national politics—including the suffrage movement—than White women attending Normal Schools in Virginia. And in direct contrast to all the previous schools in Virginia, men and women at Howard University—because it was co-educational—routinely served together as officers in many campus organizations. This was particularly the case during the establishment, in 1913, of a

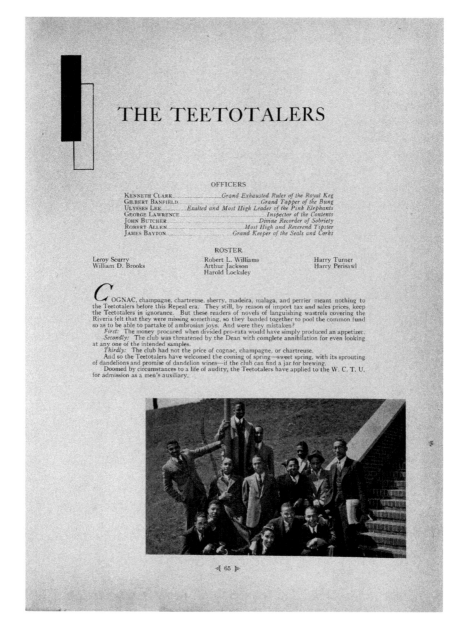

THE TEETOTALERS

OFFICERS

KENNETH CLARK..................................*Grand Exhausted Ruler of the Royal Keg*
GILBERT BANFIELD...*Grand Tapper of the Bung*
ULYSSES LEE...............*Exalted and Most High Leader of the Pink Elephants*
GEORGE LAWRENCE...................................*Inspector of the Contents*
JOHN BUTCHER...*Divine Recorder of Sobriety*
ROBERT ALLEN.............................*Most High and Reverend Tipster*
JAMES BAYTON.........................*Grand Keeper of the Seals and Corks*

ROSTER

Leroy Scurry   Robert L. Williams   Harry Turner
William D. Brooks   Arthur Jackson   Harry Perisawl
                            Harold Locksley

*C*OGNAC, champagne, chartreuse, sherry, madeira, malaga, and perrier meant nothing to the Teetotalers before this Repeal era. They still, by reason of import tax and sales prices, keep the Teetotalers in ignorance. But these readers of novels of languishing wastrels covering the Riveria felt that they were missing something, so they banded together to pool the common fund so as to be able to partake of ambrosian joys. And were they mistaken?

First: The money procured when divided pro-rata would have simply produced an appetizer.

Secondly: The club was threatened by the Dean with complete annihilation for even looking at any one of the intended samples.

Thirdly: The club had not the price of cognac, champagne, or chartreuse.

And so the Teetotalers have welcomed the coming of spring—sweet spring, with its sprouting of dandelions and promise of dandelion wines—if the club can find a jar for brewing.

Doomed by circumstances to a life of aridity, the Teetotalers have applied to the W. C. T. U. for admission as a men's auxiliary.

⊰{ 65 }⊱

FIGURE 3.4 Humor at Howard University. The Teetotalers Club members (*The Bison* 1934, 65) are presented far more informally—not strictly lined up, for example—than members of the other clubs. The names of the club officers also appear to lampoon the club culture at the university.

branch of the NAACP on campus. For example, Eulalia Layne (Howard class of 1916) was the 1915–16 secretary of the NAACP. Alongside her yearbook picture she chose to quote, "The suffrage must be ours," which references a popular rally song written by E.R. Bennett for the suffrage movement (Bennett 1915).

The same year Eulalia Layne was secretary of the campus NAACP the organization created a student petition that solicited local officials to stop a screening of the film *Birth of a Nation* (see *Howard Yearbook* 1916, 107). This now notorious movie, directed by D.W. Griffith, was based on *The Clansman*, written by Thomas Dixon. The movie provided a fantastical history of post–Civil War Reconstruction in which the Ku Klux Klan (KKK) are portrayed as heroic figures fighting to restore order after a period of Black governance and Northern occupation. The film had profound and lasting effects on American culture and politics. For example, it appears that after being screened in Charlottesville, it helped inspire the creation of two chapters of the KKK—one actually located on the UVA campus (von Daacke and Schmidt 2019).

The Howard NAACP was likely following the example of other regional groups that were calling for similar boycotts. This was particularly the case in Boston under the leadership of early civil rights activist William Monroe Trotter (Puttkammer and Worthy 1958). This was also one of the first periods of activism associated with the NAACP, established shortly after the Niagara Conference of 1905. Below is the text that appeared in the 1916 Howard yearbook that outlined these and other activities. As is typical of the Howard yearbooks, the NAACP's club page offers a detailed chronicle of the activities undertaken during the year.

> The work done by the chapter this year has been commendable. It has sent thirty dollars to the national organization. It sent a strong letter of protest, signed by a majority of the student body to the Commissioners in order to secure the prevention of "The Birth of a Nation" from being shown here. It has presented such prominent speakers as Prof. William Pickens, Dr. Charles Edward Russell, Hon. Archibald Grimke and Dean Miller. Student meetings in which the conditions and progress of the Negroes in various cities were given, have also been held. In co-operation with the Social Science Club and Chapter has presented Prof. Alain Locke in a series of lectures on "Race Contacts and Inter-Racial Relations." (*Howard Yearbook* 1916, 107)

Judging from the yearbook content, Howard University administrators and students have long been particularly proud of both the law school and the medical school. And the motivation for establishing the law program, it is clear, was to train lawyers who would work to protect and increase the rights of the Black community in the United States. The school struggled somewhat before gaining more prominence during the deanship of Charles Hamilton Houston (1929–1935), who believed that law was a mechanism that could be used to enable social reform (McNeil 1983). During this period Howard University trained many of the lawyers who formed the nucleus of the NAACP. Foremost among its graduates was Thurgood Marshall, who as chief counsel for the NAACP Legal Defense and Educational Fund argued several cases before the Supreme Court. The best-known case, *Brown v. Board of Education of Topeka*, effectively dismantled the "separate but equal" standard as applied to education in the Southern United States (Williams 2011).

But before this Howard University was among the first law schools in the country that admitted women. Regarding this fact, and indicative of the optimistic tone that is evident in much Howard University yearbook content generally, is an extraordinary essay penned by Zephyr Abigail Moore, who graduated from the law program in 1922. Previously, she had—with eight other women enrolled in the program—established Epsilon Sigma Iota, a professional sorority designed to support women who wanted to study the law and help provide them with meaningful law careers afterward. Moore was later admitted to the California Bar in 1930 but soon after returned to Washington, DC, to work for the Federal Emergency Relief Administration. Following World War II she returned to Pasadena, California, and practiced law (see Smith 2000).

In an essay titled "Law and Its Call to Women," in the Howard College yearbook, Moore (1924) begins with lines from a poem by A. Cleveland Coxe, which frames the period as "a grand and awful time." Moore argues that despite ongoing violence directed toward Black communities in the South, the American system of law has the capacity to be reformed and ensure, in the future, greater equality—a common theme throughout the Howard yearbooks.

> We are living, we are dwelling,
> In a grand and an awful time,
> In an age on age is telling,
> To be living is sublime.

While noting that men in law and medicine have often felt "theirs is a man's profession," Moore nonetheless argues there are now greater opportunities for women to study the law. She makes note that an increasing number of the best law schools were now accepting women and that there were currently 1,500 women lawyers in the country. While her essay mostly concerns the reasons why women should enter law, it is also clear that this motivation should be understood within the larger context of working toward racial equality. Here, she includes the following reasons why Black lawyers are important:

> I have just been forcibly reminded, by glaring headlines in the daily paper, that in our America, "the land of the free and the brave," that grim monster, mob violence, still exists. This monster is grappling at the throat of the civilization of this great government and means its sure destruction. Our constitution forbids the taking of life, liberty or prosperity of citizens

without the due process of law. Again three Negroes, American citizens, were deprived of life without due process of law in the state of Texas. They met an awful death,—burned at the stake at the hands of an angry mob. 'Tis to horrible to contemplate. Civilization in this country cannot hope to long survive, if such acts of reckless disregard for law and order continue. Progress is inconceivable where anarchy and disorder prevail.

Do I mean that we must despair of American civilization? Men should never despair. Indeed the task is great, but the foundation is laid—we have the basic law. It only remains for the Negro lawyer to secure its protection to his own people. All of the important statutes that have been enacted to meet every great crisis have been drafted by lawyers. All the constitutions that have advanced the liberties of people have been written by lawyers....

So civilization and the law are inseparable. That is why Auguste Comte laid such stress upon the tremendous question of public order. Let us adopt his motto, "Order and Progress," and hasten the realization of an ideal civilization. (Moore 1924)

By way of comparison to the legal philosophy dominant in Virginia at the time, just two years after Moore's essay was written, the Virginia state legislature—after being lobbied by groups that included UVA graduates— passed the Racial Integrity Act. This established the so-called one-drop rule of racial categorization designed mostly to severely curtail the rights of Black Virginians (Reynolds 2020).

"The race is on trial": participation of Howard faculty and students in World War I

The most important national event that occurred during the period examined was the American entry into World War I in 1917. Over the course of the war as many as 700,000 African Americans registered for military service. While the armed forces would not be completely integrated until after World War II, Black Americans did serve in nearly all branches of the US Army during World War I, although barred from serving in the US Marines and in fighting units in the US Navy (Williams 2010). From the beginning of the conflict, Howard University students and faculty—both men and women—were active in the war effort.

At the forefront was Professor of English and dramatist T. Montgomery Gregory—later a proponent of the Negro theater who co-founded the acclaimed Howard Players (discussed below). In particular, Gregory started the campaign by writing to regional newspapers advocating for a plan to train Black army officers. He eventually led a group, the Central Committee of Negro College Men, that lobbied members of the US Congress to establish a training camp for Black army officers (Gregory 2015). The group met in the basement of the Howard University Chapel. It included graduates from other colleges but was

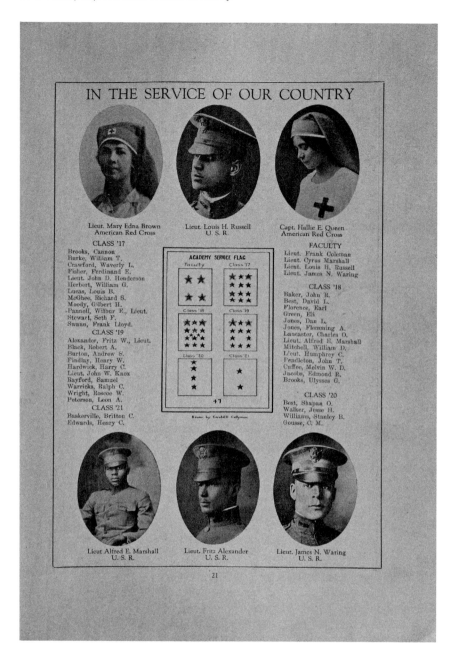

FIGURE 3.5 Yearbook page dedicated to Howard University students and faculty, both men and women, serving in the armed forces and Red Cross (*The Howard Academy Yearbook* 1918, 21).

dominated by Howard students and alumni (Kelly 2019). Ultimately, the lobbying was successful, and the War Department established the 17th Provisional Training Regiment for Black officer candidates at Fort Des Moines, Iowa. Howard students and faculty were well represented among the officers trained at this camp (Matthews 2018). Of particular note is that this group included over 100 medical officers, many trained at Howard University, to care for Black army units. Concurrently, women attending Howard used their medical training in service to the American Red Cross (Matthews 2018).

The Central Committee was extremely active is recruiting African Americans to serve in the army. Here, the message was clear: the war offered an opportunity to demonstrate both loyalty to the nation and courage during a period of conflict. In short, the war was framed as an opportunity to demonstrate that Black men and women could be, and should be, allowed to participate as full citizens in the effort. Or more bluntly, as quoted in the recruitment pitch below, African Americans should join because "the race is on trial" (Kelly 2019):

> Let us not mince matters; the race is on trial. It needs every one of its red-blooded, sober minded men. Doctors, lawyers, teachers, business men, and all men who have graduated from high school. Let the college student and graduate come and demonstrate by their presence the principles of virtue and courage learned in the academic halls. Up, brother, our race is calling.

In the picture shown in Figure 3.5, published in the 1918 Howard yearbook (21), the students and faculty, both men and women, serving during the war are recognized.

Importantly, it appears that this officer-training experience was directly responsible for the establishment of the first military science and Reserve Officer Training Corps (ROTC) program on campus. Later, after World War II, ROTC training was expanded and became mandatory for men. This mandatory training would later become a source of student-administration conflict during a series of student protests in the tumultuous year of 1968 (see chapter 5).

Race and extracurricular campus life: the performing arts and sports

The performing arts

In chapter 2 it was noted that minstrelsy and blackface performances were often predominant forms of entertainment associated with theater and choral performances on Virginia campuses. In fact, some blackface productions continued to be annual events—apparently a highlight of the academic year—well into the 1960s. For example, at the Virginia Military Institute (VMI) the Monogram

Minstrel Show was staged annually—into the 1960s—often on Thanksgiving before the VMI versus VPI (Virginia Polytechnic and State University) football game (see *The Bomb* 1962, 275). While there were often other performances staged at Virginia schools, it appears that the blackface performances were the most anticipated, and probably the most popular. At Howard, obviously, there were no blackface productions, but it is notable that even their acclaimed theater program could not fully escape the staging of plays that reinforced some racial stereotypes of the period.

There were other types of theatrical productions staged at the White colleges too. These include Greek tragedies, the occasional Shakespeare, and even a few performances of more modern material written during the 20th century. The quality of these performances is hard to judge from yearbook pictures. Sometimes the sets and costuming look quite good, other times kitschy. Mostly, none of the theater departments or performing groups appear to stand out from what might be considered a routine theatrical performance that one would expect to see at a college. The fact that some of these Virginia schools now have excellent programs is an indication that there may be a history of excellence not well captured in these schools' older yearbooks.

I mention the previous because the performing arts at Howard University—while apparently long considered excellent—had acclaim, and an extraordinarily creative period, beginning in the 1920s. This largely corresponded with the establishment of the Howard Players, who often performed at the 1,200-seat Howard Theatre (not directly affiliated with Howard University). This group was co-founded by T. Montgomery Gregory, discussed previously concerning his leadership in lobbying for a Black officer corps in World War I. He is considered one of the early advocates and developers of Black theater. He also co-edited *Plays of Negro Life* (1927) with his sometime collaborator Alain Locke, often considered "the Dean of the Harlem Renaissance" (Stewart 2018). Many of the plays included in this volume were written by students he mentored at Howard, and Gregory is credited with helping to sustain and advance the emerging Black theater throughout his life. Notably, it appears that three plays, of varying quality, by Zora Neale Hurston were written when she was a student of Gregory's, although there is no indication that any of these plays were staged (Speisman 1998).

During this period Howard University was among the first to establish a professional theater program, one that awarded college credit for performance and the other technical aspects (costuming and set design) associated with staging professional productions. In effect, the Howard University Department of Dramatic Art was running a successful professional theater troupe where students could also earn credit through their participation (as writers, actors, directors and set makers) for these productions. Soon enough, this professional model was adopted by other university programs. These early developments are first characterized in the 1920 Howard yearbook (106) as follows:

The Department of Dramatic Art is today not only the center of interest at the university but it is also the center of interest for the entire dramatic world. The merging of the famous old College Dramatics Club into the Department of Dramatics, has given forth the rapidly rising Howard Players.

The Department of Dramatic Art of Howard University is formed after Harvard's Department of Dramatics. It has, according to the *New York Times*, gone a step further, however, in that it gives a full academic credit for its work. The practical work of acting and character portrayal, the technical work of the stages, the making of costumes, and the managing of productions come under the course in Dramatic Art. It has its own business offices, costume rooms, and scenic work shop....

This is the most cultural and dramatic program ever presented by a Negro organization. The Department of Dramatics expects to stimulate and develop a national effort and work among Negroes in the art of drama.

After the establishment of the Howard Players the breadth and scale of productions increased each academic year. The company produced plays written by European authors, but also more modern one-act plays, including the production of race plays. For example, in 1923 this included a production of *Mortgaged* by Willis Richardson, a prominent African American playwright whose previous play had been staged on Broadway (*The Bison* 1924, 250).

The double-bind of the Howard Players: the enabling and problematic aspects of the acclaimed Emperor Jones performance

Not only were some of the Howard University productions regionally acclaimed, on occasion they were covered by the national press. This was the case in an early Howard Players production, in 1920, of Eugene O'Neill's first widely popular play, *The Emperor Jones*. The play tells the story of a charismatic Black railroad porter who, after killing a man in a gambling dispute, flees to a Caribbean island, where he becomes the self-styled emperor (O'Neill 1998). Later, the play was made into a movie and helped launch the career of Black actor and singer Paul Robeson, who acted the part of Brutus Jones on stage and in movie productions. It appears that the critical acclaim the Howard theater program received after staging this play helped launch its innovative performing arts program, outlined above.

To be clear, *The Emperor Jones* is deeply problematic in its use of racial tropes. The play would be considered retrograde if viewed by the public today. Practically, for some White viewers at the time, it likely had some of the same appeal—in terms of presenting and reinforcing Black stereotypes—that minstrel productions had. But during this period Black intellectuals tended to laud the play because it was, compared to other portrayals of Black men and women on stage, a serious (as opposed to comical) representation. It also allowed Black actors, such as Paul Robeson, to perform in prominent venues. Alain Locke ([1925] 1968, 157), for example, described the play as a "Tour de Force of Genius" that marked "the breakwater plunge of the Negro drama into the mainstream of American drama." But as one modern critic has summarized:

> The acknowledgment of the thinly veiled, eroticized quality of the play in combination with the overdetermined racial qualities of Brutus Jones (the patois with which he speaks, the conflation of his personal history with that of a primitive, collective past, the seemingly inevitable and inescapable influence of ritual on Jones's internal trajectory over the course of the play) have led to a profound discomfort towards O'Neill's piece. Credited by some Black artists for providing rich dramatic matter, the play has not enjoyed universal praise. (Steen 2000)

Here, it is interesting to contemplate the ongoing double-bind that faculty and Howard University students had to navigate as they established a world-class theater program. On largely practical terms, it is impossible to fault the motives of either Montgomery Gregory or Alain Locke in the decision to stage *The Emperor Jones* during the period they lived in. And judging from Locke's comments on the play, he sincerely regarded it as a breakthrough in Black cinema. At times, the Howard Players performed for both Black and White audiences— often the productions of the Howard Players seemed designed to have crossover appeal—even though Gregory was also an advocate for a new kind of theater whose appeal would be primarily to Black audiences.

It is interesting to contemplate how the arc of the Howard theater program might have progressed without the initial success of *The Emperor Jones*. Practically, the yearbooks do indicate a clear break in the type of material staged before and after this event and the establishment of the Howard Players. Afterward, the content of the plays changed. While the Howard Players still staged classics, far more modern material was included too. And, importantly, new plays by Black writers—sometimes students—were also staged. Here, Gregory was an early advocate for creating an attitude that cultivated "race pride" in theater, and he specifically disliked trying to "un-race" Black performances. While the Howard yearbooks indicates that the previous Dramatics Club was always considered excellent, judging from their performances (see Figure 3.6), always work penned by well-known European playwrights, Gregory might have regarded these earlier productions as trying to "un-race" the performers.

Race and sports at Howard

One theme developed in this chapter is that the international contingent of Howard students often made the school culture more worldly than the Virginia

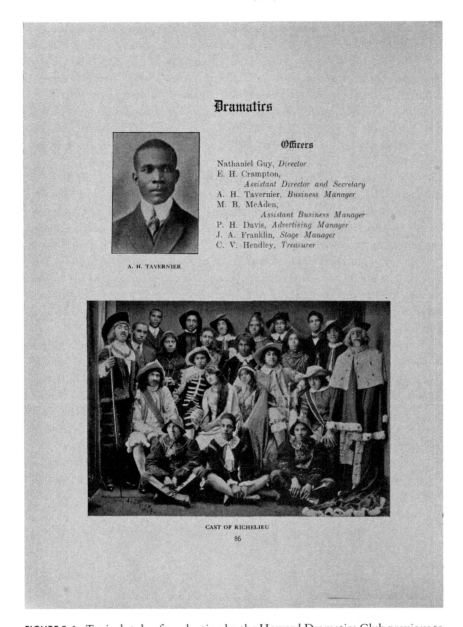

Dramatics

Officers

Nathaniel Guy, *Director*
E. H. Crampton,
    Assistant Director and Secretary
A. H. Tavernier, *Business Manager*
M. B. McAden,
    Assistant Business Manager
P. H. Davis, *Advertising Manager*
J. A. Franklin, *Stage Manager*
C. V. Hendley, *Treasurer*

A. H. TAVERNIER

CAST OF RICHELIEU
86

FIGURE 3.6 Typical style of production by the Howard Dramatics Club previous to the establishment of the performing arts program (*The Mirror* 1915, 86). The play, *Richelieu*, is a historical drama written by Edward Bulwer-Lytton that portrays the life of 17th-century French statesman Cardinal Richelieu. Other plays staged during this period include *She Stoops to Conquer* (1908–09), *The Rivals* (1909–10), *The Merry Wives of Windsor* (1910–11), *For One Night Only* (1911–12), *The Lady of Lyons* (1912–13), *Richelieu* (1913–14), *The Merchant of Venice* (1914–15) and *Herod* (1915–16).

schools. This is also the case concerning a few of the sporting clubs encountered at the university. For example, Howard was the only school studied that had a cricket team. At first, this sport might seem incongruous with any American college, but the team was dominated by Black Caribbean students who sometimes fielded a formidable club. Figure 3.7 is a picture of the Howard cricket team in 1916.

Importantly, many have commented on the racial hierarchy of cricket as it was established in the West Indies during the period of the British Empire. Foremost would be C.L.R. James (2013), a Marxist academic from Trinidad who wrote the acclaimed *Beyond a Boundary*. James used the game as a metaphor for the racial politics of the region. Basically, while the sport was rigidly ordered by race as a result of the colonial experience—to the extent that there were distinctions between light-skinned teams and dark-skinned teams in Trinidad—James also argues the sport, as well as other aspects of the colonial experience, did help create a Pan-Caribbean identity. Here, at Howard, while the Caribbean students made Howard a more cosmopolitan college, it seems clear these students were also navigating the colonial experience. This experience was clearly different compared to that of the American students, and the interaction with these foreign students acted to broaden their own worldviews significantly.

Overall, it appears that Caribbean students at Howard also excelled at all the British lawn sports, including tennis, and that the foreign students also founded a very successful Soccer Club team in 1929. The yearbooks (1929–1932) indicate the team did not lose a game during the first three seasons it played. Of note, in 1961 the Howard soccer team was the first from an HBCU to win a national championship—Howard's first national championship in any sport (*The Bison* 1962, 138). In the early 1970s, also fielding players from around the world, Howard scoccer was consistently one of the best programs in the country. During this period the team became the first HBCU to win a National Collegiate Athletic Association national championship (Seium 2019).

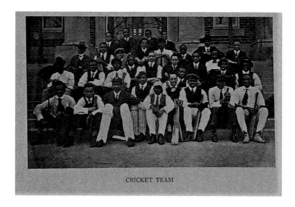

FIGURE 3.7 The cricket team at Howard was often dominated by players from Caribbean countries (*The Howard Yearbook* 1916, 125).

At times, Howard athletes—particularly in track—had an opportunity to participate in sports against White athletes, but these events were relatively uncommon and usually associated with regional events in which many schools participated. For example, the yearbooks indicate that in 1920, Howard track athletes—along with those of other HBCUs—began competing in the Penn Relays, hosted annually—starting April 21, 1895—by the University of Pennsylvania. This is the oldest track-and-field competition in the United States. Howard and other HBCUs were first invited to participate in 1920 ("Penn Relays" 2020).

More often, the teams that Howard played against were other HBCUs in the region, with some ongoing rivalries dating back to this early period. Currently, the biggest rivalry is probably with another HBCU, Hampton University (HU)—where competition is described as a battle for the "real HU." During the period surveyed it was the football rivalry with Lincoln College that dominated yearbook coverage (Rodgers 2015).

Scholarly debate on race at Howard University as compared to Virginia universities

One of the remarkable features of the early Howard yearbooks is that they routinely include both popular and academic sentiment characterizing American race relations that would later become increasingly accepted by more White Americans over time. In effect, the Howard University yearbook content is more prescient concerning the politics of future race relations in America when compared to information presented in the yearbooks at White Virginia universities during the same period. Within the Howard yearbooks it is routine to encounter intellectual arguments associated with the necessity of Black political activism, the egalitarian foundations of American constitutional governance, all combined with ongoing commentary about the increasing violence being directed toward the Black community in the South. Here, the portrayal of race relations during this period is far more accurate when compared to the fantastical imagery and texts presented in the Virginia yearbooks. Moreover, the students and faculty at Howard University offer prescriptions for solving racial violence and racial inequality—most often an argument for equal protection under the law—that later became the foundational legal strategy undertaken by the NAACP to dismantle the institutions associated with the Jim Crow South.

It is also notable how the field of sociology was embraced and used to great effect by a small but increasingly significant group of Black intellectuals at the turn of the century. Two of the better-known academics during this period are E. Franklin Frazier and W.E.B. Du Bois. Frazier was a Howard undergraduate (class of 1916) who later received a PhD in sociology from the University of Chicago. He eventually returned to Howard as a professor of sociology (1934–1962). Popularized interpretations of his work later gained wide currency among the Black community and are explored in greater detail below.

It is important to understand the general outlines of intellectual debate at Howard University and the Virginia schools to provide context for the dramatic differences in their yearbook content. Here, as in so many cases, the Black experience in America appears to have made Black intellectuals like E. Franklin Frasier—and the students he was teaching—much more insightful observers of the entire American experience compared to most of their White counterparts. Notably, the Howard worldview and academic tradition appear to have made Howard scholars far more likely to routinely tackle difficult topics when compared to most of their White counterparts. And when they did confront the nettlesome questions of race and poverty, they were far more insightful than their White counterparts. To put this another way, it is hard to imagine a White scholar in the South conducting an inquiry into White poverty that might have mirrored the approach used by W.E.B. Du Bois (2007 [1899]) in his study of Black poverty in Philadelphia. That work, *The Philadelphia Negro*, published in 1899, is now considered a classic, an enduring work of early sociology. Although Du Bois was never a professor at Howard (he declined an offer), his work was clearly a part of the scholarly tradition Howard students were working within, and he is routinely referenced in the Howard yearbooks (see Figure 3.3. above).

During this period there were very few White sociologists—Robert Park at the University of Chicago is probably the most notable—making inquiries into Black and White poverty, social stratification and ethnic stratification. Here, Park stands out because of his long association with the Tuskegee Institute and his collaboration with Booker T. Washington. In this case, his collaboration with Washington resulted in the text *The Man Farthest Down: A Record of Observation and Study in Europe* (1913). Importantly, Robert Park was at the University of Chicago when E. Franklin Frasier was trained as a sociologist. Notwithstanding some groundbreaking work being done by Northern sociologists such as Robert Park and his associates at the University of Chicago (see Raushenbush 1979), at White universities in the South social scientists nearly always gravitated toward a "hierarchy of races" perspective directly connected with the growing popularity of eugenics. And this was not just a Southern tradition—there were plenty of Northern social scientists who likewise followed this line of reasoning. For example, two years previous to the publication of *The Philadelphia Negro* (1899), Carlos Closson (1897) published "The Hierarchy of European Races" in the *American Journal of Sociology*—the flagship journal of American sociology. In this study he extended Georges Vacher de Lapouge's (1889) argument that statistics and social science could help scientifically establish the superiority of certain races. De Lapouge's (1889) most notable work, *The Aryan: His Social Role*, became part of the basis for much Nazi political and social doctrine.

In Virginia, at the turn of the century and well into the 1930s, academic study of eugenics essentially saturated the major colleges, with the work done at UVA being the most notable. Previously, in chapter 2, the example of Dr. Paul B. Barringer (1901) was discussed—a professor at UVA who helped establish the study of eugenics in the UVA Medical School before moving to Virginia Tech to become its sixth president. He actively recruited prominent eugenicists to the UVA faculty during this period (see Dorr 1999; Dorr 2008). Here, the popularity of eugenics, combined with the more populist sentiments perpetuated by prominent UVA alumni such as Thomas Nelson Page (1904), helped to support the establishment of Virginia's infamous Racial Integrity Act, which established the one-drop standard in terms of determining racial categories (Dorr 1999).

Probably the most significant difference between Howard University and the University of Virginia was the attitudes of their prominent scholars—and certainly the students they taught—concerning racial identity and racial politics. From the beginning, Thomas Jefferson (1984) himself espoused ideas associated with a hierarchy of races, and the later eugenics-based ideas adopted by the UVA faculty can be read as the inevitable extension of his ideas. By way of contrast, Howard University was founded on explicitly egalitarian principles, racially grounded but also clearly progressive at the time, which inevitably caused professors and students at Howard to make evidence-based observations that were aided by prominent sociological perspectives.

As a consequence, Howard University scholars—and particularly lawyers trained during this period who used social psychology in their legal arguments against the "separate but equal" standard—ultimately changed the trajectory of American politics toward better realizing the American ideal of equality. Here, Howard University deserves credit for making these changes possible. And while the alumni of the university know this history, it is a story that has rarely been widely disseminated to citizens throughout the United States. Conversely, it seems notable that there has never really been a similar accounting of the role that an institution like UVA played in subverting the progressive racial agenda that those at Howard, and elsewhere, were advancing. Perhaps the best specific example of how these conflicting intellectual ideas were later debated in a public setting concerns the lawsuit (*Gregory Hayes Swanson v. Rector & Visitors of the University of Virginia*) brought by the Virginia NAACP. With Howard alumnus Thurgood Marshall as part of the NAACP team, this was the lawsuit that ultimately forced the University of Virginia to accept Black students to its law school (discussed in the following chapter).

The exemplary Howard alumni and faculty: E. Franklin Frazier and perspectives on race relations

Previously, this text described a few prominent alumni and professors associated with UVA and W&L and their opinions on race relations and Black labor. Here, the focus is on the life and work of E. Franklin Frazier, a Howard graduate who later returned as a sociology professor. The goal is to provide a comparison of exemplary alumni who were prominent concerning their views on race relations. For example, on E. Franklin Frazier's Howard University yearbook page, the year he graduated, he is given the nickname "Plato," which hints he is someone inclined toward academic thought. His college record—president of his class, president of the Social Science Club, and vice president of the NAACP chapter—indicates a young man with a bright future. His plans after graduating state simply that he "will teach" (*Howard Yearbook* 1916, 29). Ultimately, Frazier did teach at a few universities, both before and after earning a PhD in sociology at the University of Chicago. Before receiving his doctorate he taught at Morehouse College in Atlanta. Afterward, he spent most of his career teaching at Howard University (1934–1961), but sometimes he took visiting appointments at colleges throughout the United States and Europe. During his career, in 1948, he became the first Black president of the American Sociological Association (see Cromwell 2002). He also authored several influential articles and texts on the Black family, racial prejudice and the Black middle class. The two most influential were *The Negro in the United States* (1949) and the *Black Bourgeoisie* ([1962] 1997).

Below is an early, extended excerpt of Frazier's indictment of White prejudice, published in 1927, in which he offers a clinical diagnosis of the "Negro-complex." This piece, written before he received his PhD in sociology, is probably best read as a half-serious argument of social satire. Using new terminology associated with psychology, Frazier directly compares Southern attitudes toward the Negro as similar to disorders associated with insanity. The article, published in a Georgia periodical, was considered radical. The work was not embraced by administrators at Morehouse College, where he was teaching at the time. In fact, when excerpts—largely taken out of context—appeared in the *Atlanta Constitution*, the Morehouse Board of Directors, both the White and the Black members, quickly agreed to terminate Frazier's contract with the school. Fortunately, he had been offered admittance to the University of Chicago sociology program, at that time one of the most influential programs in the country (Cromwell 2002; Teele 2002).

The argument, notwithstanding its use of psychological terms, is not particularly indicative of Frasier's later sociological work. It is, however, indicative of a sometimes pugnacious style he employed as a public figure discussing issues of the day. In this case, it employs a stinging wit in order to demonstrate the dangerous banality with which Southern Whites—including popular White literary figures—characterized the Black community. Frazier's criticism of Southern literature can be read as a direct indictment of the type of work that had made Thomas Nelson Page (1898; 1904) renowned, particularly regarding his claim that he was well placed to understand the Negro mind and temperament.

> When one surveys Southern literature dealing with the Negro, one finds him accused of all the failings of mankind. When we reflect, however, that the Negro, in spite of his ignorance and poverty, does not in most places contribute more than his share to crime and,—even in the opinion of his most violent disparagers,—possesses certain admirable qualities, we are forced to seek the cause of these excessive accusations in the minds of the accusers themselves. Here, too, we find striking similarities to the mental processes of the insane. Where the conflict between the personality as a

whole and the unacceptable complex is not resolved within the mind of the subject, the extremely repugnant system of dissociated ideas is projected upon some real or imaginary individual. Except in the case of those who, as we have seen, charge the Negro with an inherent impulse to rape as an unconscious defense of their own murderous impulses, the persistence,— in the face of contrary evidence,—of the delusion that the Negro is a ravisher can only be taken as a projection. According to this view, the Southern White man, who has,—arbitrarily without censure,—enjoyed the right to use colored women, projects this insistent desire upon the Negro when it is no longer socially approved and his conscious personality likewise rejects it. Like the lunatic, he refuses to treat the repugnant desire as a part of himself and consequently shows an exaggerated antagonism toward the desire which he projects upon the Negro....

From a practical viewpoint, insanity means social incapacity. Southern White people afflicted with the Negro-complex show themselves incapable of performing certain social functions. They are, for instance, incapable of rendering just decisions when White and colored people are involved; and their very claim that they "know" and "understand" the Negro indicates a fixed system of ideas respecting him,—whereas a sane and just appraisal of the situation would involve the assimilation of new data. The delusions of the sane are generally supported by the herd, while those of the insane are often antisocial. Yet,—from the point of view of Negroes, who are murdered if they believe in social equality or are maimed for asking for an ice cream soda, and of White people, who are threatened with similar violence for not subscribing to the Southerner's delusions,—such behavior is distinctively antisocial. The inmates of a madhouse are not judged insane by themselves, but by those outside. The fact that abnormal behavior towards Negroes is characteristic of a whole group may be an example illustrating Nietzsche's observation that "insanity in individuals is something rare,— but in groups, parties, nations, and epochs it is the rule." (Frazier 1927, 856–862)

I am not sure how much Frazier actually believed in his diagnostic criteria associated with the "Negro-complex," but it seems fair to conclude he often understood the motives of White Southerners regarding their prejudices far better than most of these men and women themselves. Notable is that the style in the excerpt, somewhat more moderated, is evident in the second half of Frazier's ([1962] 1997) much-debated *Black Bourgeoisie*. Like the analysis above, it tends toward the language of pathology. Importantly, Frazier's tendency to explore pathology—in all his academic work—was often considered the weakest aspect of his academic arguments.

E. Franklin Frazier's (1949) work on the Black family, *The Negro in the United States*, has become more contentious in the past three decades. For some, Frasier is regarded primarily as an economic sociologist who placed the post–Civil

War structure of the Black family into an economic context. He argues that the structure of the Black family was related to patterns of post-war economic deprivation. Similarly, he believed that Black migration into urban centers after the Civil War was a condition that also placed strain on the Black family—particularly as it concerns the labor of Black men as compared to Black women. Defenders of Frazier have indicated that they regard his description of the matriarchal family—the role that mothers and grandmothers play in organizing and heading Black families—as reasonably nuanced. Further, they claim he never directly implied a matriarchal family organization was a pathological state. For those who regard his work as nuanced, he is credited with describing how Black women were uniquely equipped for this role coming out of slavery (see Semmes 2001; Platt 1989).

For critics, they assert his language implies that a woman-headed family is pathological. Here, his work is linked to what is generally described as the "pathology disorganization" perspective in which a woman-centered family is considered a cause for Black family disorganization (see Roberts 1997). Most prominently, this line of reasoning underpins ideas that were presented by Patrick Moynihan (1965) in the now infamous *Moynihan Report* (Acs et al. 2013) on the Black family. Moreover, Moynihan explicitly linked his ideas—fairly or not—to work done by E. Franklin Frazier.[2]

Finally, there are a few important reasons to briefly introduce Frazier's ([1962] 1997) controversial *Black Bourgeoisie*. Foremost is that a wider audience—and later a group of young Black activists at Howard during the 1960s—largely reimagined Frasier's work through their own activism and this helped fashion a Black Power movement that regarded the Black bourgeoisie as a barrier to realizing real political power in America. Frazier's text was published in the 1950s—it is a discussed further in chapter 5, but for continuity it is presented here because Frazier's career spanned both periods examined in this text. Here, Frazier's text offers a nice transition concerning ideas that were more commonly represented in the post–World War II Howard yearbook content explored in the following chapter. In particular, the student movement at Howard University in the late 1960s was largely articulated as a reaction against the bourgeois sentiments and goals of the previous generation—the generation that Frazier belonged to. The new movement largely rejected these values—expressed as a tendency for the Black middle class to favor assimilation by acting White—in favor of a movement that articulated the distinctiveness, and beauty, of Black American culture.

Conclusion: race relations at Howard University as compared to campus life in Virginia

Howard University students and professors, as represented in yearbook material, were usually much more nuanced in their analysis of race relations in the United States compared to students and professors at White universities in

Virginia. Particularly striking is that within the Virginia university yearbooks previously examined there are essentially no progressive opinions associated with improving race relations. Indeed, it was not until well after World War II that a very few progressive voices appeared on these campuses (discussed further in chapter 5). Further, while the Howard yearbooks routinely pay homage to the most progressive voices on race relations—Black as well as White—the most prominent Virginia colleges just as often featured alumni whose views on race were among the most retrograde of the period.

The argument made in this chapter, using material from the Howard University yearbooks, is that Howard University was, in all matters, a much better university—particularly as it relates to the study of the law and the social scientific inquiry into race relations—than the schools in Virginia that were examined previously. The faculty—small in number—appear more energetic and engaged. The students appear to have been more serious minded, more generous and far more worldly because of their Howard experience too. They often appeared better trained in the humanities, particularly in the performing arts. Probably had Howard been given the chance to compete against these neighboring schools in sports—at least as they concern cricket and soccer—they would have proved better in this arena too.

The last section of this chapter outlined the career trajectory of a single man, E. Franklin Frazier, who graduated from Howard in 1916 and later returned to the university as a professor of sociology. Ultimately, although his work was controversial, he was largely at the center of important intellectual debates associated with race relations. Here, while E. Franklin Frasier is just one person, he is also exactly the sort of person you would expect to be produced by the academic culture at Howard University at roughly the turn of the century. Ideally, this chapter has presented enough Howard yearbook content to enable readers to intuitively understand why so many Howard University students, faculty and alumni were at the center of intellectual debates that were necessary for the social change that later took place during the civil rights period. Howard students, throughout the history of the school, had important impacts on race relations because this was an important part of their intellectual life at the institution. Here, it is not surprising that future Howard students would have a significant impact on the trajectory of the civil rights movement in the 1950s and 1960s.

By way of comparison, the yearbooks produced by the Virginia institutions during this period tell a sad story about ongoing race relations. To be clear, these schools produced some fine students who likely had meaningful impacts on their communities. But the overall culture of these Virginia schools also helped—to varying degrees—maintain the violent structural racism of the South. Further, these schools helped manufacture the ideals that were used to maintain racial segregation in Virginia well into the 1960s. In short, the Virginia schools in this study were largely a part of the problem—not part of the solution—on issues of race relations during the period examined.

The next chapter explores social change at the Virginia institutions following the post–World War II period. Here, the story for the White universities in this study continues to be a largely desultory tale. Were there any Virginia colleges where students and faculty were at the forefront of the civil rights movement? No, there were not. Worse than that, some of these schools essentially became the target for school desegregation campaigns in the 1950s and 1960s. Here, many people at these schools actively fought to maintain racial segregation during the Virginia state government's campaign of massive resistance to school desegregation. By way of contrast, it was students from HBCUs throughout the country—sometimes with help from White students attending elite colleges in the North—who became an important mobilizing force of the Black civil rights movement.

Notes

1 For example, the yearbooks in this period chronicle the establishment of five fraternities that are usually referred to as part of the "Divine Nine" by the National Pan-Hellenic Council, which was itself established at Howard University in 1930. These five include Alpha Kappa Alpha sorority, founded in 1908; Omega Psi Phi fraternity, founded in 1911; Delta Sigma Theta sorority, founded in 1913; Phi Beta Sigma fraternity, founded in 1914; Zeta Phi Beta sorority, founded in 1920.
2 The maternal Black family being portrayed as pathology is part of an important ongoing debate that has been nicely summarized by Ta-Nehisi Coates, "The Black Family in the Age of Mass Incarceration," *The Atlantic* 316, no. 3 (2015). Basically, an assumption of pathology has important negative implications as it relates to public policy. Coates offers a nuanced argument as to how Moynihan's (1965) perspective was drawn from work done by sociologists like E. Franklin Frazier when he directed the congressional committee that produced the report *The Negro Family: The Case for National Action*. See Gregory Acs, Kenneth Braswell, Elaine Sorensen and Margery Austin Turner, *The Moynihan Report Revisited* (Washington, DC: Urban Institute, 2013).

References

Acs, Gregory, Kenneth Braswell, Elaine Shaw Sorensen and Margery Austin Turner, 2013. *The Moynihan Report Revisited*. Washington, DC: Urban Institute.

Aptheker, Herbert. 1969. "The Negro College Student in the 1920s—Years of Preparation and Protest: An Introduction." *Science & Society* 33 (2): 150–167.

Barringer, Paul B. 1901. "The American Negro: His Past and Future." Presented at the *Negro Education in the South* session during the Tenth Annual Meeting of the Southern Education Association Proceedings, 133–146. Richmond, VA: The Education Association. Available at: https://archive.org/details/american negro his00barr/page/6/mode/2up.

Bennett, E.R. 1915. "The Suffrage Must Be Ours." *Rally Song*. Camden, NJ: Bennett & Bennett.

The Bison.1923–2012. Howard University Library Yearbook Digital Archive. https://dh.howard.edu/bison_yearbooks/index.4.html.

Boyd, Valerie. 2003. "Zora Neale Hurston: The Howard University Years." *Journal of Blacks in Higher Education* 39: 104–108.

Carter, Robert L. 1988. "The NAACP's Legal Strategy against Segregated Education." *Michigan Law Review* 86 (6): 1083–1095.

Chetty, Raj, John N. Friedman, Emmanuel Saez, Nicholas Turner and Danny Yagan. 2017. "Mobility Report Cards: The Role of Colleges in Intergenerational Mobility." National Bureau of Economic Research Working Paper No. 23618, July 2017.

Closson, Carlos C. 1897. "The Hierarchy of European Races." *American Journal of Sociology* 3 (3): 314–327.

Coates, Ta-Nehisi. 2015. "The Black Family in the Age of Mass Incarceration." *The Atlantic* 316 (3).

Cook, Mercer. 1938. "The Teaching of French in Negro Schools." *Journal of Negro Education* 7 (2): 147–154.

Coolidge, Calvin. 1924. "Speech at Howard University," Calvin Coolidge Foundation, June 6. https://www.coolidgefoundation.org/resources/speeches-as-president-1923-1928-7/.

Cromwell, Adelaide M. 2002. "Frazier's Background and an Overview." *E. Franklin Frazier and Black Bourgeoisie*, edited by James E. Teele, 33–35. Columbia MO: University of Missouri Press.

De Lapouge, Georges Vacher. 1889. *L'Aryen: Son rôle social*. Paris: Libraire des Ecoles Francaises.

Dorr, Gregory Michael. 2008. *Segregation's Science: Eugenics and Society in Virginia*. Charlottesville, VA: University of Virginia Press.

Dorr, Lisa Lindquist. 1999. "Arm in Arm: Gender, Eugenics, and Virginia's Racial Integrity Acts of the 1920s." *Journal of Women's History* 11 (1): 143–166.

Du Bois, William Edward Burghardt. [1899] 2007. *The Philadelphia Negro*. New York: Cosimo.

Du Bois, William Edward Burghardt. 1995. *W.E.B. Du Bois: A Reader*. New York: Macmillan Press.

"Economic Diversity and Student Outcomes at America's Colleges and Universities: Find Your College." *New York Times*. https://www. nytimes.com/interactive/projects/college-mobility/.

Frazier, E Franklin. 1927. "The Pathology of Race Prejudice." *The Forum*. June 1927, 856–862.

Frazier, E. Franklin 1949. *The Negro in the United States*. New York: Macmillan Press.

Frazier, E. Franklin. [1962] 1997. *Black Bourgeoisie: The Book That Brought the Shock of Self-Revelation to Middle-Class Blacks in America*. New York: Free Press.

Gregory, Thomas Montgomery. 2015. "List of Personal Correspondence." Howard University Library. Manuscript Division Finding Aids, 82. https://dh.howard.edu/finaid _manu/82 https://dh.howard.edu/finaid_manu/82. "Thomas Montgomery Gregory."

Howard Yearbook. 1916. Howard University Library Yearbook Digital Archive. https://dh.howard.edu/bison_yearbooks/index.4.html.

Howard Academy Yearbook. 1918. Howard University Library Yearbook Digital Archive. https://dh.howard.edu/bison_yearbooks/index.4.html.

"Howard at a Glance." Howard University. https://www2.howard.edu/about/ howard-glance.

"Howard University." DATA USA. https://datausa.io/profile/university/howard-university.

James, Cyril Lionel Robert. 2013. *Beyond a Boundary*. Durham, NC: Duke University Press.

Jefferson, Thomas. 1984. *Notes on the State of Virginia*. Chapel Hill. NC: University of North Carolina Press.

Kelly, John. 2019. "When World War I Raged, a D.C. Professor Fought for Black Officers' Participation," *Washington Post*, February 5. LexisNexis Academic.

Locke, Alain. [1925] 1968). *The New Negro*. New York: Arno.

Locke, Alain LeRoy, and Montgomery Gregory, eds. 1927. *Plays of Negro Life: A Source-Book of Native American Drama*. New York: Harper & Brothers.

Logan, Rayford W. 1969. *Howard University: The First Hundred Years, 1867–1967*. New York: NYU Press.

Matthews, Lopez D. 2018. *Howard University in the World Wars: Men and Women Serving the Nation*. Cheltenham, UK: The History Press.

McKinney, Richard Ishmael. 1997. *Mordecai, the Man and His Message: The Story of Mordecai Wyatt Johnson*. Washington, DC: Howard University Press.

McNeil, Genna Rae. 1983. *Groundwork: Charles Hamilton Houston and the Struggle for Civil Rights*. Philadelphia, PA: University of Pennsylvania Press.

The Mirror. 1915. Howard University Library Yearbook Digital Archive. https://dh.howard.edu/bison_yearbooks/index.4.html.

Moore, Zephyr Abigail. 1924. "Law and Its Call to Women." *Intium*, pp. 147–150.

Moore, Zephyr Abigail. 2000 [1924]. "Law and Its Call to Women." *Rebels in Law: Voices in History of Black Women Lawyers*, edited by J. Clay Smith, 13–16. Ann Arbor, MI: University of Michigan Press.

Moynihan, Daniel Patrick. 1965. *The Negro Family: The Case for National Action*, No. 31–33. Washington, DC: US Government Printing Office.

NIKH Yearbook. 1915. Howard University Library Yearbook Digital Archive. https://dh.howard.edu/bison_yearbooks/index.4.html.

Norell, Robert Jefferson. 2009. *Up from History: The Life of Booker T. Washington*. Boston: Harvard University Press.

O'Neill, Eugene. 1998. "The Emperor Jones." In *Four Plays by Eugene O'Neill*, 109–153. New York: Signet Classic.

Page, Thomas Nelson. 1898. *Social Life in Old Virginia before the War*. New York: Charles Scribner's Sons.

Page, Thomas Nelson. 1904. *The Negro: The Southerner's Problem*. New York: Charles Scribner's Sons.

"Penn Relays to Showcase 100 Years of HBCU Competition." 2020. *Penn State Athletics*. https://pennathletics.com/news/2020/1/23/general-2020-penn-relays-to-showcase-100-years-of-hbcu-competition.

Platt, Tony. 1989. "E. Franklin Frazier Reconsidered." *Social Justice* 16 (4): 186–195.

Puttkammer, Charles W., and Ruth Worthy. 1958. "William Monroe Trotter, 1872–1934." *Journal of Negro History* 43 (4): 298–316.

Raushenbush, Winifred. 1979. *Robert E. Park: Biography of a Sociologist*. Durham, NC: Duke University Press.

Reynolds, P. Preston. 2020. "UVA and the History of Race: Eugenics, the Racial Integrity Act, Health Disparities." *UVA Today*. https://news.virginia.edu/content/uva-and-history-race-eugenics-racial-integrity-act-health-disparities.

Roberts, Dorothy E. 1997. *Killing the Black Body: Race, Reproduction and the Meaning of Liberty*. New York: Pantheon.

Rodgers, P.R. 2015. "It's HBCU Classic Time!" In *The Athletic Experience at Historically Black Colleges and Universities: Past, Present, and Persistence*," edited by Billy Hawkins, Joseph Cooper, Akilah Carter-Francique and J. Kenyatta Cavil, 145–165. Lanham, MD: Rowman & Littlefield.

Seium, Michael. 2019. "NCAA Soccer Champions Howard University: The Triumphs and Tribulations of Reclaiming a Historic National Title." Master of Science thesis, George Mason University.

Semmes, Clovis. 2001. "E. Franklin Frazier's Theory of the Black Family: Vindication and Sociological Insight." *Journal of Sociology & Social Welfare.* 28 (2): Article 2. Available at: https://scholarworks.wmich.edu/jssw/vol28/iss2/2.

Smith, John Clay, ed. 2000. *Rebels in Law: Voices in History of Black Women Lawyers.* Ann Arbor: University of Michigan Press.

Speisman, Barbara. 1998. "From 'Spears' to 'The Great Day': Zora Neale Hurston's Vision of a Real Negro Theater." *Southern Quarterly* 36 (3): 34–46.

Steen, Shannon. 2000. "Melancholy Bodies: Racial Subjectivity and Whiteness in O'Neill's *The Emperor Jones.*" *Theatre Journal* 52 (3): 339–359.

Stewart, Jeffrey C. Stewart. 2018. *The New Negro: The Life of Alain Locke.* New York: Oxford University Press.

Tushnet, Mark V. 1994. *Making Civil Rights Law: Thurgood Marshall and the Supreme Court, 1936–1961.* New York: Oxford University Press.

von Daacke, Kirt, and AshleySchmidt. 2019. "UVA and the History of Race: When the KKK Flourished in Charlottesville." *UVA Today,* September 25. Available at: https://news. virginia.edu/content/uva-and-history-race-when-kkk-flourished-charlottesville.

Washington, Booker Taliaferro, and Robert Ezra Park. 1913. *The Man Farthest Down: A Record of Observation and Study in Europe.* New York: Transaction Publishers.

Weishan, Michael. 2014. "The Real Gentleman's C." Franklin Delano Roosevelt Foundation. June 30. https://fdrfoundation.org/the-real-gentlemans-c/.

Williams, Chad. 2010. *Torchbearers of Democracy: African American Soldiers in the World War I Era.* Chapel Hill, NC: University of North Carolina Press.

Williams, Juan. 2011. *Thurgood Marshall: American Revolutionary.* New York: Three Rivers Press.

4

RESISTANCE TO RACIAL INTEGRATION AT VIRGINIA COLLEGES AFTER WORLD WAR II (1945–2000)

Past historical studies of race relations in the United States often regard the period directly after World War II as a defining moment in racial progress within the country. Usually, the integration of the American armed forces by President Truman in 1948 is considered a watershed moment—one that indicated that the United States was changing its policies of racial segregation (see Taylor 2013). Here, Black men returning from the war—having experienced a largely desegregated Europe—expected that having fought against tyranny abroad, they might expect race relations at home to have improved (Quarles and Nalty 2014).

No doubt the previous indicates important political and cultural shifts in some areas of the country, but in most respects these events did not immediately compel significant changes at the Virginia colleges examined in this study. Practically, all these schools remained segregated directly after the war. On a few campuses there were modest changes following the *Gregory Hayes Swanson v. the Rector and Visitors of the University of Virginia* (in 1950) court ruling in Virginia. This case forced the UVA law school and other graduate programs to begin accepting Black students (Picott 1958; Sky Lark 2017). But most schools in this study—including UVA—did not admit Black undergraduate students until the 1960s, with some—Virginia Military Institute (VMI), Longwood College, Hampden-Sydney College—not admitting Black students until 1968, four years after the Virginia state legislature officially abandoned its program of massive resistance to school desegregation. At most schools, significant numbers of Black students were not enrolled until the 1970s.

After World War II there was very little change concerning the service roles of African Americans at these institutions. Black men (and increasingly Black women) continued to be employed as janitors and other support staff that served

DOI: 10.4324/9781003134480-4

White students. While these service workers were not maligned as much in yearbooks following the war, they were still largely taken for granted by White students and staff. In some cases, student attitudes toward Black staff began to shift in the 1970s—the staff is more often recognized with some appreciation during this period—and there are tentative signs that some students began regarding the segmented labor market on campus as problematic.

One change following the war was that the most egregiously offensive forms of racial caricatures—the pencil and line drawings often presented on "State Clubs" pages—did largely disappear (along with the state clubs) from yearbooks. But it was still common to find racialized entertainment—blackface musicals, for example—being staged at some of these schools well into the 1960s. In other cases there was an appreciable uptick in symbolic representations designed to associate many of these schools with the "Old South." Most evident is that representations of Confederate flags increased dramatically during the post-war period. Perhaps this is related to students being able to editorialize more in these yearbooks—maybe the flags were always there—but more likely is that these flags were increasingly adopted to represent Virginia universities' "Southern-ness" during specific school events (see Nehls 2002). Importantly, even as these schools desegregated in the late 1960s and 1970s there were pockets of resistance—well known on these campuses. This was particularly the case at certain fraternities.

Focus colleges: Hampden-Sydney College and Virginia Military Institute

This chapter continues to consider the three schools—University of Virginia (UVA), Washington and Lee (W&L) and James Madison University (JMU)—that were the focus schools in chapter 2, but it also focuses on two other Virginia schools: Hampden-Sydney College and the Virginia Military Institute (VMI). Virginia Military Institute was selected because it is the only military college in the study. While it is not a federal service academy, it is organized in a somewhat similar manner. All VMI students enter the Reserve Officer Training Corps (ROTC) program and have the option of being commissioned as officers when they graduate, although graduates can also choose civilian careers. Usually, over 50% of VMI students enlist in the armed services after graduation. While VMI is not directly affiliated with the federal service academies, it is a good indicator of how Southerners inclined to military service regarded desegregation. Importantly, VMI has a history directly connected to the Civil War—students, faculty and alumni participated in several regional battles that are memorialized to this day.

Hampden-Sydney College is comparable to Washington and Lee in terms of its early history. It was founded in 1775, just before the Revolutionary War, and is the tenth-oldest college in the nation. It is one of the last remaining small liberal arts colleges that focuses on men's education. It currently enrolls about 1,000 men each academic year. The school was founded on egalitarian political principles—with a literal who's who of Virginia revolutionary figures serving on its first Board of Trustees ("History" Hampden-Sydney). At the same time, the school is located in Prince Edward County, which was central with respect to the Virginia campaign of massive resistance to school desegregation undertaken in the 1950s and 1960s.

Brief history Hampden-Sydney College

The principles on which Hampden-Sydney College were founded are notably egalitarian. The first president of the college chose the names "Hampden" and "Sydney" to recognize John Hampden (1594–1643) and Algernon Sydney (1622–1683), both advocates for representative government and religious freedom who were killed during two separate constitutional crises in England. In 1775, as the movement for American succession from England grew, the name explicitly aligned the college with the cause of American independence. Prominent Virginians—including James Madison and Patrick Henry—served on the Board of Trustees. The school also has a long affiliation with the Presbyterian Church ("History" Hampden-Sydney).

The college enjoyed a steadily rising academic profile over time, consistently being considered a traditional but excellent liberal arts college in Virginia. It founded a medical department in 1838 that eventually became the Medical College of Virginia (MCV), now affiliated with Virginia Commonwealth University (VCU) (Dabney 1987). The issue of slavery was debated before the Civil War by the faculty, particularly during meetings of the Literary and Philosophical Society (Morrison [1824–1835] 1917), but once the war began campus sentiment was almost entirely Confederate, and students quickly mustered a band of recruits. In a history of the school, the modest exploits of the "Hampden-Sydney Boys" during the war are described as follows:

> These men, officially mustered as Company G, 20th Virginia Regiment, "The Hampden-Sydney Boys," saw action in the disaster of Rich Mountain (July, 1861). They were captured and later paroled by General George B. McClellan on the condition that they return to their studies. ("History" Hampden-Sydney)

The college has been closely associated with the Virginia elite. To this day it is considered a "preppy" school—a place that draws disproportionately from regional preparatory schools. In the 1980s it was routinely described as one of the "preppiest" colleges in the country, and students largely embraced the characterization that they were "preppy." For example, in the 1981 yearbook—labeled the "Official Preppy Yearbook"—Lisa Birnbach (1980), the author of the *Official Preppy Handbook*, was invited to write an introduction (Birnbach 1981:5–6).

"Do you really need to ask why I have called Hampden-Sydney the preppiest college in the United States?....Why? Because nobody would believe it. There *is* still a College that time forgot, still a breeding ground for the right boys, with beautiful surroundings, and southern gentility. Hampden-Sydney is one of the few schools that hasn't bowed to ugly pre-professionalism. There students can actually study the liberal arts because they will be able to mooch off their parents for the rest of their lives" (5).

In 1981 the yearbook cover (and much of the contents) is fashioned directly after the *Official Preppy Handbook*.

Hampden-Sydney College also has the reputation of being very conservative. And, less charitably, it was among those lampooned in a classic *Spy* article, "Colleges of the Dumb Rich" (Handy 1987, 61). The curriculum has tended to emphasize the Western classics. There is also an emphasis on honor (the long-standing honor code is administered by students) and civility. Since 1978, the school has given incoming freshmen *To Manner Born, To Manners Bred: A Hip-Pocket Guide to Etiquette for the Hampden–Sydney Man* (Shomo 1978). The book is a compendium of old-school etiquette related to making introductions, what to wear for different occasions, and also a how-to guide concerning, among other things, wear a tie.

The college is located near Farmville, Virginia, in Prince Edward County. In the early 1950s the unequal status of the segregated public schools in this county was litigated in the case of *Davis v. County School Board of Prince Edward County*. It was eventually incorporated into the *Brown v. Board of Education of Topeka* case, where, in 1954, the Supreme Court ruled school segregation was illegal (Turner 2004). As a result, the county was at the center of the Virginia state government's program of massive resistance to school desegregation. Hampden-Sydney College was officially neutral on the issue of school desegregation during these events. It admitted its first Black student to the college in 1968. Notably, although still predominantly White, in 2009 the school hired Christopher B. Howard, the first Black president of the school (Kapsidelis 2009).

Currently, the college has a well-regarded liberal arts curriculum. Its current motto is "Forming good men and good citizens since 1776." The college has graduated a long list of notable alumni in the fields of politics, art, entertainment and business. Although he did not graduate from the school, Stephen Colbert, comedian and host of *The Late Show*, attended for two years. He tends to embody that "*je ne sais quoi*" quality—the erudition, the snappy dress, the witty repartee—that characterizes the ideal Hampden-Sydney man (at least by the men's own reckoning) (Howard, Deis and Frye 2012). Like many of the other Virginia schools in this study, most students who attend Hampden-Sydney College come from reasonably well-heeled families. The mean family income was $126,900 for the class of 2013 in 2015 dollars. And true to its reputation, it did have (in 2013) a disproportionately high number of students from the top 1% of income earners, with 6.1% of families earning more than $630,000 a year. About 40% of the student body came from families in the top 10% of income earners. The mean family income ranked it 23 out of 614 "selective colleges" in its peer group (see Chetty et al. 2017; "Economic Diversity" *New York Times*). In 2020 the school was 85.6% White, 4.9% Black, and 3.8% Hispanic ("Demographics and Retention" Hampden-Sydney).

Brief history Virginia Military Institute

Virginia Military Institute is a public military college located in Lexington, Virginia, the same community where Washington & Lee University is located. In fact, the two campuses are directly adjacent to each other. Founded in 1839, it currently enrolls about 1,700 students. All the VMI cadets participate in a physically rigorous ROTC program while pursuing their college studies. Most are commissioned as officers after they graduate. The school's most celebrated professor is Thomas "Stonewall" Jackson, who taught at the college before the Civil War and became a Southern hero during the Shenandoah Valley campaign. His intimate knowledge of the surrounding mountain typography gave him a considerable advantage during a series of nearby battles.[1]

In terms of Civil War memorialization in Virginia, Thomas "Stonewall" Jackson is second to Robert E. Lee in the number of statues, public memorials and public buildings that have been erected or named after him ("Whose Heritage?" SPLC). For example, a main highway (State Route 11) that runs nearly the length of the Shenandoah Valley (and through Lexington) is officially the Lee-Jackson Highway. Importantly, VMI cadets were involved in several regional battles during the Civil War. The most notable was the Battle of New Market, which took place in the Shenandoah Valley about 100 miles from where the school is located. The VMI students, after marching through the valley, were integral to a Confederate victory and also suffered a relatively high number of fatalities (10) and wounded (41 to 53)—the total representing about 25% of the of the group that marched to New Market ("Battle Report" VMI 1864). The event is still memorialized by the institution, six of the dead are buried at a campus memorial, and VMI also operates the museum located near the battlefield. In an annual ceremony there is a roll call of the names of the VMI cadets killed in the battle. In an older ceremony the band played "Dixie" and the Confederate flag was prominently displayed. The song and flag were apparently retired, by a vote of the entire student corps, when Black cadets raised objections in 1973 (Finn 1997).

Several VMI graduates became prominent officers during the Civil War. Afterward, many prominent ex-Confederate officers, such as Matthew Fontaine Maury—the Maury River that runs through Lexington is named after him— also took academic appointments at the college. Not surprisingly, Civil War memorialization is still prominent on campus, sometimes resulting in what, to outsiders, are bizarre displays of reverence. For example, the VMI military museum on campus displays the "stuffed" hide of Jackson's horse, Little Sorrel, who died in 1886. The horse's bones were buried, in 1997, in front of a prominent statue of Jackson at VMI ("VMI Museum" VMI). The statue was removed from campus in 2020. Little Sorrel outlived Jackson by over a decade as the cavalryman was killed, shot by mistake by Confederate troops the day before the Battle of Chancellorsville. At the museum, close to the horse, is a display of the raincoat that Jackson was wearing when he was mortally wounded ("VMI Museum" VMI). Jackson is buried in Lexington, Virginia—he died of pneumonia after having his arm amputated at Chancellorsville. Of note, Jackson's private chaplain decided to give his amputated arm a "full Christian burial" at a private cemetery near Chancellorsville, which has proven to be a curiosity that annually attracts tourists to the arm's burial site (Martinez 2012). Little Sorrel, the stuffed horse, tends to generate the same type of enthusiasm for some.

In the modern period, VMI is an institution where many prominent Virginia politicians have matriculated, including, at this writing, the current governor of Virginia, Ralph Northam. It boasts alumni of national stature who served in the armed forces, General George Patton among the most prominent. The school was integrated in 1968 when five Black cadets were enrolled. During an interview with three of these men, during their 25th class reunion, they generally commented that they had little trouble with discrimination as it concerned treatment by White cadets but that they were sometimes troubled by the symbols of the Confederacy—in particular, the ceremony memorializing the New Market battle in which "Dixie" was played and the Confederate battle flag publicly displayed. They were also supposed to salute when they passed Lee Chapel—the site of Robert E. Lee's family crypt located on the nearby W&L campus. Some also avoided the campus ceremonies replete with Confederate symbols, but another "swallowed his resentments for the sake of military cohesion" (Finn1997).

VMI had a long period of resistance with respect to admitting women. On June 26, 1996—following the Supreme Court case *United States v. Virginia*—the trustees of the school, because it accepted state and federal assistance, decided to admit women (Kovacic-Fleisher 1997). At first some trustees considered taking the school private so that it could remain a men's college, but it appeared this would cause the school to lose the money and support associated with the ROTC program. The students at VMI generally come from affluent families. The median family income of a student attending the Virginia Military Institute in 2013 (in 2015 dollars) was $120,500, and 58% came from the top 20% of income earners. This ranked the median family income at 17 out of 377 selective colleges. It ranked 360 out of 377 in admitting students from the bottom fifth in family income (see Chetty et al. 2017; "Economic Diversity" *New York Times*). The school is roughly 78% White, 7.4% Hispanic, 6.5% Black and 4.2% Asian ("VMI Student Population," VMI).

During the preparation of this text, throughout the year 2020, the *Washington Post* reported that systemic racism on the VMI campus was still prevalent and interviewed a number of Black students and recent alumni who described their

COLOR PLATE 5 A picture of the Thomas "Stonewall" Jackson statue that once stood at VMI (*The Bomb* 1960, 11). It bears the inscription, "The Virginia Military Institute Will Be Heard From Today" and states these words were spoken on "May 3," the day of the decisive civil war battle at Chancellorsville. The statue was removed in December 2020.

experiences. As a result, Superintendent James Peay, a retired four-star general in the armed forces, resigned in October 2020. This followed a move by state officials and the governor of Virginia to open an investigation into allegations of racism on campus. Shortly after, the Board of Visitors voted to remove a statue of Stonewall Jackson that stood on the main quad of the campus directly in front of barracks also named after Jackson (see Shapira 2020a; 2020b; 2020c; 2020d). A picture of that statue is represented in Color Plate 5 on the previous page.

Massive resistance (1954–1964) in Prince Edward County: Longwood College and Hampden-Sydney College

Very few White Virginia college students were directly engaged in the student-organized civil rights campaigns of the 1960s. These include the sit-in campaigns directed by the Student Non-Violent Coordinating Committee (SNCC) in 1960 and the later Freedom Summer campaign in 1964 (see Michel 2004).[2] These events are discussed in greater detail in the following chapter. Still, one might expect that even if Virginia students were not involved directly in these events—or were not staging similar events on their own campuses—that yearbook content might still recognize that the civil rights movement was an ongoing event during this period of time. Here, what is remarkable is the extent to which landmark civil rights events were essentially "non-events" as it concerns the Virginia yearbook content of this period. Perhaps most poignant, the assassination of Martin Luther King Jr. in 1968 is almost entirely absent from the content of the all 1968–69 Virginia yearbooks in this study. This lack of memorialization differs dramatically with the content of the Howard University yearbooks examined in the following chapter.

Mostly, the Virginia yearbooks of this period give an indication that many of these campuses were essentially "islands" (and at times fortresses) in which the disturbances of the wider world associated with the civil rights movement were largely cordoned off from the campus experience. Perhaps, at some schools—where the student and faculty remained all White—these events were not considered as relevant enough in students' day-to-day lives to merit a mention. But notably, some of the colleges in this study were located at sites where ongoing civil rights protests throughout the 1950s and 1960s were common—enough so that it would seem impossible that students could manage to entirely ignore these events when they occurred in the communities where their campuses were located. But nonetheless, it was common to discover that the yearbook content at these schools usually made no mention of these historical, and often dramatic, social protests.

Two schools in this study—Hampden-Sydney College and Longwood College—are located at the epicenter of several important events that largely defined the civil rights struggle in Virginia. Here, Farmville, Virginia, was the site of one of the first entirely student-organized protests of the civil rights period when, in 1951, Black students collectively decided to walk out of their all-Black high school to protest the poor quality of the building and other school materials. The case brought on behalf of these students, *Davis v. County School Board of Prince Edward County* (1952–1954), was later incorporated into the Supreme Court proceedings concerning *Brown v. Board of Education,* the case that ended legal segregation in 1954 (Smith 1965).

Following the *Brown* decision, over the course of the next decade Prince Edward County became a center of local and state government policies associated with a campaign of massive resistance to school desegregation. During this period, Prince Edward County officially closed its public school system rather than desegregate. No provision was made for educating Black students. For White students, the county established a system of segregated private schools in which the county and state provided funding used previously for public education to provide grants to residents to pay for tuition. After five years this practice was eventually ruled unconstitutional in the state courts and formally abandoned in 1964 (Smith 1965).

Probably the most dramatic event during this period occurred during the summer of 1963 when the Black community in Farmville, Virginia, staged several demonstrations against the segregated private schools and segregated businesses in the community. These protests, labeled a "Program of Action," were organized by Reverend L. Griffin, pastor at First Baptist Church. He was aided by members of SNCC who were veterans of previous direct action and sit-in campaigns; they helped train the Farmville activists, many of whom were later arrested. The VCU library houses a repository of pictures documenting this event. A few are presented in Figures 4.1 and 4.2. The largest number were taken by a photographer hired by the Farmville Police Department, which intended to use them as evidence if charges were brought against the protestors ("Farmville 1963" VCU).

Later, in May 1964, Attorney General Robert Kennedy visited the community in support of the activists after he helped establish the "Free Schools" that were educating black students in the county. Neither the Hampden-Sydney College nor Longwood College yearbooks, in the years during and immediately following these events, provide information associated with these ongoing protests. None, for example, directly indicate that Attorney General Robert Kennedy visited Farmville and Hampden-Sydney College in May 1964, except for one small picture, with no accompanying information, that shows Kennedy receiving a portrait of his recently slain brother by an admiring Hampden-Sydney student (*Kaleidoscope* 1965: 165). But mostly, if judging only from the Hampden-Sydney yearbook, it can be assumed life preceded as it always had. There are the student club activities, the usual fraternity high jinks and hazing— all organized by a White faculty and student body in the same largely self-satisfied manner, with no indication that civil rights protests were occurring locally or nationally. Notably, there are two pages in the 1964 Hampden-Sydney yearbook that show Black women. Both picture the singing group the Shirelles, who played at homecoming that year for the all-White

FIGURE 4.1 The Program of Action protest in Farmville, Virginia, against school segregation that also targeted Whites-only businesses in the community. At the time of the protest the Farmville public schools had been closed for three years. Photograph made available by the James Cabell Library, Special Collections and Archives, VCU Libraries.

FIGURE 4.2 Sit-in at a lunch counter in downtown Farmville during the 1963 Program of Action protesting school segregation and businesses in Farmville, Virginia. Protesters also targeted the downtown College Shoppe. From the James Cabell Library, Special Collections and Archives, VCU Libraries.

student body (*Kaleidoscope* 1964, 113 & 115). Black bands played on campus the following year too. The increasing number of Black bands performing on all-White campuses during this period is discussed further below.

Brain Lee (2009) has conducted a thorough study of Robert Kennedy's personal involvement in the desegregation of Prince Edward County. Here, he cites an internal survey of Longwood faculty during the period in which: "one-third of the faculty supported segregation, one-third opposed the school closings, and one-third favored integration but were afraid to express their opinions" (52). Notably, another survey indicated that the roughly 75% of students at Longwood College, often women training to be teachers, were willing to teach in segregated classrooms.

The one faculty member at Longwood who was outspoken on the issue, Dr. C. Gordon Moss (1899-1982) was essentially "blackballed" from the Farmville community and subsequently threatened with termination from the college. He appears to have been among the very few white activist within the Farmville community that spoke out publicly on the desegregation issue. Or, as Lee (2009) put it: "White dissent became a virtual one man crusade" (53). Previously, Moss had been chairman of the History Department and the Academic Dean of the college from 1960-64. When Moss managed to retain an academic appointment at the college, Congressman Watkins M. Abbitt pressed the State Superintendent of Instruction to fire Moss. He also used his influence to have the House Un-American Activities Committee investigate community activists, including the American Friends Service Committee (AFSC), which had begun educating the displaced black students (Lee 2009, 53-54). Moss characterized his treatment in the community as:

> "I have been snubbed on Main Street by virtually lifetime friends," lamented Dr. Moss. "I sit in the pew by myself in church every Sunday. I am not allowed to serve on the vestry, although my work as treasurer of the church is quite willingly accepted."

Further:

> "Within a matter of days after my first public speech for public schools," Dr. Moss reflected, "a delegation was in the office of the president of Longwood College demanding that I be fired" (quoted in Lee 2009, 53-54).

Lee (2009, 54) summarizes: "The treatment of Dr. Moss served as an example to all who considered challenging the decisions of the power structure."

Given the conservative reputation of the faculty and students at Hampden-Sydney, on balance it seems safe to assume that many (likely most) were not supportive of school integration. Indeed, this was the indication Robert Kennedy was given when he received a less then "warm" welcome during his May 1964 address at Johns Auditorium (Lee 2009, 13-14):

Kennedy entered Johns Auditorium under a homemade placard, which read: "GOLDWATER To Whip Mass[achusetts] Socialism!" The "hostile" students "began to hiss and grumble" as the Attorney General moved to the lectern. Kennedy removed his jacket, rolled up his sleeves, discarded his prepared remarks, and stated: "I believe you gentlemen may have a few questions." For forty-five minutes, Kennedy fielded questions on his political future, Vietnam, and the civil rights bill. Asked who favored the civil rights bill, the crowd responded with "moderate applause." Asked who opposed the bill, applause filled the hall. "I don't understand your opposition," replied Kennedy. "Go over to Prince Edward County, as I have just done, and see the children put their hands over their hearts and swear allegiance to the American flag and sing 'America the Beautiful.'"

Some prominent members of the Hampden-Sydney community were clearly active in the fight against desegregation. For example, Paul Tulane Atkinson (1887-1963) was a graduate and later the Treasurer the college from 1919-1957 and afterwards the alumni director until 1960. He was also the seventh superintendent of Prince Edward County public schools from 1909-1918. During the period of massive resistance he was on the Board of Directors of the private school system that was attempting to claim the public school buildings as "surplus property" for the white private schools in the county (Lee 2009, 33). His wife, referred to affectionately as "Mrs P.T."—was later credited with establishing the Hampden-Sydney History museum which is now named the Esther Thomas Atkins Museum.

In Lee's (2009) study he indicates there were Hampden-Sydney faculty who, while not activists, personally did not support closing the Prince Edward public schools. Taylor Reveley II, president of Hampden-Sydney College at the time, is said to have been a supporter of racial integration —at least according to his son (a former president of William and Mary College) and grandson (the current president of Longwood College). His grandson noted this when commenting that his grandfather, unlike the Longwood president at the time, was responsible for inviting Attorney General Robert F. Kennedy to the Hampden Sydney campus in 1964 (Anderson 2015). Practically, though, Hampden Sydney—still being guided by Taylor Reveley II—remained segregated for a number of years after this event, accepting its first Black student in 1968.

Importantly, Longwood College has taken tentative steps in recognizing its institutional policies during this period of Farmville history. In 2015, the college issued a formal apology for its actions during the civil rights era. This resolution states, in part, "As an institution Longwood failed to stand up publicly for these ideals [equal protection under the law and educational opportunity for all], resulting in support to those who opposed desegregation, and falling short in its duty to provide strong moral leadership in the community" (Anderson 2015). Nick Anderson (2015), reporting for the *Washington Post*, collected responses to this statement by long-time Black activists in the community:

The statement came as "quite a shock," said the Rev. J. Samuel Williams Jr., 81, a Baptist minister who was one of the 1951 student strikers at Robert Russa Moton High School. "Something that was long overdue." Williams said that when he was growing up, Black residents viewed Longwood as a place that was "totally off limits unless you were an employee in a menial position."

Social change and resistance to desegregation at state universities in Virginia: the civil rights period (1950–1964)

Some Virginia schools—the campuses themselves—were also the battlegrounds on which civil rights lawyers, during the 1950s, waged their fight to dismantle the "separate but equal" standard in the state. For example, one of the earliest tactics of the National Association for the Advancement of Colored People (NAACP) was to have well-qualified Black applicants apply to Whites-only state law schools where no comparable institution existed for Black students. Thurgood Marshall, a Howard University School of Law graduate, first used this tactic in a suit directed toward the University of Maryland School of Law in a 1936 case, *Murray v. Pearson*. In this case, Marshall demonstrated that the state of Maryland had no facilities to educate Black lawyers, and consequently the University of Maryland was forced to desegregate its law school. Eventually, the same tactic was used by NAACP lawyers, including Marshall, against the University of Virginia School of Law. In this case, Gregory Hayes Swanson, a Howard law school graduate, applied to the University of Virginia law school and was denied admittance based on his race. In *Gregory Hayes Swanson v. the Rector and Visitors of the University of Virginia*, like the Maryland case that preceded, it was also demonstrated that Virginia had no Black law schools, which forced the desegregation of the University of Virginia law school in 1950. Practically, it also desegregated any program at a public university where there was not an equivalent degree being offered by a historically Black college or university (HBCU) in Virginia (Tushnet 1994). As a result, shortly afterward an extremely small number of Black students were admitted to the law program and some graduate programs in education. The undergraduate programs at UVA remained segregated until 1960.

Following the *Swanson* case, there was a reluctant desegregation of a few other programs at state universities, such as the undergraduate engineering program at Virginia Tech (VPI), because there was no comparable program available for Black students in the state. As a result, a very small number of Black students began to trickle into these programs in the 1950s. The other undergraduate colleges in this study—public and private—remained largely segregated until after the period of massive resistance in 1964. By all accounts, the experience for these first Black students was extremely difficult, particularly in that the campus facilities and communities remained segregated during the period they were admitted. Here, the experience of Irving Peddrew, the first Black student admitted to Virginia Tech (in 1953) in the undergraduate engineering program, largely mirrors the experience of the very few Black students who were admitted to VPI and UVA at this time (Peddrew 2017). Peddrew, like most others, reports he was extremely isolated when on campus—unlike other VPI students, he was not allowed to live in the dorms on campus or eat his meals with other students. As a result, Peddrew left the university after three years of study. In an interview conducted many years later Peddrew (2017) reported:

> I couldn't eat in any of the restaurants in the city here. If I wanted to go to a movie, I had to sit up in the balcony. There were just—I couldn't get a haircut downtown in Blacksburg, although friends of mine owned the barbershop, but they catered only to Whites, but they were owned by Blacks. I mean the barbershop was. I just knew that there were things that I couldn't do, places I couldn't go, and you had to accept that. I couldn't go into the soda shop, into the drug store and eat and sit at the soda fountain. I knew that I couldn't do that.

Notably, there is no significant VPI and UVA yearbook content that indicates that some programs at these schools were desegregated during the 1950s. In a very few cases, Virginia school yearbooks indicate wider discussion of ongoing national events associated with the civil rights movement—but these are not well documented in terms of yearbook content. Further, the few times the yearbooks address issues associated with civil rights are usually peripheral to a wider debate that concerns an increase in student activism in general. Later this became particularly associated with student protest against the war in Vietnam (see chapter 5).

A typical example of the previous would be the opening content of the 1954 *Corks and Curls* (11–13). Here, as the editors are summarizing the school year, they note that there was a campus-wide discussion concerning the Students for America (SFA) organization established that year. The SFA was largely established to counter Students for Democratic Action (SDA). Further, in "America's Conservative Revolution," the author states that the SFA "stands for the 'Constitution, religious freedom and free enterprise' and is pledged to combat 'socialist expansion, appeasement and subversive elements'" (Hall 1955). Campus debate concerning the organization began after a *Cavalier Daily* editorial described the SFA as "kindergarten Ku Klux Klan" (*Corks and Curls* 1955, 13). Afterward, for several months, the "SFA controversy" continued "to rage on the editorial page with many students contributing many more letters to the editor than could be printed" (13). As it turns out, the UVA organization did eventually divorce itself from the national organization during the school year—a move that apparently ended the controversy (13).

With respect to the foregoing debate, there is never really a reference to the ongoing civil rights movement. Nor, is there a discussion of racial politics generally on campus. But the indictment of the SFA as a "kindergarten Ku Klux Klan" indicates some social sanction associated with the organization. The previous is notable insofar as it was only a few decades before that a picture of the KKK—on horseback and marauding at night—was used to introduce the "Clubs and Organizations" section of *Corks and Curls* (1922, 359). Here, this debate is indicative of a slowly changing culture on the UVA campus—actually more evident in comparison to the yearbook content presented at the other Virginia schools during the same period.

Martin Luther King Jr. speaks at the University of Virginia

This study is based on an idea that the content of university yearbooks—the types and composition of student clubs, who is doing what type of work, and what the student body "looks like"—reflects institutional norms and culture. But here it is time to again reflect upon the fact that during momentous events associated with the civil rights movement—often occurring in the communities where some of these schools were located—there is usually no yearbook content that chronicles these events. In these cases, the content that is omitted is as enlightening as what is chosen to be included.

For example, there was clearly some modest change in the attitudes of students and faculty "creeping into" these Virginia campuses during the early civil rights period, but this was nearly always met with active resistance by most in the administration and student body. Here, it is notable that none of the Virginia yearbooks mention any of the seminal events associated with the civil rights movement. Perhaps the most damning "sin of omission" is the complete lack of memorialization of Martin Luther King Jr. in the Virginia yearbooks the year he was assassinated (in 1968)—even though, for instance, the event was apparently recognized on the UVA campus, with a flag lowered and a memorial service held at Cabell Hall ("A Life" *Virginia Magazine*).

Another example is that well-meaning people at UVA recently resurrected an institutional history associated with what is now considered a groundbreaking speech that Martin Luther King Jr. gave to approximately 900 people at old Cabell Hall in March 1963. In particular, on January 23, 2017, a plaque was dedicated at the auditorium that commemorates this speech. The plaque was donated by one of the UVA activists, Wesley Harris (along with his brother), who had invited King to UVA. Its purpose is to "forever be a reminder of the speech that brought Dr. King's legacy to UVA and Charlottesville." During the 2017 event a well-known political scientist, Larry Sabato, "called the speech 'a signal event at a place that needed to be shaken up'" (Newman 2018). A year later—on the 55th anniversary of the event—King's son retraced his father's steps in another ceremony (Newman 2018).

While Martin Luther King Jr.'s speech at Cabell Hall is an event of importance—one that needs to be remembered—the style of memorializing tends to obscure how the speech was actually received among many students.

Although at the time attended by many like-minded supporters—many of whom apparently came from the Charlottesville community—the event, in the near term, appears not to have shaken up the institution of UVA at all, though it clearly inspired some of the very few activists working for change at UVA during this period. For example, there appears to have been no representatives from the student body government or the administration at the speech. It appears no yearbook staff attended the event as neither King's visit nor his speech are represented in the 1963 *Corks and Curls*. In effect, this was not a fully sanctioned university event: King received no stipend for his talk, and he drove from his home in Georgia at his own expense after a handful of students asked him to come. In fact, the UVA administration was concerned about the event, but not enough to stop it. So, this was not a triumphant speech that marked significant progress at UVA. Nor was this a moment when a significant number of students afterward immediately rallied around the larger cause of civil rights or even acknowledged there were problems associated with the policies of UVA itself (see the *Cavalier Daily* response below). In fact, while King was on campus the group that invited him was very much on edge for most of the visit, afraid throughout that violence might be directed toward King or themselves. As Paul Gaston, a UVA professor and one of the organizers, put it, "King was not someone who was really safe to celebrate" (Barnett 2008). Another UVA student, Wesley Harris—the man who sponsored the memorial plaque—commented of the period: "This was, in my eyes as I remember it, some very dark times on Grounds." Harris recalled, "Walking through Grounds on an evening at night, you would be presented with cigarette butts thrown from cars driving by, the N-word being yelled from cars being driven by" (Kelly 2018).

How did UVA students respond to the King speech? Here, it is impossible to generalize to the entire campus, although it is clear that the small group of activists who brought King to campus were heartened by the visit. But judging from other sources available at the time, many used King's speech to advance their own arguments that everything at UVA, as related to race relations, was just fine. Further, they argued that the course of action outlined by King—particularly the strategy of non-violent resistance—was an affront to an individual's right to form voluntary associations. That segregated restaurants, for example, were not an important social justice issue. These arguments were made clear in the following largely mocking editorial published after King's visit in the *Cavalier Daily* (1963, 4) (italics added):

> In listening to the would-be heir to the sacred traditions of faith inspired by the original Martin Luther, we can find little to criticize—or even analyze. *What is more important: we can find no final indictment of University policy as related to the turmoil of racial struggle....*
>
> The abstract basis of his sermon may be exemplified by his plea that the tensions and conflict which exist are not actually between Negroes and

White, but between justice and injustice. *We should all question such shaky correlation: does this not tend to equate the Negro cause with Justice?*

Like the Supreme Court, Mr. King's philosophy makes use of that muddying term of child psychology: maladjustment. Mr. King may not have cited any acts or policy of discrimination here, but those who advocate better human relations never fail to point to segregation at the Corner restaurants. *To those who continue to hold that "non-violent" methods of coercion through sanctions should be employed by the University as well as by the government, we would recommend that they pay more attention to the rights of individuals and less concern to Negro maladjustment.* The rights of individual association should never be violated forcefully on such a basis.

The pattern outlined above, a seemingly willful ambivalence—if not outright hostility—toward the very small numbers of campus activists (when they existed at all) in Virginia seems to be, for the most part, the most common characteristic of many White students who attended the Virginia schools during the civil rights period from 1954 to 1964. At schools where there were no Black students—still the majority of these Virginia colleges at the time—there is essentially no record of the ongoing activities associated with the civil rights movement. Mostly, while it seems clear the world around these students was changing—sometimes in the very communities where these schools are located—this does not appear to have had dramatic impacts on campus life, at least as reflected by the yearbook content. Here, while there was clearly change occurring all around these students during the period examined, one has to dig deep to see even modest indications of this reflected in the yearbook content before the year 1968.

Race relations on campus: representations of university staff

Previously, several pictures from Virginia yearbooks, but particularly *Corks and Curls*, were used to illustrate the jobs that Black staff workers performed on campus. In the post-war period, and for many years after, what is notable is how *little* the roles of Black staff changed concerning the service work done on campuses. Here, it appears that Black staff, well into the 1980s, had largely the same occupations they had previously filled on campus. Mostly, these involved serving White students in some capacity or another. One exception is that more Black women—cooks, housekeepers and cleaning staff—begin to appear more routinely in the photographs during the post–World War II period.

Figure 4.3 shows a picture of a UVA fraternity published in the 1954 edition of *Corks and Curls*. As in pre-war photographs, the members are formally arranged, seated and standing with their hands in front of their bodies. In this case, three Black staff are clustered at the back. Of note, it was now more routine to include Black staff in these fraternity pictures as compared to pictures taken before World War II.

ALPHA TAU OMEGA

FIGURE 4.3 Typical picture of a University of Virginia fraternity in 1954 (*Corks and Curls* 1954, 194). Like pre–World War II photographs, the members are seated and standing with their hands in front of their bodies. The Black staff are clustered at the back. As in previous photographs, their names are informal and listed in quotation marks.

During the 1960s and 1970s some of the fraternity pictures became more informally arranged, with the members not as neatly aligned. Often, the Black staff are included in these photographs too. Notably, more Black women are present in pictures over time (see Figure 4.4).

At VMI there are not many pictures of staff in the yearbooks, but when they do appear there is an indication that the supprt staff was, as in other Virginia colleges, disproportionately Black and concentrated in service roles (see Figure 4.5). Of particular note are reocurring pictures of "Tom and Snake," who worked in the press shop for many years during the 1950s—they can be seen in the montage in Figure 4.5, in the picture labeled "Snake and Tom of the Pressing Shop" (*The Bomb* 1950, 32–33). This shop is where the student uniforms were cleaned and pressed. Their immediate succesors were both African American men too. It appears that both "Tom" and "Snake" (the latter's real name was never identified in the yearbooks) were themselves veterans of the armed forces. In particular, there is a ongoing joke during this period that one or the other (it shifts over different years) is said to be the "leader" of the "Outrage" section of the yearbook staff (see Figure 4.6). In both cases, these men appear in uniform and look

MU CHAPTER OF ALPHA EPSILON PI ESTABLISHED 1924

FIGURE 4.4 Some University of Virginia fraternity pictures became more informal during the 1960s, with Black staff pictured among members (*Corks and Curls* 1969, 225). The Mu chapter of Alpha Epsilon Pi is exemplary in this regard, over a few years appearing as one of the more informally arranged groups in the chapter's annual picture. Black staff are also pictured in various locations beside, and sometimes among, the members.

younger than they do in pictures of them working in the Press Shop (see *The Bomb* 1954, 213). Notably, the uniformed pictures do not definitively identify the men as either "Tom" or "Snake"—but comparisons of several photographs[3] indicate that the pictures are of these two men.

The "Outrage" section of the student yearbook includes student humor such as limericks, poems, stories and cartoons. Much of this content is focused on women, of whom the VMI men clearly spent a considerable amount of time thinking. Mostly, there are pin-ups, pencil drawings of nudes that express adolescent longing, and a considerble number of pictures of men dressed in drag too (see *The Bomb* 1954, 215–219). Notwithstanding the idea that these young military men are gallants and gentlemen—the sort of men that would offer a

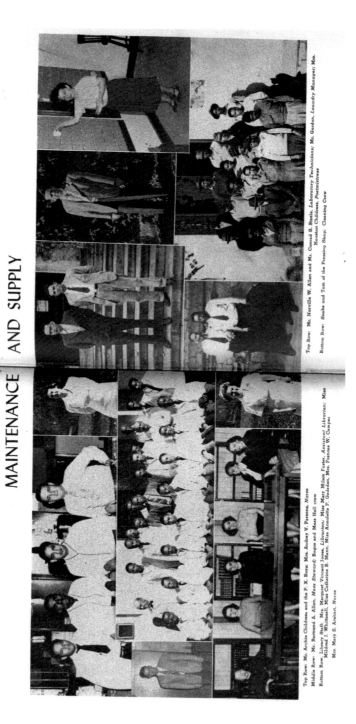

FIGURE 4.5   Montage of VMI support staff showing the strict separation of jobs on campus according to both race and gender (*The Bomb* 1950, 32–33). Black men are the only group represented in the cleaning crew and the "Mess Crew," and unlike the White support staff they are not identified by name. The "PX Crew" consisted of three Black men, apparently managed by a White man, Archie Childress, who is named.

IT'S AN
OUTRAGE!

With great pride the "Outrage" Staff dedicates its section to our beloved Leader
... What an Outrage!

FIGURE 4.6 "Snake," who worked in the VMI Press Shop, shown in uniform (*The Bomb* 1954, 213). During the 1950s "Snake" worked together with "Tom" in the Press Shop, and the two men are sometimes designated, in an ongoing joke, as the "leaders" of the "Outrage" editorial staff, the group that assembled the "Outrage" section of the VMI yearbook. This section consisted of student humor, including limericks, poems, stories and cartoons. Both men are shown in uniform, so it is likely that they were, at one time, service members of the military (*The Bomb* 1954, 213).

woman their coat, hold the door open for her and so on—the general discourse that accompanies this material concerning women is usually not flattering (see *The Bomb* 1954, 215–219; 1956, 233).

At Hampden-Sydney College in the 1950s and 1960s there are few pictures of staff, but they also indicate that much of the support staff was Black (see Figure 4.7 below). Beginning in the 1970s the yearbooks begin to have content where it appears the ongoing state of race relations is being discussed at campus venues. This content is infrequent but provides some context as to race relations on campus during different periods. Of particular importance is an essay written by Vinston Goldman, published in the 1975 *Kaleidoscope*, "On Being Black at Hampden-Sydney" (71). Goldman, after graduating from Hampden-Sydney, trained to be a clinical psychologist at Duke University and is currently an associate professor at North Carolina Central University (NCCU), a historically Black college. As a student he had the following comment concerning the informal manner that Black staff was treated at the college:

> One aspect of Hampden-Sydney which is very distasteful is the fact that students as well as many of the White employees of the College address

FIGURE 4.7 One of the few pictures in *Kaleidoscope* (1972, 8–9) that probably shows Black staff at Hampden-Sydney College although their names are not identified. There appears to be some recognition of racial inequality during the period—the quotes reference the failure of Southern Reconstruction and racial segregation in Prince Edward County.

Black employees by their first name. All my life I have heard Black parents and elders address White persons as "Mr." and "Mrs." but who are denied that due courtesy from Whites. Hampden-Sydney still clings to one aspect of White supremacy!

In the 1972 *Kaleidoscope* (8–9) on the previous page, are yearbook pages that appear to show Black staff, although none are identified by name. The yearbook also includes a quote concerning the failure of Southern Reconstruction to aide Black citizens. That quote is attributed to Dr. Heinneman, a professor at the college. In a fairly recent fundraising video (2013) made with a colleague—they indicate both have taught at the college for over 40 years—Dr. Heinneman is described as one of the few liberal professors on campus, and also that students "like him anyway" ("A Conversation" 2013). Another quote on the yearbook page states, "On the contrary, the White man is the Negro's chief problem," and is attributed to Eric Hoffer (1992), at the time a prominent moral philosopher and social theorist. There is also an enigmatic reference to the role that Prince Edward County played in Virginia's campaign of massive resistance to school desegregation: "Thanks a lot, Prince Edward County."

As shown in Figure 4.7, there is a noticeable shift—on a few campuses—concerning how the Black staff are characterized, roughly beginning in 1970 after a series of student protests that took place following the Kent State shootings (discussed further in chapter 5). Much of the content is still patronizing, but much was undertaken in the spirit of fostering a greater understanding and respect for the Black workers on campus. This shift was particularly noticeable in the 1971 *Corks and Curls* yearbook, where under the title "It Wasn't Easy, but Scott Will Find a Better Life" (74–75) there are several pages dedicated to "unseen" UVA staff. One essay focuses on Foster Lowe and his wife, Grace, who are both employed as custodians at UVA. The portrayal is somewhat maudlin—and still represents the power that White students have in characterizing Black staff—but appears motivated by a sincere attempt to understand Foster's life and work. To a greater extent the piece uses Foster's own words when compared to portrayals of previous Black staff. Here, the student writing this account first encountered Foster during the second job Foster works, as a dish washer, at the Dutch Pantry Restaurant. Apparently, the student and Foster sometimes work together at this restaurant, so the student is surprised when he encounters Foster working at UVA too. Soon, he realizes Foster works two jobs. He then asks the rhetorical question, "But why? Nobody works that hard" (74). The answer is that Foster and his wife have worked long hours to put their son, Scott, through medical school following his graduation from Virginia Union. Figure 4.8 is the second page of this narrative that has two pictures of Foster. Importantly, while the editorial staff of the 1971 *Corks and Curls* was clearly liberal minded, there are sections in the yearbook (see discussion of fraternities below) where negative racialized images are still presented.

Jefferson Hall, and the Chapel.

During his last eight years, Foster has seen quite a few changes in the university community, and in his own job. Several years ago, for example, "B and G" granted retirement to maintenance personnel, by giving them full-time, eight-hour day employment, rather than the previous seven hours a day without any retirement benefits.

Then when asked about the student strike last spring, Foster simply said, "if you're doing it for the right reasons, it's alright."

What can anyone say about this man and his wife? That although these people are employed in seemingly menial tasks, they have achieved in large measure for their son what most parents only dream for their children in a lifetime? An attempt at answering this question and understanding Foster and Grace Lowe would be a specious understatement. Rather than in words, the answers lie in the simplistic beauty of the tools of Foster's trade — his hands . . .

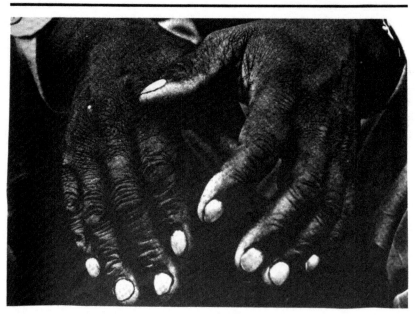

FIGURE 4.8 Narrative account with pictures of Foster Lowe's life and work as a custodian at the University of Virginia. Unlike previous portrayals of Black staff at UVA, this piece largely treats the subject with respect. It was published in *Corks and Curls* (1971, 75) following the 1970 UVA student protest strike which seems to have inspired significant changes in the 1971 yearbook content, although racist pictures and text do sometime appear in this yearbook edition.

Race and extracurricular campus life: fraternities and entertainment

Like the pre–World War II period, the post-war period also provides ample evidence that both formal and informal blackface performances continued on nearly all these campuses into the 1950s, with some campus-wide productions ocurring into the 1960s and 1970s. Over time, in general, it does appear annual blackface shows began to slowly dissappear during this period. By the late 1970s there is no evidence of *campus-wide* blackface productions, but it was still routine to find students in blackface at other informal events—especially at Halloween parties and during annual events held by fraternities (particularly by Kappa Alpha; see examples below).

In stark contrast to yearbooks published before World War II, the post-war yearbooks indicate that Black entertainment—in particular performances by Black bands—became increasingly routine throughout the 1950s and were incredibly commonplace, on all campus venues, in the late 1960s and early 1970s. In the 1950s, when Black performances appear to have become more common, most of these schools had entirely White undergraduate student populations. And in the 1960s—when these performances appear to increase dramatically—most of these schools still had all-White student bodies, or very few Black students.

This section also includes an exploration of the symbolism that increasingly associated these institutions as proudly "Southern," particulalry evident during sporting performances. Here, Confederate flags became increasingly common at many of these schools during pep rallies and at football games. These flags might also be considered part of "memorializing the Confederacy," and that content category is presented in greater detail after this section.

Minstrelsy and blackface performances

One well-chronicled annual event in the VMI yearbooks is the Monogram Minstrel Club performances, which became an annual production in the fall of 1948 (see *The Bomb* 1949, 148). The Monogram Club was composed of cadets that had lettered in a varsity sport and was designed to promote sports and also organize banquets and picnics. It appears the minstrel show was the highlight of the club's activities during the year. Figure 4.9 is a picture in *The Bomb* (1953) that details the 1952–53 school-year production. Specific references to the "Monogram" show in the VMI yearbook appear to end in the 1962–63 school year (see Figure 4.10 below), although unattributed pictures indicate the performance (or similar performances) were staged afterwards (for example, see *The Bomb* 1963, 97).

While the Monogram Minstrel program at VMI was among the most thoroughly documented in the yearbooks examined, it was also routine to find incidences of other blackface productions at other Virginia schools well into the 1960s and sometimes into the 1970s. Often, these appeared associated with

THE MONOGRAM MINSTREL

Every so often the Institute must bear the brunt of some sort of satire, and the greatest leg-puller round the Institute is the annual Monogram Minstrel. Nothing is so sacred or hallowed that comment cannot be made upon it by the cavorting end-men, and the authorities always receive a dusting that they never forget. It is all in fun, however, and those who are the targets of withering remarks from the stage go off laughing as much as any other member of the audience. From Colonel Pancake's whip-lashing entrance to the take-off on the current comedy team of Dean Martin and Jerry Lewis old J. M. Hall rocked with laughter, proving that this year's Minstrel was as much fun (or more) than those in the past.

FIGURE 4.9 The Merry Monogram Minstrel show began production at VMI in the fall of 1948. The Monogram Club was composed of cadets that had lettered in a varsity sport at the college. It appears the minstrel show was the highlight of the club's activities during the year. This is a picture of the 1952 production (*The Bomb* 1953, 163).

FIGURE 4.10 A campus-wide production of the Merry Monogram Minstrel show at VMI in the 1961–62 school year (*The Bomb* 1962, 275).

specific fraternities and sororities. Perhaps most surprising is that this tradition continued at a nearby women's college, James Madison University, well into the 1960s. At Longwood College, the other women's college in this study, a staged blackface performance is documented in the 1974 yearbook (*The Virginian* 1974, 152). The example shown in Figure 4.11 is from *The Bluestone* (1963) yearbook and indicates the performance was associated with a JMU women's sorority.

FIGURE 4.11 The Phi Mu sorority page at Madison College (later James Madison University) showing members in blackface in *The Bluestone* (1963, 185). The two bottom pictures appear to be side-by-side representations of the sorority members, and annual blackface performances by this sorority may have been common at the college.

Notably, even after these performances were no longer being staged as campus-wide productions, it was still common to find what appear to be more impromptu blackface performances at costume parties, Halloween dances and so on. Sometimes there were school-wide events that referenced slavery in a facile and offhand manner, completely absent any historical context in terms of

Slave Day

The Slave Day chorus line trips across the quadrangle.

Pete Forame, pres of the Pep Club, auctions off the GMC slaves.

Yes, I am the Mademoiselle from Armentiers.

71

Do you like my ironing bonnet?

FIGURE 4.12 "Slave Day" at George Mason University was an annual event held by the Pep Club for a few years in the late 1960s. It appears that students dressed in a range of costumes and were then auctioned as "slaves" (*The Advocate* 1968, 71).

what the system of slavery was like in America. An exemplary case took place at George Mason University, just previous to its establishment as an independent four-year college, where for several years there was an annual "Slave Day" in which the Pep Club auctioned students as slaves (see *The Advocate* 1968, 71). It is portrayed in the yearbooks as a largely whimsical and lighthearted event, designed to increase school spirit (see Figure 4.12).

COLOR PLATE 6   Black performers during "The Hop" weekend at VMI in 1966, two years before the school was integrated. The caption (on the following page) states, "The abandon of a hop weekend" (*The Bomb* 1966, 18–19).

Black entertainment on campus

It was routine to find Black bands performing on Virginia campuses with increasing frequency during the 1950s. Often, the performances by Black bands appear more numerous (or at least more documented) than those by

FIGURE 4.13 An event at VMI where a band—it appears integrated—performs for the White student body and their guests. Here, unlike the picture in Color Plate 6, the men appear to be in uniform (*The Bomb* 1967, 33).

White bands during the same periods. Many of these Black performers were nationally renowned at the time. A good example of this trend is a period at Virginia Tech during two academic years (1967–68 and 1968–69) in which the following national acts performed: Marvin Gaye and Tammy Terril, Wilson Pickett, Count Basie, The Supremes, Percy Sledge and Duke Ellington's Band (*The Bugle* 1968, 66, 69, 70, 119; 1969, 48 & 74). In addition to the previous, a host of local Black performers appeared in smaller venues, often at fraternity formals, for example.

Often, the composition of these pictures shows the sharp juxtoposition of Black musicians performing in front of an entirely White student body. The pictures in Color Plate 6 and Figure 4.13 are from VMI in the 1960s, but they are representative of the type of pictures that were found in nearly all the Virginia yearbooks during this period. These two were selected because they offer a wide shot of the audience that is likely (although not definitively) entirely White. At least, both these performances occurred before the school was desegregated during the 1968–69 school year.

Civil War memorialization, Confederate flags and sports

The yearbook content does indicate one obvious increase concerning Civil War memorialization that took place directly after World War II: the incidences in which Confederate flags appeared. During the post-war period it became increasingly common to find Confederate flags on campus and particularly during football games. This appears to have been a common practice at many Virginia schools that had football teams—and the flags are also commonly pictured at pep rallies associated with important annual events, such as Homecoming. Mostly, the Virginia university yearbooks indicate that Confederate flags were often everywhere on these campus. There were flags in dorm rooms. There were flags at dances. There were flags at pep rallies. And there were definitely flags directly associated with certain "Southern" fraternities and sororities. Foremost among these, the Kappa Alpha Order (KA) commonly had Confederate flags represented on its yearbook pages.

An end to the "Gentlemen's Agreement"—an increase in Confederate flags

Christopher Nehls (2002) has conducted a study that provides evidence that the widespread adoption of Confederate flags by fans during football games may have originated with the UVA football program during and directly after World War II. Here, UVA students appear to be among the first to popularize the practice, which later became widely associated with other schools in the South. Nehls believes the first instance of Confederate flag waving at a football game occurred in 1941, when the UVA team traveled to Yale University and many of the UVA supporters followed the team to New Haven. In this case, a local paper indicated that the Confederate flag was raised from "a thousand hands" during the game (469). Here, the tactic was apparently employed only when the UVA team was playing teams from the North.

The previous chapter discussed how the W&L and UVA football teams became closely associated with the "Gentlemen's Agreement" in which opposing teams agreed to sit their Black players during football games. Notably, in 1947 the UVA football team gained national exposure when it ended the Gentlemen's Agreement by playing a Harvard team that refused to sit a Black player, Chester Pierce. The end of the agreement at UVA, during a game held in Charlottesville, was covered by both the national press and the regional Black press. Apparently, there were attempts by UVA administrators to provide separate accommodations for Pierce from those of his Harvard teammates—to maintain the "local customs"—but the Harvard coach quickly moved his entire team into the same hotel and also refused a request that Pierce be served his meals separately too (Nehls 2002).

Throughout the game Confederate flags were enthusiastically waved by the UVA fans, who also engaged in racial taunting. The band played "Dixie" repeatedly throughout—a tradition that was also soon adopted by other regional schools (e.g. VMI). Later that season, the team traveled to the University of Pennsylvania (UP), and some supporters living in the state apparently asked UVA supporters not to bring Confederate flags to the game, mostly because they feared it would antagonize UP fans. Apparently, this fueled the Virginia fans' desire to bring the flags (Nehls 2002). That year the *Corks and Curls* (1947) yearbook makes a reference to the "invasion" of Pennsylvania by UVA: "Cavaliers Invade Philadelphia: And Who Could Forget the Weekend in November When the Rebels Invaded Yankeeland?" (138). Later, the yearbook shows a picture of a fan with a large Confederate flag boarding a train to the game (139).

Notably, Nehls's (2002) study also offers a range of editorial opinions published that indicate there was some ambiguity as to what the flag-waving meant to participants and observers. For example, some Southern White commentators actually regarded the flag as "sacred" and initially found its use at a football game akin to a sacrilegious event. Others said it simply reflected school spirit. But, undoubtedly, at least for some—given its prominence at the game that ended the Gentlemen's Agreement—it was sometimes a statement of defiance, an insistence that the customs of the South were not really changing (even when they were). Probably the ambiguity over the meaning of Confederate flags made them more widely appealing, over time, for more White students in the South (discussed further below).

Two William and Mary Bravettes remind fellow students

of our "Southern Heritage".

COLOR PLATE 7 "Two William and Mary Bravettes remind fellow students of our 'Southern Heritage'" (*The Chieftain* 1961, 13). Taken at the Norfolk division of William and Mary College, a few years before it became the independent college Old Dominion University. Negative stereotypes associated with Native Americans were common at schools in the Tidewater region. The Bravettes is a reference to the William and Mary Indian mascot. This mascot has since been retired, but the school's sports teams are still referred to as "The Tribe."

School spirit: Confederate flags at dances and pep rallies

There were sometimes campus events—sanctioned by the administration—that used the Confederate flag to generally associate the university with pride in its "Southern Heritage." For example, a photograph (see Color Plate 7) published by the Norfolk campus of William and Mary College shows two women, dressed as William and Mary Bravettes (a reference to the Indian mascot), in the process of raising the Confederate flag up a campus flagpole. Judging from past yearbook pictures, this was an annual event. The title states: "Two William and Mary Bravettes remind fellow students of our 'Southern Heritage'" (*The Chieftain* 1961, 13).

Using only yearbook content, it is hard to make a fine-grained judgment as to how routinized and centralized the act of flag-waving was during athletic contests and annual campus events at all the Virginia schools in this study. But there is often yearbook content that shows flags at football games and pep rallies, in what appears to be a loosely organized undertaking in which a few students routinely decide to bring Confederate flags. On occasions, there also appears to be a more centralized effort associated with flag-waving during specific school rituals. And when accompanied by bonfires or torches (e.g. during a pep rally), the overall purpose seems clear. Figure 4.14 is an example of a pep rally in which there are several Confederate flags and students carrying torches. The VMI yearbook also directly associates athletics with a Civil War battle. The composition of the picture, whatever the specific intention of the participants, appears menacing, and it seems likely it was meant to be so.

On one level, it seems the Confederate flag became associated, over time, with school spirit at many of these colleges. Other times there are references to the "Lost Cause" narratives associated with Civil War. For example, in the picture presented previously of a VMI pep rally the Battle of New Market is referenced. In a few cases, at the colleges that most fully embraced Lost Cause mythology, flags were continually displayed on campus in institutional settings. For example, within Lee Chapel at Washington and Lee University there was a constant rotating retinue of different Confederate battle flags (first the originals and then reproductions) displayed from 1930 until 2014, when the administration, over the objections of many, finally retired the practice. Many of these flags were donated by the United Daughters of the Confederacy (UDC) and the Confederate Memorial Literacy Society (CMLS), located in Richmond, Virginia ("History of Flags" W&L).

Confederate flags in dorm rooms

Probably the most common place that flags were displayed on campus were in dorm rooms. Often, the flags in dorm rooms are in the background and not the primary focus of a picture. But there are also many examples in which the flag

THE
ATHLETICS

More rain and mud. The Corps comes under a heavy barrage of artillery and musket fire as it advances through an orchard just 500 yards from the enemy. While friends fall to the ground around them, the cadets begin to fire on the enemy from the cover of a fence.

FIGURE 4.14 Picture of a pep rally with torches and Confederate flags published in *The Bomb* (1956, 160–161), the VMI yearbook, introducing the "Athletics" section of the yearbook. This was probably a student rally associated with a sporting contest. But the use of torches, combined with the display of Confederate flags, evokes rituals commonly associated with the KKK. Also notable is that the picture appears beside an account of the VMI cadets' actions during the Battle of New Market, implying that the spirit of war and sports are synonymous.

FIGURE 4.15 Confederate flags were routinely hung in student dorms at all Virginia universities in this study. They are often represented in the W&L year-book. Often they are associated with drinking, pep rallies and parties (*The Calyx* 1975, 263).

appears to have been part of the composition as intended by the photographer. An exemplary picture, taken on the W&L campus, is presented in Figure 4.15.

Notably, flags also appear in the Madison College (later JMU) yearbook when the school was still primarily a women's college that often trained teachers (see Figure 4.16).

These common-place representations of Confederate flags, as when flags were used during campus "pep rallies," represent a more "generalized" form of Lost Cause memorialization. Here, what is different than the past yearbook content is that popular Lost Cause narratives became more and more a part of the culture of the South, and also the culture on these campuses. For exam-ple, at VMI football games it was routine—it happened at every game during much of this period—to hear "Dixie" played at halftime.[4] But while this type of popular memorialization increased, other types appear to have waned at many Virginia colleges. For example, campus-wide Lee Literary Societies were no longer a part of the campus club scene at JMU. Further, specific instances associated with the founding of statues and naming of buildings on these campuses is far less evident during this period too. Here, it appears the buildings named for Confederates on these campuses were mostly events that occurred from 1890 to 1930. For example, three buildings at James Madison University—Maury Hall, Jackson Hall and Ashby Hall—were all renamed

FIGURE 4.16 Confederate flag that appears to be in a women's dorm, shown in the 1952 Madison College (later James Madison University) yearbook (*The Bluestone* 1952, 16). Flags were commonly represented in the yearbooks issued by women's colleges.

after the Confederate generals during this period ("History of the Quad" JMU).[5] Indeed, this corresponds with a well-documented rush of memorialization that took place in Virginia at roughly the turn of the century through the 1920s ("Whose Heritage" SPLC). At the same time, the exceptions are that Washington and Lee University and Virginia Military Institute remained closely associated with Civil War memorialization. Below, a discussion of civil war iconography as associated with VMI is presented. Here, unlike most of the other schools studied, there were, until recently, daily and annual rituals associated with Civil War memorialization that were integral to the campus culture during the period examined.

Lost Cause memorialization at Virginia Military Institute

Virginia Military Institute (VMI) represents a special case as it relates to Civil War memorialization. Importantly, during that war VMI students—while matriculating at the school—participated in regional battles. Specifically, the Battle at New Market is the most memorialized. Here, as shown in Figure 4.17, the VMI cadets, after marching for three days from the VMI campus, arrived at the battle in time to help turn the tide in the Confederates' favor. About 25% of the students who participated were killed or wounded during the battle

FIGURE 4.17 An account of the bravery of the VMI student corps of cadets during the Battle of New Market. VMI students were credited with ensuring victory through their bravery, and this mural was once on the VMI campus. About 25% of the students were killed or wounded in the battle (*The Bomb* 1948, 20–21).

("Battle of New Market Report" 1864). Practically, there is no need to embellish the previous story in order to understand this was a remarkable feat of endurance, undertaken before a hard-fought battle in which many were killed. But the more detailed version of this account, codified in school lore, tends toward the apocryphal. For example, it states the group visited the grave of Thomas "Stonewall" Jackson, buried a year previously in Lexington, and then recalled his words, supposedly spoken before the Battle at Chancellorsville, that "the Virginia Military Institute will be heard from today," and this "re-doubled their courage" (*The Bomb* 1948, 21). As shown in Figure 4.17, the "standard" telling of this story is recounted in the 1948 yearbook and accompanied by a style of artwork—this is a mural located on the VMI campus—typically associated with Lost Cause narratives.

Not surprisingly, given Stonewall Jackson's fame—combined with the fact he was a VMI instructor— he is much memorialized on the VMI campus. There is, of course, Jackson Hall. And until December, 2020, in front of the building stood a life-size statue of Jackson (pictured in Color Plate 5 as it appeared in the 1960 yearbook). On the statue's base are written his apocryphal words, supposedly uttered before the Battle of Chancellorsville. Here, the VMI Stonewall Jackson website FAQ helpfully notes that his actual words began with "The Institute" and not "The Virginia Military Institute." The FAQ also helpfully informs that the remark was actually made on May 2, not on the date of May 3 that is indicated below the statue ("Stonewall Jackson FAQ" VMI). The FAQ also notes Jackson was "overcome by emotion" when he uttered these words—an interesting rhetorical flourish in that other accounts of the event do not usually describe Jackson in this manner ("Stonewall Jackson FAQ" VMI). Notably, Jackson's troops did undertake a relatively modest engagement on May 2—during a flanking move they essentially routed some Union forces (most ran away as Jackson's men approached)—and afterward was when Jackson was accidentally wounded while trying to determine how far these men had scattered.

To be clear, there appears to be no definitive evidence one way or the other as to whether Jackson actually said, "The Institute will be heard from today." But the entire account has the feel (the convoluted "facts" often rearranged, the strange phraseology of the words themselves etc.) of many other now largely debunked accounts of Southern chivalry, gallantry and nobleness undertaken during the Civil War.[6] Moreover, all these accounts—true or not—obscure the most fundamental aspects of fighting during the Civil War. In particular, because the war was fought in a largely traditional manner using more modern weapons, the fatality rates and the number of wounded far exceeded those associated with previous conflicts. Mostly, compared to wars undertaken previously, the Civil War was a uniquely barbarous and inhumane undertaking. Many see it as a precursor to the trench warfare fought during World War I (see McWhiney and Jamieson 1984). And notwithstanding innovations such as Jackson's much-lauded hit-and-run tactics, these were battles in which the ability to capture land—often the high ground and land reinforced using trenches etc.—depended mostly on marching thousands of men at heavily fortified positions. Here, the strategy was related to a willingness to have thousands of men mercilessly cut down by gunfire until, somewhat improbably, they might prevail (McWhiney and Jamieson 1984). Other times, there was a lot of waiting—for months at a time—until the other side, weakened and sick from lack of food and medicine, began to slowly abandon its fortified positions in large enough numbers that the other army might advance. Some participants in these endeavors state in their correspondence that these acts—particularly with respect to battles in which men were marched into gunfire with no real prospect for success—"were not war, they were murder" (Ferguson 2000; McWhiney and Jamieson 1984, 2).[7]

But to give readers an idea of how events of the Civil War can be reimagined as a chivalrous and vainglorious adventure—particularly as applied to the culture at VMI—we should re-examine a classic print that depicts the Battle of Chancellorsville (see Color Plate 1 represented in chapter 1). First, this battle is often cited as an indication of Robert E. Lee's genius because he engaged in a series of tactics—mostly dividing his army and fighting on different fronts—credited with manufacturing an improbable Confederate victory (see Stackpole [1958] 1988). Practically, while the Confederates won the battle, the casualties were so high that some modern historians regard this as an example of how "winning a battle" can contribute to "losing a war" (see Gallagher 2012). It was a brutal undertaking. In fact, popular Lost Cause accounts often state that the casualties at Chancellorsville—in excess of 20,000 men in the May 3 fighting—represent the second-highest total (the highest was the Battle at Antietam) of American fatalities experienced in the history of the country.[8]

In *The Battle of Chancellorsville* print represented in Color Plate 1 (in the opening chapter), Stonewall Jackson is the focus of the painting. He is portrayed on horseback, the central figure of the fight, in which he appears mortally wounded—he is falling from his horse—while other officers rush to his aid. As stated previously, Jackson was actually killed by Confederate troops when he was scouting in advance to see where the Union army was stationed. He did not participate, as the print would indicate, in the definitive fighting that took place the next day.

That an institution like VMI—and really all institutions to some extent—participate in myth making concerning the exploits of its founders, former faculty and notable students is probably inevitable. But the problem here is that it is impossible to understand the politics and culture of the United States today—including ongoing patterns of racism—without also understanding the real history of the Civil War too. What is notable about W&L and VMI is the difficulty in creating a truthful institutional accounting of this period because it cannot take place without also delegitimizing the once bedrock principles—at least as they existed in the past—upon which these institutions were built. In effect, a truthful institutional accounting of the Civil War—along with Jackson's and Lee's roles in it—will force these institutions to reconcile the facts with the Lost Cause narratives upon which these institutions were built. The word "built" is intentional here: in the past these universities attracted students, attracted supporters and raised money by anchoring their missions—and even daily practices—to the logics associated with the Lost Cause. And notwithstanding the fact that both these institutions claim to value "truth seeking" and "honor"—within the context of the Lost Cause ideology that permeates these institutions, the "honorable" act usually becomes some manner of tinkering with the apocryphal accounts of Jackson's and Lee's lives and philosophies. In effect, considering a logical alternative—contemplating that the apocryphal stories associated with both Lee and Jackson may not be true—is currently (even as the statue of Jackson is being removed from campus) an impossibly difficult task within the context of the VMI institutional culture. It means admitting that an important anchor upon which VMI culture was built—and which cadets dutifully followed for over 100 years—was based on falsehoods too.

But change is coming to VMI. Beginning in October 2020, VMI was rocked by a series of *Washington Post* reports that documented ongoing institutional racism on the campus. Shortly after, the Board of Visitors voted to remove the statue of Stonewall Jackson that stood on the main quad of the campus (Shapira 2020a; 2020b; 2020c; 2020d). This was not, among many older alumni, a popularly supported decision.[9] Notwithstanding this important symbolic change, a fuller accounting of how the academic culture was largely constructed using the mythology of Lost Cause ideology will be a considerably more difficult endeavor.

At the other Virginia schools in this study the type of Civil War memorialization discussed above—even as the flag waving increased—tended to slowly diminish during the post–World War II period. But importantly, by the time this decline took place the Lost Cause myths were so firmly entrenched in educational curriculum of the South that these more vainglorious forms of memorialization were also largely beside the point. Practically, the Lost Cause narrative, in the immediate aftermath of the post–World War II period in Virginia, was now accepted as truth. They were also a part of "built" physical landscape—Virginia still has more commemorative statues of Civil War figures than any other state by far (Whose Heritage" SPLC). These myths clearly underpinned the culture at VMI—a place where the institution completely embraced, and then embellished, these accounts in order to make its role in the Civil War a noble endeavor. Here, Stonewall Jackson was literally front and center: he functioned as the face of the institution, the exemplary figure that all VMI cadets were told they should emulate.

Southern fraternities and historic preservation societies: the Kappa Alpha Order and others

There are fraternities that were established at Southern colleges whose explicit purpose was to maintain ideas associated with Southern manhood and chivalry. These often remained informally segregated even as schools integrated. The most notable among these are the so-called Lexington Triad, three fraternities all established after the Civil War by W&L and VMI students and alumni. The triad includes Alpha Tau Omega (ATO), founded in 1869 by VMI alumni in Richmond; the Kappa Alpha Order (KA), founded in 1865 by W&L students in Lexington; and Sigma Nu, founded at VMI in 1865. At VMI, fraternities were abolished in the 1880s because they were considered to be an impediment to cohesion among the corps of cadets, but ATO now has around 250 chapters nationwide. Sigma Nu currently has about the same number of chapters. Kappa Alpha, still based in Lexington, has around 150 active and inactive chapters in the United States (see James 2008; Edmondson 2020).

The Kappa Alpha Order has probably been the most thoroughly examined in terms of its founding history. The organization regarded Robert E. Lee—alive and in residence in Lexington when the first chapter was founded—as its spiritual leader. Both Robert E. Lee and Thomas "Stonewall" Jackson are considered exemplary figures, literally the template fraternity members should use in terms of their own conceptions of honor and ethics. It also appears that the fraternity once routinely used the symbols and organizational structure closely associated with the Ku Klux Klan. For example, individual chapters were referred to as "Klans" into the 1950s. They often adopted the Confederate flag as an explicit symbol of protest against school desegregation (see James 2008; Ross 2016: Edmondson 2020).

A few academic studies and commentaries have associated KA as maintaining "neo-Confederate" ideals and "fostering a racially hostile environment" on college campuses and within its chapters (James 2008; Edmondson 2020). During the period examined in his study, the Virginia KA chapters routinely held events such as "Old South" balls in which the members and guests dressed in the period of the antebellum South. It appears to have been open knowledge—during the period of integration at Virginia colleges in the 1970s—that the KA chapters in Virginia would not admit Black pledges. More recently, after a series of KA fraternity events received negative press coverage, the national chapter banned the use of Confederate symbols, although it appears that some chapters have not complied (Edmondson 2020). In terms of this inquiry, while Confederate flags and provocative Lost Cause imagery were associated with several fraternities, this was far more often the case with respect to the KA yearbook pages.

During this study it was sometimes jarring to encounter tentative signs of racial progress on campuses as represented in yearbook material and then—in the very same yearbook edition—encounter extraordinary examples of institutional racism. One example of this occurred while coding the 1975 *Kaleidoscope*, the Hampden-Sydney yearbook. In this edition, as previously mentioned, was a forthright account written by Vinston Goldman, now an associate professor of psychology, about being Black at Hampden-Sydney. Its publication could be construed as a tentative sign that people at the institution were grappling with the need to improve race relations on campus. In that essay, as it relates to social life on campus and fraternities, Goldman (1975, 71) wrote the following:

> Social life for Blacks at Hampden-Sydney is practically nil. Of course fraternities are on campus and Longwood College is only five miles away.... Though I was not a member of a fraternity at Hampden-Sydney, I feel fairly confident that the majority of Blacks would feel uncomfortable in one there. Fraternities at Hampden-Sydney as well as many throughout the United States, have not reached the point where Black and White individuals can socialize without at some point making a reference (verbally or otherwise) to the Black individuals' "inferiority." ... To expand upon why Whites behave as if they are superior to Blacks is not the purpose of the present article. I refer to racial tension only to show that it does exist at Hampden-Sydney.

In the same edition of the 1975 *Kaleidoscope* the following picture of the KA fraternity appeared with the legend representing the students as members of the KKK (see Figure 4.18). Notably, it may not be the case that the members themselves created this legend—it appears likely that the yearbook editors were responsible for this—so this could be a case of how the KA fraternity was perceived by others at the college. The KA picture is followed by another (Figure 4.19) published in *Corks and Curls* (1971) in which much of the yearbook content also indicated tentative signs of racial progress, but the yearbook still included a picture of a mock hanging that was staged by Chi Psi fraternity. On the page opposite this picture is a quote by Frank Zappa: "You know I am not Black, but there are a whole lot of times I wish'd I wasn't White" (141). The final picture presented (Figure 4.20) appeared in the Old Dominion University yearbook (*Troubadour* 1968, 235) and shows the ATO fraternity (one of the Lexington Triad) "string[ing] up 'Black Bart' in honor of the Bar-T." Notably, this appears to have been an annual event, as a previous yearbook picture shows the "Bar-T Cowboys" hanging a "runaway Indian" (*The Chieftain* 1961, 109).

It was also routine to find pictures in which KA fraternity members were associated with the antebellum South, the Civil War, and where Confederate flags were also commonly displayed. For example, Figure 4.21 is a 1990 picture from Washington and Lee taken during one of the chapter's "Old South" events.

FIGURE 4.18 The Kappa Alpha Order, founded at Washington and Lee University, regards Confederate leaders Robert E. Lee and Thomas "Stonewall" Jackson as exemplary figures associated with chivalry and Southern honor. Some have associated its founding with symbols and structure used by the Ku Klux Klan. That connection is made explicit in this example from the KA chapter at Hampden-Sydney College (*Kaleidoscope* 1975, 142–143). The KKK legend may not have been created by the fraternity members themselves but rather may represent how the yearbook editors perceived the group.

Following this picture is another (Figure 4.22) from the University of Richmond KA chapter in which its members stand in front of the towering statue of Robert E. Lee. This was the first Confederate statue erected on Memorial Avenue in Richmond, Virginia.

Importantly, while the KA chapters were consistently shown with symbols associated with the Civil War, other fraternities—not directly associated with the South in terms of their founding—nonetheless adopted these symbols too. Figure 4.23 shows an example, published in 1981, from the Lambda Chi Alpha fraternity at Hampden-Sydney College.

Finally, on some Virginia campuses—likely in response to an increase in academic debate concerning the historical context in which the Confederacy should be placed—there was in increase in ostensibly academic clubs and associations that appear, for the most part, to be defending long-standing Lost Cause narratives. In Figure 4.24, a yearbook page shows a presentation by

FIGURE 4.19 A mock hanging staged by Chi Psi fraternity at UVA (*Corks and Curls* 1971, 140). On the page opposite this picture is a quote by Frank Zappa: "You know I am not Black, but there are a whole lot of times I wish'd I wasn't White" (41). Notably, the editors of this yearbook edition did tackle a range of important social justice issues on campus—they make a tentative case for progress and also argue for greater campus-wide change—but pictures like this indicate that racism was still common on campus during this period.

the Society for the Preservation of Southern Heritage, "Black Confederates in the War between the States," that took place at Hampden-Sydney College on February 23, 1999. This society appears to have been active at the college for the next couple of years before disappearing from the annual yearbooks.

ATO strings up "Black Bart" in honor of the Bar-T.

FIGURE 4.20 Alpha Tau Omega members involved in a mock hanging. The picture, with the caption "ATO strings up 'Black Bart,'" appeared in the 1968 Old Dominion yearbook (*Troubadour* 1968, 235). The fraternity was founded in 1869 by VMI alumni in Richmond. It is one of the Lexington Triad established after the Civil War by VMI and W&L students.

FIGURE 4.21 A picture of the Kappa Alpha fraternity at Washington and Lee during one of its annual Confederate-themed events (*The Calyx* 1990, 261). These events were held by many chapters during the period examined.

FIGURE 4.22 The University of Richmond KA chapter assembled in front of the towering statue of Robert E. Lee, the first Confederate statue erected on Monument Avenue in Richmond (*The Web* 1971, 286–287). The statue, in separate pieces, was pulled by thousands of residents to the site when it arrived by rail from Paris. It was reassembled and officially unveiled on May 29, 1890. It was the first of a series of statues of US Civil War figures to be erected on this wide boulevard. All the statues on Monument Avenue, except this one—currently the subject of a court case—were removed following the Black Lives Matter protest in 2020.

LAMBDA CHI ALPHA

111

FIGURE 4.23 Hampden-Sydney College chapter of Lambda Chi Alpha, a fraternity founded in Boston, with KKK figure in the fraternity yearbook picture (*Kaleidoscope* 1981, 111). Even fraternities that were not explicitly founded with connections to the antebellum South sometimes used symbols associated with the Ku Klux Klan, probably meant as a form of "humor."

Black Confederates in the War Between the States Feb. 23

Presented by The Society for the Preservation of Southern Heritage

FIGURE 4.24 Presentation concerning "Black Confederates" made at Hampden-Sydney College by the Society for the Preservation of Southern Heritage (*Kaleidoscope* 1999, 82). As academic debate increased concerning the historical context in which the Confederacy should be placed, some clubs and associations appear to defend long-standing Lost Cause narratives, as shown here.

Conclusion

Often, World War II is considered a symbolic dividing point after which more progressive race relations in the United States were increasingly established. That, for the most part, is not a good description of the history of the Virginia universities in this study. Instead—most notably at the UVA law school—these schools continued to insist on a policy of legal segregation and became the targets of the NAACP in their ongoing fight to dismantle the "separate but equal" standard. All these universities remained active sites of resistance to desegregation well after the *Brown v. Board of Education* Supreme Court ruling ended school segregation within the state. And while UVA was forced to desegregate its law school and some graduate programs after a 1950 court ruling, the other schools in this study largely adhered to the state program of massive resistance for a decade after the 1954 *Brown* decision. Also notable was the degree to which the Black civil rights movement was ignored in campus yearbooks until the late 1960s. Indeed, it was not until this period, usually following litigation, that these schools began to admit, in very small numbers, their first Black undergraduate students. And even after this modest period of advancement, many of these schools maintained pockets of resistance to desegregation—places where Black students were informally barred from participating in campus organizations, particularly specific fraternities.

The following chapter investigates the periods of increasing social movement activism at Howard University during the civil rights period and throughout Virginia during the anti–Vietnam War movement. For the most part, this is when modest cultural shifts associated with race relations were observed on some Virginia campuses. Here, the landmark year marking the beginning of widespread social change on all the Virginia campuses appears to have been 1970, a period when student protest against the Vietnam War became widespread throughout the United States. While Black civil rights were not the primary focus of this student movement, demands associated with greater Black student and faculty representation on campus became more commonplace at this time. Often, it appears that university administrations—some more than others—began to increase Black student enrollment on campus during this period and also modestly extended efforts to hire more Black faculty.

Notes

1 I am intimately familiar with many of Jackson's battles during his famous "Valley Campaign." I once lived in the Village of Port Republic, only a few doors from his headquarters (now a local museum) during his battles at Cross Keys and Port Republic. In the early 1990s, I was prevailed upon to become a member of the Board of Directors of the Port Republic Museum. During this period I also lobbied for the Battlefield Preservation Act, sponsored by Congressman Frank Wolfe, which helped preserve endangered battlefields in the region. But unlike many Civil War enthusiasts and re-enactors I encountered during this period, I never became enamored of the Lost Cause mythology. Mostly, the more I walked and studied the local battlefields

and battles identified for preservation—a friend of mine actually lived near one these at Cross Keys—the more the brutality (as opposed to chivalry or gallantry) of the entire endeavor was impressed upon me.

2 These student movements are discussed further in the next chapter. Mostly, it appears a few students from UVA were active in the Freedom Summer campaign—probably the only representatives from the schools in this study. See Gregg Michel, *Struggle for a Better South: The Southern Student Organizing Committee, 1964–1969* (New York: Springer, 2004).

3 See the picture of "Snake" in *The Bomb*, 1955, 252, as compared to the picture in this chapter to see the resemblance.

4 Several VMI alumni, who attended in the 1970s, told me that "Dixie" was played at all the home games when they were cadets. They also indicated that it was routine for students to state that: "The Institute will be heard from today" previous to football games.

5 The buildings named after confederates were recently renamed again in 2021. One was named for Sheary Darcus Johnson, the first black woman to attend JMU. Another for two popular members of the faculty (Drs. Joanne V. and Alexander Gabbin). The last for a prominent black community activist (Doris Harper Allen) and long serving black staff member (Robert Walker Lee). The renaming effort began before the 2020 Black Live Matter protests, but this event appears to have expedited what had been a slow moving process.

6 I tried to find the original source for this Jackson quote. The quote is not usually accompanied by a citation, and when cited it does not reference the original source. For example, a few citations refer to a text published by the Virginia Military Institute: *The Spirit*, ed. William Butler and William Strode (Prospect, KY: Harmony House, 1989). This is basically a "history for hire" text, and the editors indicate that the quote is from VMI founder John Thomas Lewis Preston, a Lexington attorney. In a few other cases, the specific account is retold with enough detail to posit that Colonel Tom Mumford—attributed with making the observation about the number of VMI men in the field—would be the logical original source, but even these detailed accounts do not provide the original source. For an example see Samuel C. Gwynne, *Rebel Yell: The Violence, Passion, and Redemption of Stonewall Jackson* (New York: Simon & Schuster, 2014). Here, the account states that "Jackson, pleased with this notion, turned to Munford and said, 'Colonel, the Institute will be heard from today'" (521). Other citations refer to Colonel William Couper, *One Hundred Years at V.M.I.* (Richmond, VA: Garrett and Massie, 1939). Perhaps, some industrious Civil War sleuth has triangulated direct accounts so that the quote rises to the level of fact—but if this is the case, the academic work validating this quote is not easily found.

7 This quote, likewise apocryphal, is attributed to different sources and different battles too. See Ernest B. Ferguson, *Not War but Murder: Cold Harbor* (New York: Alfred A. Knopf, 2000), and specifically Grady McWhiney and Perry D. Jamieson, *Attack and Die* (1984, 2). Here, the "It was not war, it was murder" phrase appears in the correspondence of General D.H. Hill, a Southerner, when describing the Battle at Malvern Hill outside Richmond.

8 For example, at this writing this comparison is made on the Wikipedia page of "The Battle of Chancellorsville," https://en.wikipedia.org/wiki/Battle_of_Chancellorsville.

9 My neighbor is a VMI alumnus who attended the school when the first Black cadets were admitted. His has been an active alumnus voice in terms of reforming the campus culture and is also active on VMI alumni LISTSERV and Facebook pages. Following this decision he reported, as did the *Washington Post* (see Shapira 2020c), that the racist rhetoric among VMI alumni increased dramatically. Initially, a common refrain was that Virginia Governor Northam—a VMI graduate—should lose his diploma because he called for a state investigation of the allegations. At the most extreme, some alumni indicated—at least rhetorically—that they believed Northam should be "dragged from the governor's mansion and shot." In a later conversation, as some initial changes

to the campus were being instituted and following the removal of the Jackson statue, he indicated that the official alumni association was increasingly supportive of these changes, although many of his classmates (from the early 1970s) were not. For his part, he is entirely supportive of the recent changes. From two personal conversations with the same alumni held on October 29, 2020 and on May 27, 2021.

References

"A Conversation with Professors Ron Heinemann & Jim Simms." 2013. Hampden-Sydney College. Youtube.com, June 19. https://www.youtube.com/watch?v=5VFimgJkth0.

"A Life, a Legacy: Honoring Martin Luther King Jr." 2011. *Virginia Magazine*, Spring. https://uvamagazine.org/articles/a_life_a_legacy.

Anderson, Nick. 2015. "Longwood U. in Va. Expresses Regret for Actions in Civil Rights Era, Apologizes." *Washington Post*, January 18. LexisNexis Academic.

Barnett, Todd. 2008. "Failure's Brink: How MLK Snatched Success in Charlottesville." *The Hook*, April 3. http://www.readthehook.com/81986/cover-failures-brink-how-mlk-snatched-success-charlottesville.

"Battle of New Market: Annual Report Excerpt." 1864. Virginia Military Institute. https://www.vmi.edu/archives/civil-war-and-new-market/battle-of-new-market/battle-of-new-market-annual-report-excerpt1864/.

The Bluestone. 1962–2010. James Madison University Library Digital Yearbook Archive. https://commons.lib.jmu.edu/allyearbooks/39/.

Birnbach, Lisa, ed. 1980. *The Official Preppy Handbook*. New York: Workman Publishing.

Birnbach, Lisa. 1981. "Fanning the Flame: An Introduction by Lisa Birnbach." *Kaleidoscope*. Hampden-Sydney College Yearbook.

The Bomb.1885–2010. Virginia Military Institute Library Digital Yearbook Archive. https://www.vmi.edu/archives/digital-collections/vmi-yearbook-digital-archives/

Butler, William, and William Strode, eds. 1989. *Virginia Military Institute—The Spirit*. Prospect, KY: Harmony House Publishers.

The Calyx. 1895–2019. Washington and Lee Library Digital Yearbook Archive. https://dspace.wlu.edu/handle/11021/26929.

Chetty, Raj, John N. Friedman, Emmanuel Saez, Nicholas Turner and Danny Yagan. 2017. "Mobility Report Cards: The Role of Colleges in Intergenerational Mobility." National Bureau of Economic Research Working Paper No. 23618, July 2017.

Chieftain. 1953–1961. Old Dominion University Library Digital Yearbook Archive. https://digitalcommons.odu.edu/scua_yearbooks/index.html.

Corks and Curls. 1888–2018. University of Virginia Library Digital Yearbook Archive. https://v3.lib.virginia.edu/catalog/ u126747.

Couper, William. 1939. *One Hundred Years at V.M.I.* Richmond, VA: Garrett and Massie.

Dabney, Benjamin. 1987. *Virginia Commonwealth University: A Sesquicentennial History*. Charlottesville, VA: University Press of Virginia.

"Demographics and Retention." Hampden Sydney College. http://www.hsc.edu/institutional-effectiveness/demographics-and-retention.

"Economic Diversity and Student Outcomes at America's Colleges and Universities: Find Your College." 2017. *New York Times*. https://www. nytimes.com/interactive/projects/college-mobility/.

Edmondson, Taulby. 2020. "The Campus Confederate Legacy We're Not Talking About: Kappa Alpha, Washington and Lee University, and the Ku Klux Klan." *Chronicle of Higher Education*. July 8. https://www.chronicle.com/article/the-racist-fraternity-that-tried-to-shut-me-up?cid2=gen_login_refresh&cid=gen_sign_in.

"Farmville 1963 Civil Rights Protests." VCU Libraries Digital Collections. https:// digital.library.vcu.edu/islandora/object/vcu%3Afar.

Ferguson, Ernest B. 2000. *Not War but Murder: Cold Harbor.* New York: Alfred A. Knopf.

Finn, Peter. 1997. "At VMI, Pioneers Recall Breaking Earlier Barrier." *Washington Post,* October 5. LexisNexis Academic.

Gallagher, Gary W. ed. 2012. *Chancellorsville: The Battle and Its Aftermath.* Chapel Hill, NC: University North Carolina Press.

Gates, Robbins L. 2009. *The Making of Massive Resistance: Virginia's Politics of Public School Desegregation, 1954–1956.* Chapel Hill, NC: University of North Carolina Press.

Goldman, Vincent 1975. "On Being Black at Hampden-Sydney." *Kaleidoscope.* Hampden-Sydney College, 71.

Gwynne, Samuel C. 2014. *Rebel Yell: The Violence, Passion, and Redemption of Stonewall Jackson.* New York: Simon & Schuster.

Hall, Chadwick. 1955. "America's Conservative Revolution." *The Antioch Review* 15 (2): 204–216.

Handy, Bruce. 1987. "Colleges of the Dumb Rich." *Spy Magazine,* May, 58–63.

"History of Hampden-Sydney College." Hampden-Sydney College. www.hsc.edu/ about-h-sc/history.

"History of the Flags in Lee Chapel and Museum: President Ruscio's July 8, 2014 Message." 2014. Washington and Lee University website. https://my.wlu.edu/ lee-chapel-and-museum/about-the-chapel/history-of-lee-chapel-flags.

"History of the JMU Quad." JMU Website. https://sites.lib.jmu.edu/historyandcontext/ quad-storymap/.

Hoffer, Eric. 1992. *The Temper of Our Time.* New York: Buccaneer Books.

Howard, Chris, Elizabeth J. Deis and Lowell T Frye. 2012. "What Aristotle and Stephen Colbert Have in Common." *The Atlantic Monthly,* October 5. www.theatlantic.com › national › archive › 2012/10.

Lee, Brian. 2009. "A Matter of National Concern: The Kennedy Administration and Prince Edward County, Virginia." MA Thesis. Virginia Commonwealth University.

James, Anthony. 2008. "Political Parties: College Social Fraternities, Manhood, and the Defense of Southern Traditionalism, 1945–1960." In *White Masculinity in the Recent South,* edited by T. Watts, 62–85. Baton Rouge, LA: LSU Press.

Kaleidoscope. 1907–2010. Hampden-Sydney College Yearbook Internet Archive. https:// archive. org/search.php?query=collection%3Ahampdensydneycollege+AND+subject% 3A%22College+yearbooks-Virginia-Hampden-Sydney%22&page=2.

Kapsidelis, Karin. 2009. "Hampden-Sydney College Adds Chapter to Its Long History." *Richmond Times-Dispatch,* July 19. https://richmond.com/news/hampden-sydney-college-adds-chapter-to-its-long-history/article_641d02c2-c387-5785-89b3-b639704be90f.html.

Kelly, Jane. 2018. "This Is How the Rev. Martin Luther King Jr. Came to Speak at UVA in 1963." *UVA Today,* January 12. https://news. virginia.edu/content/how-rev-martin-luther-king-jr-came-speak-uva-1963.

Kovacic-Fleischer, Candace S. 1997. "United States v. Virginia's New Gender Equal Protection: Analysis with Ramifications for Pregnancy, Parenting, and Title VII." *Vanderbilt Law Review* 50: 843.

Martinez, Ramona. 2012. "The Curious Fate of Stonewall Jackson's Arm." Morning Edition Radio Broadcast. *National Public Radio.* https://www.npr. org/2012/06/28/155804965/ the-curious-fate-of-stonewall-jacksons-arm#:~:text= Jackson%20is%20informed%20that %20the,Despite%20Mrs.

McWhiney, Grady, and Perry D. Jamieson. 1984. *Attack and Die: Civil War Military Tactics and the Southern Heritage.* Tuscaloosa, AL: University of Alabama Press.

Michel, Gregg. 2004. *Struggle for a Better South: The Southern Student Organizing Committee, 1964–1969.* New York: Springer, 2004.

Morrison, A.J., ed. [1824–1835] 1917. *Six Addresses on the State of Letters and Science in Virginia 3–4.* Lectures Delivered to the Literary and Philosophy Society at Hampden-Sydney College. Roanoke, VA: Stone Printing and Manufacturing. https://blurblawg.typepad.com/files/ hampden-sydney-6-addresses.pdf.

Nehls, Christopher C. 2002. "Flag-Waving Wahoos: Confederate Symbols at the University of Virginia, 1941–51." *Virginia Magazine of History and Biography* 110 (4): 461–488.

Newman, Caroline. 2018. "Martin Luther King III Retraces His Father's Footsteps at Old Cabell Hall." *UVA Today,* November 4. https://news.virginia.edu/content/martin-luther-king-iii-retraces-his-fathers-footsteps-old-cabell-hall.

Peddrew, Irving Linwood. 2017. "Oral History Interview with Irving Linwood Peddrew, III." Interview. Virginia Tech Library Archives. https://web.archive.org/web/20170403191202/http://spec.lib.vt.edu/ archives/Blackhistory/oralhistory/peddrew/.

Picott, J. Rupert. 1958. "Desegregation of Higher Education in Virginia." *Journal of Negro Education* 27 (3): 324–331.

Quarles, Benjamin, and Bernard C. Nalty. 2014. *Taps for a Jim Crow Army: Letters from Black Soldiers in World War II.* Lexington, KY: University Press of Kentucky.

Ross, Lawrence. 2016. *Blackballed: The Black and White Politics of Race on America's Campuses.* New York: Macmillan Press.

Shapira, Ian. 2020a. "VMI Votes to Remove Stonewall Jackson Statue amid Racism Accusations by Black Cadets." *Washington Post,* October 29. LexisNexis Academic.

Shapira, Ian. 2020b. VMI Superintendent Resigns after Black Cadets Describe Relentless Racism." *Washington Post,* October 26. LexisNexis Academic.

Shapira, Ian. 2020c. "Northam Calls for VMI Investigation after Black Cadets Describe Relentless Racism." *Washington Post,* October 19. LexisNexis Academic.

Shapira, Ian. 2020d. "At VMI, Black Cadets Endure Lynching Threats, Klan Memories and Confederacy Veneration." *Washington Post,* October 17. LexisNexis Academic.

Shomo, Thomas H. 1978. *To Manner Born, to Manners Bred.* Hampden-Sydney College, VA: Office of the Dean of Students.

Sky Lark, Taj'ullah X. 2017. "Unlocking Doors: How Gregory Swanson Challenged the University of Virginia's Resistance to Desegregation. A Case Study." *Spectrum: A Journal on Black Men* 5 (2): 71–84.

Smith, Robert Collins. 1965. *They Closed Their Schools: Prince Edward County, Virginia, 1951–1964.* Chapel Hill, NC: University of North Carolina Press.

Stackpole, Edward James. [1958] 1988. *Chancellorsville: Lee's Greatest Battle.* Harrisburg, PA: Stackpole Books.

"Stonewall Jackson FAQ." VMI website. https://www.vmi.edu/archives/stonewall-jackson-resources/stonewall-jackson-faq/.

Taylor, Jon E. 2013. *Freedom to Serve: Truman, Civil Rights, and Executive Order 9981.* New York: Routledge, 2013.

Troubadour. 1962–1972. Old Dominion University Library Digital Yearbook Archive. https://digitalcommons.odu.edu/scua_yearbooks/index.html.

Turner, Kara Miles. 2004. "Both Victors and Victims: Prince Edward County, Virginia, the NAACP, and 'Brown.'" *Virginia Law Review* 90 (6): 1667–1691.

Tushnet, Mark V. 1994 *Making Civil Rights Law: Thurgood Marshall and the Supreme Court, 1936–1961.* New York: Oxford University Press.

The Virginian. 1900-2006. Longwood College Digital Yearbook Archives. https://digitalcommons.longwood.edu/yearbooks/.

"VMI Museum." Virginia Military Institute. https://www.vmi.edu/museums-and-archives/vmi-museum/.

"VMI Student Population." Virginia Military Institute. https://www.univstats.com/colleges/virginia-military-institute/student-population/.

The Web. 1922–2002. University of Richmond Library Digital Yearbook Archive. https://scholarship.richmond.edu/the-web/.

"Whose Heritage? Public Symbols of the Confederacy." 2019. Report. *Southern Poverty Law Center*. https://www.splcenter.org/20190201/whose-heritage-public-symbols-Confederacy.

5

SOCIAL MOVEMENT ACTIVISM AT HOWARD UNIVERSITY AND VIRGINIA COLLEGES

This chapter concentrates on Black civil rights activism and its aftermath at Howard University and the Virginia colleges in this study. Here, there was not much significant change directly after World War II on the Virginia campuses in terms of the composition of the student body, or the widespread use of Black labor to support White students and faculty (see previous chapter). In a few cases, court decisions in the early 1950s—one directly associated with admitting Black law students to the University of Virginia—did force a few state universities to accept very few Black students in a few programs, but most Virginia colleges either actively or passively complied with the program of "massive resistance" to school desegregation until it became untenable in the period of 1964–1968.[1] Hereafter, colleges began to tentatively admit Black undergraduate students (see Sky Lark 2017). In the year 1968, all the Virginia schools in this study had admitted at least one Black student. But even when institutional change was taking place, there remained pockets of institutional racism on these campuses.

More signs of change began to take place following the tumultuous political year of 1968. That was the year both Martin Luther King Jr. and Robert Kennedy were assassinated. That was also a year when widespread racial unrest took place in many cities (including Washington, DC). Throughout this period more students became vocal opponents of the Vietnam War. Soon after, the high point for progressive activism at many Virginia schools occurred directly after four Kent State students were killed by the Ohio National Guard, on April 30, 1970, during an anti-war protest. This precipitated nationwide campus strikes against the Vietnam War, and most Virginia schools in this study participated, to varying degrees, in these protests.

Afterward, a general consensus emerged in the early 1970s that increasing Black student enrollment and Black faculty was needed on many Virginia campuses.

DOI: 10.4324/9781003134480-5

At the same time, substantive institutional change with respect to increasing Black presence on campuses—50 years after this consensus emerged—has usually been disappointing. Most notable is that student demographics and the average family income of students attending these schools—with the exception of Old Dominion University (ODU) and Virginia Commonwealth University (VCU)—indicate that most of these institutions still cater to relatively affluent White students. In sum, notwithstanding a few significant changes made over time, most of the Virginia institutions in this study are still a reflection of White privilege (see Chetty et al. 2017; "Economic Diversity" *New York Times*).

Howard University: a social movement machine

Founded on egalitarian principles emphasizing the importance of being committed to a lifetime of community service, Howard University produced an extraordinary number of prominent Black activists during the civil rights movement. Most well know is the judicial activism of the National Association for the Advancement of Colored People (NAACP), led by Howard University graduate Thurgood Marshall, which was responsible for overturning the "separate but equal" standard in American law. But Howard students, along with others attending historically Black colleges and universities (HBCUs) throughout the South, were also leaders in the Student Non-Violent Coordinating Committee (SNCC), which coordinated a highly successful sit-in campaign in the 1960s and a voter registration drive in Mississippi in 1964, during Freedom Summer. Finally, Howard was an intellectual center from which the Black Power movement emerged in the 1970s.

Howard students were also at the forefront of advocating for changes to the university curriculum, for changing governing structures to create more student input into campus-wide decision-making, and active in the anti-war movement. In particular, in 1968 Howard students staged a well-documented takeover of the Howard administration building while pressing demands to create more courses associated with the Black experience. That same year, well before the Kent State demonstrations in 1970, Howard students demanded that Reserve Officer Training Corps (ROTC) training at the university be made optional.

Howard law school alumni: the end of "separate but equal" as a legal standard

Beginning in the late 1930s and culminating with the 1954 *Brown v. Board of Education of Topeka* Supreme Court decision, Howard graduates working in the NAACP systematically pursued court cases that attacked the separate but equal standard concerning educational opportunities for Blacks. The early tactic was to have well-qualified Black applicants—many were Howard graduates—apply to Whites-only state law schools where no comparable institution existed for Black students. Thurgood Marshall first used this tactic in a suit directed against the University of Maryland (UMD) in the 1936 case *Murray v. Pearson*. Here, Marshall demonstrated that the state of Maryland had no facilities to educate Black lawyers, and consequently UMD was forced to desegregate its law program. Eventually, the same tactic was used by the NAACP against the University of Virginia (UVA) law program when Gregory Swanson, another Howard law school graduate, applied to the UVA program and was denied admittance based on his race. In *Gregory Hayes Swanson v. the Rector and Visitors of the University of Virginia* it was demonstrated that the state of Virginia had no Black law schools, which forced the desegregation of the UVA program in 1950 (Taj'ullah 2017). Practically, this case also desegregated other graduate programs when there was not an equivalent degree being offered by a Virginia HBCU. As a result, small groups of Black students were admitted to the law program and some graduate programs at White Virginia colleges. A few years later, in 1953, Virginia Tech (VPI) was forced to admit its first Black undergraduate student to the engineering program (see "Irving Peddrew" VPI).

Howard University yearbooks often recognize these ongoing events. For example, the 1955 Howard University yearbook is dedicated to the law school graduates and the yearbook theme is "Howard—The Leader on the Frontier of Democratic Education" (*The Bison* 1955, 2):

> In days of rapid social change in our nation and in the world at large the leadership of Howard University in this movement gives us a deep feeling of pride. Changes which today are stirring our country have been in process at our Alma Mater for many years. The world looks to Howard for leadership, and we, its graduates, drawn from all quarters of the globe, are grateful for the training and guidance given us. Realizing the beneficial results of exposure to the unique character of democratic education at Howard and profoundly thankful for the opportunity offered us, we have chosen as the theme of this yearbook: "Howard—The Leader on the Frontier of Democratic Education."

The yearbook page that precedes the graduating class of law students that year is shown in Figure 5.1, along with the following description: "Among the most courageous fighters for human rights in our country today are the graduates of the School of Law. We are happy to go forth and join them" (*The Bison* 1955, 145).

The Howard yearbook content stands in direct contrast to the yearbook content at all the Virginia colleges during the same 1954–55 period. Here, the *Brown* decision is essentially a non-event. There is no indication in the yearbooks at any Virginia colleges that school segregation had been legally abolished. Sometimes there are veiled references to "change"—most often an indication that conservative groups on campus are reacting to events (see chapter 4).

Among the most courageous fighters for human rights in our country today are the graduates of the School of Law. We are happy to go forth to join them.

FIGURE 5.1 Howard University yearbook dedication to the law class of 1955 (*The Bison* 1955, 145). Howard law school graduates were instrumental in dismantling the legal standard of "separate but equal" in the United States through their judicial activism and support for the NAACP. Foremost, Howard alumnus Thurgood Marshall spearheaded a series of cases that culminated in the *Brown v. Board of Education of Topeka* Supreme Court decision that ended legal segregation. Howard University yearbooks reflect these achievements.

The student sit-in campaign in the early 1960s

Activism at Howard University continued into the 1960s as Black students throughout the South began using the sit-in tactic to desegregate lunch counters and restaurants. Similar tactics had been used previously by Howard students. For example, in 1943 a few Howard faculty and students protested against the segregation of commercial establishments in Washington, DC, but had little long-term success desegregating these establishments (Brown 2000). In 1950 another faculty member, Ralph Bunche (who was then chair of the Department of Political Science) organized a protest against the National Theatre, which temporarily ended its Whites-only policy. Notably, some of the Howard administration, including President Mordecai Johnson, did not always approve of this type of activism (Brown 2000).

In the early 1960s there was an increase in sit-ins led by students at HBCUs throughout the South. Most known, the "Greensboro Four" sit-in at a local Woolworth lunch counter, in July 1960, was undertaken by North Carolina A&T students Joseph McNeil, Franklin McCain, Ezell Blair Jr., and David Richmond. Aldon Morris (1981) has demonstrated that these protests were not spontaneous and that the sit-in tactic had been widely discussed previously, and even work-shopped in Miami, Florida, during a Congress of Racial Equality (CORE) meeting a year previously. But soon after the Greensboro sit-in the tactic became more widespread and was often used by students at other HBCUs.

At Howard the primary activist using the sit-in tactic was Laurence Henry, a divinity student who single-handedly organized protests that desegregated scores of restaurants and lunch counters in northern Virginia and southern Maryland (see Figure 5.2). In one case, he was beaten and arrested during a campaign to desegregate an amusement park in Glen Echo, Maryland, but he was released after a hunger strike (Hardin 2015). He also lobbied at the Capitol Building for the passage of the Civil Rights Bill. This activism is commented on in the 1961 Howard yearbook: "This young knight is King of the sit-ins, kneel-ins, bowl-ins, and drive-ins. As Chairman of the Social Action Committee of Washington, a non-violent action group, he has ably piloted the youthful organization through many a stormy sea" (*The Bison* 1961, 203). Also recognized is Howard activist Samuel Garner, who appears to be operating more along the lines of the traditional community uplift model. Here, Garner primarily organizes activities for disadvantaged Black youth in the community.

During this period there were sometimes collaborations between White and Black students, particularly during the Freedom Summer campaign in 1964 in which students established "Freedom Schools" in Mississippi. The campaign was centered on voter registration; at the time fewer than 6% of Black Mississippi voters were registered to vote (McAdam 1986). Here, Doug McAdam (1986) investigated applications to the program to determine the backgrounds of White students who participated. Often, the White students had very little

Lawrence Henry — This young knight is King of the sit-ins, kneel-ins, bowl-ins, wade-ins, and drive-ins. As Chairman of the Social Action Committee of the Washington area non-violent action group, he has ably piloted the youthful organization through many a stormy sea.

These two knights of Howard U.
Whose wealth are tears and sorrows
Their trumpeters are what they do
Their men at arms are prayers

Their castles are unkind words
Whereon they hand so high
Their banners suffer many a loss
Yet, they still touch the sky.

Samuel Garner — From the beginning, this young knight from Chicago, Illinois had his finger on the pulse of the situation in the 9th and P Street area. Derelicts, juveniles, and social outcasts, will always remember him as the man "Who Cares." His conscious awareness of the unhealthy conditions in this area has led him to establish prayer meetings, bible study groups, and enlisting the aid of such resource groups as Alcoholics Anonymous, The Sociology Club, and recreation facilities.

203

FIGURE 5.2 Howard University students were active during the student sit-in movement of the early 1960s. Pictured is Laurence Henry, a divinity student who organized protests that desegregated scores of restaurants and lunch counters in northern Virginia and southern Maryland (*The Bison* 1961, 203). In one case, he was beaten and arrested during a campaign to desegregate an amusement park in Glen Echo, Maryland.

in common with the Black student participants, who were mostly attending Southern HBCUs. Most White activists were from affluent families located in the North, with 40% coming from Harvard, Yale, Stanford and Princeton. Also well represented were state universities such as the University of California at Berkeley and Michigan State. At the beginning of this campaign two White students from New York, Michael Schwerner and Andrew Goodman, along with a Black man from Mississippi, James Chaney—after investigating a church arson in Mississippi—were beaten and killed by members of the local Citizen's Council after being stopped and then released by the local police in Philadelphia, Mississippi (see Chaney 2000).

Very few White student activists directly involved in Freedom Summer came from universities located in the South—probably around 20–25 students total (Michel 2004).[2] Here, there were a few UVA student activists in the Southern Student Organizing Committee (SSOC)—a group of White Southern students initially aligned with SNCC during Freedom Summer—who later moved into the anti-war movement and a partnership with Students for a Democratic Society (SDS) (Michel 2004). While there was apparently some student activism on a few Virginia campuses during this period, these relatively modest activities are not chronicled in Virginia yearbooks. For example, a few UVA students began an alternative press associated mostly with anti-war positions in the mid-1960s, and a few also participated in an NAACP staged sit-in at the popular Charlottesville restaurant Buddy's (McKenzie 2013). None of the Virginia yearbooks studied reference Freedom Summer or the student sit-in movement directly. Perhaps most remarkable, none of these schools make direct reference to the events that occurred in 1968 either, including the assassinations of Martin Luther King Jr. and Robert Kennedy. This is true for the UVA yearbook, even though other sources do indicate that the flag at UVA was lowered and that a mass was held on campus the day after King's assassination (see "A Life" *Virginia Magazine*). Notably, unlike the Howard yearbooks, there is essentially no Virginia yearbook content that indicates any sustained—and widely supported—period of student activism on any Virginia campuses until the 1970 nationwide anti-war protest (discussed below).

Jonathan Myrick Daniels: an exceptional White activist and Virginia Military Institute graduate

While there appears to have been little student activism on Virginia campuses in support of the civil rights movement in the 1950s and 1960—the exception being a modest group of supporters at the University of Virginia[3]—there were some-times people associated with these schools who did become activists largely on their own. Perhaps the most well known was a VMI graduate, Jonathan Myrick Daniels—valedictorian of his class of 1961—who was killed while participat-ing with SNCC students attempting to desegregate local businesses and register Black voters in Lowndes County, Alabama.

Jonathan Daniels was born in New Hampshire, and after attending VMI he returned to New England, where he was training to be an Episcopal minister. Notwithstanding his accomplishments at VMI, his personal correspondence indicates that he found many of the rituals associated with the VMI "Rat Line" barbaric ("Here I Am" PBS; Daniels 1992). Probably much of his personal familiarity with Southern racism was directly related to his experiences living in Lexington, Virginia, as a VMI student. While attending seminary he was inspired by Martin Luther King Jr.'s call for the clergy to join the 1965 protest in Selma, Alabama ("Here I Am" PBS). Later, while working with SNCC activists (including Howard graduate Stokely Carmichael—later named Kwame Ture), he was one of several protesters arrested in Fort Deposit, Alabama, while picketing a store that served only White customers. After being released, on August 20, 1965, nearly a week after being arrested, the group was confronted by Tom L. Coleman, who brandished a shotgun and pointed it in the direction of Ruby Sales, a 17-year-old Black SNCC activist. Daniels pulled Sales out of the way but was himself mortally wounded by Coleman. Another activist, Father Richard F. Morris, was wounded by Coleman as he ran from the scene ("Jonathan Daniels" VMI).

Soon after this event, news of Jonathan Daniels's bravery became one of the heroic stories associated with those who died during the civil rights movement. The acquittal of the man who killed him by an all-White jury inspired several congressional laws associated with jury reform ("Here I Am" PBS). He was later officially recognized as a martyr by the Episcopal Church. Eventually, the VMI Board of Visitors, in December 1997, established the Jonathan M. Daniels '61 Humanitarian Award "to recognize individuals who have made significant personal sacrifices to protect or improve the lives of others" ("Jonathan Daniels" VMI). Notwithstanding this recognition by VMI, it is notable that the award was established over 30 years following his death—well after Daniels had been recognized by others associated with the civil rights movement. Despite widespread national attention concerning his death, he was not memorialized in the 1966 VMI yearbook, the first published after his death.

Activism at Howard in 1968

The activism that took place at Howard University in March 1968 is well documented (see Azore and Cohon 2018), particularly the student takeover of the administration building that shut down the campus for a roughly a week. Here, students pressed demands for more diverse course offerings that described the Black experience. They also demanded that the mandatory ROTC training be made optional and for an increase in student decision-making concerning campus policy. The demand associated with ROTC training is indicative of the more radical positions that many Howard students were gravitating toward at this time. In particular, Stokely Carmichael (Kwame Ture), a former SNCC field officer and leader of the organization, was actively advocating for an anti–Vietnam War position (Carmichael 1971). Carmichael's position was based on academic arguments associated with neo–imperialism and war fighting. Mostly, he argued that a disproportionate number of Black men were serving, and dying, during the conflict (Carmichael 1971). Practically, this position was later adopted by Martin Luther King Jr. (1967) and a few years later became widely accepted on predominately White campuses throughout the country during a coordinated series of anti-war protests. These protests—many directed against the ROTC—are when the four Kent State students were killed by the Ohio National Guard.

While student activism at Howard is entirely in character with the culture of the university, it did surprise the Howard administration, which included an older generation of civil rights activists. Here, the Howard protests mark a break between the style of activism pursued by past civil rights leaders and that pursued by younger activists associated with the Black Power movement. Howard yearbooks document this protest—and many other events that took place in 1968—in a forthright manner. In particular, the first 16 pages of the 1969 yearbook open with a photo-essay and news headlines detailing the Howard student activism of the past year. Below is provided a summary of headlines in *The Bison* (1969, 5–21), along with one page to show how this photomontage and essay was arranged (see also Figure 5.3).

PHOTOGRAPHIC ESSAY: *THE BISON* (1969)

OPENING PAGE: THIS IS THE TIME OF A NEW AMERICAN REVOLUTION....

(Pictures of Black protesters and Black Panther leader Huey Newton, along with a counter-protester holding the sign "Go to Hell with the Red Clergy! Fight Against the Communist Menace")

PAGE 2: A REVOLUTION BROUGHT ABOUT BY THE INADEQUACY OF A 200 YEAR OLD SYSTEM....

(Pictures of Capitol Building and the American flag. Newspaper headlines: "Black Hero Carlos Given Huge Welcome" and "Black Killed on 14th St.; Neighbors Threaten Riot")

PAGE 3. AN IMPOTENT SYSTEM, INCAPABLE OF SOLVING SOCIAL, POLITICAL AND ECONOMIC PROBLEMS... (this page is reproduced below).

PAGE 4. PROBLEMS FOSTERED BY HATE, BIGOTRY, DISCRIMINATION AND INDIFFERENCE....

(Pictures of Ronald Reagan and Richard Nixon)

PAGE 5. INDIFFERENCE WHICH HAS INVITED MOLD AND DECAY....

(Pictures of people sleeping in the streets and protests associated with Dr. King's assassination. One man holds a sign: "Our King is Slain!!: No Class." Another picture shows the Poor People's March and signs associated with hunger in America.)

PAGE 6. A DECAYING SYSTEM THAT MUST BE REVAMPED...

(Picture of a "Give a Damn" Poster. Two newspaper headlines: "Gov't Dept. to Study Black Group Problems" and "Q.T. Admonishes University at Formal Exercises")

PAGE 7. OR WILL BE TOTALLY DESTROYED....

(Pictures of D.C. unrest in 1968 and of police officers and military in the streets)

PAGE 8. WE ACCEPT THE CHALLENGE OF CHANGE...

(Headline: "Student Demands Result in New Black Courses." Bottom left picture shows Stokely Carmichael—Kwame Ture—a Howard graduate and a past president of SNCC.)

PAGE 9. WE DEMONSTRATE OUR CONCERN IN MAJOR SOCIAL ISSUES

(Headline: "Yippies Mock HUAC Hearing: See proceedings as ludicrous." Pictures of protesters and a discussion outside on campus)

PAGE 10. WE DISSENT WITH REASON AND RESPONSIBILITY

(Headline: "Bowie Students Blasts Agnew, Cite His Past History of Racism." Pictures of protesters and a classroom discussion)

PAGE 11. WE CHALLENGE THE AUTHORITY OF THE ADMINISTRATIVE SYSTEM

(Pictures of the Howard student strike)

PAGE 13. WE CHALLENGE THE RELEVANCY OF THE EXISTING CURRICULUM....

(Picture of a professor lecturing in a classroom. Two pictures of students talking together outside the classroom)

PAGE 14. WE CHALLENGE OUR CRITICS WHO SEE NO REASON FOR CHANGE....

(Picture of Vice President Spiro Agnew and another of police standing together)

PAGE 15. WE CHALLENGE YOU TO JOIN US...

(Pictures: "Black is Beautiful"; demonstration with fist in the air; a bison (the school mascot); students on campus)

PAGE 16. FOR THE REVOLUTION HAS COME TO HOWARD.

(A picture of Howard buildings and another of a sundial. A picture of Howard student protesters with fist raised in the air. Headline: "Will Howard University Meet the Challenges of the Times?") (*The Bison* 1969, 5–21).

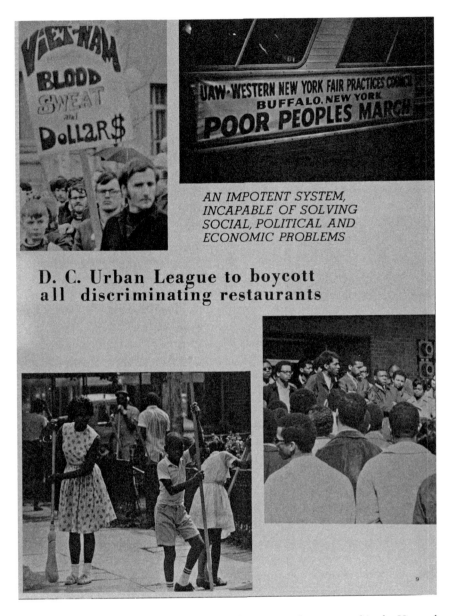

FIGURE 5.3 The third picture in a 16-page photo-essay that appeared in the Howard yearbook (*The Bison* 1969, 9) reviewing the student protest at Howard in 1968 and the tumultuous events that occurred that year. It shows an anti-war protest, scenes from the "Poor Peoples" march in New York, along with a headline concerning the DC Urban Leagues boycott of "discriminating restaurants."

Following this 1969 photo-essay, the Howard yearbook diligently surveys the events of the past year, including the aforementioned press for an increase in Black studies coursework and the policy change that would make ROTC training optional. When some students interrupted the Charter Day celebration in early March, they were quickly threatened with expulsion. This prompted other students to take over the administrative building from March 19 through March 23, 1968, in support of these students and to make demands associated with student governance.

The yearbook also discusses other social protests that took place through-out the country, the assassination of Martin Luther King, and the subsequent role that Howard University students played in supporting DC residents during the unrest that occurred afterward. The picture in Figure 5.4 documents the student takeover of the administration building.

Later, in the direct aftermath of the assassination of Martin Luther King Jr. (April 4, 1968), civil uprisings took place regionally in Washington, DC, and Baltimore, Maryland, and other cities throughout the country. As shown in Figure 5.5, Howard students actively supported the DC community and organized the Howard Relief Center, which "operated for 24 hours a day over 12 days" and "provided food, clothing and shelter for D.C. residents." Apparently, it was the "only center that remained in operation throughout the disorders." But it was "never 'officially' recognized by the press or authorities" (*The Bison* 1969, 137).

More generally—and in direct contrast to the Virginia schools in this study—Dr. King (along with Robert Kennedy) was memorialized in the Howard yearbooks soon after he was assassinated in 1968 (*The Bison* 1969, 145).

The difference between the Howard University content during this period (1968–69) and the yearbook content of the Virginia schools is stark. Here, the manner with which the Howard editors chronicled the extraordinary events of 1968, in the first 30 pages of the 1969 edition, provides far more information than all the other Virginia yearbooks combined during the same year. As in the past, the Howard yearbook content gives the impression that Howard students, as compared to their Virginia peers, were generally far more cosmopolitan and engaged American citizens concerning a range of ongoing political events that were often, but not always, associated with civil rights.

Black Power and "Black Is Beautiful": generational difference and the Black bourgeoisie

Howard activists, during this period, were also becoming more influenced by academic work associated with anti-colonialization and neo-Marxist philoso-phies. One aspect of the movement was the reimagining of E. Franklin Frasier's 1997 work, *Black Bourgeoisie*. Here, leaders associated with the Black Power movement regarded the Black bourgeoisie as a barrier to realizing real political

STUDENTS TAKE OVER ADMINISTRATION BUILDING

When the sit-in began, most people thought it would last for a few hours, and then everyone would pack up and go home. They did not believe that Howard students were organized well enough to put forth a united front for any length of time. Many students who were skeptical at the start had joined in by the second day. It had really happened: a well-organized and well disciplined group of students had peacefully taken control of the University. Support for the Sit-in came from Alumni Associations, Universities, religious groups and interested people throughout the country.

Before going to the Administration Building, the students are told what the problems are.

HUSA President Ewart Brown explains the status of the students who were involved in the Charter Day incident.

FIGURE 5.4 Howard students standing in front of the administrative building during a strike in 1968 (*The Bison* 1969, 122). In 1967 Howard students began to press for an increase in Black Studies coursework and a policy change that would make ROTC training optional. When some students interrupted the "Charter Day" in early March 1968, they were quickly threatened with expulsion from Howard by administrators. Later, students occupied the administrative building from March 19 through March 23, 1968, in support of these demands and students.

STUDENTS OPERATE
EMERGENCY CENTER

Although the University was closed by the riots,
several students sacrificed their spring break to
operate an emergency relief center in the University
Center.

The center was open 24 hours a day for twelve
days. The students mobilized all available resources
to provide food, clothing and shelter for District
residents. Volunteer drivers picked up and delivered
food; after being given permission by the Mayor to
remain on the streets after curfew.

When the crisis ended, the Howard center was
the only one that had remained in operation throughout the disorders. Ironically, it was never "officially"
recognized by the press or the authorities.

Any student with a car was asked to deliver food

Make-shift signs like this one appeared all over campus

137

FIGURE 5.5 The Howard Relief Center organized by students provided food, clothing and shelter for the city's residents during unrest in Washington, DC, following
Martin Luther King Jr.'s assassination. The center "operated for 24 hours a day over
12 days." The yearbook entry states it "was the only center to remain in operation
during the unrest, but was never 'officially' recognized by the press or authorities"
(*The Bison* 1969, 137).

power in America (Kelley 1998). Many in the student movement at Howard University saw their activism as a reaction against the bourgeois sentiments and goals of the previous generation. This was often characterized as a tendency for the Black middle class to favor assimilation by acting White. Instead, these students wanted a movement that articulated the distinctiveness, and beauty, of Black American culture (Kelly 1998).

In his work Frazier (1997) had used a class-based analysis—one that fits neatly with a neo-Marxist perspective—when describing the Black middle class in the United States. Here, the chapters of *The Black Bourgeoisie* are divided into two sections: (1) "The World of Reality" and (2) "The World of Make Believe." Notwithstanding some Black achievements, Franklin assesses the post-war period as a failure in terms of real Black integration into American society, and particularly into the American economy. He states a very small Black middle class has achieved "half-a-man status in White Man's country" (138–146).

In the "World of Make Believe" section, Frazier (1997:153–229) explores how the Black middle class creates a "make believe world" in which the achievements of the Black race (economically, socially, artistically etc.) are over-amplified in order to create a mythology of Black advancement. Frazier asserts that the "half-a-man status" of the Black middle class has caused many to have an inferiority complex marked by insecurity, frustration, self-hatred and guilt. Further, he contends that the constant struggle for status and recognition tends to manifest itself in the conspicuous consumption of the goods that are regarded as markers of a respectable middle-class life. Essentially, the Black bourgeoisie delude themselves into believing that the acquisition of these material goods marks their acceptance into American White society.

It is hard to know how many Black activists actually read E. Franklin Frazier's (1997) text, but there is no doubt that his general argument was perfectly aligned with ideas associated with Black nationalists such as Malcom X. For example, the idea that the Black middle class could achieve only half-a-man status in White society essentially echoes the same arguments that Malcolm X often made (see Kelly 1998). More generally, the rejection of White norms associated with middle-class life clearly underpinned many of acts characterized as cultural re-appropriation by Black students at Howard.

All the previous contributed to a new look and style among Howard students beginning roughly in 1968. Howard, in the past, was largely a buttoned-up and formal place (see chapter 3), but it appears that students loosened up considerably during this period. Many of the differences in style were directly associated with the Black Power and Black Is Beautiful themes. The first example below describes the activism among *The Hilltop* editorial staff, specifically how style issues are closely associated with Black Power activism and a rejection of the Black bourgeoisie (*The Bison* 1968, 166).

HILLTOP EMPHASIZES BLACK AWARENESS

This year's **Hilltop** was truly a Black oriented newspaper, evidenced not only by coverage of the numerous issues confronting Black people, but also by the fact that the entire staff adapted the Afro look and by the countless pro-Black slogans which decorated the walls of the office.

Having received a first-class honor rating for the past several years, **The Hilltop** has been dedicated to extensively reporting campus issues, affairs and events. This year, in addition to this, the Hilltop was dedicated to creating an awareness on the part of Howard University of the unique problems confronting Black America today....

The March 1968 issue of **The Atlantic** quotes a staff member as saying, "The Howard paper last year created an atmosphere of militancy on campus." "We had an editorial against the War in Viet Nam and in support of Black Power. The Administration was surprised by the Black Power editorial. *In it we said it was time for the students to start acknowledging that they were Black and stop trying to be bourgeois....* We stopped publishing a lot of public relations garbage."

On the following page, in Figure 5.6, is a two-page pictorial from *The Bison* (1968, 80–81) that comments on changing student style and ends with "And It's Beautiful to Be Black."

Overall, and in direct contrast to the Virginia schools surveyed below, many Howard University students were active—from the beginning—in civil rights protests that began in the 1950s and 1960s. The Howard yearbook forthrightly chronicles not just the important national events of the day as associated with civil rights but also the growing activism of Howard University students themselves in terms of having a say in university curriculum and judicial policies on their campus. Here, as in the past, they were largely out in front of their White peers in terms of advocating for progressive national policies.

Social change at Virginia universities: the anti-war movement and race relations

Often, in the years following 1965, on more Virginia campuses, speakers and events associated with controversial issues became more common. Usually, these are speakers associated with the anti-war movement, although there are occasionally those who discuss the "changing" South, an indirect reference to

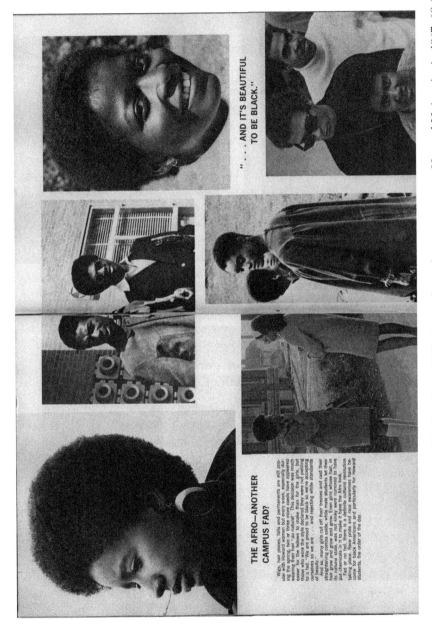

FIGURE 5.6   Cultural trends associated with "Black Is Beautiful" during the student movement at Howard University in 1967–68 (*The Bison* 1968, 180–181).

desegregation in Virginia. While the topic that generated the most student activism was the war in Vietnam, peripheral to this concern was that students should have more say in campus-wide policies. Once in a while there is also an indication that race relations on campus were being more widely discussed too.

Culture and conflict at Virginia Tech

A little ahead of the curve compared to other Virginia colleges in terms of institutionalizing a lecture series that tackled controversial events was the "Culture and Conflict" series established at Virginia Tech in 1965–66 (see Figure 5.7). The format was designed to present both sides of controversial issues. For example, the first year the series brought Ray Wilkins, president of the NAACP, and James Kilpatrick, at the time a Richmond newspaper editor who supported the program of massive resistance. The event was titled "The Rights and Responsibilities of the States." Later that same year Norman Thomas and George Cabot Lodge discussed the "U.S. Involvement in Viet Nam" (*The Bugle* 1966, 68).

A few years later, the series was focused on the draft. The speakers included Carl Oglesby, former leader of the SDS, who spoke about the student protest movement. Also appearing was Strom Thurmond, Senator from South Carolina and noted segregationist during this period (*The Bugle* 1969, 58). That same year State Senator Henry Howell—a populist Virginia politician who helped dismantle the Virginia campaign of massive resistance—also spoke on campus (*The Bugle* 1969, 33).

Campus activism at the University of Virginia: from "Old U" to "New U"—an end to the "Gentleman's C"

During this period (1965–69) the UVA yearbooks indicate more student activism too. For example, *Corks and Curls* (1969, 28) includes a few pictures of anti-war protesters in the 1969 yearbook. There are modest indications that race relations—while not central to this activism—were sometimes part of these discussions too. Mostly, the UVA yearbooks are preoccupied with changes to the traditional campus culture. For example, in 1968 the yearbook editor begins with a summary of events of the past year, and most of his remarks are directed toward the fact that the Gentlemen's Club—and the norms associated with the "Gentleman's C" (discussed in chapter 2)—were disappearing at UVA (*Corks and Curls* 1968, 16):

> The Virginia man, likewise, was once known chiefly for his legendary abilities at drinking Jack Daniels, rolling to Sweet Briar or Hollins, and choosing the "gut" courses that guaranteed his "gentleman's C". Individuals still exists that fit this description, and the ABC stores and girls' schools certainly haven't gone out of business. Yet as an archetype, this sporting fellow has gone the way of parties on the Quad, formal dances in the gym and party weekends that began on Tuesday.

Roy Wilkins, executive director of the National Association for the Advancement of Colored People.

George Cabot Lodge, consultant to the State Department on South Vietnamese rural problems.

The Czechoslovakia Philharmonic Orchestra presented a community concert in Burruss Hall Nov. 9.

Culture and Conflict

Come to VPI

It has often been said that education does not totally come from books. The greatest chapter in life itself, that of the years associated with one's university, can be considered the most educational of all. All universities are surrounded by many opportunities outside the classroom for the student to learn. Virginia Tech students have a variety of chances each year to broaden their cultural interests.

Winter quarter, '65-'66, provided much entertainment in the arts for Techmen. The Chicago Opera Ballet Company presented "Camille" from "La Traviata" and also the "The Merry Widow." The University Players, otherwise known as the Maroon Mask, gave outstanding performances of "The Chinese Wall," a farce by Max Frisch. Slated for the remainder of the year, the University Players also plan to bring "Look Homeward, Angel" to the Tech campus. The National Players, who visit the university annually, acted "Romeo and Juliet" this year.

A new idea in cultural and educational expansion has appeared in the form of CONFLICT. Sponsored by the YMCA, CONFLICT invites to VPI world-famous figures to speak on controversial subjects. National politics and civil rights are the topics for discussion in this year's programs. Roy Wilkins and James Kilpatrick will comment on "The Rights and Responsibilities of the States," while Norman Thomas and George Cabot Lodge will speak on "U.S. Involvement in Viet Nam."

68

FIGURE 5.7 The first "Culture and Conflict" lecture series at Virginia Tech in 1965 included a debate on the civil rights movement and states' rights issues (*The Bugle* 1966, 68). During this period more Virginia colleges institutionalized campus lecture series designed to debate controversial issues of the day.

Later, a picture in the 1969 yearbook indicates there was a protest associated with an end to the Gentlemen's Club—the exact nature of the event is not specified—but other sources indicate that about 150 students, associated with a "Coat and Tie Rebellion," pressed demands that included increasing the representation of both women and African Americans on campus (Gates 2018). At this time, UVA administrators were making plans to begin phasing in the admittance of women to the university. Also, this essay indicates that UVA students were beginning to engage in other social issues and also demanding more say in terms of campus governance (*Corks and Curls* 1969, 17):

> The faculty's complete control over academic rules, the administration's final authority over dispensing student funds, Charlottesville's neglect of its poor and ill-educated, the "generation gap"—these are just a few of the issues students are discussing—and doing something about.

Here, it is notable that Jim Roebuck, a Black UVA student, is pictured as a member of the 1969 Student Council (*Corks and Curls* 1969, 37). The following year he would be elected Student Council president and played a pivotal role in negotiating student demands with the administration during the 1970 student strikes discussed further below.

Finally, there were also increasing criticisms of the fraternity system too. In the past, membership in a fraternity at UVA was largely a social obligation, but many were growing disenchanted with the cliquishness of these groups and also the hazing rituals associated with pledging. There is also, for the first time, the indictment that some fraternities "would never pledge a Black" (*Corks and Curls* 1970, 175).

Widespread social activism on Virginia campuses: the 1970 student anti-war protest

While there was some modest social movement activism on a few Virginia campuses previous to 1970—William and Mary students protested a visit to campus by Richard Nixon in 1969, for example (*Colonial Echo* 1969, 151)—in May 1970 there were widespread anti-war protests on most of the Virginia campuses in this study. These were part of nationwide campus strikes that began shortly after President Nixon announced the United States had invaded Cambodia on April 30, 1970. These protests accelerated dramatically when four student protesters at Kent State University were killed by Ohio National Guardsmen on May 4, 1970. The Virginia universities in this study that had significant student strike activity included the University of Virginia, George Mason University, Washington and Lee College, Old Dominion University, University of Richmond, James Madison University, Virginia Commonwealth University and Virginia Tech ("May 1970" UW). There is little evidence of widespread activity on the Hampden-Sydney, Longwood or Virginia Military Institute campuses, although some later evidence exists (in yearbooks) that a few students on these campuses were discussing and actively watching these events (see below). This section will concentrate on the yearbook content at UVA and W&L, two universities that had widespread student strikes on their campuses that are well documented in their yearbooks. The student strike at Virginia Tech was also well covered in the state media, but it ended quickly when Virginia state police forcefully evicted and arrested student protestors who were occupying the administration building (see "Protest!" VPI).

FIGURE 5.8 Cover of the 1970 George Mason University yearbook. In May of that year there were widespread student protests throughout the country and on most of the Virginia campuses in this study (*The Advocate* 1970).

An important difference between the strikes at Washington and Lee and the University of Virginia is that at UVA students pressed demands that included the need for greater diversity on campus. These appear to be an extension of a previous protest on campus, in 1969, which had called for an increase in Black enrollment, a Black assistant dean of admissions and a Black Studies program (Gates 2018). These types of demands, judging from yearbook material, were entirely absent during the W&L student protests.

Many other Virginia university yearbooks indicate there were student strikes and a general increase in anti-war sentiment—but these are usually presented in a haphazard manner, often showing student demonstrations without much context. Perhaps yearbook editors assumed that the students on the campus during these events would understand what the pictures represented. For example, the George Mason University yearbook in 1970 does not have much specific information concerning student activism, but it did have the picture on the following page (Figure 5.8) on its cover (*The Advocate* 1970).

Similarly, there are a few yearbook pictures in the Madison College (later JMU) yearbook that show student demonstrations on campus, and the entire yearbook is indicative of the more activist-minded student population in 1970–71 (see *The Bluestone* 1971, 26, 32). On the cover is a dove that periodically appears throughout the yearbook. The editors also reference the environmental movement—the first Earth Day had also taken place that year (*The Bluestone* 1971, 491). The last page of the yearbook ends with a popular protest slogan "Give a Damn" and the following picture (Figure 5.9):

The sudden activism at Washington and Lee surprised some because it was considered a conservative campus. For example, *The Calyx* editors summarized events in 1970: "Following a national trend, the antiwar movement at W&L reached new heights this year (It was finally formed)" (124). Here, while anti-war activism at W&L was not long established, the movement appears to have galvanized considerable student support. As shown in Figure 5.10, the yearbook juxtaposes a picture of the empty main quad with another that shows it occupied by student demonstrators during the 1970 May strike.

The most radical and far-flung campus movement during this period occurred at the University of Virginia from May 1 until May 11. Over this period—after students were killed during the Kent State protests—UVA students presented a series of escalating demands to the administration, most associated with anti-war activism, but also including demands for significant changes to university policy. Over the course of the week, during a series of escalating conflicts, there was also increasing tension between the state police—at times entering the campus intent on establishing order—and a somewhat chaotic coalition of student protesters whose strategies ranged from occupying the ROTC building (from which they were quickly evicted) to pressing for a campus-wide vote to have a strike of classes. In the middle of many of these events—acting as a liaison between the students making demands and the UVA administration—was Jim Roebuck, a Black UVA student who was also Student Council president (Gates 2018).

FIGURE 5.9 "Give a Damn" poster on the last page of the Madison College (later JMU) yearbook in 1971 (*The Bluestone* 1971, 492). Depicting a popular slogan during the student movements of 1970, this picture follows a long stream-of-consciousness essay concerning social unrest and social problems.

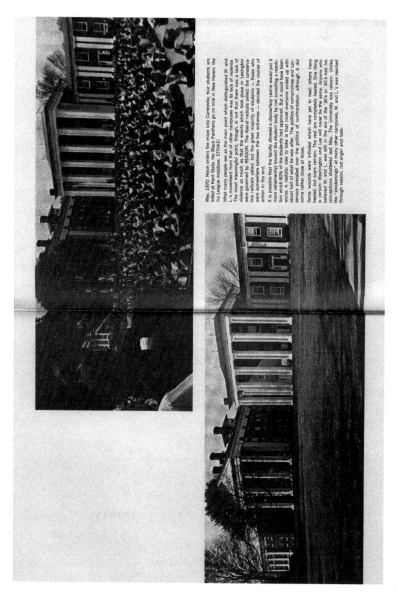

May, 1970. Nixon orders the move into Cambodia; four students are killed at Kent State; the Black Panthers go on trial in New Haven; the Ivy League mobilizes. STRIKE!

What many people see as the main point which distinguished W and L's movement from that of other campuses was its lack of violence. The most meaningful point, though, is not that there was a lack of violence so much as that the events which took place in Lexington were governed by REASON. The liberal radicals yelled; the conservative radicals yelled; but the great majority of students — those who were somewhere between the two extremes — decided the course of action in the end.

It is possible that the faculty showed a discourtesy (some would put it more vehemently toward the student body by not accepting a resolution which 80% of the students had approved. But it could have been worse. A realistic view to take is that most everyone ended up with about half of what he was after. The politics of compromise and consensus prevailed over the politics of confrontation, although it did come rather close at times.

Some wounds were inflicted which have yet to heal; others have healed, but scars remain. The rest are completely healed. One thing is certain: Washington and Lee will never be the same. Anyone who believed W. and L. was still in the era of the '30s or '40s had his conceptions shattered last May. The University was reborn. Unlike the "awakenings" at many other campuses, W. and L.'s was reached through reason, not anger and hate.

FIGURE 5.10 The 1971 W&L yearbook picture of the May 1970 anti–Vietnam War general strike on campus that many students participated in. The yearbook devoted several pages to the strike. The editors noted that a "lack of violence" and a politics of "consensus" prevailed over the politics of "confrontation" (*The Calyx* 1971, 4–5 [front]).

This activism culminated in an address by President Edgar Shannon to 4,000 students on the Lawn in which he reiterated his own anti-war position and agreed to send a letter to Virginia politicians—which students could sign— outlining his concerns over the Vietnam War and increasing "militarization" on campus. Later, when Shannon's response was criticized by Governor Linwood Holton and Senator Harry F. Byrd Jr.—combined with calls from some members of the Board of Visitors for his resignation—students rallied in support of the UVA president (see Gates 2018).

Notably, UVA was one of the few Virginia campuses that had a few students who had participated in earlier civil rights campaigns (see Gardner 2018). Many had since migrated into the anti-war movement (see Michel 2004). Here, it is also notable that Jim Roebuck, the Black Student Council president, was intimately involved in the negotiations between students, administrators and state politicians. It seems likely his presence helped ensure that increasing student and faculty diversity was included in student demands. Indeed, the list of demands he presented on behalf of students—narrowly ratified by the Student Council— included increasing the Black student population to 20%, which would have mirrored the Black population in Virginia at that time (see Gates 2018). Also notable—and unlike other Virginia yearbooks during this period—is that there are pictures of Black protesters on campus who appear to have prominent roles in the student movement and student government.

Both the W&L and UVA strikes began as anti-war movements, but once students decided to shut down their respective campuses, debate inevitably shifted to negotiating the appropriate roles that students should have in campus governance. For example, should they have a say in curriculum discussions? Should they have a greater role in disciplinary proceedings? Here, the presence of Black activists on campus at UVA—combined with Jim Roebuck as the Student Council president—caused issues associated with diversity on campus to be part of the discussions. This contrasts markedly, for example, with the list of demands—ultimately modest in nature—that the W&L students pressed for during their strike (see *The Calyx* 1970, 4–5; 1971, 11).

By way of contrast, the Washington and Lee movement took place among an almost entirely White student body with apparently no prominent Black activists on campus.[4] The students shared some concerns about curriculum—among their demands was that the programs of study at W&L be updated—but modernizing the curriculum (from these students' perspective) did not include creating a Black Studies program. Here, increasing student freedom at W&L tended to be concerned with loosening the rules at the dorms and also being allowed to bring a car to campus. Practically, at least as indicated by yearbook content, at W&L there were no demands associated with increasing either student or faculty diversity on campus. Probably, unlike the UVA campus, there were simply not enough students of color on campus in a position to articulate this demand.

Figures 5.11 and 5.12 show yearbook pictures from the *Corks and Curls* (1970, 10) that chronicles the student strike that year and indicate a greater

The young men of this land are not, as they are often called, a "lost" race — they are a race that never yet has been discovered. And the whole secret, power, and knowledge of their own discovery is locked within them — they know it, feel it, have the whole thing in them — and they cannot utter it.

Thomas Wolfe

10

FIGURE 5.11 Anti–Vietnam War student activism on the UVA campus in May 1970. The protests were primarily associated with the anti-war movement, but the UVA student demands, unlike other Virginia campus movements, included increasing the diversity of the students and faculty on campus (*Corks & Curls* 1970, 10).

Injustice anywhere is a threat to justice everywhere.
Martin Luther King Jr.

13

FIGURE 5.12 Scenes from the UVA student strike in May 1970. Predominantly an anti-war strike, the UVA movement did press issues associated with increasing campus diversity in a series of formal demands delivered by the Student Council to the UVA administration (*Corks & Curls* 1970, 13).

level of diversity among the activists on the UVA campus as compared to others in Virginia.

In the aftermath of these strikes, it is notable how self-satisfied the W&L yearbook editors were in comparison to those at UVA. Here, the UVA editors tend to be looking forward to the work that needs to be done, although a year later the yearbook editors (*Corks and Curls*, 1971) also indicate that students on campus were no longer as committed as in the past. By way of contrast, *The Calyx* editors felt they had accomplished much—but the changes the administration agreed to seem, in the modern context, remarkably modest. As the president of W&L summarized in *The Calyx* (1971, 11):

> In the social sphere, the past year has seen significant departures from the concept of *in loco parentis* that has prevailed for so long on this campus. The liberalized dormitory and fraternity regulations and the removal of the last restrictions on student ownership and control of automobiles indicate an increasing regard for student maturity, as well as greater reliance on individual student responsibility for his actions outside the classroom. (*The Calyx* 1971, 11)

One theme the yearbook editors of *The Calyx* (1971) repeatedly return to is that these protests were not violent but driven by "REASON" (sometimes "reason" appears in capitals). Specifically: "The University was reborn. Unlike the 'awakenings' at many other campuses. W. and L.'s was reached through reason, not anger and hate" (4–5). Here, being reborn or awakened at W&L did not necessitate any attempt to think about, or reconcile, a problematic campus history as associated with race relations. Indeed, much of the May movement at W&L was recast to fit the traditionalism of the campus culture—it was not considered a break with the past. It was not, as compared to UVA, considered as a dramatic shift from the "Old U" to the "New U."

The modest progress on improving race relations on Virginia campuses (1970 to present)

Following the period of student activism in the early 1970s it became increasingly normative, in fits and starts, for administrators, faculty and students—particularly at public institutions in Virginia—to argue that increasing campus diversity through affirmative action was important. Further, they argued that non-discrimination—first based on race but increasingly also encompassing gender, sexuality, military service, disability and so on—should be a hallmark of university life. Importantly, during this period all the Virginia university yearbooks studied indicate an increase in the number of Black students on Virginia campuses. Soon after, the first Black fraternities and sororities were established (see Figure 5.13). Black student unions became more common.

The post-1970 yearbooks also indicate a steady increase in campus dialogue associated with race relations, often in direct response to ongoing acts of racism at these universities. Here, even the Whitest colleges—and some of the Virginia colleges, at this writing, remain very White in terms of their demographic makeup—established administrative offices and student campus groups where there was a recognition of diversity on campus. Usually, implicit within

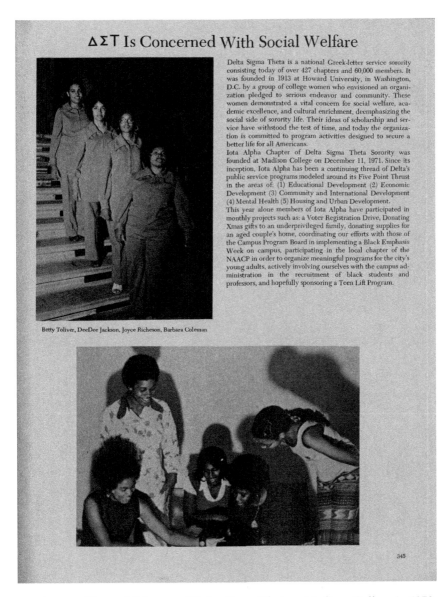

ΔΣΤ Is Concerned With Social Welfare

Delta Sigma Theta is a national Greek-letter service sorority consisting today of over 427 chapters and 60,000 members. It was founded in 1913 at Howard University, in Washington, D.C. by a group of college women who envisioned an organization pledged to serious endeavor and community. These women demonstrated a vital concern for social welfare, academic excellence, and cultural enrichment, deemphasizing the social side of sorority life. Their ideas of scholarship and service have withstood the test of time, and today the organization is committed to program activities designed to secure a better life for all Americans.

Iota Alpha Chapter of Delta Sigma Theta Sorority was founded at Madison College on December 11, 1971. Since its inception, Iota Alpha has been a continuing thread of Delta's public service programs modeled around its Five Point Thrust in the areas of: (1) Educational Development (2) Economic Development (3) Community and International Development (4) Mental Health (5) Housing and Urban Development.

This year alone members of Iota Alpha have participated in monthly projects such as: a Voter Registration Drive, Donating Xmas gifts to an underprivileged family, donating supplies for an aged couple's home, coordinating our efforts with those of the Campus Program Board in implementing a Black Emphasis Week on campus, participating in the local chapter of the NAACP in order to organize meaningful programs for the city's young adults, actively involving ourselves with the campus administration in the recruitment of black students and professors, and hopefully sponsoring a Teen Lift Program.

Betty Toliver, DeeDee Jackson, Joyce Richeson, Barbara Coleman

FIGURE 5.13   The establishment of Delta Sigma Theta at Madison College in 1972, probably the first Black sorority on this campus. The sorority was first established at Howard University in 1913 (*The Bluestone* 1973, 345).

the logics of these offices and organizations is the idea that diversity should be celebrated and increased at the institution (see "Office of Access and Inclusion" JMU).

At the same time, during this period it is still common to find progressive institutional imagery—even tentative reckonings with the dark history of race

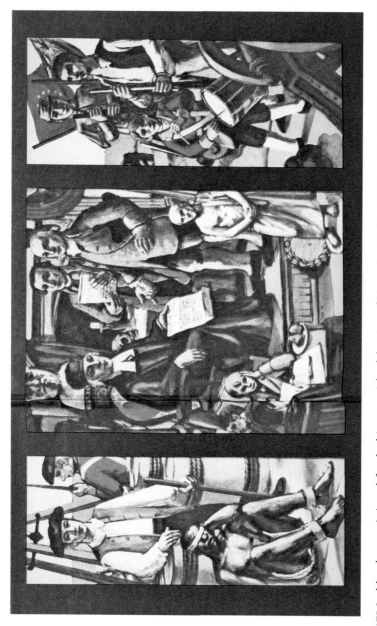

COLOR PLATE 8 Mural commissioned for the bicentennial celebration of Hampden-Sydney College, founded the same year as the American Declaration of Independence. It depicts events associated with the founding of the United States—but it also includes, in the first panel, a picture of men engaging in the slave trade (*Kaleidoscope*, 1975, inside cover).

prejudice that existed on these campuses—being presented alongside cultural tropes and symbolism that link these institutions to a problematic Southern racial history. While the previous whipsaw effect—one where the yearbook content simultaneously presents progressive racial imagery along with negative racial tropes—is hard to capture when presenting just a few pictures and content, one good example concerns the 1975 Hampden-Sydney *Kaleidoscope*. In the previous chapter a forthright essay in this yearbook by Vinston Goldman (1975) discussed the problematic aspects of being Black at Hampden-Sydney, but the same edition included a Kappa Alpha photograph in which the members are represented as members of the Ku Klux Klan (see chapter 4).

Notably, in this same yearbook, it documents the bicentennial anniversary of Hampden-Sydney College. Because the college was founded at the same period as the Revolutionary War, its institutional history, beginning with the college name, has long been associated with American independence. Not surprisingly, the yearbook content that year offers accounts of Hampden-Sydney's institutional history. Most prominently, on the inside cover of the yearbook is a picture of a mural, painted by Morton Sacks, that was commissioned for the anniversary year (see *Kaleidoscope* 1975, 282–283). A picture of this mural is presented in Color Plate 8. It represents standard tropes associated with the founding of the United States—the Constitutional Convention is portrayed, for example—but also includes, in the first panel of the triptych, a picture of men engaging in the slave trade (*Kaleidoscope*, 1975, inside cover). The modest representation of this history—at the time rarely identified with the official founding histories of the Virginia colleges—most definitely stands out as exceptional during this period.

Another notable aspect about the yearbook content that year is that the editor, Pat Manson (1975), appears more liberal minded than his predecessors. For example, he penned an essay (likely autobiographical) where he comments on seminal events of the past decade associated with civil rights activism. He may have assumed these events were at the forefront of past Hampden-Sydney yearbooks—but practically, this appears to be the first time most of these events are directly referenced in an institutional yearbook. Basically, he states that the graduating Hampden-Sydney students watched the progressive movement of the 1960s with admiration before arriving at college, but then largely reverted to "normal" (returned to conservatism) during their four-year stay at the college. Here, his chronicle of progress that graduating seniors experienced includes this observation:

> "When you were in seventh grade ... there was a March in Selma."... "When you were in ninth grade, Martin Luther King Jr. and Robert Kennedy were slain."... "When you were in the eleventh grade ... college and university students from coast to coast rioted, boycotted classes, occupied administration offices, and in general, raised hell in protest.... It was known as the Movement, or even worse, the Revolution, and a lot more

of you then will now admit were impressed, possibly sympathetic, even influenced, or, Heaven help us, in favor of this phenomenon."

Following this opening, he then describes how, in 1972 (the year after the graduating class arrived on campus) most students decided to vote for Nixon because he: "promised nothing weird, or untested like tax reform, minimum income, or pot decriminalization." Finally, the return to normalcy becomes complete when Henry Howell—a firebrand and populist liberal in the Virginia state legislature—apparently received a less than favorable welcome when he visited the college (Manson 1975, 74–77).

While the previous is a stylized account of how apathy often follows activism, it does capture the zigzag nature as it relates to establishing more inclusivity on campus following the 1970s activism. With the previous in mind, how much has Hampden-Sydney—among the most conservative colleges in this study—changed in terms of its racial composition in the 50 years following the activism chronicled in this text? As noted previously, the campus was not integrated until 1968. And judging from the yearbooks, there was probably only one Black professor shortly after this period for much of the 1970s. So, practically, it would have been nearly impossible not to have improved Black representation on campus somewhat in the intervening 50 years. Here, there are indications concerning the stutter-step nature of racial progress on campus. For example, one high-water mark might be when, in 2009, the school hired Christopher B. Howard as the first Black president (Kapsidelis 2009). At the same time, the racial and ethnic composition of Hampden-Sydney College in 2020 was 85.6% White, 4.9% Black, 3.8% Hispanic and 0.7% Asian ("Demographics and Retention" Hampden-Sydney). The small town of Farmville, Virginia, a few miles from campus, was a center of Black protest in 1963 against the Virginia program of massive resistance to school desegregation and is about 27% Black. The surrounding county is 32% Black ("Quick Facts" US Census).

Notably, it would be hard to intuit the Whiteness of the Hampden-Sydney student body if one simply glanced at the college's institutional website. At this writing (August 30, 2020) the front page of this website prominently features nine Hampden-Sydney students—three are Black. To be clear, Hampden-Sydney is far from the only college in Virginia that engages in this kind of sleight-of-hand concerning its front-stage presentation of the racial demographics on its campus. And perhaps the previous represents a convoluted manner of progress insofar as Black students—even when they are few in number—are now so often prominently displayed on college materials. Maybe these websites represent an institutional aspiration—a future-looking statement that widespread diversity on campus may be possible. But practically, even the most generous assessment of racial progress at Hampden-Sydney College—in terms of racial diversity on its campus—is that there have been remarkably modest accomplishments over the past 50 years. Probably the magical thinking concerning campus diversity represented on the institution's website (in the absence of real policies for minority recruitment) is unlikely to help ameliorate this problem in the future.

The few Virginia schools that largely reflect the demographic character of the state—or the region where the college is located—are public universities that have made long-standing administrative efforts to attract a diverse student body. Here, for example, Old Dominion University (ODU)—located in Hampton Roads (the Tidewater region of the state)—in its student demographics tends to reflect the community it serves. Usually, the White student population is a little below 50% of the total and the Black population around 27%–30%, close to the Black population in the region. The Hispanic population is around 8%, and the Asian population close to 5%, both also close to the regional population. In comparison to the state, the Black student population is actually over-represented at ODU (Black Virginians have represented around 19%–20% of Virginia residents for the past 50 years) and the White population under-represented (about 55% of Virginians are non-Hispanic White). The school ranks very high on measures of social mobility too (see Chetty et al. 2017; "Center for Social Mobility" ODU).

Importantly, the demographic changes over time at ODU have been considerable. For example, in a 1979 article about the desegregation process at ODU, the researchers indicated they had to over-sample the Black student population because it was only 6% of the total (Rosenthal 1979). At times, the yearbook content during this period does indicate bumps in the road in terms of campus racial conflict occurring during this transition. For example, in 1989—when the ODU student population was apparently about 10% Black—as shown in Figure 5.14, *The Laureate* yearbook indicates there was a panel discussion among faculty and students concerning racial discrimination on campus (Shiner 1989, 36–37). Here, it was noted that the audience was largely Black—disappointing because the panel members regarded this as outreach directed toward the White community at ODU. But the experience was still judged a "productive way to allow students to voice their views" (Shiner 1989, 36–37).

Over time, many students at Virginia schools—even when these schools remain predominantly White—appeared increasingly willing to engage in pro-active discussions concerning race relations on these campuses. Unfortunately, the yearbook content also indicates that these community discussions are often associated with confronting racism that was actively occurring at these schools and in the wider community. Importantly, incidences of racism on these campuses continue to the present day (see Murphy and Welch 2020).

Sometimes yearbooks during this period indicate that students mobilized to confront racism in the wider community. For example, over the course of two years a diverse group of students from James Madison University (JMU)—a school with an extraordinarily low Black student enrollment for a public university in Virginia—actively confronted a local chapter of the Ku Klux Klan that periodically marched, from 1987 to 1990, in nearby Staunton, Virginia (see Fritz 2017). Here, Staunton is actually about 30 miles away from the JMU

DISCRIMINATION?
Black And White Examines Grays

Racial Tension. Does it exist at ODU? How may we further examine the issue? Possibly by creating a comfortable learning/sharing situation where students may express their feelings on the subject. Hmmm . . . so midway through first semester a meeting led by a panel of four students, all male, two white, two black, with a black moderator was held in the Midrise "Pit." Sounds discriminatory just by the make-up of the panel. Having neither women nor international students represented should raise a few eyebrows.

Student Body President, Doug Tudor; Commentary Editor of *The Mace and Crown*, Robert Lewis; Past President of the Black Greek Council, now called National Panhellenic, Kevin McNeill; and Midrise Resident Advisor Joe Pauldine were our panel members led by moderator Jason Duley, who is a former National Panhellenic president. Faculty members were present and did partici-

pate in the discussion a great deal, but the focus was on students. The audience was composed of approximately 130 persons. Ten percent of ODU's student population is black, but the audience consisted of only 20 whites, which was discouraging according to Jason Carter who added, "It's the whites we were really trying to reach."

The meeting was a positive experience and some thought-provoking parallels were drawn. How does it feel to be a black student at ODU? How would it feel to be a white student at Norfolk State University? Of the Communications majors I spoke with, all found the classes they take at Norfolk State are a really neat learning experience.

Although some changes would be made before another panel convened with increased publicity and a more diverse selection of panel members, this was a productive way to allow students to voice their views and continue reaching students.

Heidi Shiner

Stephanie Snowden listens intently as her question is answered. (C. Thomas)

36   STUDENT LIFE

FIGURE 5.14 Panel discussion concerning campus race relations at ODU in 1989 (*The Laureate* 1989, 36–37). As some campuses increased Black enrollment, there is evidence in many yearbooks that seminars, talks and panel discussions concerning campus race relations increased. This panel session occurred when Black enrollment at the college was about 10% of the student population.

It's as simple as

◀ BLACK & WHITE ▶

or is it?

Let's discuss blacks and whites on campus! MONDAY NITE 7:30

Standing Room Only! Crowds of students completely filled the Midrise "Pit." (C. Thomas)

Student Body President Doug Tudor measures every word as Kevin McNeal looks on. (C. Thomas)

mesmerized crowd watches the Black and White scussion with thoughtful reserve. (C. Thomas)

BLACK/WHITE TALK   37

FIGURE 5.14   *(Continued)*

campus in Harrisonburg, but students traveled to the community to participate in anti-Klan demonstrations. Figure 5.15 is a picture of the students as they appeared in *The Bluestone* (1989, 362). It appears another group also protested the following year—that group appears larger, with perhaps as many as 20 students (*The Bluestone* 1990, 89).

FIGURE 5.15 Students of James Madison University protesting against a local Ku Klux Klan chapter (*The Bluestone* 1989, 362). There were often periods when students appear to be more actively confronting racism at their college and also in the wider community. For at least two years, in 1989 and 1990, JMU students traveled to nearby Staunton, Virginia—about 30 miles from campus—to protest against the Ku Klux Klan chapter that marched in the downtown.

Notwithstanding the indications of racial progress represented in these student yearbooks, increasing Black student and faculty representation on many Virginia campuses has been problematic. For example, the previous picture associated with positive race activism took place at James Madison University, but at this writing about 5% of the undergraduate student population at JMU is Black, among the lowest rate for a public university in Virginia ("Institutional Research" JMU). While the Shenandoah Valley does not have a large Black population (about 7.5% in the Harrisonburg community), the rate of Black enrollment is still low, given that the university has oriented itself toward providing educational opportunities to Virginia residents statewide. Here, while there has been a rhetorical acceptance of diversity and now increasingly inclusivity—combined with the establishment of student clubs and administrative offices directly associated with increasing diversity on campus (see "The Office for Inclusion" JMU)—to date neither has translated into significant changes in Black representation at James Madison University over time. And JMU is not the only Virginia institution where Black representation on campus is low. Virginia Tech, located in a similarly rural region of the state—but considered the flagship university, as it concerns science and engineering studies—has a similar rate of Black enrollment (between 4% and 5%) ("Fact Book" VPI). George Mason University, the largest public university in Virginia, looks inclusive concerning many ethnic groups represented in Virginia, but its Black student population is low compared to the state representation, usually around 11% ("Diversity" GMU).

Other state universities in this study, like Virginia Commonwealth (VCU), do look more like Virginia in terms of Black representation—over 18% of the VCU student population is Black, which is close to Black representation in the state ("Fact Card" VCU). And while VCU looks inclusive compared to the other Research I universities in the state, the number of Black students appears low, given that the city of Richmond, Virginia—where VCU is located—is a community where approximately 50% of residents are Black. Notably, while VCU is among the best Virginia colleges in terms of student diversity, the administration also appears to be pro-actively initiating policy designed to recruit a diverse faculty (Nasim 2020).

And how about what many consider the flagship university in the state, the University of Virginia? What does its campus look like in 2020? As noted previously, this was a place where there was significant student activism associated with issues of diversity in 1970. At that time, one student demand was that 20% of the future UVA student population should be Black—roughly proportional to the representation of Black Virginians in the state. Currently, UVA enrolls a Black student population that is close to 7% of the total student population ("Diversity Dashboard" UVA)—well short of the 20% goal articulated 50 years ago.

Not surprising is that the elite private schools in this study are—on average— even less diverse than most state universities. Here, for example, Washington and Lee currently has a Black student population that over the past few years has been between 2% and 3% of the undergraduate student body ("Facts and Stats" W&L). With respect to the representation of other ethnic and racial groups, W&L and Hampden-Sydney College are among the least inclusive (or the most White) of all the schools included in this study, with over 80% of the student population non-Hispanic White. Somewhat better, the University of Richmond (UR)—located near a city that is over 50% Black—has a Black student population of 7%. It has relatively high levels of Latinx (9%) and Asian (8%) students, with 58% White ("Student Diversity," UR).

Finally, among the schools chronicled in this study the Virginia Military Institute has been the institution most recently in the news concerning ongoing race relations on campus. The Black student body on campus is currently around 7%–8%. The school has—as chronicled in this study—maintained a close association with "Lost Cause" mythology in general, and the adulation of Thomas "Stonewall" Jackson in particular. As this text was being completed (in late October 2020) the *Washington Post* published a series of articles that documented routine incidences of racism on the VMI campus (see Shapira 2020a; 2020b; 2020c; 2020d; 2020e). Perhaps most disturbing was an account of a classroom discussion, led by an adjunct professor of business, E. Susan Kellogg, that was ostensibly supposed to demonstrate the changes that had taken place over her own life-course. Here, the professor described her own father's partic-ipation in the KKK.[5] Among the accounts chronicled by a Black student in the class and later confirmed by the *Washington Post* were that Kellogg stated, "KKK parties were the best parties ever, they had candy, clowns, games, and meetings were held there." Further, she said that "she and her high school friends in Ohio drove around their all-White neighborhood 'looking for people who didn't belong'—racial minorities—in order to 'bop' them on the head." Finally, she claimed that when she was young, "I didn't know if they bathed, what clothes they wore, how they ate, what they ate, if they could read, study, or even had the ability to learn" (Shapira 2020a). Following this discussion, Keniya Lee, a Black woman in the class who graduated from VMI in 2019, wrote a memo out-lining this content and asked her classmates to confirm the account to admin-istrators. None agreed—so she reported the teacher herself. Eventually Kellog was asked to apologize to Lee (see Shapira 2020a).

Just as problematic is that following these accounts, much of the outrage felt among both current VMI students and alumni was related to the fact that Governor Northam—a VMI graduate—had the audacity to commission a state-wide investigation into allegations and patterns of racism at VMI. Moreover, ver-bal attacks against current Black students—charged as being responsible for the new oversight—increased on social media in the aftermath of this reporting (see Shapira 2020b). During this time I encountered one VMI alumnus who attended the school while the first Black cadets were in attendance in the early 1970s; he became increasingly despondent (and later angry) as he discovered that a com-mon refrain among his classmates on social media was that Virginia Governor Northam should lose his VMI diploma because he called for the state inves-tigation. At the most extreme, some alumni indicated—at least rhetorically—that they believe Northam should be "dragged from the governor's mansion and shot" ("Conversation" 2020). Still, a more positive sign is that Cedric T. Wins—a Black retired major general and 1985 VMI graduate—was later named as the interim superintendent of the school on November 12, 2020. Soon after, as a result of a state government investigation, a number of symbolic changes—most notably the removal of a prominent statue of Stonewall Jackson—began to take place on campus.

To be clear, the reason why Virginia Military Institute appeared last in this summary is not because the events described previously are particularly out of the ordinary, but rather because they are the most recent to be reported in the media as this text was being prepared for publication. Of course, VMI has always been among those Virginia colleges—along with neighboring Washington and Lee—most closely associated with Lost Cause mythology. Indeed, myths associated with the US Civil War were literally observable in the day-to-day culture of the institution. But most of the Virginia campuses in this study have, during recent times, had reports of incidences of racial discrimination. And just as important—as indicated by the institutional demo-graphics concerning the student and faculty populations at these schools—most

Virginia colleges in this study clearly continue to reinforce long-established patterns of White privilege.

Conclusion

For much of the civil rights period examined in this chapter, the Virginia colleges in this study were active sites of resistance to racial integration. Sometimes they were literally the campuses on which the desegregation battle was fought. Many only grudgingly began to desegregate during the 1960s. At that time, the campus climate for the very few Black students who entered these colleges was extraordinarily inhospitable. And notwithstanding the modest changes on these campuses in the 1950s and 1960s—precipitated by the activism of the NAACP in the courts—none of these schools significantly increased the enrollment of Black undergraduate students during this period. Mostly, these schools acquiesced to an ongoing program of massive resistance to school integration pursued by the state of Virginia. It was not until the 1968–69 academic year that all the Virginia schools in this study had admitted at least one Black undergraduate student. By way of comparison, Howard University students were activists in the civil rights movement—affecting significant changes not only on the Howard campus but throughout the entire United States.

The most significant period of student activism on Virginia campuses were the May 1970 protests against the Vietnam War. While these protests mostly concerned anti-war activism, some included demands for an increase in student freedom on campus and greater input on campus-wide policies. In a few cases, this included formal demands for an increase in the recruitment of Black students and faculty. At the same time there were also campuses with significant anti-war movements in which increasing racial equity was never associated with this activism.

Generally, following the previous period of activism, the Virginia yearbooks do indicate modest advancements concerning race relations on campus. Black student organizations were established as Black enrollment modestly increased. Administrative offices associated with affirmative action, and later inclusivity, became normative at all the colleges examined in this study. The yearbook content indicates that there was at times on these campuses widespread dialogue concerning racial discrimination—often undertaken in response to events taking place on campus or in the wider community. But notwithstanding the increase in pro-social racial imagery within these school yearbooks, at many of these schools there was a continued association with past narrative tropes that reinforced "Southern-ness" and, in some cases, continued the memorialization of specific Civil War figures.

In terms of changes with respect to Black student and faculty representation on these campuses during the past 50 years, most of these Virginias schools—with a few important exceptions—have at best made only modest progress. Notably, this stands in direct contrast to much of the messaging that these schools have adopted as related to campus diversity and inclusivity. Here, it seems, a rhetorical acceptance of diversity—associated with more pro-social imagery in yearbooks—does not ensure that meaningful change always follows. The previous is important because during the 2020 Black Lives Matter protests there was clearly an increase in student activism on Virginia campuses as concerns Black representation on campus. Here, a number of schools—certainly not all—have also recently undertaken largely symbolic changes on campus associated with greater inclusivity. For example, James Madison University recently renamed three buildings after black community and campus leaders that were previously named after Confederate generals associated with Lost Cause memorialization ("JMU Board" *JMU News*).

Obviously, this study did not examine the 2021 yearbooks—but I expect the Black Lives Matter movement will, to varying degrees, make an appearance in this yearbook content. Perhaps, years from now, some intrepid social scientist might wade through these yearbooks and, inevitably, come to the conclusion that 2020 was clearly different than other years in establishing better race relations on these Virginia campuses. But a question with respect to the future is the degree to which these largely symbolic policy changes and events—some clearly important in terms of reconciling the largely idealized history of these institutions with past acts of racism—is actually followed by real policy changes in terms of recruiting Black students and faculty to these campuses. Previously, the outcomes since the May 1970 protests—50 years later—are somewhat mixed. Here, there are a few Virginia colleges that look more like the state in terms of Black student enrollment and are working toward having a similarly diverse faculty. But the cautionary tale is that most, on balance, have largely failed to significantly increase Black representation on campus over the past 50 years.

Notes

1 In 1966, the Virginia state government ended the subsidy that allowed students to attend private Whites-only schools. In 1968, the US Supreme Court declared other massive resistance strategies as illegal in *Green v. County School Board of New Kent County.*

2 A headcount of Southern White activists directly associated with the Freedom Summer campaign organized through the Southern Student Organizing Committee (SSOC) is estimated by Gregg Michel at around 19 students. See Gregg Michel, *Struggle for a Better South: The Southern Student Organizing Committee, 1964–1969.* (New York: Springer, 2004). Probably a few more Southerners joined the larger group of activists who gathered in Ohio before the campaign, but the McAdam (1986) study "Recruitment to High-Risk Activism" indicates those from Southern schools were very few in number.

3 While not represented in the yearbook, Michel Gregg, *Struggle for the South*, details a few modest campaigns undertaken at UVA by the SSOC. Beginning in 1966 there also appears to be some student activism associated with a few alternative newsletters that were mostly focused on the anti-war movement but also addressed issues associated with the civil rights movement. See *The Virginia Patriot*, October 3, 1966 (Charlottesville, VA: Patrick Henry Society, University of Virginia), available in the "Social Movements Collection," Special Collections Department, UVA Libraries.

4 This is judging from the W&L yearbook content, where the very few Black students on campus do not appear to have been central to the protest effort.
5 Kellogg's sister stated that their father was not a member of the KKK and also that her sister was a habitual liar.

References

"A Life, a Legacy: Honoring Martin Luther King Jr." 2011. *Virginia Magazine,* Spring. https://uvamagazine.org/articles/a_life_a_legacy.

Azore, Kyra, and Justin Cohon. 2018. "50 Years Later: The Demonstration That Changed Howard and the Legacy It Left." *The Hilltop*, March 31. https://thehilltoponline.com/2018/03/31/50-years-later-the-demonstration-that-changed-howard-and-the-legacy-it-left/.

The Bison.1923–2012. Howard University Library Yearbook Digital Archive. https://dh.howard.edu/bison_yearbooks/index.4.html.

The Bluestone. 1962–2015. James Madison University Yearbook Digital Archive. https://commons.lib.jmu.edu/allyearbooks/index.html.

Brown, Flora Bryant. 2000. "NAACP Sponsored Sit-ins by Howard University Students in Washington, DC, 1943–1944." *Journal of Negro History* 85 (4): 274–286.

The Bugle. 1895–2020. Virginia Tech Library Digital Yearbook Archive. https://vtechworks.lib.vt.edu/handle/10919/11349.

Carmichael, Stokely. 1971. "*Stokely Speaks: Black Power to Pan-Africanism.*" New York: Random House, Vintage Books.

The Calyx. 1895–2019. Washington and Lee Library Digital Yearbook Archive. https://dspace.wlu.edu/handle/11021/26929.

"Center for Social Mobility." Old Dominion University. https://www.odu.edu/sees/social-mobility

Chaney, Ben. 2000. "Schwerner, Chaney, and Goodman: The Struggle for Justice." *Human Rights* 27: 3–7.

Chetty, Raj, John N. Friedman, Emmanuel Saez, Nicholas Turner and Danny Yagan. 2017. "Mobility Report Cards: The Role of Colleges in Intergenerational Mobility." National Bureau of Economic Research Working Paper No. 23618, July 2017.

Colonial Echo 1969. William and Mary Library Digital Archive. https://digitalarchive.wm.edu/.

"Conversation with VMI Alumni." 2020. Private conversation Oct. 29, 2020. Note: this was reconstructed from memory; the conversation was not recorded or transcribed.

Corks and Curls. 1888–2018. University of Virginia Library Digital Yearbook Archive. https://v3.lib.virginia.edu/catalog/u126747.

Daniels, Jonathan Myrick. 1992. *American Martyr: The Johnathan Daniels Story.* Atlanta, GA: Morehouse Publishing Company.

"Demographics and Retention." Hampden Sydney College website. http://www.hsc.edu/institutional-effectiveness/demographics-and-retention.

"Diversity Dashboard." University of Virginia. https://diversitydata.virginia.edu/Home/Details/Undergraduate%20Students.

"Fact Book: Student Overview." Virginia Tech. "Fact Book: Student Overview." https://vt.edu/about/facts-about-virginia-tech/factbook/student-overview.html.

"Fact Card." Virginia Commonwealth University. https://irds.vcu.edu/media/decision-support/pdf/fact-cards/FinalADAweb2-10-21.pdf

"Facts and Stats: Enrollment Reports." Washington and Lee University. https://my.wlu.edu/strategic-analysis-and-institutional-research/facts-and-stats.

Frazier, E. Franklin. 1997. *Black Bourgeoisie: The Book That Brought the Shock of Self-Revelation to Middle-Class Blacks in America.* New York: Free Press.

Fritz, David. 2017. "KKK Has Long History of Local Appearances." *Staunton News Leader,* July 11. https://www.newsleader.com/story/news/local/2017/07/11/kkk-marched-area-1987/468567001/.

Gardner, Tom. 2018. *From Rebel Yell to Revolution: My Four Years at UVA, 1966–70.* Richmond, VA: Brandylane Publishers.

Gates, Ernie. 2018. "Antiwar Stories—May Days, 1970: The Week That Would Change UVA Forever." *Virginia Magazine,* March. https://uvamagazine.org/articles/antiwar_stories.

George Mason University. "Diversity." https://diversity.gmu.edu/ diversity.

Goldman, Vincent. 1975. "On Being Black at Hampden-Sydney." *Kaleidoscope,* 70–71.

Hampden Sydney College website. http://www.hsc.edu/. Accessed on August 30, 2020.

Hardin, Daniel. 2015. "Contradictions in the Cause: Glen Echo, Maryland, 1960," *The Spark* Blog Post. https://washingtonareaspark.com/2015/06/26/contradictions-in-the-cause-glen-echo-maryland-1960/.

"Here Am I, Send Me: The Story of Johnathan Daniels." *PBS Documentary,* January 16, 2020. https://www.pbs.org/video/here-am-i-send-me-the-story-of-jonathan-daniels-bkneej/.

"Irving Linwood Peddrew III, First Black Student at VPI." Virginia Tech Special Collections and Archives. October 3, 2013. https://vtspecialcollections.wordpress.com/2013/10/03/irving-linwood-peddrew-iii-first-Black-student-at-vpi/.

"Institutional Research: Fact Book." University of Richmond. 2020. https://ifx.richmond.edu/research/fact-book.html

"Institutional Research: Fact Book, 2019-2020." 2020. James Madison University. https://www.jmu.edu/oir/oir-research/statsum/2019-20/2019-20toc.shtml#STUDENT.

"JMU Board of Visitors Approves Renaming Three Buildings Named for Confederate Leaders." *JMU News.* https://www.jmu.edu/news/2020/07/07-bov-approves-renaming.shtml.

"Jonathan M. Daniels: VMI Class of 1961." VMI website. https://www.vmi.edu/ media/content-assets/documents/communications-and-marketing/media-relations/VMI_Daniels_ Fact_Sheet_2019.pdf.

Kaleidoscope. 1907–2010. Hampden-Sydney College Yearbook Internet Archive. https://archive. org/search.php?query=collection%3Ahampdensydneycollege+AND+subject%3A%22College+yearbooks-Virginia-Hampden-Sydney%22&page=2.

Kapsidelis, Karin. 2009. "Hampden-Sydney College Adds Chapter to Its Long History." *Richmond Times-Dispatch,* July 19.

Kelley, Robin D.G. 1998. "House Negroes on the Loose: Malcolm X and the Black Bourgeoisie." *Callaloo* 21 (2): 419–435.

King Jr., Martin Luther. 1967. "Beyond Vietnam: A Time to Break Silence." Speech. Riverside Church, New York, April 4. Martin Luther King Jr. Research and Education Institute. Stanford University. https://kinginstitute.stanford.edu/king-papers/documents/beyond-vietnam.

The Laureate. 1988–2007. Old Dominion University Digital Yearbook Archives. https://digitalcommons.odu.edu/scua_yearbooks/index.html.

Manson, Pat. 1975. "To the Class of '75." *Kaleidoscope,* 74–77.

"May 1970 Student Antiwar Strikes." Mapping Social Movements Project. The University of Washington. https://depts.washington.edu/moves/antiwar_ may1970.shtml.

McAdam, Doug. 1986. "Recruitment to High-Risk Activism: The Case of Freedom Summer." *American Journal of Sociology* 92 (1): 64–90.

McKenzie, Bryan. 2013. "Civil Rights Leaders Reflect on Charlottesville Segregation 50 Years After King Speech," *Daily Progress*, August 24. https://daily progress.com/news/local/civil-rights-leaders-reflect-on-charlottesville-segregation-50-years-after-king-speech/article_ 6d420fa4-0d00-11e3-b22c-0019bb30f31a.html.

Michel, Gregg. 2004. *Struggle for a Better South: The Southern Student Organizing Committee, 1964–1969.* New York: Springer.

Morris, Aldon. 1981. "Black Southern Student Sit-in Movement: An Analysis of Internal Organization." *American Sociological Review* 46 (6): 744–767.

Murphy, Connor, and Carley Welch. 2020. "JMU Community Reacts to Defaced 'Black Lives Matter' Spirit Rock." *The Breeze*, August 22. https://www. breezejmu. org/news/jmu-community-reacts-to-defaced-Black-lives-matter-spirit-rock/article_6ebcbab8-e495-11ea-afda-cb4f792d1850.html.

Nasim, Aashir. 2020. "A Brief Report on the State of VCU's Black Faculty." Virginia Commonwealth University: Office of Institutional Equity, Effectiveness and Success. https://inclusive.vcu.edu/Black-facultyreport/ief.

"Office of Access and Inclusion." James Madison University. https://www. jmu.edu/diversity/.

Protest! Remaking Virginia Tech in the Era of Civil Rights and Vietnam. "Vietnam War," and "Occupying Williams Hall." Exhibition. Visualizing Virginia Tech History. https://vt150.omeka.net/exhibits/show/vtprotest/vietnam-war.

"Quick Facts: Farmville, Virginia." US Census. https://www.census.gov/quickfacts/fact/table/farmvilletownvirginia/AGE295219.

Rosenthal, Steven J. 1979. "Racism and Desegregation at Old Dominion University." *Integrated Education* 17 (1–2): 40–42.

Shapira, Ian. 2020a. "VMI Votes to Remove Stonewall Jackson Statue amid Racism Accusations by Black Cadets." *Washington Post,* October 29. LexisNexis Academic.

Shapira, Ian. 2020b. VMI Superintendent Resigns After Black Cadets Describe Relentless Racism." *Washington Post*, October 26. LexisNexis Academic.

Shapira, Ian. 2020c. "Northam Calls for VMI Investigation After Black Cadets Describe Relentless Racism." *Washington Post*, October 19. LexisNexis Academic.

Shapira, Ian. 2020d. "At VMI, Black Cadets Endure Lynching Threats, Klan Memories and Confederacy Veneration." *Washington Post*, October 17. LexisNexis Academic.

Shapira, Ian. 2020e. "VMI Cadets Attack Black Students, Women on Anonymous Chat App as Furor over Racism Grows." *Washington Post*, October 27. LexisNexis Academic.

Shiner, Heidi. 1989. "Discrimination?: Black and White Examines Grey." *The Laureate*, 36–37.

Sky Lark, Taj'ullah X. 2017. "Unlocking Doors: How Gregory Swanson Challenged the University of Virginia's Resistance to Desegregation. A Case Study." *Spectrum: A Journal on Black Men* 5 (2): 71–84.

"Student Diversity." University of Richmond. https://www.richmond.edu/about/consumer-info/diversity.html.

The Virginia Patriot. 1966. UVA Protest Newsletter. October 3. Charlottesville: Patrick Henry Society, University of Virginia. Available in the "Social Movements Collection," Special Collections Department, UVA Libraries.

6

CONCLUSION AND FUTURE QUESTIONS

The case for reparations

This study used institutional yearbook content—pictures and texts—to demonstrate that on Virginia campuses, during much of their histories, a hierarchy of races ordered all aspects of university life, including work, study and leisure. Importantly, these schools—acting as incubators, hubs, sieves and temples—were complicit in the construction and maintenance of this racial hierarchy. These schools not only maintained segregation on their campuses but also were places where destructive norms associated with race were created, reinforced and then widely disseminated. Here, elite Virginia schools, those with medical schools and law programs established before the Civil War, often had prominent faculty and alumni who advocated for the most pernicious statewide race polices. Few on Virginia campuses questioned institutionalized racial inequality, which was maintained until well after World War II.

Some tentative change began in the 1960s after Black Virginians successfully challenged the program of massive resistance to school desegregation implemented by the Virginia legislature following the 1954 *Brown v. Board of Education of Topeka* Supreme Court decision. Beginning in the late 1960s—and accelerating during the 1970s—some White students, faculty and administrators at these schools began to recognize the importance of increasing the number of Black students on campus. Black student organizations were established and Black enrollment modestly increased at many of these schools. Administrative offices associated with affirmative action, and later inclusivity, became normative at all the colleges examined in this study. But most of these Virginia schools—with a few important exceptions—have, at best, made only modest progress in terms of educating Black Virginians. Notably, this now stands in direct contrast to much of the messaging that these schools have recently adopted as relates to campus diversity and inclusivity.

DOI: 10.4324/9781003134480-6

Importantly, a rhetorical acceptance of diversity and inclusivity—associated with more pro-social imagery in yearbooks (and other campus publications)—does not ensure that meaningful change will follow as it relates to increasing Black students and faculty on Virginia campuses. Here, there are a few Virginia colleges that reflect state demographics in terms of Black student enrollment, but on balance most have largely failed to significantly increase Black representation on campus over the past 50 years. On many campuses, particularly those with a long-standing connection to Civil War memorialization such as the Virginia Military Institute, there is evidence that racial discrimination remains a part of the campus culture.

Recently, in 2020, many students on Virginia campuses engaged in social protests following the killing of George Floyd by a Minneapolis, Minnesota, police officer. Unfortunately, that event was preceded by other Black men and women being killed by police. They included Eric Garner, Tamir Rice, Jamar Clark, Philando Castile, Dreasjon "Sean" Reed, and Breonna Taylor. Here, the groundwork for widespread national protests was laid by a loose coalition of activists—connected through a decentralized Black Lives Matter movement—that brought increasing scrutiny to these events (Elgin 2020; Buchanan, Bui and Patel 2020). During the same period, video recordings of Black men and women being routinely harassed while engaging in innocuous activities—running, barbequing, birding in Central Park, New York—were also consistently being discovered and released (see Nir 2020).

Some campus protests were associated with policing, but most were focused on a wider public debate concerning institutional racism in all aspects of American life—including racism that still existed on these college campuses. In the state of Virginia, much of the protest activity became focused on the symbols of the confederacy that were largely constructed just after the turn of the century. Soon after these events, the mayor of Richmond, Virginia, Levar Stoney, removed all the confederate monuments that the city controlled (Vozzella and Schneider 2020; Ortiz 2020). Of note, Mayor Stoney is a graduate (class of 2004) of James Madison University (JMU), where he was also the first African American man elected president of the student government (DeSimone 2017). Currently, in the wake of this activism, there has been a rapid move, after years of debate, to remove confederate names from Virginia university buildings. For example, at JMU three buildings named after Confederates were renamed after black community and campus leaders (Kolinech 2021). By way of contrast, the Board of Visitors at Washington and Lee University recently refused to act on a faculty petition that supported removing "Lee" from the university's name (see Toscano 2017).

Whether symbolic changes on campuses will be followed by a sustained and long-term program designed to increase the recruitment of Black students and faculty is an open question.[1] Previously, it is clear, some of these institutions have engaged in well-meaning but somewhat incongruous efforts to reconcile the past wrongs done to the Black community by these institutions. Often, the outcome has resulted in an institution identifying an improbable Black figure—a freed Black man who managed to get a degree from the institution, a former enslaved servant (e.g. Paul Jennings) of a great man (e.g. James Madison) who later made good—and then name a new building on campus (dorms are popular) after this individual (see "JMU to Name" JMU). Another recent example was the re-naming of three buildings at JMU that memorialized confederate leaders. One was re-named for Sheary Darcus Johnson, the first black woman to attend JMU. Another, for two popular members of the faculty (Drs. Joanne V. and Alexander Gabbin). The last for a prominent black community activist, Doris Harper Allen, and a long serving black staff member, Robert Walker Lee (Kolinech 2021). At Virginia Tech, Hoge Hall was recently named after William and Janie Hoge who hosted the first Black students admitted to Virginia Tech—including Irving L. Peddrew (discussed in chapter 4)—when Black students were not allowed to be residents on campus. Barringer Hall at Virginia Tech, named after prominent eugenicist Paul Barringer—a faculty member at the University of Virginia and later a president of VPI—has also recently been renamed (see Gendreau 2020).

Another strategy undertaken by administrators at these universities—also well meaning—is to erect markers, monuments and memorials that describe and recognize the slaves who built and maintained these campuses (see "Memorial" UVA). The previous acts are all well and good—they are certainly meaningful acts too—but these gestures do very little to remedy the past injustice done to the Black community by these colleges. Clearly, that will require some form of compensation. And if the compensation approaches the level of harm these institutions did to the Black community, then we should expect, in the future, a program of redress—a redistribution of institutional wealth and opportunity directed toward Black citizens living in Virginia—to be implemented over a very long period time.

Importantly, calculating the damage done to the Black community—the first step in constructing a reasonable program of redress—is no longer an abstract idea among current scholars in the fields of sociology, political science and economics. Indeed, studies that calculate the "cost of being Black" are now well established in the academic literature of all these disciplines (see Falk and Rankin 1992 for an early example). Currently, the most interesting work being done in the field of economics concerns how social structure—sometimes including the cost of being Black—affects opportunities during someone's life-course (see Chetty et. al. 2020; 2011). Here, it is inevitable that enterprising academics will eventually calculate the amount of wealth that was appropriated from Black men and women by these institutions during much of their histories. Probably the most straightforward cases involve the descendants of former slaves whose ancestors labored at these institutions. In a few cases, such as at Georgetown University, compensation—usually in the form of scholarships—is being offered to the descendants of these men and women (Jones 2020). Indeed, the need for this sort of compensation is so clear that there is no moral position that argues otherwise.

But compensation for slavery is not a full accounting of the costs that Black men and women bore in maintaining these institutions. Rather, the fuller account would follow the framework outlined by Ta-Nehisi Coates (2014) regarding a case for reparations being made to the broader Black community in the United States. Here, Coates (2014) makes a convincing argument that the expropriation of Black wealth and labor continued long after slavery was abolished—the particular example he uses is the amount of wealth expropriated from Black men and women as associated with the policy of red-lining mortgages in Chicago. Importantly, as more scholars adopt a labor-based approach to calculating harm—one that calculates exactly the degrees to which of these institutions were built and maintained by discounted Black labor—the future questions associated with racism on campus will become remarkably straightforward. The first is simply: How much money did these institutions "make" (or "take") by expropriating the labor of Black men and women? Another: How much money did these institutions prevent the Black community from gaining by excluding them as students?

I regard the previous questions as among the most important that need to be explored in future studies in the field of higher education. In effect, what was the real cost of segregation in higher education? How much did these institutions contribute to the maintenance of segregation as an ideal? What programs of redress—and for how long—should these institutions undertake to make meaningful reparation to the Black community in Virginia?

To be clear, this study did not tackle these questions directly. Rather, it demonstrated using visual artifacts that these institutions were culpable—in terms of their day-to-day operations—in creating a system of racial hierarchy that ordered life on these campuses in the past. Moreover, the faculty, administrators and students at these schools were not particularly active in working to end racism on their campuses either. Importantly, to this day this past history continues to have effects on access to higher education, where Black representation on most Virginia campuses remains low. Here, while this study did not calculate the specific cost of being Black in Virginia—or the specific amount of money that these institutions made exploiting the labor of Black men and women—it did show, in human terms, what this past history looked like on campus. It gave an indication that appropriate redress to the Black community in Virginia is considerably more than the naming rights to a few buildings, or the placement of placards that retroactively recognizes Black labor on campus, or even the modest support extended to the direct descendants of the slaves that these institutions once owned. The debt is clearly much larger.

While all the institutions in this study are all, to some degrees, culpable with respect to the harm done to the Black community in Virginia in the past, some clearly did more harm than others. Moreover, if institutions do adopt a real plan for redress—if they adopt programs to make good on this debt—the amount owed will be considerable. For example, the benefits of cheap Black labor were realized over many lifetimes, so we should expect that paying this debt might take just as long. Not surprising, though, is that the institutions that probably expropriated the most wealth and labor in the past—where it can be argued, in good faith, that much of the institutional wealth was literally built on the backs of Black men and women—also appear to be those with the largest financial endowments.

What would such an academic inquiry look like? Here, two of the most prestigious schools in this study—the University of Virginia and Washington and Lee University—are good examples of institutions that were literally and metaphorically built with Black labor. Notably, these schools—and particularly UVA—have begun an accounting of how enslaved labor was used to build and maintain these early institutions. To date, scholars at UVA are further along in systematically investigating how discounted Black labor helped support the institution for much of its history. This is largely because a past UVA president, sociologist Theresa Sullivan, formed two presidential commissions to study UVA policy during the period of slavery and also during massive resistance to school desegregation ("Presidential Commission" UVA).

But what exactly should be included in the calculation of the debt to the Black community? Probably a true accounting of the Black contribution to maintaining these schools would have to tackle the nettlesome problem of how much tuition paid by the White elite—and also the endowments these universities received from Virginia planters and later from the new South industrialists who often attended these schools—was made possible by the labor of Black men and women. Here, Washington and Lee University (W&L) is an exemplary case—it drew much of its early financial support from this class of people—so I offer a few simple examples by way of a process for calculating the contribution that Black labor made with respect to building the institution.

One obvious place to start, given how much the event is discussed in the W&L institutional history, would be the gift of 100 shares of James River Canal stock that George Washington gave the Liberty Hall Academy, a gift often credited with saving the institution. Washington himself had actually received this stock as a gift from the Virginia state legislature a year previously. In W&L institutional lore the gift was so important that soon after the college was renamed Washington College to honor the former US president's largesse ("University History: Our Name" W&L). Practically, although it is not nearly as romantic a story, one might also make the argument that notwithstanding the financial importance of this gift—among the largest to date ever given to an institution of higher learning—this institutional renaming also presaged a canny strategy of W&L administrators "hitching their wagon" to the great men of the period. Here, the school undoubtedly benefited from its later association with Robert E. Lee following the Civil War too. But to the case in point, the clear-eyed question concerning this gift of stock, following Ta-Nehisi Coates's (2014) line of reasoning, is relatively straightforward: How much of Washington's fortune in general, and this gift in particular, was made possible by the labor of Black men and women?

The answer, I expect, is quite a bit. First, it appears that much of the canal was built with enslaved labor, particularly after nearly all Irish and German workers left the project in 1838 following an outbreak of disease that killed many of them (Robertson 1999). Indeed, it appears Virginia planters along the canal route also profited handsomely by leasing slaves to the canal company. Later, the company itself decided it was more profitable to purchase slaves and then sell them, ideally for a profit, once the work was completed (Robertson 1999). Peter Way (2009) quotes an unnamed official as stating: "The negroes being your own (or hired) you can command their service when you please—when your work is completed, if you have not further occasion for them, they can be sold for nearly as much, or probably more than they cost you" (as referenced in Robertson 1999).

As it turns out, W&L actually kept the canal stock, collecting an annual dividend from the state until 1927, when it was essentially forced to sell the stock back to the state of Virginia for $50,000. The school quickly reinvested this money, and the W&L institutional website states: "It remains part of the institution's endowment to this day, contributing to the University's operating budget" ("Our History" W&L).

Importantly, like most of the large-scale agricultural and industrial enterprises in the South at that time, cheap Black labor largely underpinned the value of the James River Canal stock. Moreover, Black labor was certainly responsible for Washington's wealth generally—it can be argued that this fact allowed him to make this generous gift to the college. So here, the first step in any historic accounting of the Black financial contribution to the maintenance of W&L would be to recognize that much of this gift—and many, many others—was made possible not by the industry and thrift of the Southern White planter class but far more so by the sweat and toil of thousands of Black bodies laboring over many, many years. Of course, fortunes were also built on the backs of Black men and women after the Civil War—this is actually Coates's (2014) primary argument—whether it was because Black men and women had to sell their labor at a discount or because they had to purchase services (e.g. a mortgage) at a premium. Here, without doubt, all the colleges in this study took advantage of the fact that Black labor was cheap—that is clearly one reason why so many Black men and women were employed at these schools.

Currently, it remains to be seen whether there will be a full institutional accounting of the harm done to the Black community by these schools. Further, if following such an inquiry, whether these institutions might institute a program of redress that is designed to help "make whole" the Black community in Virginia, which clearly continues to suffer the consequences from this past period of institutional racism. If the past actually does presage the future, then this study is probably an indication that many of these schools—far from being in front of this process—are just as likely to be among those that actively resist any attempt to institutionalize a program that offers redress to the Black community in Virginia. But change is possible, perhaps currently more possible on university campuses than at other institutions, so perhaps, in the future, more of these institutions will "look like Virginia" in the racial and ethnic composition of students and faculty on campus.

Note

1 I am most familiar with policy at James Madison University, where I was a student in the 1980s, adjunct faculty in the 1990s, and a fulltime member of the faculty since 2004. I am currently a professor in the sociology at the school. Just previous to the Black Lives Matter protests, after a series of unflattering national reports concerning campus diversity at JMU (and other colleges throughout the country), there was clearly a renewed attempt to increase inclusivity on campus, not just as it relates to race and ethnicity but also as concerns social class. It remains to be seen whether this effort will be sustained over time. I expect that recent events have compelled most other state institutions in this study to undertake a similar "burst" in affirmative action programs designed to increase diversity on campus.

References

Buchanan, Larry, Quoctrung Bui and Jugal K. Patel. 2020. "Black Lives Matter May Be the Largest Movement in US History." *New York Times*, July 3. LexisNexis Academic.

Chetty, Raj, John N. Friedman, Nathaniel Hilger, Emmanuel Saez, Diane Whitmore Schanzenbach and Danny Yagan. 2011. "How Does Your Kindergarten Classroom Affect Your Earnings? Evidence from Project STAR." *Quarterly Journal of Economics* 126 (4): 1593–1660.

Chetty, Raj, Nathaniel Hendren, Maggie R. Jones and Sonya R. Porter. 2020. "Race and Economic Opportunity in the United States: An Intergenerational Perspective." *Quarterly Journal of Economics* 135 (2): 711–783.

Coates, Ta-Nehisi. 2014. "The Case for Reparations." *The Atlantic* 313 (5): 54–71.

DeSimone, Tim. 2017. "JMU Alumnus Levar Stoney Serves as Richmond's Mayor," *The Breeze*, September 28. https://www.breezejmu.org/news/jmu-alumnus-levar-stoney-serves-as-richmond-s-mayor/article_36c201ba-a3f5-11e7-b923-abd57cdeaf12.html.

Eligion, John. 2020. "Black Lives Matter Grows as Movement While Facing New Challenges." *New York Times*, August 28. LexisNexis Academic.

Falk, William W., and Bruce H. Rankin. 1992. "The Cost of Being Black in the Black Belt." *Social Problems* 39 (3): 299–313.

Gendreau, Henri. 2020. "Virginia Tech Committee Backs Renaming Dorms for Black Life Campus Pioneers." *Roanoke Times*, August 13. https://roanoke.com/news/local/education/virginia-tech-committee-backs-renaming-dorms-for-Black-life-campus-pioneers/article_ac539960-ec 37-52bb-9e8c-e96c771657f1.html.

"JMU to Name New Residence Hall after Paul Jennings, a Madison Family Slave." 2019. *JMU News*. James Madison University. https://www.jmu.edu/news/2019/02/11-jenningshall.shtml.

Jones, Thai. 2020. "Slavery Reparations Seem Impossible. In Many Places, They're Already Happening." *Washington Post*, January 31. LexisNexis Academic.

Kolenich, Eric. 2021. "Three JMU buildings honoring Confederate leaders will be renamed for prominent Black members of the community." *Richmond Times Dispatch*, February 26. https://richmond.com/news/state-and-regional/three-jmu-buildings-honoring-confederate-leaders-will-be-renamed-for-prominent-black-members-of-the/article_9a4defe3-546b-55c5-9d68-4dd408e130e5.html

"Memorial to Enslaved Laborers at the University of Virginia." University of Virginia. https://www2.virginia.edu/slaverymemorial/design.html.

Nir, Sarah Maslin. 2020. "How Two Lives Collided in Central Park, Rattling the Nation." *New York Times*, June 15. LexisNexis Academic.

"Presidential Commission on Slavery and the University." University of Virginia. https://slavery.virginia.edu/.

Robertson, Gary. 1999. "Canal Was Carved with Slave Labor / Waterway's Construction Was a Demanding Task." *Richmond Times-Dispatch*, September 26. https://archive.vcu.edu/english/engweb/Rivertime/canal0926.html.

Toscano, Pasquale S. 2017. "My University Is Named for Robert E. Lee. What Now?" *New York Times*, August 22. LexisNexis Academic.

Vozzella, Laura, and Gregory S. Schneider. 2020. "Confederate Stonewall Jackson Statue Removed in Richmond; City Says Others Will Come Down 'Soon.'" *Washington Post*, July 1. LexisNexis Academic

"University History: Our Name." Washington and Lee University. https://www.wlu.edu/the-w-l-story/university-history/#:~:text=Liberty%20Hall%20Academy%20was%20in,his%20service%20to%20the%20commonwealth.

Way, Peter. 2009. *Common Labour: Workers and the Digging of North American Canals, 1780–1860*. Cambridge: Cambridge University Press.

INDEX

Notes: Folios in italics indicate figures and with "n" indicates endnotes in the text.

Pontius Pilate

INTERFACES

Series Editor: Barbara Green, O.P.

Pontius Pilate

Portraits of a Roman Governor

Warren Carter

A Michael Glazier Book

LITURGICAL PRESS

Collegeville, Minnesota

www.litpress.org

A Michael Glazier Book published by the Liturgical Press.

Cover design by Ann Blattner. Watercolor by Ethel Boyle.

1   2   3   4   5   6   7   8

Library of Congress Cataloging-in-Publication Data

Carter, Warren, 1955–
    Pontius Pilate : portraits of a Roman governor / Warren Carter.
      p. cm. — (Interfaces)
    "A Michael Glazier book."
    Includes bibliographical references.
    ISBN 0-8146-5113-5 (alk. paper)
      1. Pilate, Pontius, 1st cent.   I. Title.   II. Interfaces (Collegeville, Minn.)
BS2520.P55 37 2003
226'.092—dc21

                                2002069481

CONTENTS

PREFACE

The book you hold in your hand is one of six volumes in a new set. This series, called INTERFACES, is a curriculum and scholarly adventure, a creative opportunity in teaching and learning, presented at this moment in the long story of how the Bible has been studied, interpreted, and appropriated.

The INTERFACES project was prompted by a number of experiences that you, perhaps, share. When I first taught undergraduates the college had just received a substantial grant from the National Endowment for the Humanities, and one of the recurring courses designed within the grant was called Great Figures in Pursuit of Excellence. Three courses would be taught, each centering on a figure from some academic discipline or other, with a common seminar section to provide occasion for some integration. Some triads were more successful than others, as you might imagine. But the opportunity to concentrate on a single individual—whether historical or literary—to team teach, to make links to another pair of figures, and to learn new things about other disciplines was stimulating and fun for all involved. A second experience that gave rise to the present series came at the same time, connected also with undergraduates. It was my frequent experience to have Roman Catholic students feel quite put out about taking "more" biblical studies since, as they confidently affirmed, they had already been there many times and done it all. That was, of course, not true; as we well know, there is always more to learn. And often those who felt most informed were the least likely to take on new information when offered it.

A stimulus as primary as my experience with students was the familiarity of listening to friends and colleagues at professional meetings talking about the research that excites us most. I often wondered: Do her undergraduate students know about this? Or how does he bring these ideas—clearly so energizing to him—into the college classroom? Perhaps some of us have felt bored with classes that seem wholly unrelated to research, that rehash the same familiar material repeatedly. Hence the idea for this series of books to bring to the fore and combine some of our research interest with our teaching and learning. Accordingly, this series is not so much

about creating texts *for* student audiences, but rather about *sharing* our scholarly passions with them. Because these volumes are intended each as a piece of original scholarship they are geared to be stimulating to both students and established scholars, perhaps resulting in some fruitful collaborative learning adventures.

The series also developed from a widely-shared sense that all academic fields are expanding and exploding, and that to contemplate "covering" even a testament (let alone the whole Bible or Western monotheistic religions) needs to be abandoned in favor of something with greater depth. At the same time the links between our fields are becoming increasingly obvious as well, and we glimpse exciting possibilities for ways of working that will draw together academic realms that once seemed separate. Finally, the spark of enthusiasm that almost always ignites when I mention to colleagues and students the idea of single figures in combination—interfacing—encourages me that this is an idea worth trying.

And so with the leadership and help of Liturgical Press Academic Editor Linda Maloney, as well as with the encouragement and support of Managing Editor Mark Twomey, the series has begun to take shape.

Each volume in the INTERFACES series focuses clearly on a biblical character (or perhaps a pair of them). The characters are in some cases powerful (King Saul, Pontius Pilate) and familiar (John the Baptist, Joseph) though in other cases they will strike many as minor and little-known (the Cannibal Mothers, Herodias). In any case, each of them has been chosen to open up a set of worlds for consideration. The named (or unnamed) character interfaces with his or her historical-cultural world and its many issues, with other characters from biblical literature; each character has drawn forth the creativity of the author, who has taken on the challenge of engaging many readers. The books are specifically designed for college students (though we think suitable for some graduate work as well), planned to provide young adults with relevant information and at a level of critical sophistication that matches the rest of the undergraduate curriculum. In fact, the expectation is that what students are learning in other classes on historiography, literary theory, and cultural anthropology will find an echo in these books, each of which is explicit about at least two relevant methodologies. It is surely the case that biblical studies is in a methodology-conscious moment, and the INTERFACES series embraces it enthusiastically. Our hope is for students (and teachers) to continue to see the relationship between their best questions and their most valuable insights, between how they approach texts and what they find there. The volumes go well beyond familiar paraphrase of narratives to ask questions that are relevant in our era. At the same time the series authors have each dealt

with the notion of the Bible as Scripture in a way that is comfortable for them. None of the books is preachy or hortatory, and yet the self-implicating aspects of working with the revelatory text are handled frankly. The assumption is, again, that college can be a good time for students to rethink their beliefs and assumptions, and they need to do so in good company.

The INTERFACES volumes are not substitutes for the Bible. In every case they are to be read with the text. Quoting has been kept to a minimum for that very reason. The volumes, when used in a classroom setting, are accompanied by a companion volume, *From Earth's Creation to John's Revelation: The INTERFACES Biblical Storyline Companion,* which provides a quick, straightforward overview of the whole storyline into which the characters under special study fit. Web links will also be available through the Liturgical Press website: www.litpress.org.

The series challenge—for publisher, writers, teachers, and students—is to combine the volumes creatively, to "interface" them well so that the vast potential of the biblical text continues to unfold for all of us. The first six volumes: in Old Testament/Hebrew Bible featuring Saul, the Cannibal Mothers, and Joseph; in New Testament focusing on John the Baptist, Herodias, and Pontius Pilate, offer a foretaste of other volumes currently in preparation. It has been a pleasure, and a richly informative privilege, to work with the authors of these first volumes as well as the series consultants: Carleen Mandolfo for Hebrew Bible and Catherine Murphy for New Testament. It is the hope of all of us that you will find the series useful and stimulating for your own teaching and learning.

Barbara Green, O.P.
INTERFACES Series Editor
June 29, 2002
Berkeley, California

INTRODUCTION

This study examines the portraits of Pontius Pilate, Roman governor of the province of Judea from 26–37 C.E., found in the four gospels of the Christian Scriptures.

Chapter One offers a rationale for this focus and Chapter Two outlines the methods that guide the study. Chapter Three provides an overview of the structure of the Roman empire and the roles of a Roman governor, knowledge that the gospels assume their audiences have. Chapters Four through Seven examine the portrait of Pilate that emerges from the gospels of Mark, Matthew, Luke, and John. Each of these chapters focuses on one gospel. Each chapter begins by outlining the circumstances of the audience for which the particular gospel was written, then details the gospel's larger emphases that provide the context for the scene with Pilate. Finally, it discusses the portrait of Pilate that emerges from his confrontation with Jesus. The conclusion considers some of the ethical and theological issues that the scenes involving Pilate raise for contemporary readers.

In addition to its specific focus on Pilate, the study contributes to the understanding of the gospels in six ways.

1. It attends to the historical circumstances out of which and for which the gospels were written in the late first century.

2. It draws attention to the often-neglected Roman imperial context of the gospels, inviting both the recognition and evaluation of this context.

3. It takes the gospels seriously as narratives that tell a story.

4. It recognizes that the four gospels have significant similarities and differences.

5. It takes seriously the theological and pastoral address of the gospels to believing communities, without artificially separating these crucial functions from the lived, socio-political realities of first-century daily life.

6. It locates both the causes and effects of Jesus' death in this first-century world, while recognizing the gospels' claims concerning the significance of Jesus' death in revealing God's salvific purposes.

The study, then, employs historical criticism, social-scientific work, and post-colonial perspectives along with literary criticism (especially audience-oriented criticism), to examine the portraits of Pilate in the four gospels. While this range of scholarship informs the work, I have kept notes to an absolute minimum (though the less-familiar material of Chapter Three has somewhat more extensive notation). This book is written for college and seminary students, for interested lay people, for clergy, and even for scholars. It builds on and develops my recent work in *Matthew and the Margins: A SocioPolitical and Religious Reading* (Maryknoll, N.Y.: Orbis, 2000), and in *Matthew and Empire: Initial Explorations* (Harrisburg, Pa.: Trinity Press International, 2001). Both can be consulted for more extensive discussion and bibliography.

I want to thank Barbara Green for the opportunity to contribute to this series, George Wiley, Robert R. and Clarice D. Osborne Professor of Religion at Baker University, Baldwin City, Kansas, who graciously provided very helpful feedback on the manuscript, and my student assistant, LeeAnn Ahern, who has yet again rendered valuable and astute assistance.

Warren Carter
December 2001

ABBREVIATIONS

ABD *Anchor Bible Dictionary*

BAGD Walter Bauer, W. F. Arndt, F. W. Gingrich, and Frederick W. Danker, *Greek-English Lexicon of the New Testament and Other Early Christian Literature.* 3d ed. Chicago: University of Chicago Press, 1979

CBA Catholic Biblical Association

CBQ *Catholic Biblical Quarterly*

JJS *Journal of Jewish Studies*

JSJ *Journal for the Study of Judaism in the Persian, Hellenistic, and Roman Periods*

LCL Loeb Classical Library

MSSNTS Society for New Testament Studies Monograph Series

NICNT New International Commentary on the New Testament

NRSV New Revised Standard Version

SBLDS Society of Biblical Literature Dissertation Series

CHAPTER ONE

Would the Real Pilate Please Stand Up?

In the Christian tradition, Pontius Pilate is forever associated with one event. He was the Roman governor of the province of Judea between 26 and 37 C.E. who used his life-and-death power as governor to execute Jesus of Nazareth in Jerusalem around the year 30 C.E. The New Testament accounts of Pilate's role in crucifying Jesus will be our focus in this study.

Pilate's name has been memorialized among Christian people in creed and gospel. For nearly two millennia, Christians throughout the world have recited the words of the Apostles' Creed that link Pilate with Jesus:

> I believe in God the Father Almighty, maker of heaven and earth,
> And in Jesus Christ, his only son our Lord,
> Who was conceived by the Holy Spirit,
> born of the virgin Mary,
> suffered under Pontius Pilate,
> was crucified, died, and was buried;
> he descended to the dead.
> On the third day he rose again . . .

And in the Easter season they have heard the words of the gospels' accounts of Jesus' final hours, including his "trial" before Pilate.

They bound Jesus, led him away, and handed him over to Pilate. (Mark 15:1b)	They bound him, led him away, and handed him over to Pilate, the governor. (Matt 27:2)

Then the assembly arose as a body and they brought Jesus before Pilate. (Luke 23:1)	Then they took Jesus from Caiaphas' house to Pilate's headquarters. (John 18:28)

Matthew's account ends with the memorable image of the Roman governor Pilate washing his hands before authorizing Jesus' crucifixion (Matt 27:24). John's account has Pilate ask the very famous question, "What is truth?" (John 18:38), a question for which, as Francis Bacon noted in his 1625 essay, Pilate "would not stay for an answer!"

As with most figures caught up in human dramas, Pilate's role in Jesus' execution as well as Pilate's character have been much debated through the ages by historians and scholars, preachers and common folks. What motivated him to kill Jesus—hatred for Jews, patriotic fervor for Rome, intolerance of any opposition? As a political figure, he has to answer the "character" question. What sort of character did Pilate exhibit in these events? Did Pilate play a willing part in the events or was he just the front man for the "real" villains, the Jewish leaders? One of the tragic consequences of this later view has been an undeniable and destructive tradition of anti-semitic actions and attitudes in western civilization and Christianity. Was Pilate weak and manipulated, as many have suggested, in condemning an "innocent" man, or was he arrogant and skillfully manipulative in protecting the interests of the ruling elite? What sort of political and socio-economic system, what sort of world did Pilate represent and defend in his actions? And since Jesus' death is usually understood as a religious event, what significance is there to the involvement of a political figure like Pilate, a representative of Rome's empire? How did Jesus threaten Rome's interests, provoking the empire to strike back? What does Jesus' death say about Rome's way of ruling? What visions of human society collide when Pilate confronts Jesus?

Of course, as with any character in a novel or movie, questions about Pilate's character, motivations, commitments, actions, and imperial world raise questions about our own commitments and ways of living. What sort of "world," what sort of empire do we support and promote? And for people who identify themselves as Christians, there is a further question of what it might mean to live as followers of Jesus "crucified under Pontius Pilate."

History has delivered at least five very different verdicts on Pilate. Is he a Villain or a Saint? Or somewhere in between? We will briefly consider each verdict in turn.

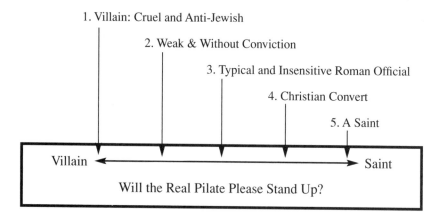

1. Pilate the Villain: A Cruel Anti-Jewish Tyrant

This very negative verdict sees Pilate's complicity in Jesus' death as a consequence of his cruel hatred of Jewish people. Pilate was, so the theory goes, allied with and inspired by the enormously powerful figure Sejanus, the Praetorian Prefect who commanded the troops in Rome responsible for the protection of the emperor and imperial family, as well as for maintaining order and loyalty. Supposedly Sejanus was very anti-semitic, so he sent Pilate as governor to Judea in 26 C.E. to provoke Jews into revolt so that they could be crushed with military might and the race exterminated.[1]

Advocates of this view highlight conflicts between Jews and Pilate as evidence that Pilate actively sought to provoke this conflict. Ignoring Jewish sensitivities, Pilate tried to introduce into Jerusalem shields that honored the emperor Tiberius. He also used funds from the Jerusalem Temple to build an aqueduct that ran through a cemetery and violated Jewish purity concerns.[2] And in the years 29–31 he depicted on Jewish coins for the first time sacred objects associated with Roman worship and power.

But things change significantly in the year 31, when Sejanus is executed. Now without his protector in Rome, Pilate considerably modifies his

---

[1] Proponents of this view include Ethelbert Stauffer, *Christ and the Caesars: Historical Sketches.* Translated by K. and R. Gregor Smith (London: S.C.M., 1955); Ernst Bammel, "Syrian Coinage and Pilate," *JJS* 2 (1950–51) 108–10; Paul Winter, *On the Trial of Jesus* (Berlin: Walter de Gruyter, 1961); Haim Cohn, *The Trial and Death of Jesus* (London: Weidenfeld & Nicholson, 1972); Harold W. Hoehner, "Pilate," *Dictionary of Jesus and the Gospels* (Downers Grove: Intervarsity Press, 1992) 615–16.

[2] Josephus, *Jewish War* 2.169-74; *Jewish Antiquities* 18.55-60; Philo, *Legatio ad Gaium* 299-305.

actions and seeks a less hostile relationship with his Jewish subjects. This view of Pilate claims that his weak actions in Jesus' death result from the time after Sejanus' death in 33 C.E. when he was more interested in trying to secure favor with the Jewish leaders and crowds.

It is interesting to note that this view of Pilate was strongly advocated after the Second World War (1939–45) and may have been influenced by the larger context of Nazi attempts to exterminate European Jews. Most scholars have not been convinced that it is an accurate or fair picture of Pilate. The evidence for Sejanus' anti-Jewish hatred is slim, deriving from only one source about Pilate (Philo's *Embassy to Gaius*). Without trying to defend what Pilate did, it can be said that Pilate could have minted much more offensive coins (such as those with the emperor's image) and committed much more offensive acts if he was trying to provoke violent conflict.[3] If his goal was to provoke warfare, he was not very good at accomplishing it! The coins he did mint don't seem to have provoked outbursts of violence, and his rule was not marked by extraordinary conflict when it is compared to the administrations of other governors. Others have recognized his cultural and religious insensitivity but have explained it not by this conspiracy theory, but by deficiencies in Pilate's personality and/or administrative policies. Others have noted his difficult situation of representing Roman rule over a subjugated people who understood themselves to be God's special people and over land that the occupants regarded as given to them by God.[4]

2. Pilate: Weak and Without Conviction

A second, very common view of Pilate focuses particularly on his role in Jesus' death. He has noble intentions to release the "innocent" Jesus, but he is too weak, lacks conviction, and gives in to stronger voices.

Readers of the gospel accounts of Jesus' trial have noticed that Pilate makes statements such as these:

> "I find no basis for an accusation against this man . . . and here I have examined him in your presence and have not found this man guilty of any of your charges against him . . ." And Pilate, wanting to release

[3] Helen Bond, "The Coins of Pontius Pilate: Part of an Attempt to Provoke the People or to Integrate them into the Empire?" *JSJ* 27 (1996) 241–62.

[4] So Jean-Pierre Lémonon, *Pilate et le gouvernement de la Judée: textes et monuments* (Paris: Gabalda, 1981); Raymond E. Brown, *The Death of the Messiah* (New York: Doubleday, 1994) 695–705.

Jesus, addressed them again; but they kept shouting, "Crucify, Crucify him!" A third time he said to them, "Why, what evil has he done? I have found in him no ground for the sentence of death. I will therefore have him flogged and then release him." (Luke 23:4, 14, 22)

All of them said, "Let him be crucified!" Then he asked, "Why, what evil has he done?" But they shouted all the more, "Let him be crucified!" (Matt 27:23; cf. Mark 15:13-14)

Pilate went out again and said to them, "Look, I am bringing him out to you to let you know that I find no case against him." (John 19:4, also 6)

This view understands these verses to mean that Pilate does not seem to find Jesus guilty of anything and is not convinced that Jesus merits the death sentence. Yet though he thinks Jesus is innocent and nobly wants to release him, he ends up handing Jesus over to be whipped, mocked, and crucified. Unable to resist the pressures of the Jewish leaders and of the shouting crowds, he does not have the strength of his own convictions to release the innocent Jesus. Instead of doing what he knows is right, he weakly capitulates to their demands in order to maintain both public order and his own political neck.

We will consider in Chapters Four through Seven whether this is an adequate view of the role of Pilate the Roman governor as we discuss each gospel account. I will suggest there that for most of the accounts it is not adequate, partly because it ignores crucial ways in which the Roman empire operated and so misreads the gospel texts. But for now we can note it is a very common, negative view of Pilate.

3. Pilate: A Typical and Culturally Insensitive Roman Official

This third view of Pilate gives him a mixed review. It rejects Verdict 1, that Pilate was motivated by an anti-Jewish extermination agenda, and Verdict 2, that Pilate was weak and lacking conviction. Instead, this view sees Pilate as trying to fulfill the roles and requirements of being Roman governor of the difficult province of Judea as ably as he can. Trying to avoid direct conflict, Pilate attempts to strengthen Jewish recognition of and loyalty to Roman rule. So he makes Rome's presence, claims, and rewards more visible through displaying symbols of Roman control in Jerusalem and on coins. But he makes a mistake in not realizing how religiously insensitive such actions are and does not anticipate the strong resistance. His responses to the resistance—either employing military force to maintain

control or changing his plans—further fuel the cycle of alienation rather than securing his subjects' loyalty to Rome.

This view essentially sees Pilate as competent but somewhat out of his depth personally and politically. He lacks the cultural knowledge and respect as well as the political acumen and administrative mechanisms to rule effectively. According to one writer he is "a loyal governor (loyal to the emperor), ignorant of and insensitive to the rigorous and varying demands of Judaism . . . Pilate's stubbornness is a very noticeable feature of his character, but it is coupled with a degree of indecision . . . [He was] a typical Roman officer of the type."[5]

But whether personality and policies adequately account for Pilate's actions is debatable. Also to be considered is Pilate's no-win situation. Longstanding Jewish traditions meant many Jews understood themselves as God's chosen people and their land as God's gift to them. Any representative of any power that claimed control contrary to God's purposes was in for a difficult time.[6]

4. Pilate: A Christian Convert

This is a very old verdict on Pilate, and one that modern readers of the gospels may find difficult to understand at first glance. But in some ways it develops an aspect of the second verdict, that Pilate finds Jesus innocent of any charges and not properly to be condemned to die as a criminal. This fourth view places all the responsibility for Jesus' death on the Jews, while maintaining that Pilate knew Jesus was innocent. But in addition to exonerating him from any blame, this verdict claims that during Jesus' trial Pilate recognizes Jesus' special identity and so becomes a Christian. Pilate plays a crucial role in accomplishing God's purposes.

This view came to the fore in the late second century, some 150 years or so after Pilate's term as governor ended. The early church leader Tertullian, writing around the year 200 C.E., claimed that the emperor Tiberius, emperor from 14–37 C.E. and Pilate's boss, received and believed a report "from Syria Palestine which had revealed the truth of Christ's divinity" (*Apologeticus* 5.2). Later Tertullian says that the report came from Pilate, who was a Christian:

---

⁵ Brian C. McGing, "Pontius Pilate and the Sources," *CBQ* 53 (1991) 416–38, especially 434–35, 438.
⁶ Daniel R. Schwartz, "Pontius Pilate," *ABD* 5:395–401.

This whole story of Christ was reported to Caesar (at that time it was Tiberius) by Pilate, himself in his secret heart already a Christian (*Apologeticus* 21.24).

Tertullian does not say how he knows Pilate was a Christian, especially since Pilate was a Christian "in his secret heart."

Over subsequent centuries some Christian traditions develop these claims about Pilate. These developing traditions, perhaps written down in the late fourth or fifth century at the earliest, some three hundred or so years after Pilate, probably have no historical basis. Instead, they expand the gospel accounts of Jesus' trial before Pilate by adding dialogue, writing letters between Pilate and other characters involved, elaborating Pilate's interaction with the emperor.[7] Pilate emerges as a repentant Christian, blessed by God, while the Jewish leaders are depicted as the sole villains.

- The long narrative called the *Acts of Pilate* removes any responsibility from Pilate by having Jesus give him permission to proceed with the execution! Pilate recognizes Jesus' identity as a king and his superiority by exclaiming, "Tell me! How can I, a governor, examine a king?" (1.2). But Jesus kindly excuses him from any responsibility by telling Pilate that he must execute Jesus "because Moses and the prophets foretold my death and resurrection" (4.3). Throughout, responsibility is placed on the hostile Jewish leaders.

- In a work called *Paradosis Pilati* there is hostility toward Pilate for ordering Jesus' death as well as recognition of Pilate as a Christian. The emperor Tiberius receives a report of Jesus' crucifixion and has Pilate brought to Rome to defend his actions. Tiberius appears as a believer and is furious with Pilate. Pilate defends himself by blaming the "lawlessness and sedition of the lawless and godless Jews."[8] He also confesses, "Truly the charges made against him (Jesus) are true. For I myself was convinced by his deeds, that he is greater than all the gods whom we worship." Tiberius orders troops to attack, enslave, and scatter Jews from Judea since they committed "a lawless crime in forcing Pilate to crucify Jesus, who was acknowledged as God." Tiberius also orders Pilate to be executed for his terrible act against "the righteous man called Christ." As he is about to be

---

[7] These texts can be found in John K. Elliott, *The Apocryphal New Testament* (Oxford: Clarendon Press, 1993) 164–225. For some discussion see Clayton N. Jefford, "Acts of Pilate," *ABD* 5:371–72.

[8] Elliott, *Apocryphal New Testament* 210.

beheaded,[9] Pilate prays for himself and his wife that Jesus, now exalted and ascended in heaven with God, will not condemn them because of their sin, "but pardon us and number us among your righteous ones." The prayer moves the exalted Jesus to speak words of blessing and forgiveness to Pilate from heaven. Speaking from heaven, Jesus says:[10]

> "All generations and families of the Gentiles shall call you blessed, because in your governorship everything was fulfilled which the prophets foretold about me. And you yourself shall appear as my witness at my second coming, when I shall judge the twelve tribes of Israel and those who have not confessed my name." And the prefect cut off Pilate's head, and behold, an angel of the Lord received it.

- In another writing, *The Letter of Pilate to Herod,* Pilate meets the risen Jesus and receives his blessing. The letter begins with Pilate confessing to Herod, "it was no good thing that I did at your persuasion when I crucified Jesus." Pilate tells Herod that subsequently Pilate and his wife Procla and other believers found the risen Jesus teaching in a field. In the midst of supernatural signs that depict God's presence, Pilate says:[11]

> We fell on our faces and the Lord (the risen Jesus) came and raised us up, and I saw on him the scars of the passion, and he laid his hands on my shoulders, saying, "All generations and families shall call you blessed, because in thy days the Son of Man died and rose again."

In these texts that develop in the fourth century and following Pilate is clearly presented as a repentant, believing Christian and, amazingly, a blessed martyr! He does God's will in ensuring Jesus' crucifixion, fulfills God's purposes, and is put to death for doing so. Jesus encourages Pilate before the crucifixion to do God's will. After his death, the risen Jesus meets him and blesses him for faithfully doing God's will. Before Pilate's execution, Jesus blesses him from heaven. Pilate is among the righteous who do God's will and find God's favor. But his exoneration goes hand in hand with greatly increased blame placed on the Jews, who are presented as wickedly rejecting God.

[9] Other traditions depict Pilate being punished by exile, not death. Those that mention death differ considerably: He is drowned; he is shot with an arrow; he is forced to commit suicide.

[10] Elliott, *Apocryphal New Testament* 211.

[11] Ibid. 223.

Such claims are usually understood to have developed in a double context of defining the relationship of the early Christian movement to Roman imperial control and of debates and disputes (including with Jewish groups) about the identity, specifically the divinity, of Jesus. The account of Jesus' crucifixion by Rome was problematic for these followers of Jesus. Living as disciples of a crucified person within the empire, they could be understood by outsiders to be opposed to Roman rule. Some, though not all, members of the minority Christian movement made great efforts to convince themselves and others that in fact Jesus had posed no threat to Rome at all, and that the Jewish leaders were responsible for his death. In retelling the story they presented Roman officials like Tiberius and Pilate not only as recognizing that Jesus had not posed any threat, but also as confessing Jesus' special identity in relation to God. The presentation of Pilate the Christian who confesses Jesus' divinity, who does God's will and is accepted by Jesus and God serves to show that the church poses no threat to the empire. Making Pilate into a Christian is an attempt to protect the church from Rome's hostile attention. But, as we have seen, these attempts were often matched, regrettably, by increased hostility toward Jews.

IS MATTHEW'S PILATE A CHRISTIAN?

Matthew's gospel was written in the 80s of the first century, several centuries before these traditions making Pilate a Christian developed. A modern interpreter of Matthew's gospel, Robert Gundry, argues that already late in the first century, some fifty years after Jesus' death, Matthew's gospel presents Pilate as a Christian.[12] Gundry sees the first sign of this Christianizing in Matthew's presentation when Pilate asks the crowd if they want him to release "Jesus Barabbas or Jesus who is called the Christ?" (Matt 27:17). Gundry thinks that in this statement Pilate not only takes the initiative in seeking Jesus' release but also genuinely confesses that Jesus is the Christ.

The second sign of Pilate being a Christian, according to this view, is the word from Mrs. Pilate to Pilate:

> Have nothing to do with that innocent man, for today I have suffered a great deal because of a dream about him. (Matt 27:19)

Gundry claims that Mrs. Pilate makes a "Christian confession" in testifying to Jesus' righteous behavior, and Pilate will in v. 24 follow her advice

---

[12] Robert H. Gundry, *Matthew: A Commentary on His Handbook for a Mixed Church Under Persecution* (2nd ed. Grand Rapids: Eerdmans, 1994) 561–65.

to have nothing to do with Jesus. His handwashing attests his innocence of Jesus' blood. Gundry says:

> Thus, in a preview of wholesale conversion among all the nations, Pilate's wife and Pilate himself become Gentile disciples of Jesus . . . The Christianizing of Pilate and his wife makes them a foil to the Jewish leaders, whose guilt stands out all the more.

Most Matthean scholars are not at all convinced by Gundry's analysis, and I will offer a very different approach in Chapter Four. Gundry claims too much in arguing that Pilate's description of Jesus as "Jesus who is called the Christ" (27:17) should be read as a personal confession. He also fails to explain just how Mrs. Pilate's instruction to Pilate to "have nothing to do with" Jesus is at all appropriate for Christian discipleship. Gundry does not take into account the dynamics of Roman imperial power that are central to the scene when he places all the blame for Jesus' death on the Jews. Nevertheless, his interpretation belongs with a very old Christian tradition that has excused Pilate and Rome from any responsibility for Jesus' death and has instead placed all blame for it on "the Jews." In addition to being an inadequate analysis of Matthew's text, this very old verdict on Pilate as the converted Christian has had tragic consequences for the treatment of Jews through the centuries.

5. Pilate the Saint

It is only a short step from this fourth verdict on Pilate as a Christian and martyr to the fifth verdict. This approach venerates Pilate as a saint. Its emergence is evident, for instance, in a letter that later Christian traditions attributed to Herod as his reply to a letter from Pilate.[13] Herod responds to Pilate's remorse for crucifying Jesus and Pilate's account of his meeting with the risen Jesus. He describes numerous tragedies that have befallen his family: His daughter Herodias has her head cut off (ironically because Herod had John the Baptist's head cut off after Herodias requested it); his son Lesbonax is dying; Herod himself is afflicted with "dropsy, and worms are coming out of my mouth;" his wife is blinded through weeping. Herod

---

[13] Elliott, *Apocryphal New Testament* 222–24. The author of this "letter" either did not know or did not care that there were a number of "Herods" in the gospel accounts, details of whose lives have been combined into a single "Herod" who is supposedly writing the letter. For example, Herod the Great (d. 4 C.E.), who is supposed to have massacred the Innocents, was the father of Herod Antipas (d. 39 C.E.), who beheaded John the Baptist, and the grandfather of Herod Agrippa, who (according to Acts 12:23) "was eaten by worms and died" (in 44 C.E.).

recognizes these tragedies as God's punishment "because we mocked at the eye of the righteous." Herod begs Pilate to pray for him:

> I am in great distress of mind at the death of Jesus, and reflecting on my sins in killing John Baptist and massacring the Innocents. Since, then, you are able to see the man Jesus again, strive for me and intercede for me; for to you Gentiles the kingdom is given, according to the prophets and Christ.

In the traditions of the very old Ethiopian churches Pilate has been canonized, or made a saint. He and his wife Procula are honored with a feast day, June 19.

Why So Many and So Different Views?

These five verdicts on Pilate are very different. At least six factors explain why interpreters have come to such diverse conclusions about Pilate's roles and character.

1. Time Gap

Pilate has been dead for two thousand years. He did not leave us a diary or letters. Creating these written accounts, especially letters, was one of the key ways that the tradition about him grew. As with all historical work, our reconstructions of events and people from across the ages are always at best partial and incomplete.

2. Different Interests of Readers

The five verdicts come from readers who have lived at different times in very different circumstances and with very different reasons for being interested in Pilate. These circumstances and interests shape what interpreters see in the various sources about Pilate. I have noted above that the view of Pilate as a converted Christian (Verdict 4) was probably shaped initially by concern over the risk of Roman actions against Christians and by attempts to define Christians as a group separate from Jews. I also suggested that the context of Nazi atrocities against Jews in the 1930s and 1940s may have impacted the first verdict. Some interpreters are historians who are trying to develop as full a picture of Pilate as possible from as many sources as possible (Verdicts 1 and 2). Other interpreters focus only on the gospels or on one gospel or source and have special Christian commitments and church interests uppermost in their approaches (Verdicts 3-5). As with all

acts of interpretation, readers in diverse circumstances notice different things in the sources and make sense of their observations in various ways.

3. Readers' Limited Knowledge

A further factor influences some of these verdicts. Christian readers of the gospels, for example, often read them with particular religious questions in view and with an eye on their own religious experience. Often they do not realize that the gospel texts assume knowledge of significant cultural and political structures. In many cases we who live two thousand years after the time of the gospels, and in a very different world, do not have this knowledge unless we do some special study. Without it we can form some inadequate conclusions about what is happening in the texts. One of the things I will do in this book is fill in some of the knowledge about Pilate's world that the gospel texts take for granted.

4. The Limited Number of Sources

Information about Pilate is not extensive, though we know a little more about him than about other governors of Judea. Six texts comprise the main sources for information about him. These texts consist of four Christian gospels of Matthew, Mark, Luke, and John, and references in the works of the first-century Jewish writers Philo and Josephus. The texts I discussed above that present Pilate as a Christian and saint with their obviously Christian agenda are in all likelihood fourth- to eighth-century texts, too late to be used as reliable historical sources.[14] Tacitus makes a very brief, passing reference to Pilate while describing the emperor Nero's attack on some Christians in Rome in the 60s C.E. Nero is suspected of starting the fire himself, so he punishes some Christians as scapegoats:

> Christus, the founder of the name, had undergone the death penalty in the reign of Tiberius, by sentence of the procurator Pontius Pilate, and the pernicious superstition was checked for a moment. . . . (Tacitus, *Annals* 15.44)

Apart from these literary texts, some coins that Pilate minted in the years 29–31 have survived. There is also a stone inscription that names Pilate. This inscription, consisting of three incomplete lines, was discovered in the port city of Caesarea in 1961. It is difficult to reconstruct its full

---

[14] Note also the brief references to Pilate's involvement in Jesus' death in Acts 3:13; 4:27; 13:28; and 1 Tim 6:13.

form with certainty, but the three existing partial lines establish three things. The first line links Pilate somehow to Tiberius, Rome's emperor from 14–37 C.E. who appointed Pilate as governor of Judea from 26–37 C.E. This line suggests that the inscription marks an attempt to honor Tiberius (and Pilate?) in some way. The second line names Pontius Pilate, and the third identifies him as Prefect or governor of Judea.

Thus with six short written texts, a few coins, and an incomplete and short inscription, the database for information about Pilate is very limited.

5. Limited Information

Not only is the number of sources about Pilate few, but the information the written texts present is also very limited and sketchy.

- The gospel references are concerned almost exclusively with Pilate's role in Jesus' trial and crucifixion. The only exception occurs in Luke 13:1-2 where a brief and strange reference is made to Pilate killing some Galileans "whose blood Pilate had mingled with their sacrifices."

- The Jewish writer Philo (ca. 30 B.C.E.–45 C.E.), a leader of the large Jewish community in Alexandria in Egypt, offers the earliest information about Pilate from around the year 41, just after Claudius had become emperor and about four years after Pilate's governorship ended. But Philo is not writing a biography of Pilate. He deals with just one episode from Pilate's governorship (*Embassy to Gaius* 299-305). Pilate attempts to set up shields in Jerusalem to honor the emperor Tiberius, but Jewish leaders complain to Tiberius, who severely rebukes Pilate and orders their removal. The incident is described in a letter ascribed to King Agrippa, who also mentions Pilate's other shortcomings: "briberies, insults, robberies, outrages, wanton injuries, constantly repeated executions without trial, ceaseless and supremely grievous cruelty" (*Embassy to Gaius* 302).

- The Jewish historian Josephus, writing some forty to sixty years after the end of Pilate's governorship, narrates two incidents about Pilate's rule in one of his works (*Jewish War* 2.169-77, written about 75–79 C.E.). In a second work Josephus covers the same two episodes and adds a third (*Jewish Antiquities* 18.55-59, 60-62,[15] 85-89,

---

[15] I omit the reference to Jesus in *Jewish Antiquities* 18.63-64 since its authenticity is greatly disputed.

published about 93–94 C.E.). The incidents that Josephus describes include the placing of images of the emperor in Jerusalem (similar to what is narrated by Philo), paying for an aqueduct with money from the sacred treasury, and a bloody attack on prophet-led Samaritans on Mt. Gerizim. Complaints about this attack result in Pilate being ordered to return to Rome to explain his actions to the emperor. But Tiberius dies in 37 C.E. before Pilate arrives in Rome.

Each incident demonstrates Pilate's insensitivity to Jewish religious traditions and customs. Opposition, riots, and conflict usually result. Pilate restores order, sometimes with considerable violence from his soldiers. And several times Pilate has to back down. Because of some duplication of material among the four gospels and between Josephus' two works (and perhaps between Josephus and Philo also), together these six sources give us insight into five or six moments in Pilate's governorship.

AUTHOR	REFERENCE	INCIDENT
Philo	*Embassy to Gaius* 299-305	Pilate tries to set up shields, probably identifying the emperor as divine, in the Jerusalem Temple.
Josephus	*Jewish War* 2.169-74 *Antiquities* 18.55-59	Pilate tries to introduce standards bearing the emperor's image into Jerusalem.
Josephus	*Jewish War* 2.175-77 *Antiquities* 18.60-62	Pilate takes sacred Temple funds to finance an aqueduct.
Josephus	*Antiquities* 18.85-89	Pilate's troops attack a group of armed Samaritans, led by a prophet, on the sacred Mt. Gerizim. Many die. Pilate is called to Rome to give account.
Luke	Luke 13:1-2	Pilate kills some Galileans, "whose blood Pilate mingled with their sacrifices."
Gospels	Mark 15:1-15; Matt 27:1-26; Luke 23:1-25; John 18:28–19:22	Pilate condemns Jesus to death.

These sources, then, highlight some conflict between Pilate and his subjects, but given that Pilate governed for eleven years in Judea, that is not much information. And it is difficult to know how much weight to place on these episodes. Do they record typical events in his rule or exceptional happenings? No one gives us a biographical sketch of his life. What about his life before (and after) being governor? When was he born? And where? How and where did he die? How did he get to be appointed to Judea? How old was he? What prepared him for his duties as governor, and how well did he do? Who were his friends and enemies?

On the basis of information about other governors and about how the Roman imperial system maintained control (which I outline in Chapter Two), we can reasonably guess that Pilate probably had some sort of military career in which he most likely distinguished himself in some way as an officer. We can also be fairly confident that he belonged to the upper stratum of Roman society, that his family was wealthy (though not the most wealthy), that it was very well connected socially and politically, that Pilate was well educated, and that he was married (Matt 27:19). But such generalities do not tell us a great deal about him.

One thing is certain. With this limited information we cannot write a biography of Pilate, get inside his head, understand how he ticked. We simply do not have basic information about him, let alone anything that would enable us to understand his psychological makeup and workings.[16]

But there is another issue with the sources to be identified first.

6. Diverse Views in Diverse Sources

Perhaps the major reason for the diverse views of Pilate we noted above is that the sources present him in diverse ways. None of the sources is trying to write a biography of Pilate. In none of them is Pilate even the central character. In each source he is a minor part of, an example for, a larger project. Each source has its own agenda, its own purpose, its own reasons for mentioning Pilate at all. Each presents him in a particular way as it makes its larger points. And these perspectives differ greatly from one another.

PHILO'S PILATE

For instance, Philo, a leader of the large Jewish community in Alexandria in Egypt, is quite negative in his presentation of Pilate. He is writing

---

[16] For a recent attempt (with some awareness of the obstacles) see Ann Wroe, *Pontius Pilate* (New York: Random House, 1999). As interesting as it may be, such imaginary writing cannot be confused with anything like a reliable historical biography of Pilate.

around 41 C.E. to the new emperor Claudius to persuade him to protect Jews in Alexandria from attacks by Roman governors. He does not want Claudius to continue the policy of hostility to Jews associated with his predecessor, the emperor Gaius Caligula (37–41 C.E.). Caligula had tried to force Jews in Alexandria to worship his image. They boldly refused. He also tried to set up his own image in the Jerusalem Temple (also courageously resisted). Philo wants Claudius to follow the less confrontational, more tolerant policy of the previous emperor, Tiberius (who had died in 37).

Philo uses Pilate as an example of how not to rule over the Jews. Philo describes Pilate's misguided attempt to set up shields honoring the emperor Tiberius in Jerusalem (*Embassy to Gaius* 299-305). Jewish opposition is met by stubborn determination and perseverance from Pilate. So Jewish leaders write, a letter to the emperor Tiberius. The emperor is appalled at Pilate's insensitivity, rebukes him severely, and orders him to remove the shields. Tiberius offers a good model for Claudius to follow!

Philo is very careful to show that the Jewish opposition is to Pilate's insensitivity and not to the emperor or to Roman rule in general. In contrast to the insensitive and rebuked Pilate, Philo presents the emperor Tiberius as one who virtuously honors and protects Jewish traditions. Written after Tiberius' death in 37 C.E., Philo's negative presentation of Pilate's actions and positive presentation of the virtuous and noble emperor Tiberius serve Philo's purpose of urging the new emperor Claudius to follow Tiberius' actions and continue to protect Jewish traditions.

Moreover, it is very significant that Philo describes Pilate as doing the same sorts of things that he attributes to other Roman officials who have not treated Jews well! Philo presents officials like Pilate, Sejanus, Capito, and the emperor Gaius Caligula as typically hating Jews, exhibiting fear, and devising false accusations. Like other governors, Pilate receives bribes, engages in violence against his subjects, and is cruel. That is, what Philo says about Pilate is not specific to Pilate. It is part of a stereotypical presentation of numerous Roman officials that identifies them as opponents of Jews. This device of using standard rhetorical features to depict negative characters casts doubts on the historical accuracy of Philo's presentation of Pilate. But it clarifies Philo's agenda. Philo is using Pilate to make his political and religious points in order to protect Jewish groups against unjust treatment, and in order to show that such treatment was the mark of good emperors like Augustus and Tiberius.[17]

---

[17] For details see McGing, "Pontius Pilate and the Sources," 430–33.

Another Jewish writer, Josephus, is less negative in what he chooses to say about Pilate, but he is not consistent in his two works. In the earlier work, *The Jewish War,* written in the 70s C.E., Josephus explains to his patron, the Emperor Vespasian, how the war against Rome of 66–70 C.E. happened. It was, in his view, largely caused by internal dissension among Jewish groups, by small factions of rebels, and by God's will. But he also claims that the last two Roman governors—Albinus (62–64 C.E.) and Florus (64–66 C.E.)—contributed significantly to the outbreak of war by their excessive greed and misuse of power. By comparison, the governor Pilate, though guilty of two instances of religious insensitivity (*Jewish War* 2.169-77), did not contribute to the revolt with greedy or violent misrule. Pilate comes off quite well.

But in Josephus' *Jewish Antiquities,* written some twenty or so years later, he places more responsibility on Roman governors in general for causing the revolt. Particularly he is concerned to show that the governors violated religious customs and in doing so not only offended the Jewish people, but also risked God's wrath and punishment for violating God's decrees (e.g., *Ant.* 1.14). In this regard Pilate, who otherwise seems to be presented as a moderate and basically competent ruler, does not appear in a good light. His three actions—trying to introduce images of the emperor into Jerusalem, misusing sacred funds for an aqueduct, and attacking Samaritan worshipers on Mt. Gerizim—violate God's will. Pilate begins a line of similar actions by governors that results in war (*Ant.* 18.55-59, 60-62, 85-89).

Such major differences between Philo and Josephus over Pilate's actions and character cause considerable difficulties for anyone trying to build an integrated and coherent picture of Pilate. Some have tried to integrate the sources. Others have tried to reconcile them by ascribing Philo's very negative view to the time when Pilate was supposedly under Sejanus' influence, and Josephus' more positive view to the time after Sejanus' death (Verdict 1 above). But this approach is complicated by the fact that within Josephus' own work a significant development takes place in the twenty years between one source and the next. With limited and diverse information, it is not surprising that different images and evaluations of Pilate will emerge. Will the real Pilate please stand up?

PILATE AND THE GOSPELS

Similar problems exist with the gospels and their presentations of Pilate. Often readers see little difference among the four gospels' presentations of Pilate and think that all the gospels present Pilate as weak and

indecisive (Verdict 2 above). And even among those who do recognize some discrepancies among the gospel accounts Pilate is usually understood to be presented in relatively harmless terms.[18]

But is such a summary accurate for the gospels, or does each gospel offer a quite distinct presentation of Pilate? Research on the gospels over recent centuries has established that they are more likely to be distinct in their presentations, though with some common ground.[19] The discussions in Chapters Four through Seven will demonstrate these distinctive features. Like the writings of Philo and Josephus, each gospel has a specific agenda. The gospels are not eyewitness accounts of Jesus' ministry. No one was making a video; no one was recording his words. Rather, they were written late in the first century, some forty to fifty years after the time of Jesus, around or in the decades after the time of the fall of Jerusalem in the year 70 C.E. to which they all refer (Mark 13:2, 7-8; Matt 22:7; Luke 21:20-24; John 2:18-21; 11:47-50). Late in the first century they tell the story of Jesus not primarily as some sort of objective, historical study, nor as a modern biography that seeks to discover how Jesus "ticked." Rather, they resemble ancient biographies that presented a selective account of a notable figure's life in order to provide readers with an understanding of the figure's teaching and with a pattern to copy for virtuous living.

The gospels are written not by outsiders who are investigating Jesus for historical reasons or out of general interest. Their authors themselves are committed followers of Jesus. They shape, combine, and expand traditions about him from the perspective of being profoundly committed to him. They write not for outsiders but for an audience that comprises his followers. They are "in-house" writings. Their authors write to shape the identity and way of life of Jesus' followers. That is, they have primarily *pastoral* goals. Gospels were written to instruct and encourage small communities of followers of Jesus to be faithful disciples.

Moreover, while gospels utilize historical material about Jesus, they present Jesus from a *theological* perspective. Written forty to fifty years after Jesus' crucifixion, they show the importance of Jesus in relation to God's purposes and his significance for the lived discipleship of small groups of followers in the Roman empire. The gospels are story-sermons

---

[18] Compare McGing's presentation ("Pontius Pilate," 416–17): "Philo is extremely hostile to Pilate, Josephus comparatively neutral, and the Gospel authors, even allowing for the discrepancies between them, comparatively friendly."

[19] For discussion of gospels see Warren Carter, *Matthew: Storyteller, Interpreter, Evangelist* (Peabody, Mass.: Hendrickson, 1996). For the question of genre see especially pp. 35–54.

in that they proclaim what God was doing in Jesus. They do not begin by trying to persuade their readers that God exists, or what God is like. They assume these realities and tell the story of Jesus to show God's purposes at work in and through him and to shape the identity and way of life of their audiences as faithful followers of Jesus. The gospels are theological in that they are concerned to show God's purposes being worked out in Jesus. They are pastoral in that they address this understanding to the situations and lives of followers of Jesus. In this context we can expect the presentations of Pilate in each gospel to be impacted by the larger theological and pastoral commitments of each gospel.

How to Proceed?

We have so far identified five distinct verdicts that history has handed down on Pilate, and we have identified at least six factors that contribute to these different verdicts, noting that:

- A large time gap separates us from him.

- Interpreters notice and give significance to different things in the sources.

- The sources assume cultural and religious knowledge on our part that we do not always possess.

- There are only six main written sources of information about Pilate.

- They offer a limited amount and type of information about Pilate.

- They offer diverse views of Pilate in accord with the agenda of each work.

a. Clearly it is not possible to write a biography of Pilate, given the lack of and type of information about him. We have noticed that the sources are few and sketchy in that they present Pilate in ways that are appropriate to their larger purposes and perspectives. None of them is particularly interested in Pilate as its main focus, but only in relation to how he serves a larger purpose.

b. We have observed that trying to reconcile the information in these different accounts is very difficult. We do not have enough to form a comprehensive picture of Pilate with any confidence.

c. We have also observed the theological and pastoral nature of the gospel accounts about Jesus in that each gospel shows the significance of

Jesus in relation to God's purposes and in ways that are appropriate to their respective audiences of followers of Jesus.

These observations shape the questions, focus, and approach that I will employ in this book. Given restrictions on length, I am going to put Philo and Josephus aside, as well as the post-gospel Christian traditions that both oppose and rehabilitate Pilate. Rather, I will take a different and more limited approach that focuses on *Pilate as a character in each of the gospel narratives in the New Testament.* My goal is not to form a composite picture of Pilate by combining the four accounts. Instead I will treat Pilate as a character in each gospel scene. I will discuss each gospel account involving Pilate separately, respecting its own particular presentation of him as a character in the narrative, and observing the different images of Pilate that emerge. In the final chapter I will consider some of the questions and implications that emerge from these presentations of Pilate's character for us as contemporary readers of these gospel accounts.

CHAPTER TWO

Reading the Gospel Accounts of Pilate

At the end of Chapter One I outlined the questions I am addressing in this book. After identifying five quite different verdicts history has rendered on Pilate, and after describing six factors that in part account for those distinct verdicts, I concluded that we do not have enough information in the six brief sources that mention Pilate to attempt a "biographical sketch." Instead, I will focus on the way each gospel presents Pilate as a character in the story of Jesus' death. I will discuss each gospel account involving Pilate separately, respecting its particular presentation of him as a character and observing the different images of Pilate that emerge. I will not try to combine them into one. My central questions will be:

- How does each gospel present Pilate as it narrates the story of Jesus' crucifixion?

- What sort of role/s does he play?

- What sort of character is he in each of the gospel narratives?

- What sort of world does he inhabit and how do the texts, and we as readers, evaluate that world?

How Shall We Answer These Questions?

In framing the questions in this way I understand each gospel to be a story in its own right, with its own plot, distinct characters, settings, and themes. This understanding is shaped by a set of perspectives or questions derived from literary theory. Literary criticism reflects on various aspects of the act of reading: how texts are structured, how texts function in various contexts, what sorts of worlds and characters texts depict, how audiences

make meaning of texts. The last question belongs to a type of literary criticism or interpretation called audience-oriented criticism. The term "criticism" does not refer to a mean attack or to tearing something to pieces, as the word is popularly used. Rather, it refers to an approach or set of questions and perspectives that is employed to interpret a text. The term "audience-oriented" indicates a focus on how audiences or readers make meaning from a text rather than on what an author does to create a text.[1]

In this chapter I will briefly discuss several dimensions of this approach that are important factors in understanding Pilate's roles as a character in each of the gospel accounts. One dimension has to do with how we read gospel texts. Our only access to Pilate is as a character in these gospel texts, so it will be helpful to be aware of what we as readers do with the gospel texts when we read them. A second dimension concerns how we think about characters in a story, what they are, and how we construct and interact with them. And a third dimension is crucial: Pilate is a member of the Roman imperial world and in these stories he represents their power and commitments. We will need to be aware of how this system works, discern its impact in these texts, and evaluate the texts' perspectives on it.

1. What Happens When We Read Gospel Texts?

In Chapter One I described gospels as stories about Jesus written late in the first century, some forty to fifty years after Jesus' crucifixion. They are

- written from a particular perspective (by followers of Jesus)

- written for a particular audience (small communities of followers of Jesus)

- written with a theological agenda (to understand Jesus in relation to God's purposes)

- and written for a pastoral purpose (to shape the identity and way of life of Christian audiences).

---

[1] The literature is extensive. See Wolfgang Iser, *The Act of Reading: A Theory of Aesthetic Response* (Baltimore: The Johns Hopkins University Press, 1978); Peter J. Rabinowitz, "Whirl without End: Audience-Oriented Criticism," in G. Douglas Atkins and Laura Morrow, eds., *Contemporary Literary Theory* (Amherst, Mass.: University of Massachusetts Press, 1989) 81–100; Mark Allan Powell, *What is Narrative Criticism?* Guides to Biblical Scholarship (Minneapolis: Fortress, 1990); Warren Carter, *Matthew: Storyteller, Interpreter, Evangelist* (Peabody, Mass.: Hendrickson, 1996); Warren Carter and John Paul Heil, *Matthew's Parables: Audience-Oriented Perspectives.* CBA Monograph Series 30 (Washington, D.C.: Catholic Biblical Association, 1998).

A gospel, like any written text, is an act of communication. This act of communication involves an author who chooses certain words and puts them on the page in a particular order. It also involves an audience or reader who engages the words and makes sense of them. An author writes with some sense of this audience in mind. An author imagines an audience that is able to follow what is being written, to understand it, and to agree with or appreciate it. How the author imagines this audience is going to influence what the author chooses to say and how he or she says it—how difficult the words, how theoretical the content, how complex the style of writing. I, for example, am imagining an English-speaking audience, so I am not going to start writing in French. I am also imagining an audience that has not studied the gospel accounts of Pilate in any great detail. In addition, I am imagining a reasonably intelligent, adult audience. I am also imagining an audience capable of understanding the concepts and processing the information as it appears in this book in order to follow my argument.

This imagined audience, of course, exists only in an author's mind. While I can imagine the sorts of people for whom I am writing, I cannot see them or receive immediate feedback from them that will influence the next sentence that I type. But while this "authorial audience" exists in an author's mind, there is significant overlap between the audience for whom I imagine I am writing and the actual readers of this book. The competencies and interests that I assume of my authorial audience will be necessary competencies and interests for an actual audience.[2]

Reading, then, is a partnership. Authors choose the words to put on the page. But audiences have to make sense of them. Doing so can be a considerable challenge, especially when we are reading a gospel written some two thousand years ago.

READING A GOSPEL

Reading a gospel is like any act of reading. It is complex work that demands much of readers if we are going to understand what we are reading. The gospel authors assume we are competent or skilled enough to do a whole range of tasks.[3]

One task concerns the language. We have to notice the words they select, and connect them together, being attentive to how they might have been used previously in the gospel, whether they echo other biblical stories

---

[2] On the notion of an "authorial audience" see Carter, *Matthew: Storyteller,* and Carter and Heil, *Matthew's Parables* 8–17.

[3] Carter, *Matthew: Storyteller.*

and traditions, whether they are positive or negative terms, whether they are using language in a literal or figurative sense. Of course the language they wrote in was Greek, not English. Our English translations give us access to what they wrote, but at one step removed. Translation always involves some degree of interpretation.

Another task concerns the events or actions in the gospel. We have to work out the relationships between events. What time sequences are involved? What causal relationships, if any, link events? Determining these relationships and sequences enables us to construct the gospel's plot or story about Jesus. Filling in these "gaps" or "blanks" is crucial work. We also have to take note of the settings for events, who is involved, what happens, when, and where events happen, with what consequences. We have to decide the relative importance of any one event in relation to others.

A further task involves identifying the different points of view about Jesus that are offered throughout each gospel, evaluating them, and deciding whether to accept or reject them. Clearly, the more carefully we read, the more skilled we are in noticing and assembling the material we encounter in the gospel, the better our understanding will be. But without our efforts as hardworking and careful readers there will be no communication.

As we read a gospel we are constantly assembling pieces of information, impressions, and details into a larger whole. We read looking for consistency, though there is no guarantee we will find it. We try to build a world that makes sense of the actions (plot), characters, settings, and points of view we have identified in reading the text. Reading is, then, like putting together a jigsaw puzzle or assembling pre-cut furniture. We try to fit all the pieces together and to find the right place for all the bits!

And all of this happens in a process of ongoing discovery. Reading a gospel involves a temporal progression as we move through the text. We have to do these tasks over and over again as we read because we keep getting new information with each new episode and chapter. This new information causes us to be always looking back ready to revise, expand, or reinforce what we have already pieced together, yet we are also always moving forward, picking up new pieces of information that have to be connected to or integrated with what we have already put in place. Reading involves a constant progression through retrospection and anticipation, revision and integration, consolidation and expansion.

To What End?

The goal of this reading process is not just to know some more stuff. As far as the gospel writers are concerned, the goal is that gospel readers

might become more faithful followers of Jesus. Near the end of John's gospel we find these words:

> But these things are written so that you may come to believe that Jesus is the Messiah, the Son of God, and that through believing you may have life in his name. (John 20:31)

Luke's gospel begins with the author explaining that he writes his account about Jesus so that Theophilus and readers like him (his name means "one who loves God")

> may know security concerning the things about which you have been catechized or received previous (religious) instruction. (Luke 1:4, author's translation)

Christian readers have read the gospels in this way for two millennia now. Through the process and numerous tasks involved in reading they have sought better understanding of God's purposes manifested in Jesus. And Christian readers have sought to allow these texts to shape their thinking and living. The gospels use lots of literary or storytelling techniques—repetition, contrasts between scenes, direct teaching from Jesus, appropriate actions, words from God, for example—to accomplish these purposes.

But the gospel cannot guarantee that such believing, security, and way of life will be the outcome of our reading. Such outcomes are by no means inevitable. We can read carefully and skillfully, doing all the active and creative work I have outlined above. We can understand the gospel, the significance of Jesus, the required way of life of disciples. But we can still decline to adopt this perspective and way of life.

Readers and audiences always have this choice. For instance, if we read one of Adolf Hitler's terrible anti-Jewish speeches from Nazi Germany in the 1930s we can work out fairly easily whom we are supposed to hate, how we should express our hatred, and why. But while we can understand the rhetorical devices and follow the argument, we do not have to be persuaded to act and live that way. We can reject the argument and refuse to assent to the claims being made. We cannot plead, "The text made me do it."

As we read each of the gospel narratives about Pilate we will be attentive to these sorts of tasks that any responsible reader undertakes. We will try to work out how Pilate fits into the gospel plots. We will be attentive to the points of view about him that are being offered. We will want to work out what sort of character he is and what sort of world he represents.

And we can think about how any of this might relate to how we live. We might, for instance, examine our attitudes to and actions concerning the exercise of power, what justice looks like, how God might be at work in the world.

2. Reading as Character-Building Work: Assembling Pilate

Constructing characters is one of the tasks readers are expected to undertake. Pilate was a real human being in the first century. We meet him, though, as a character in the gospel scenes. How do audiences construct characters?[4]

We do not meet Pilate already assembled! As with everything else in the gospels, we as readers are going to have to do our construction work. Just as we connect events together to form a coherent plot, just as we interpret the significance of settings, so we also link features, words, and actions together to construct characters, including Pilate.

This is, of course, what we do with "real" people we meet each day. At our first meeting we form an initial impression. Over time, with subsequent interactions, we confirm, expand, or revise those impressions (sometimes significantly). We observe traits or features from their actions and words, their relationships and conflicts, to build a sense of who they are, their character. Our knowledge will always be limited, but we will try to mold it into some sort of coherent entity.

This character-building work is something we do with all characters in a story or movie. None of the gospels, for example, gives us a complete picture of Jesus the minute he appears in the gospel. We have to read the accounts of his actions, his interactions and conflicts with other characters, his teachings, and the various interpretive perspectives used to highlight his significance (such as Scripture quotations) to assemble a picture or character. Likewise with Pilate. As we read through each gospel narrative we are going to build an image of Pilate from his actions, words, relationships, and interactions.

---

[4] On character building see Seymour Chatman, *Story and Discourse* (Ithaca, N.Y.: Cornell University Press, 1978) 107–38; Baruch Hochman, *Character in Literature* (Ithaca, N.Y.: Cornell University Press, 1985); John Darr, "Narrator as Character: Mapping a Reader-Oriented Approach to Narration in Luke-Acts," *Semeia* 63 (1993) 43–60; Carter, *Matthew: Storyteller* 189–256; William H. Shepherd, Jr., *The Narrative Function of the Holy Spirit as a Character in Luke-Acts*. SBLDS 147 (Atlanta: Scholars, 1994) 43–90.

MATTHEW'S PILATE, FOR EXAMPLE

This character-building work begins when Pilate is introduced into the gospel story. His first appearance in Matthew offers a good example of our character-building work:

> When morning came, all the chief priests and the elders of the people conferred together against Jesus in order to bring about his death. They bound him, led him away, and handed him over to Pilate the governor. (Matt 27:1-2)

What do we learn about Pilate from this first reference?

Notice that we do not get a description of what he looks like. The gospel has no interest in whether he is cute or ugly, tall or short, muscular or fat. Pilate is not introduced in relation to his parents or his favorite food or music or sports team or movie or salary or net worth or his wife or kids (did he have kids?). Rather, this first reference concentrates on only one thing, his political role. He is the governor. But the gospel does not provide any information about being governor. There is no sentence explaining his job, no sidebar, no footnote, no "Dear reader," nothing. The gospel assumes that its audience knows about Roman governors! That was a reasonable expectation for a first-century audience, but not for us. We aren't familiar with any Roman governors in our world. So we will need to find out something about the Roman empire in order to understand the system that Pilate represents and defends in executing Jesus. And we will need to investigate the role of Roman governors in that system to understand Pilate's role in it. In Chapter Three I will elaborate what governors did in the Roman imperial world. That information will show that Pilate is a very powerful character who represents and defends some very particular interests and commitments in this scene.

Moreover, knowing that Pilate is a political figure prompts further questions that will affect our understanding of him. How are other political figures and rulers presented in the gospel? What points of view have been expressed about rulers previously? Does the gospel admire or criticize rulers and governors?

For example, if we have been attentive readers of Matthew's gospel in Greek we would know that the term used to refer to Pilate as "governor" in 27:2 was used back in ch. 2 to refer to Jesus! In 2:6 Jesus is identified in a quotation from the biblical book of Micah as the "governor" or ruler (the more common English translation) who is to represent God's reign among God's people. The use of the same Greek noun for these two quite different

characters, Jesus and Pilate, is interesting. If Jesus is God's chosen representative and ruler/governor, what perspective does that offer on Pilate's governorship? We know there can't be two legitimate governors. Jesus has God's stamp of approval, and in this gospel God's perspective is the one by which everything else is assessed. It seems, then, that the gospel does not view Pilate and the Roman imperial system that he represents as friendly to God's purposes! Two quite different claims to exercise rule and to shape human society collide in this scene. This collision will cast a long shadow over the whole exchange between Pilate and Jesus.

The introduction of Pilate emphasizes two further elements of hostility and conflict between Jesus and Pilate. If we have been reading Matthew's gospel carefully we will remember that the term "governor" has also been used in another verse in the gospel, in 10:18. There Jesus warns disciples that governors in general will be hostile to them as they bear witness to God's purposes. In that verse Jesus does not specify Pilate, but that warning sets up the expectation that Pilate will be a hostile governor resisting God's agent Jesus. We will have to read on through the whole scene to see if this expectation is confirmed or revised.

And second, v. 1 of ch. 27 has established that the Jerusalem elite, the chief priests and elders, wants to kill Jesus. That is the context in which they hand him over to Pilate. We will have to think some more about the relationship between the Jerusalem elite and Pilate in the next chapter. But it is sufficient here to note the sequence. We are not told explicitly in v. 2 why they hand Jesus over to Pilate! But the sequence in which v. 1 expresses their desire to kill Jesus and then v. 2 narrates their handing over of Jesus to Pilate suggests to us what Pilate's role might be. As readers we can reasonably infer that he will be the one who brings about Jesus' death.

That is a significant piece of information for two reasons. First, it identifies Pilate as an executioner, the one with life-and-death power. We will want to inquire further about the sort of world and society Pilate is protecting as he eliminates Jesus. Why is Jesus such a threat? But further, at the very outset of the scene Pilate's role as the executioner is already being established! The trial hasn't happened yet, and already the outcome of Jesus' meeting with Pilate is being signaled. In other words, Jesus is as good as dead from the outset and without a trial! That observation does not put Roman justice in a very good light at all. It subtly expresses a very negative judgment on the one who enacts judgment in this scene.

So far we have noticed a few details from these two verses in Matthew 27, and we have started to put them together. We are using some knowledge about the historical circumstances of Rome's empire, and we are using some of the information and perspectives evident in the first part of

Matthew's gospel. As readers we are already building an image of Pilate, and it isn't very positive. From these details and traits we are starting to put Pilate's character together. But if we had missed these details, if we had not noticed them or not made the connections to the earlier sections of the gospel, or paused to think about their significance, our character-building work would not be as accurate or rich.[5]

Reading, then, is character-building work. As we read each gospel account involving Pilate, we will notice, if we read carefully, a series of character traits or aspects. In collecting these features we will have to decide how to put each trait together with the other traits. We will have to consider what importance or significance we give to each aspect. The aspects that we particularly notice or highlight will especially influence the image of Pilate that we gain. The gospel authors expect us to be competent to do this character-building work.

3. Perspectives on the Roman Empire and Assumed Knowledge

Recall the way Matthew introduces Pilate:

> They bound him, led him away, and handed him over to Pilate the governor. (Matt 27:2)

As I just pointed out, the reference to Pilate as a governor assumes that the gospel audience knows something about the Roman empire and about the place and roles of governors in that system. My view is that Matthew's gospel was probably written in the city of Antioch, the capital of the Roman province of Syria, where the Roman governor of Syria lived. Members of the gospel's audience had probably passed by the governor's administrative building and had seen the governor with his entourage of attendants or with troops in the city.

But for us, we who are readers in the twenty-first century, the assumption that we know about Roman governors and the Roman empire is of course not reasonable. If we live in the United States we know something about democratically-elected state governors who exercise some power in accord with their state's body of elected representatives. But this system is vastly different from the one in which Pilate exercises his power

---

[5] For further discussion of these Matthew references see the relevant sections in Warren Carter, *Matthew and the Margins: A Socio-Political and Religious Reading* (Maryknoll, N.Y.: Orbis, 2000).

as governor. He was not elected by anyone and was certainly not understood to be responsible to "the people." If we are going to understand the dynamics of these four gospel scenes involving Pilate we will need to learn something about Pilate's place in the Roman imperial world and the system and values he represents in these scenes.

Moreover, we are reading trial scenes. We cannot assume that Roman trials are identical to our systems of justice. What rules of evidence are operative, if any? Does everybody, including low-status people, get a "fair" hearing? How do you defend yourself? What significance does it have that the ruling elite, Pilate and his Jerusalem allies, are deciding the fate of Jesus, a provincial of low status? How significantly do those two factors determine the scene's outcome? It is not just that Jesus is on trial before Pilate for his life. A powerful governor from an occupying nation is deciding the fate of a person from the occupied people. What role do prejudices— those of the wealthy and powerful toward a low-status, poor, and powerless person like Jesus, those of a Roman official toward those not from Rome— play in this scene? Do punishments fit the crime or the person?

Likewise, we noticed that the Jerusalem elite hands Jesus over to Pilate. We will need to give some attention to the links between Pilate and the Jerusalem leaders. That question is complicated for us because when we read their titles as "chief priests," "scribes," and "Pharisees," we immediately think of them as *religious* leaders." But that view is only partly correct. We will have to adjust our modern thinking to understand them also as figures who have enormous socio-political power in Rome's imperial world and who hold their elite positions of power in alliance with Pilate and Rome. It is crucial for us to understand that there is no separation of political and religious power in these stories. That reality is often hard for Christian readers to understand, especially if we are used to reading these stories for our own private religious devotion. They are very political stories.

And we cannot forget that we are not reading court transcripts! We are reading accounts from writers who have a great interest in (and commitment to) what is happening in these scenes. What "spin" is placed on the scene by the fact that the stories are being told by people who are followers of Jesus, who is being crucified by the occupying power? Can we expect them to paint the occupiers in a good light to earn their favor? Or will they present them in a negative light in the interests of helping other followers to follow Jesus loyally?

In these matters of

- the role and place of governors,

- the nature of the Roman imperial and legal system,

- the socio-political and "religious" roles of the Jerusalem leaders,

- the "spin" or perspectives of the gospels,

the gospel narratives simply assume their audiences have the necessary information. That is because these structures were a fundamental part of the world from which the gospels originated and in which their first audiences lived. The Roman imperial world leaves its marks on these texts. But because we do not live in such a world it is often difficult for us to recognize the political structures and values assumed by the texts, and so we tend to misread or overlook these aspects. In the next chapter I will supply some of the knowledge that the gospels assume we have.

4. Post-Colonial Criticism

However, it is more than just a matter of learning some appropriate information. It is also a matter of reading with a certain perspective. For a long time scholars have paid attention to the historical contexts of the gospels. For a long time readers have known that Pilate is a Roman governor. But only recently have biblical scholars started to pay serious attention to the *dynamics* of Roman imperial rule for understanding the gospel texts and to the *societal significance* of advocating certain interpretations of the biblical material. This emphasis, a branch of cultural studies known as post-colonial criticism, has encouraged a new focus on and evaluation of the impact of imperial structures and worldviews not only on the biblical documents that so often originate from worlds dominated by empires, but also on the interpretations of this biblical material.[6]

A key question for this approach concerns how the gospels and their interpreters interact with the Roman imperial world. Since the gospels originate in an imperial world, we would expect them to be influenced by an imperial mindset and worldview. It is not surprising, then, that when Jesus talks about God's good purposes for people and for the world he uses the language of the "kingdom" or "reign" or "empire" of God. Applying that language to God's work directly reflects the influence of his empire-dominated world. And, as we will see in the narratives about Pilate, it is no surprise that the issue of Jesus' identity is expressed in questions about Jesus being "king of the Jews." In an imperial world in which Rome and its

---

[6] Rasiah S. Sugirtharajah, *Asian Biblical Hermeneutics and Postcolonialism: Contesting the Interpretations* (Maryknoll, N.Y.: Orbis, 1998); Fernando F. Segovia, *Decolonizing Biblical Studies: A View from the Margins* (Maryknoll, N.Y.: Orbis, 2000).

ruler, the emperor, claim sovereignty over Jews and Judea, questions about who is king are fundamental.

But while identifying the influence of the Roman imperial world on the gospels is important, post-colonial criticism encourages us to notice how the gospels evaluate the Roman empire. Do the gospels only mirror this world? Do they accept this way of structuring human society without question? Or do they resist it in some way? Further still, do interpretations of the gospel material promote imperial values such as submission and unquestioning consent, or do they question the impact of these structures on human lives?

I will suggest in Chapters Four through Seven that we read these scenes involving Pilate and Jesus in part as stories of resistance. I will argue that, throughout, the gospels present Jesus as resisting the Roman imperial system with a vision of an alternative structure and a set of practices that constitute a different way of life. I think that his resistance is a primary reason why he is on trial and a primary motivation for Pilate's role in removing this unwelcome challenge from Roman-controlled society. Jesus has not shown due respect for, compliance with, and submission to the system Pilate represents. The gospel emphasis on resistance and on alternative ways of organizing human interaction functions to mold followers of Jesus into communities with alternative practices and commitments.

If this claim is sustainable, it raises some interesting questions about how we read these Pilate narratives. Do we even notice the imperial structures and their destructive impact? Or do we, as I was brought up to do, think about these scenes only in relation to some very narrowly understood "religious" questions while ignoring other very important dimensions? Once we do notice the imperial structures, with whom do we side in this conflict between Pilate and Jesus, between Rome's empire and God's? Are our sympathies with Pilate, the representative of law and order, the guy who defends the way things are, the one who is merely doing his job? Or do we evaluate his actions in terms of the system that requires him to act in this way? Do we question the system he represents? Is it a system worth defending and maintaining with violence and death? Is it a fair system? Who benefits from it and who is hurt by it? Should it be changed? If so, how? If Pilate is only doing his job, is his job worth doing? And what about Jesus' role? Is he an anarchist in challenging Rome's system? Is he naïve to imagine and work for a different world? Is it worth dying for?

These sorts of questions and our responses to them will often reveal (and challenge?) personal commitments and values that have been shaped by our upbringing, religious training, various social and cultural experiences, and by how we see the world. Interpretations of these scenes will

defend or challenge, promote or criticize Pilate and the system he represents. Post-colonial criticism encourages us to examine the values and commitments promoted by our own views and advocated by the interpretations of others. Whose interests are being defended? Whose interests are being promoted?

Post-colonial criticism invites us, then, to ask such questions as we read these texts. But in doing so it does not pretend to be disinterested. It has a particular point of view or reading strategy that has at least three general emphases.[7]

1. Post-colonial criticism wants us to think about the systems of power in these gospel scenes "from below" or "from the margins." It wants us to explore how these systems work to dominate and control others in the narratives—and beyond, in our own world. It wants us to think about their impact on behalf of those who do not live at the center and who are often the victims of an empire's self-interest and actions for its own advantage.

2. Post-colonial criticism wants us to resist such ways of organizing human societies by imagining and living for alternative worlds. These worlds will be marked by a justice that embraces rightly-ordered relationships and fair access to resources like land and goods.[8] These worlds will involve new identities and arrangements of power, new societies that respect human diversity and ensure that all have adequate access to necessary resources.

3. Post-colonial criticism wants us to read texts such as these gospel accounts involving Pilate, biblical texts that have been so important in western civilization, with an eye on these complex questions. It wants us to discover in these texts the ways in which certain powerful ideas about human society have been at work, and to observe ways in which people have resisted such structures and imagined very different worlds. But reading is not just about putting words and characters together. It is also about living when we put the book down. This post-colonial approach wants us to be shaped and impacted by such inquiry so that we consider the ways in which

[7] I am working here with Sugirtharajah's helpful emphases on representation, identity, and reading posture, *Asian Biblical Hermeneutics* 16–28.

[8] For some biblical passages offering such visions centered on the establishment of God's will (though not without their own ambiguities) see Psalm 72; Isa 2:1-4; 25:1-10; 35; Matt 4:17–5:12. See Carter, *Matthew and the Margins* 119–37.

our own world is structured, and so that we live lives that resist and liberate humans from such abusive use of power.

As we think about each of the gospel stories involving Pilate in this context of Roman imperial power, we will read with these issues in mind. We will notice an understandable dual way of relating to the imperial world. At times we will notice the stories being significantly shaped by their imperial world. At times they will seem quite conformist and sympathetic in their presentations of Pilate. But at other times we will notice considerable criticism of the Roman system that Pilate represents. To offer such criticism is of course quite subversive and risky in provoking socioeconomic and even political retaliation. It is to take a bold step of daring to imagine that the world does not have to be this way. The power group, of which Pilate is a member, has much to protect and much to lose if such imagining takes hold!

CHAPTER THREE

Governors and the Roman Imperial System

The gospels originate from a world dominated by Roman imperial control.[1] They assume their audiences are familiar with such a world. When they refer to Pilate as a governor they assume we understand his role as one who maintains Roman power. In this chapter I will briefly describe some features of the Roman empire and the place of governors in it. My description is partial and broad in its emphases.

The Roman imperial world was marked by a vertical and hierarchical social structure with vast wealth and power concentrated in the hands of a very few. Most people had access to neither wealth nor power nor status. It was an "aristocratic empire"[2] in which the "aristocracy," perhaps two to five per cent of the population, ruled large areas of territory through a small bureaucracy in alliance with provincial elites. Agrarian empires like Rome's are, typically, conquest states in which a dominant central state—Rome—forcibly subjugates people and land. They operate on the principle that "force is the foundation of political sovereignty."[3] I will now elaborate these features of the Roman imperial world.

---

[1] Edward Said (*Culture and Imperialism* [New York: Vintage Books, 1994] 9) defines imperialism as "the practice, the theory, and the attitudes of a dominating metropolitan center ruling a distant territory."

[2] For good discussions see John Kautsky, *The Politics of Aristocratic Empires* (Chapel Hill: University of North Carolina Press, 1982); Gerhard E. Lenski, *Power and Privilege: A Theory of Social Stratification* (New York: McGraw-Hill, 1966) 189–296; Peter Garnsey and Richard Saller, *The Roman Empire: Economy, Society and Culture* (Berkeley: University of Carolina Press, 1987); Richard Alston, *Aspects of Roman History AD 14–117* (London: Routledge, 1998) 208–318.

[3] Lenski, *Power* 51, 195; Said, *Culture and Imperialism* xii–xiii, 78.

1. The Ruling Elite

At the top of the imperial structure, and at its center in Rome, was the emperor. He, and it was always a "he" in the first century, exercised enormous power. His position and power, along with Rome's empire, were understood to be the will of Jupiter and the gods. Virgil declares that Jupiter has decreed that Romans are "lords of the world" and has granted them "an empire without end" (*Aeneid* 1.254, 278-79, 282). The Roman writer Seneca has the emperor Nero articulate the relationship he imagines he has with the gods and the nations (*On Mercy* 1.2-3):

> Have I of all mortals found favor with Heaven and been chosen to serve on earth as vicar of the gods? I am the arbiter of life and death for the nations; it rests in my power what each man's [sic] lot and state shall be: by my lips Fortune proclaims what gift she would bestow on each human being: from my utterance peoples and cities gather reasons for rejoicing; without my favor and grace no part of the whole world can prosper; all those many thousands of swords which my peace restrains will be drawn at my nod, what nation shall be utterly destroyed, which banished, which shall receive the gift of liberty, which have it taken from them, what kings shall become slave and whose head shall be crowned with royal honor, what cities shall rise and which shall fall—this is mine to decree.

In the Roman empire, politics and religion do mix.

Legitimated by the gods, the emperor shares the benefits and rewards of this great power and wealth with the small ruling elite. He appoints them to serve as political officials, military leaders, and religious officials just as the emperor Tiberius appoints Pilate provincial governor of Judea. As a governor, Pilate represents and enforces the empire's control through tours of his province, administering justice, collecting taxes, deploying troops,[4] and securing alliances with local landowning and religious elites.[5]

Cooperation with the emperor leads to increased wealth, power, and status for members of the elite. Given that the benefits of power are so

---

[4] Peter Brunt, *Roman Imperial Themes* (Oxford: Clarendon, 1990) 53–95, 163–87, 215–54; G. P. Burton, "Proconsuls, Assizes, and the Administration of Justice under the Empire," *Journal of Roman Studies* 65 (1975) 92–106.

[5] See Vivian Nutton, "The Beneficial Ideology," in P. D. A. Garnsey and C. R. Whittaker, eds., *Imperialism in the Ancient World* (Cambridge: Cambridge University Press, 1978) 209–21; Martin Goodman, *The Ruling Class of Judea: The Origins of the Jewish Revolt Against Rome A.D. 66–70* (Cambridge: Cambridge University Press, 1987); Brunt, *Roman Imperial Themes* 267–87.

great, it is not surprising that members of the elite regularly conflict with each other and with the emperor as they struggle for "fabulous wealth and immense power . . . privilege, and prestige."[6] One sign of those tensions is found in the murder of four emperors in the first century C.E.: Gaius Caligula in 41, Claudius in 54, Vitellius in 69, Domitian in 96, while a fifth, Nero, committed suicide in 68 after being identified as a public enemy! We will notice other signs of such tensions in several of the gospel scenes involving Pilate. Particularly in the accounts in Luke and John, Pilate seems unwilling to cooperate with his allies, the Jerusalem leaders, arrogantly dismissing their concerns (Luke), and soliciting expressions of loyalty and dependency from them before he authorizes Jesus' death (John).

With control over the primary resource of land and its production, this elite group exercises great political control and acquires vast wealth through taxes, rents, and tributes. The ruling elite sees political power as something to be used not for the maximal common good of all, but for one's personal benefit and, in turn, for the good of one's heirs. The threat of the military muscle of the legions ensures most people paid the taxes. Rome regards failure to pay tax and tribute as rebellion against Rome's sovereignty and uses troops to enforce control.[7]

Along with tribute, "laws and Roman jurisdiction" are imposed on the conquered as a means of effecting and maintaining control (Tacitus, *Annales* 15.6). Virgil has Jupiter tell Mercury that Rome is to "bring all the world beneath [its] law" (*Aeneid* 4.231). But such divine sanction serves to protect elite Roman interests. Sales of favor (bribes), whether for beneficent action, legal decisions, or appointments to desirable positions, provides further income for the elite. As I will elaborate below, the Roman legal system privileges the elite and works against provincials and those of lower status like Jesus.

Taxes and military power, then, form the basis of the empire's "legionary economy."[8] Political offices and laws sanction both activities and so protect the elite's political, economic, and social inequality and privilege.[9] A huge gap exists between their power and wealth and the poverty and powerlessness of most of the population.

---

[6] Lenski, *Power,* 210–12.

[7] Stephen Dyson, "Native Revolts in the Roman Empire," *Historia* 20 (1971) 239–74. As one example, Josephus has Agrippa declare to the Jewish people in revolt against Florus in 66 C.E. that their non-payment of tribute is an "act of war." Paying the tribute would clear them of the "charge of insurrection" (*Jewish War* 2.403-404).

[8] Kautsky, *Politics* 6, 144–55.

[9] Lenski, *Power* 210; Alston, *Aspects* 227–45, 265–88.

The elite of this very vertical and hierarchical society values power, wealth, and status or public reputation above all else.[10]

- Power or the ability and means of influencing actions and decisions derives from and is expressed through alliances, patronage, friendship, and kinship; through political debate and office; through control of land and peasants, and of course through military resources and service.

- Wealth is based on (often inherited) land ownership and production.

- Status or public repute is gained in part through networks of patron-client relationships, friendship, and kinship,[11] through displays of wealth and civic influence (sponsoring games, building a bath house, giving a handout to the poor), and from the recognition by others of one's dominant position.

As provincial governor of Judea, Pilate embraces, embodies, and upholds these values. He represents a society of great hierarchy, vast inequalities of wealth and access to and exercise of power, domination by the elite, and coerced compliance for the rest.

2. Retainers

The elite creates a retainer class to assist it in governing. This group, perhaps five percent of the population, comprises "officials, professional soldiers, household servants, and personal retainers, all of whom served them in a variety of more or less specialized capacities."[12] As agents of the aristocracy, retainers personalize and represent its power among the lower orders and throughout the empire, performing its wishes, enacting its decisions, and maintaining its hold over land and people. As representatives of and associates with the aristocracy, and elevated above most people, they share in the benefits of significant power, status, and wealth.

Important for the Pilate scenes is the recognition that religious officials are part of the retainer class. They maintain and advance the interests of the

---

[10] Plutarch, "How to Tell a Flatterer," *Moralia* 58D, also 100D, 778A.

[11] K. C. Hanson and Douglas Oakman, *Palestine in the Time of Jesus: Social Structures and Social Conflicts* (Minneapolis: Fortress, 1998) 19–99; Richard Saller, *Personal Patronage under the Empire* (New York: Cambridge University Press, 1982); Garnsey and Saller, *Roman Empire* 148–59; Alston, *Aspects* 217–26.

[12] Lenski, *Power* 243–48.

ruling Roman elite.[13] When the gospels refer to chief priests, Sadducees, leading Pharisees, and scribes, with whom Jesus is in conflict, they refer to Jewish officials often based in Jerusalem and its Temple. They form the ruling aristocracy who in alliance with Rome has immense political, social, ~~have~~ and economic power. Temple worship required large supplies of agricultural products, so the priests presided over an immense Temple economy. Regular sacrifices required cattle, sheep, and birds, as well as wood (for burning offerings), oil, salt, grain, fruit crops, and incense. The Temple's ongoing construction into the 60s C.E. consumed building material (stone, wood, precious metals, linen, wool). Much was supplied through a first-fruit tithe on animals and crops (paid in goods to the priests: see Neh 10:32-39), extra taxes, and by a tax paid in money by every male (a half-shekel or two didrachma/denarii).[14] Rome did not interfere in the collection of these taxes and tributes (Josephus, *Jewish War* 6.335).

Clearly, the Jerusalem elite that administers this system does not have an exclusively "religious" agenda or role. The elite upholds and impacts the economic and societal structures for its own benefit. Josephus records that his priestly colleagues in Galilee "amassed a large sum of money from the tithes which they accepted as their priestly due" (*Life* 63). Teaching and religious practices like tithing and taxes maintain the socio-economic hierarchy (in alliance with Rome) and ensure the elite's wealth at the expense of the rest.

Josephus presents the chief priests as retainers who are the essential rulers of Judea (*Jewish Antiquities* 20.251). He consistently links these so-called "religious leaders" with the "notables" or "powerful ones/magnates" in advocating cooperation with and submission to Rome.[15] The chief priests and the "most notable Pharisees," for example, assemble with "the powerful citizens" in 66 C.E. to discuss their opposition to the lower priests' provocative act of no longer offering the daily sacrifices "for Caesar and the Roman people" (*Jewish War* 2.410-11; 197; cf 2.321-23, 336, 342). This alliance of the elite sends delegations to the governor Florus and to Agrippa exonerating itself from blame and expressing loyalty to Rome (*Jewish War* 2.418). Often allied with "the most notable Pharisees," they are consistently pro-Roman in the events leading up to the 66 C.E. war (*Jewish War* 2.320; 411). They exercise their power as retainers and gain considerable wealth at the pleasure of, in alliance with, and for the benefit of, Rome.

---

[13] Lenski, *Power* 256–66; Kautsky, *Politics* 81–83, 161–66; Anthony J. Saldarini, *Pharisees, Scribes, and Sadducees in Palestinian Society* (Wilmington, Del.: Michael Glazier, 1988) 35–49.

[14] Hanson and Oakman, *Palestine* 99–159.

[15] Josephus, *Jewish Antiquities* 18.2-3, valuation of property; *Jewish Antiquities* 20.178 on Felix; *Jewish War* 2.237-40 Cumanus.

This coalition of these Jewish leaders with the Roman officials and the intermingling of their religious and socio-political interests is evident in the gospels. For example, in Matthew's gospel in 2:4-6, King Herod, Rome's puppet king, assembles and questions his allies the "chief priests and scribes" about the Messiah's birthplace. They supply knowledge from their traditions that facilitates his violence against his subjects. At the end of the gospel the chief priests and elders assemble with Pilate's soldiers to spin a different story to explain the absence of Jesus' body (28:11-15). These actions attest a social and political alliance between the Jewish leaders and Rome's representative Pilate that is assumed in the trial of Jesus. The Jewish leaders and Pilate are allies and retainers in the Roman imperial system. We will notice, though, especially in Luke and John's scenes involving Pilate and Jesus, that the alliance between the Roman governor and the Jerusalem leaders is also marked by tensions, resentments, and struggles to maintain supremacy and dependency.

3. The Rest of the Population: Peasants and Artisans

The verticality and inequality of the empire is reflected in the large gap between the ruling class and the peasants and urban artisans. For most people this world of power, status, and wealth is far beyond their reach. Some merchants, those who gained enough commerce to elevate them above most of the population but not enough to join the aristocracy, occupy some middle ground. For those at the top, life could be very comfortable with great wealth, power, and prestige.

But it was not so for the peasants and artisans who comprise most of the population. While Roman rule provided some benefits (roads, order, etc.), life for most people was harsh and a constant struggle for survival. Given their illiteracy, these people have left few records. Nor does the elite with its perspective "from above" pay much attention in its writings to those "from below"—except to insult and despise them.[16] Poverty and low status provide an obvious motivation for such treatment.

So does place of origin. The Roman elite generally despises provincials (those who live in territory outside Rome governed by Rome). Disdain for them is evident in comments and practices. The famous orator Cicero, for example, expresses doubts about the motives and integrity of provincial witnesses (*Pro Fronteio* 27-36), and labels Africans, Spaniards, and Gauls,

---

[16] Klaus Wengst, *PAX ROMANA and the Peace of Jesus Christ* (Philadelphia: Fortress, 1987) 7–11; "A Lexicon of Snobbery," in Ramsay MacMullen, ed., *Roman Social Relations* (New Haven: Yale University Press, 1974) 138–41.

sizable populations under Roman control, "uncouth and barbarous nations" (*To his brother Quintus* 1.1.27). Roman governors treat leading provincials with disdain in inflicting on them punishments that disregard their status. Philo complains that the Roman governor Flaccus punished leading Alexandrian Jews with beatings more appropriate to low-status people (*In Flaccum* 78). Josephus is horrified that the governor Florus inflicted on leading Jews punishments such as flogging and crucifixion that were more appropriate for slaves. The use of such punishments expresses Roman arrogance and disdain for provincials.

The whole imperial system disparages, yet depends on and exploits, the poor. Rural peasants and urban artisans produce the goods and services, rendered in taxes and rents (often paid in kind), that sustain the wealth and lifestyle of the ruling elite. As much as thirty to sixty per cent of their production was claimed through various taxes.[17] Hunger, inadequate nutrition, and overwork were normal and contributed to the vast numbers of the sick who peopled the ancient world. "The great majority of peasants who lived in the various agrarian societies of the past apparently lived at, or close to, the subsistence level."[18] Akin to peasants, the smaller class of artisans in urban contexts employed varying degrees of skills to produce goods and services predominantly for the elite.[19] Slaves existed at multiple levels. Some had highly prized skills such as business management, teaching, or medical knowledge. These slaves could be well treated and could occupy positions of considerable status in doing their master's business. Other slaves, though, especially those doing manual work, were often not well treated and had no status.[20]

The very bottom layers of the social structure comprised the degraded and expendables. These groups consisted of those with no skills, but only their bodies for labor, as well as those who performed little labor such as criminals, beggars, the physically deformed, and the sick. Estimates number this group between five and ten per cent.[21]

RESISTANCE

Resistance always accompanies the assertion of power. The surviving literature from the Greco-Roman world, even though it was produced

[17] Lenski, *Power* 267.
[18] Lenski, *Power* 271.
[19] Lenski, *Power* 278–80.
[20] Thomas Wiedemann, *Greek and Roman Slavery* (Baltimore: The Johns Hopkins University Press, 1981).
[21] Lenski, *Power* 280–84.

predominantly by educated elite males, offers some glimpses of it. In a rare passage Tacitus ascribes a speech to the British chief Calgacus protesting Roman control. Calgacus describes the Romans as

> Robbers of the world . . . to plunder, butcher, steal, these things they misname empire; they make a desolation and they call it peace . . . our goods and chattels go for tribute; our lands and harvests in requisitions of grain; life and limb themselves are worn out in making roads through marsh and forest to the accompaniment of gibes and blows. (Tacitus, *Agricola* 31.1-2)

Violent and nonviolent resistance took place. In the year 66 C.E. some Jews in Judea revolted against the then Roman governor Florus. Four years later they were defeated and Jerusalem burned. Rome's puppet king Agrippa acknowledged that the revolt was sparked in part by Jews who, aware of "injustice" and "servitude," fanned hopes of "independence" and "liberty" (Josephus, *Jewish War* 2.345-49). Led by significant figures, Robin Hood-like bandit groups staked claims to independence from Roman control with attacks on aristocratic property and personnel.[22]

Other protests occurred. Tacitus narrates a scene in which Nero is aware that people are complaining about indirect taxes (*Annales* 13.50). Given the vast gap between ruler and ruled, the complaints must have been sustained and vociferous to gain the emperor's attention. Assaults on debt-record buildings in Jerusalem and Antioch around 70 C.E. indicate considerable hardship that can no longer be tolerated (Josephus, *Jewish War* 2.426-27; 7.55, 61). At various stages conquered peoples withheld taxes and tribute, an act of revolt against Roman authority.[23]

Some Jewish groups, especially after Rome's destruction of Jerusalem and its temple in 70 C.E., imagined Rome's destruction and the establishment of God's reign. A set of prayers, the Eighteen Benedictions, subversively prayed for God to restore Jerusalem, the Temple, and David's line of kings. Some apocalyptic works looked for God's agent, the messiah, to overthrow Rome, judge the wicked, and establish God's just reign (4 Ezra 7, 11-13; 2 Baruch 39-42). Such hopes clearly attest considerable dissatis-

---

[22] Lenski, *Power* 273-78; Brent Shaw, "Bandits in the Roman Empire," *Past and Present* 102 (1984) 3-52; Richard Horsley and John S. Hanson, *Bandits, Prophets, and Messiahs: Popular Movements in the Time of Jesus* (San Francisco: Harper & Row, 1988); Hanson and Oakman, *Palestine* 86-91.

[23] Stephen L. Dyson, "Native Revolts in the Roman Empire," *Historia* 20 (1971) 239-74.

faction with Rome's world. The gospels with their narratives about Jesus and his proclamation and embodiment of God's reign in anticipation of its future establishment over all belong in this context.

Nor should the "weapons of the weak" be overlooked. Peasants tried to protect their livelihood by nonviolently evading the various demands of taxes and services: hiding produce or lying about production levels to tax collectors, working slowly, pilfering, committing acts of sabotage. These small acts express dissent from the dominant aristocratic agenda and depict the hierarchical social system and its demands as unjust. They assert dignity, imagine an alternative, ensure survival.[24]

SUMMARY

A small ruling elite controlled the vast and hierarchical Roman empire. They exercised political, economic, military, and religious power over ninety per cent of the population. They defined who belonged in the decision-making processes, they controlled the production and consumption of wealth, and they exercised coercion and intimidation through military resources. This is the system and interests that Pilate represents and enforces as governor. We will look at the roles of governors in some more detail.

4. Pilate Among the Governors

Two of the gospels identify Pilate as a "governor." Matthew explicitly introduces him as "Pilate the governor" (Matt 27:2), using a term that commonly designates governors appointed from Rome (Josephus, *Jewish Antiquities* 18.170; 19.292).[25] Luke employs a related term for Pilate in Luke 3:1 ("when Pontius Pilate was governor of Judea"). Mark and John identify him with a building. Pilate encounters Jesus at the *praetorium*. The gospel writers assume that their audiences know that this building is the headquarters for a provincial governor. English versions often translate *praetorium* with the word "headquarters."

---

[24] James C. Scott, *Weapons of the Weak: Everyday Forms of Peasant Resistance* (New Haven: Yale University Press, 1985) 28–47.

[25] The term is ἡγεμών, *hegemon*. Josephus refers to governors of Syria such as Vitellius (*Jewish Antiquities* 15.405), Titius (*Jewish Antiquities* 16.270), Saturninus and Volumnius (*Jewish Antiquities* 16.344), Petronius (*Jewish Antiquities* 19.301), Marsus (*Jewish Antiquities* 19.340), Varro (*Jewish War* 1.398), and Ummidius Quadratus (*Jewish War* 2.239), as well as governors of Judea such as Florus (*Jewish Antiquities* 18.25) and Pilate (*Jewish Antiquities* 18.55), and Tiberius Alexander, governor of Egypt (*Jewish War* 2.492). Philo refers to the Egyptian governor Flaccus by this term (*In Flaccum* 31, 163) as well as by ἐπίτροπος (*In Flaccum* 43).

> Then the soldiers led [Jesus] into the courtyard of the palace, that is the governor's headquarters. (Mark 15:16)

> Then they took Jesus from Caiaphas to Pilate's headquarters. (John 18:28; also 18:33; 19:9; cf Matt 27:27)

The name *praetorium* derives in part from the title of an important Roman official who combined military and judicial functions, both of which comprised important aspects of a governor's role.

The inscription found at Caesarea in 1961, described in Chapter One, identifies Pilate as a *praefectus* or prefect. This term and its Greek equivalent are often used interchangeably with "procurator" and its Greek equivalent to denote governors (so Tacitus, *Annales* 15.44).[26] The term "prefect" has a military origin, while "procurator" is a civilian term. The use of both terms is appropriate for the variety of administrative, fiscal, legal, and military duties entrusted to governors. These terms—governor, praetorium, prefect, procurator—attest Pilate's role as governor and representative of Rome's ruling elite and the social, political, and legal structures outlined above.

The men whom emperors appointed as governors were often of the equestrian rank, the second aristocratic order below that of senators. Membership in this order required at least a certain level of wealth, usually based in land. Members of this rank occupied civilian and military positions in the empire and exerted considerable local power as magistrates and priests in the imperial cult. That is, in all likelihood Pilate, the fifth governor of Judea, came from a family of considerable status and wealth and probably had some military and/or civilian experience before being appointed governor.[27]

Governors of Judea	(Approximate) Dates (C.E.)
Coponius	6–9
M. Ambivius	9–12
Annius Rufus	12–15
Valerius Gratus	15–26

[26] See Warren Carter, *Matthew and Empire: Initial Explorations* (Harrisburg: Trinity Press International, 2001), ch. 9 n. 2 for details.

[27] Peter Brunt, "The Administrators of Roman Egypt," *Roman Imperial Themes* 215–54; "*equites*," *Oxford Classical Dictionary* 550–52.

Pontius Pilate	26–36
Marcellus	36–37
Marullus	37–41
Cuspius Fadus	44–46
Tiberius Julius Alexander	46–48
Ventidius Cumanus	48–52
M. Antonius Felix	52–60
Porcius Festus	60–62
Lucceius Albinus	62–64
Gessius Florus	64–66
(Jewish Revolt)	66–70

A GOVERNOR'S JOB DESCRIPTION

Various writers provide examples of the administrative, fiscal, military and judicial tasks entrusted to governors.[28]

- Governors settle disputes and keep order, especially among different ethnic groups (Josephus, *Jewish War* 2.487-93, in Alexandria; *Jewish Antiquities* 19.301; 20.125).

- Governors collect taxes (Albinus in Josephus, *Jewish War* 2.273) and have responsibility for fiscal administration (Philo, *In Flaccum* 4), including intervening in municipal financial affairs as necessary (Pliny, *Epistles* 10.38, 44).

- Governors engage in public works and building projects. Pilate builds a controversial aqueduct (Josephus, *Jewish War* 2.175; *Jewish Antiquities* 18.60). Pliny, the governor of Bithynia, consults the emperor Trajan about numerous building projects including aqueducts, theaters, gymnasiums, public baths (*Epistles* 10.37-44).

[28] Fergus Millar, ed., *The Roman Empire and Its Neighbours* (New York: Delacorte, 1966) 161–69; Brunt, "Administrators of Roman Egypt," *Roman Imperial Themes* 215; idem, "Procuratorial Jurisdiction," *Roman Imperial Themes* 163–87; Alston, *Aspects* 255–59. For the governor's exercise of justice as a delegated representative of and in consultation with the emperor see Peter Garnsey, *Social Status and Legal Privilege in the Roman Empire* (Oxford: Clarendon Press, 1970) 72–85.

- Governors command troops (Pilate in Josephus, *Jewish Antiquities* 18.55; Philo, *In Flaccum* 5), take military action to quell trouble-some subjects (Cestius against Galilee and Judea: Josephus, *Jewish War* 2.499-565), and engage in military action against bandits (Varro in Josephus, *Jewish War* 1.398).

- Governors administer justice. Some cases are brought to them (so Paul appears before Felix and Festus in Acts 23:24–26:30; cf. Philo, *In Flaccum* 4). Others they hear as they travel around their provinces.[29] It is very possible that Pilate is in Jerusalem because he is touring designated prominent cities in his province, such as Jerusalem, to hear civic and criminal cases.[30] Pilate likely encounters Jesus as one case among others.

- Governors have the power to put people to death. In effect this was the power to remove from society people who challenged the social order and interests of the elite. Josephus refers to governors (of senatorial provinces) who maintain control with the *fasces* (*Jewish War* 2.365-66). The *fasces,* an axe and bundle of six rods, were often ceremonially paraded to represent the administration of Roman justice. They "constituted a portable kit for flogging and decapitation. Since they were so brutally functional, they not only served as ceremonial symbols of office but also carried the potential of violent repression and execution."[31] That is, they secured the perception of the life-and-death power embodied in and executed by Rome's justice. The first governor of Judea, "Coponius, a Roman of the equestrian order, [was] entrusted by Augustus with full powers, including the infliction of capital punishment" (Josephus, *Jewish War* 2.117). Philo notes Flaccus' power to crucify people (*In Flaccum* 83-85). Clearly Pilate is assumed to have such power when Jesus is brought to him, and he exercises it in condemning Jesus to death by crucifixion.

ROMAN JUSTICE

Concern for justice is an aspect of the Roman world that is often celebrated as one of Rome's great gifts to the world. I have already noted

---

[29] Cicero and Pliny describe their traveling assizes. See also Anthony J. Marshall, "Governors on the Move," *Phoenix* 20 (1966) 231–46; Burton, "Proconsuls."

[30] Brent Kinman, "Pilate's Assize and the Timing of Jesus' Trial," *Tyndale Bulletin* 42 (1991) 282–95.

[31] Anthony J. Marshall, "Symbols and Showmanship in Roman Public Life: The *Fasces*," *Phoenix* 38 (1984) 120–41.

Rome's conviction of being chosen by the gods to spread its wonderful laws throughout the world as a precious gift to all people. In Virgil's *Aeneid* Anchises tells Aeneas in the underworld that he and Rome are commissioned "to rule the nations with your power" and "to crown peace with law" (*Aeneid* 6.851-53).

But this administration of justice by governors was also colored by the political and social structure of the empire. Roman "justice" was administered with a profound bias in favor of the elite and against those of lower status. This extensive commitment to the elite's "legal privilege" is seen, for instance, in much more lenient penalties for higher-status offenders and far greater opportunity to appeal to the emperor.[32] The whipping and crucifixion of Jesus are typical penalties for low-status offenders. By contrast, Josephus is horrified when the Governor Florus does "what none had ever done before," namely scourge and crucify members *of the Jewish elite* (*Jewish War* 2.308). Philo is similarly outraged when the Egyptian governor Flaccus ignores customs about different types of scourges for people of different social standing and treats all Alexandrian Jews as being "of the meanest rank" (*In Flaccum* 78-80). Peter Garnsey comments:

> In general it can be said that judges and juries were suspicious of, if not resentful towards, low-status plaintiffs who attacked their "betters" in court, and were prepared to believe the worst of low-status defendants, while the pleas of high-status plaintiffs or defendants . . . were given more credence.[33]

When Jesus is on trial before Pilate, these realities are at work. He is a socially low-status person on trial before the ruling elite that controls a system for its own benefit.

PILATE AND HIS ALLIES

Governors, as representatives of the Roman elite's interests, had great power and responsibilities. But their task was not easy. With small staffs, limited (though feared and very effective) military resources, and operating at a great distance from further resources and guidance in Rome, they faced a challenge in maintaining control and protecting Rome's interests. Part of Rome's strategy for social control was to secure the cooperation of the local provincial elite through alliances that emphasized their common

---

[32] Garnsey, *Social Status* 65–100, 103–52, 221–80. Wengst, *Pax Romana,* 37–40.
[33] Garnsey, *Social Status* 100.

interest in maintaining the status quo.[34] This does not mean that there were no conflicts with these elites, or that Roman officials did not treat provincial elites with prejudice and some disdain, but it does indicate a common commitment to the status quo and to protecting their mutual interests.

Pilate's allies in Judea were the Jerusalem leaders based in the Temple. One means of securing their loyalties was to involve Roman governors of Judea in appointing the chief priests. The governors also kept control of the priestly garments, the signs of their office and power. Josephus records that Pilate's predecessor, the governor Valerius Gratus, deposed and appointed at least five high priests throughout his eleven-year reign from 15–26 C.E. (*Jewish Antiquities* 18.33-35). In contrast, Caiaphas remained high priest from 18–36 C.E., throughout the whole of Pilate's administration (26–36 C.E.). This longevity suggests not only that Caiaphas enjoyed Pilate's favor but also that he was adroit at keeping the governor "happy" (which meant furthering Pilate's interests).

Both the governors and the chief priests needed each other. Governors needed cooperative priests and local landowners to maintain the hierarchical social order and ensure compliance with Rome. Pleasing the governor was the main way that the chief priests gained access to power, status, and wealth. The price for this position was to become agents of the Roman governors' interests. So later in the century, as war seemed imminent in the 60s C.E., the chief priests dutifully exhorted the people in Jerusalem to submit to, not resist, the corrupt and oppressive governor Florus (*Jewish War* 2.318-20). But as "brigands" seized power in Jerusalem the usual, hereditary ruling families who had cooperated with Rome lost power; the "brigands" elected by lot high priests who were "lowborn" (*Jewish War* 4.147-57).

Hence when the Jerusalem elite hands Jesus over to Pilate around the year 30 C.E. it would be incorrect to imagine that the scene is playing off "religious" personnel with limited interests and power against political personnel, or Jews against Romans. These are inappropriate categories for a hierarchical system that essentially allied the small Roman and local Jerusalem elite against the rest of the population. This system does not have checks and balances, burdens of proof, and a sense of public accountability. Instead, there are aristocratic alliances, "legal privilege," and bias against those of lower status.

Jesus is "handed over" to Pilate because the governor, the representative of Roman justice, is the only one entrusted in the province with powers of life and death. The limiting of the power to execute to the governor was

---

[34] Brunt, "The Romanization of the Local Ruling Classes," *Roman Imperial Themes* 272; Garnsey, *Social Status* 77–79.

another way of controlling the local elite and making it dependent on the governor. The first governor of Judea, Coponius, had been entrusted with this power in the year 6 C.E. by the emperor Augustus. Now it is Pilate's responsibility.

ABUSIVE, EXPLOITATIVE GOVERNORS

Governors represent a system that sustains the elite. They look out for the interests of the emperor, the empire, and the local elite in alliance with whom they exercise their rule. No doubt some governors did their best to fulfill a difficult role. Certainly elite writers like the orator Aristides extravagantly (and with obvious contradictions) praise governors for their devotion to the emperor and for their rule that "protects and cares for the governed":

> There is an abundant and beautiful equality of the humble with the great and of the obscure with the illustrious, and above all, of the poor man with the rich and of the commoner with the noble . . . (*Roman Oration* 31-39).

One wonders what planet Aristides inhabited.

Some have suggested that through the first century the quality of governors improved, with fewer abuses of power. But the first-century Egyptian Jew Philo did not think things had improved. He claims that the abuses of the governor prior to Flaccus in Egypt were serious but were initially repaired by the competent Flaccus (*In Flaccum* 1-5, 7). However, Flaccus deteriorates quickly and surpasses his predecessor with many excesses. And Philo can generalize:

> Some, indeed, of those who held governorships in the time of Tiberius and his father Caesar had perverted their office of guardian and protector into domination and tyranny and had spread hopeless misery through their territories with their venality, robbery, unjust sentences, expulsion and banishment of quite innocent people, and execution of magnates without trial. . . . (*In Flaccum* 105)

Tacitus, no friend to Jews, does not present a picture of gradual improvement, but seems to assume different intensities of abuse. The governor Antonius Felix (52–60 C.E.) "practiced every kind of cruelty and lust, wielding the power of king with all the instincts of a slave. . . . Still the Jews' patience lasted until Gessius Florus became procurator; in his time war began" (Tacitus, *Histories* 5.9-10).

In presenting various governors attending to their tasks, Josephus distinguishes varying levels of competency but reserves his worst criticism for Albinus and Florus, governors of Judea in 62–64 and 64–66 C.E. "The administration of Albinus, who followed Festus, was of another order; there was no form of villainy which he omitted to practice" (*Jewish War* 2.272). Josephus outlines those "villainies" as stealing property, imposing excessive taxation, freeing prisoners for a price, and stimulating social disorder by permitting attacks on the (wealthy) "peaceable citizens" to go unchecked and unpunished (*Jewish War* 2.273-76). Clearly the governor personally benefited from stealing property, attacking wealthier citizens, and imposing extra taxes. Josephus continues, "Such was the character of Albinus, but his successor, Gessius Florus, made him appear by comparison a paragon of virtue" (*Jewish War* 2.277).

Governors as Blood-Sucking Flies

Josephus attributes a significant passage about governors and a memorable image to the emperor Tiberius. The passage condemns all governors as unjust. Josephus, an ally of the Flavian emperors Vespasian, Titus, and Domitian, is commenting on Tiberius' tendency to leave governors in office for lengthy tenures. He reports Tiberius' claim to do so "out of consideration for the feelings of the subject peoples. For it was in the law of nature that governors are prone to engage in extortion." He has Tiberius argue that short-term appointments provoked governors to engage in as much exploitation for personal profit as possible. If the governor was quickly replaced, a new governor would immediately continue the process of harsh exploitation, making things continually bad for the subject people, who would not get a break from such behavior! Instead, a long tenure meant "those gorged by their robberies" would be sluggish to continue the exploitation, thereby giving the people some reprieve (*Jewish Antiquities* 18.172-73).

Josephus has the emperor Tiberius illustrate his point with a fable.

> Once a man lay wounded, and a swarm of flies hovered about his wounds. A passer-by took pity on his evil plight and, in the belief that he did not raise a hand because he could not, was about to step up and shoo them off. The wounded man, however, begged him to think no more of doing anything about it. At this the man spoke up and asked him why he was not interested in escaping from his wretched condition. "Why," said he, "you would put me in a worse position if you drove them off. For since these flies have already had their fill of

blood, they no longer feel such a pressing need to annoy me but are in some measure slack. But if others were to come with a fresh appetite, they would take over my now weakened body and that would indeed be the death of me" (*Jewish Antiquities* 18.175-76).

The fable is interpreted to show the demerits of short tenures for governors. Josephus goes on to explain that the emperor Tiberius

for the same reason took the precaution of not dispatching governors continually to the subject peoples who had been brought to ruin by so many thieves; for the governors would harry them utterly like flies. Their natural appetite for plunder would be reinforced by their expectation of being speedily deprived of that pleasure" (*Jewish Antiquities* 2.176).

The fable, whether actually spoken by Tiberius or not, is stunning for a number of reasons:

- It uses the image of flies sucking blood from an open wound to depict Roman provincial government administered by governors;
- It recognizes (in the mouth of an emperor!) that the relationship of governor and governed was one that sucked the lifeblood out of the provinces;
- It compares governors with pesky and potentially fatal flies;
- It compares governors with thieves;
- It identifies the provinces with a wounded and bleeding man who is in danger of death;
- It recognizes that such predatory and exploitative behavior is natural, inevitable, and uncontrollable;
- It has a wounded man (the provinces!) request the passer-by not to intervene lest things get worse;
- It demonstrates the wounded man's inability to request any other help;
- It shows the passer-by's inability to imagine any other intervention except to shoo flies away, but not to heal the man's wounded situation;
- It attests to the elite's advocacy of structured exploitation;

- It exists in a work authored by a Jew of priestly descent and a loyal ally of the Flavian emperors.

With this image of governors as blood-sucking flies Josephus lays bare the dominant and corrupt role of governors in the imperial system. That role is presented with a terrifying cynicism. In Josephus' narrative the emperor Tiberius presents the image without any remorse for the damage that his system causes, without any proposal for curbing the exploitation, and without any thought for its abolition. This is simply the way things are. And the alternative policy, shorter tenures, would make things a whole lot worse!

But such comments are not unusual. Juvenal advises a new governor:

> When you enter your long-expected province as its Governor, set a curb and limit to your passion, as also to your greed; have compassion on the impoverished provincials, whose very bones you see sucked dry of marrow (*Satires* 8.87-90).

Plutarch comments on "the procuratorships and governorships of provinces from which many talents may be gained" (*Moralia* 814d), while Plutarch praises Brutus' good governorship in Gaul in contrast to "other provinces [that], owing to the insolence and frivolity of their governors, were plundered as though they had been conquered in war" (*Brutus* 6). The leader Civilis complains that "we are handed over to prefects and centurions; after one band is satisfied with murder and spoils, the troops are shifted, and new purses are looked for to be filled and various pretexts for plundering are sought" (Tacitus, *Histories* 4.14). Suetonius criticizes Vespasian, emperor from 69–79, the time around which the gospels are written, for using governors to further his "love of money" (*Vespasian* 16):

> He is even believed to have had the habit of designedly advancing the most rapacious of his procurators to higher posts, that they might be the richer when he later condemned them [and confiscated their wealth through fines]; in fact it was common talk that he used these men as sponges because he, so to speak, soaked them when they were dry and squeezed them when they were wet.

Yet Rome had a vested interest in limiting the amount of plunder and keeping at least some semblance of law and order so as not to alienate the local elite and aggravate the local people into revolt.[35]

---

[35] Wengst, *Pax Romana* 35–37.

LEGAL ACTION AGAINST GOVERNORS

While it might seem that governors like Pilate had unbridled or un-accountable power, that was not the case, at least not in theory. Peter Brunt discusses the legal provision of *repetundae,* which prohibited various kinds of extortion involving force, intimidation, or fraud, undue extractions and illegal enrichment from the governed, and other oppressive acts of misgovernment.[36] Provincials did have the right of appeal. Jews in Judea could appeal first to the governor of Syria and then to Rome for redress.

But in practice exploitation was not restricted. Appeals against a governor who enjoyed the emperor's favor enough to be appointed in the first place had little chance of success. Philo cannot point to any governor removed from office in order to be tried for exploitative actions, though he knows of some punished after leaving office (*In Flaccum* 105-107). And when the Jewish citizens in Alexandria try to appeal to Rome against the governor Flaccus, they need Flaccus' permission to do so! He, predictably, obstructs the process of "justice" by omitting to pass the petition on to Rome (*In Flaccum* 97-101).

Brunt catalogues numerous obstacles to such appeals: distance from Rome, the expense of travel and accommodation while awaiting a hearing, pressure from a governor's allies in the province not to pursue action, the need even for the governor's consent for such a petition (Philo, *In Flaccum* 97-101; Josephus, *Jewish Antiquities* 20.7, 193), the influence of a governor's supportive allies in Rome, the risk of reprisal, divisions and rivalries in the province.[37]

Examples of these obstacles are readily available. We noted Flaccus' failure to pass on to Rome the petition against him. After the prosecution of Bassus, proconsul of Bithynia, the senate retaliates by attempting to prosecute Theophanes, the leader of the provincial prosecutors.[38] Some Jews from Caesarea complain against the governor Festus. Josephus comments that "he would undoubtedly have paid the penalty for his misdeeds against the Jews had not Nero yielded to the urgent entreaty of Felix's brother Pallas, whom he held in the highest honour." And in retaliation for bringing the complaint Syrian leaders successfully intervene and persuade Nero's tutor to urge the emperor to annul the grant of equal civic rights to the Jews in Caesarea (*Jewish Antiquities* 20.182).

---

[36] Brunt, "Charges of Provincial Maladministration," *Roman Imperial Themes,* 53–95, 487–506; for *repetundae* trials involving Pliny see Garnsey, *Social Status* 50–58.

[37] Brunt, "Charges of Provincial Maladministration," *Roman Imperial Themes* 71–95; Garnsey, *Social Status* 65–85; for the legal privileges of equestrians, ibid. 237–42.

[38] Garnsey, *Social Status* 55.

When Jews in Jerusalem seek an embassy to Nero against the governor Florus in 66, Agrippa tells them this action will only make matters worse. Flattery, not irritation, is the best approach. An embassy is an overreaction that "exaggerates minor errors"; it will lead to worse and open maltreatment; it will alienate the emperor who after all "cannot see in the west their officers in the east." He advises them to survive as best they can, "for the same procurator will not remain for ever, and it is probable that the successors of this one will show greater moderation in taking office" (Josephus, *Jewish War* 2.350-55). The Roman general Cerialis tells the Treviri and Lingones tribes in Gaul that they should endure "the extravagance or greed of your rulers," knowing that better ones will come, just as they endure "barren years [and] excessive rains" (Tacitus, *Histories* 4.74).

Pilate was the subject of such a complaint after attacking and killing a number of Samaritans. The Samaritans appealed to Vitellius, the governor of Syria, who ordered Pilate to "return to Rome to give the emperor his account of the matters," but Tiberius died before Pilate reached Rome (Josephus, *Jewish Antiquities* 18.88-89). This action effectively ended Pilate's governorship, but Josephus does not indicate whether any punitive action was taken against Pilate.

Conclusion

The gospel references to Pilate as a governor assume the sorts of realities I have described in this chapter. These Roman provincial administrative practices and social order provide the unspoken context for and the dynamics of the meeting between Pilate and Jesus. Pilate's role as governor is to protect and advance Rome's political and economic interests in alliance with the local elite. His role as governor in a trial assumes imperial dynamics of power, elite alliances, and legal privilege. Pilate represents and protects Rome's political, economic, military and legal interests in an exploitative and oppressive relationship over those he governs, and with little accountability on his part.

CHAPTER FOUR

Mark's Pilate

We turn now to Mark's gospel, probably the first of the gospels in the Bible to be written. What sort of portrait of Pilate do we find? As we try to answer this question it is important to remember that we are not reading a transcript of what actually happened. No one was running a video camera, no court reporter was taking it down word for word in shorthand. Rather, as the significant differences in the four accounts of the meeting between Jesus and Pilate show, the gospel writers freely interpret and recast the traditions about Jesus to present their own interpretations of these events.

As we look at each gospel account of Jesus' confrontation with Pilate, I will print the text of the episode from that gospel. But my comments about each episode will make much more sense if readers continue to refer to the gospel episode while they read the chapter. One way to do that would be to keep turning back to the text printed below. Another, perhaps better way would be to find the text in a Bible and keep an eye on the whole episode while reading my comments. I will include references to verses (15:1) to help with those connections, especially if your translation differs from the one I am using.

> **Mark 15:1** As soon as it was morning, the chief priests held a consultation with the elders and scribes and the whole council. They bound Jesus, led him away, and handed him over to Pilate.
>
> **2** Pilate asked him, "Are you the King of the Jews?" He answered him, "You say so." **3** Then the chief priests accused him of many things.
>
> **4** Pilate asked him again, "Have you no answer? See how many charges they bring against you." **5** But Jesus made no further reply, so that Pilate was amazed.

6 Now at the festival he used to release a prisoner for them, anyone for whom they asked. **7** Now a man called Barabbas was in prison with the rebels who had committed murder during the insurrection.

8 So the crowd came and began to ask Pilate to do for them according to his custom. **9** Then he answered them, "Do you want me to release for you the King of the Jews?" **10** For he realized that it was out of jealousy that the chief priests had handed him over. **11** But the chief priests stirred up the crowd to have him release Barabbas for them instead. **12** Pilate spoke to them again, "Then what do you wish me to do with the man you call the King of the Jews?" **13** They shouted back, "Crucify him!" **14** Pilate asked them, "Why, what evil has he done?" But they shouted all the more, "Crucify him!" **15** So Pilate, wishing to satisfy the crowd, released Barabbas for them; and after flogging Jesus, he handed him over to be crucified.

Often readers view Mark's Pilate as weak and indecisive (Verdict 2 in Chapter One). He knows Jesus is innocent, but, so the theory goes, he is worried about his own position and the possibility of riots if he acts on his own conviction and releases Jesus. Not wanting to anger either the Jewish leaders or the crowds, he bows to their wishes and condemns the innocent Jesus. Jesus' death is, according to this approach, the responsibility of the Jewish leaders, not Pilate. Mark's gospel supposedly tries to remove any blame from Rome. The consequence of this approach has been a long and tragic history of anti-Jewish attitudes and actions.

I will suggest that this is an unconvincing reading of Mark's scene. Apart from its tragic fostering of anti-Jewish attitudes, it ignores basic realities of Roman imperial society. Pilate is not weak. He is a Roman governor with enormous power (described in Chapter 3). The Jerusalem leaders, who have a socio-political as well as religious role, are his allies. Roman justice protects the interests of the elite against lower-status opponents like Jesus. Pilate exhibits his control by firmly and astutely guiding the scene's participants to do his will and further his interests. He perceives Jesus to be some sort of threat that he efficiently removes.[1]

Or so he thinks. We will also notice an irony created by Mark's gospel's theological perspectives. While Pilate and his allies think they have power, they are unknowingly subject to God's much greater purposes for a just world. The scene recognizes Pilate's power—he puts Jesus to death—but

---

[1] Though there are some differences, my reading is similar to those of Ched Myers, *Binding the Strong Man: A Political Reading of Mark's Story of Jesus* (Maryknoll, N.Y.: Orbis, 1988) 369–82, and Helen Bond, *Pontius Pilate in History and Interpretation.* MSSNTS 100 (Cambridge: Cambridge University Press, 1998) 94–119.

undercuts him by exposing the limits of his great power within God's cosmic scheme.

Historical Setting

Mark's gospel was probably written around the year 70 C.E., perhaps a year or two earlier, in Rome. Several pieces of data combine to suggest the gospel's likely origin in Rome, the center of the Roman empire.

- The author makes mistakes about the geography of Galilee, suggesting some distance from and lack of familiarity with Galilee. Gerasa (5:1) is actually south of the Sea of Galilee. Since Sidon is north of Tyre, one would not go through Sidon to the Sea of Galilee (7:31). At 11:1 the author incorrectly locates the village of Bethphage before Bethany.

- The author explains Jewish customs (7:3-4; 15:42) and words (5:41; 7:34; 14:36; 15:22, 34) to his audience, suggesting they are not familiar with this world.

- At 12:42 the poor widow puts "two small copper coins, which are worth a penny" into the Temple treasury. The author explains the value of the two coins to his audience by identifying them with a coin, a *kodrantes* or "penny," used in Rome and so familiar to the gospel's audience. This is one example of a number of Latin terms that appear in the gospel. Another is the term *praetorium,* which the author uses to identify the governor's headquarters or "palace" in 15:16.[2]

- Various early church traditions associate the gospel with Rome, though the historical value of this material can be difficult to assess. Perhaps more useful is the observation that the first citations of Mark appear in two works written in Rome, 1 Clement in the 90s (15:2) and Shepherd of Hermas in the early second century (5:2).

The audience for whom the gospel was written probably lived, then, in Rome. Each day they faced the challenge of living their lives faithfully as followers of Jesus in the center of the very empire whose representatives executed Jesus. More particularly, these representatives crucified him using a means of execution employed for foreigners or provincials who were judged to have rebelled against Rome's empire (Josephus *Jewish War*

---

[2] These Latin terms are often difficult to identify in English translations: 4:21, 28; 5:9, 15, 33; 6:27, 37; 7:4; 12:14; 15:15, 16, 39, 44, 45.

5.449-53). How this community of Jesus' followers understood itself in relation to Rome's power was an important issue, as was the question of how outsiders viewed the community of Christians.

In addition to daily life in the midst of Roman imperial power, two historical events in the life of this community seem especially important for understanding the gospel's story of Jesus. In the year 64 C.E. the emperor Nero attacked and killed some Christians in Rome. This event was restricted to Rome and was not an empire-wide policy of persecuting all Christians. If Tacitus, the Roman historian, is accurate, Nero's actions were motivated not by opposition to Christian affirmations and practices but by his need to find a scapegoat for the great fire of Rome in 64 C.E. Rumors suggested Nero himself had ordered the fire. So Nero deflected blame to some Christians and put them to death.[3] Some traditions include Paul and Peter among the martyrs. It seems to have been the case that these Christians happened to be in the wrong place at the wrong time, rather than there being a planned strategy to wipe out all Christians. Whatever the motivation, members of the gospel's audience know from their recent experience that they were vulnerable to the whims and terrible power of imperial officials.

Another event evidences the same power. Between 66 and 70 C.E. war broke out between Rome and Judea. By 69, about the time of the gospel's writing, the defeat and destruction of Jerusalem and its Temple seemed inevitable. The gospel seems to be aware of this imminent catastrophe. In ch. 13, Mark's Jesus predicts numerous forthcoming disasters, including the Temple's downfall. In response to a comment from a disciple about the magnificent Jerusalem Temple building, Jesus predicts:

> "Do you see these great buildings? Not one stone will be left here upon another; all will be thrown down." (Mark 13:2; see also 14:58; 15:29)

---

[3] Tacitus writes:
Therefore, to scotch the rumor, Nero substituted as culprits, and punished with the utmost refinements of cruelty, a class of people, loathed for their vices, whom the crowds styled Christians. . . . First, then, the confessed members of the sect were arrested; next, on their disclosures, vast numbers were convicted, not so much on the count of arson as for hatred of the human race. And derision accompanied their end: they were covered with wild beasts' skins and torn to death by dogs; or they were fastened on crosses, and when daylight failed were burned to serve as lamps by night (in Nero's gardens). . . . Hence, in spite of a guilt which had earned the most exemplary punishment, there arose a sentiment of pity, due to the impression that they were being sacrificed not for the welfare of the state but to the ferocity of a single man. (*Annales* 15.44, LCL)

For the gospel's audience, aware of this war and Rome's imminent triumph, Rome was doing the same sort of subjugating and death-bringing work in Judea against Jewish people that it had done some forty or so years earlier against Jesus and recently against some believers in Rome. It is no wonder that in this context the gospel presents being a follower of Jesus as a demanding challenge.

> "If any want to become my followers, let them deny themselves and take up their cross and follow me." (Mark 8:34)

While there is no empire-wide persecution of Christians in the first century, the audience of Mark's gospel in Rome lives in a hostile and unpredictable world, vulnerable to its political forces and social pressures to fit in. To take up their cross is, as Jesus demonstrates in the gospel story, to face a possible terrible death. Jesus warns his followers:

> "As for yourselves, beware for they will hand you over to councils; and you will be beaten in synagogues; and you will stand before governors and kings because of me, as a testimony to them." (Mark 13:9)

The gospel story of Jesus names these realities for his followers in Rome while encouraging them to persevere despite the cost, even of martyrdom. Their relationship with the empire is tense and difficult. Jesus does not teach them to take up arms or use violence; rather their political threat comes from their alternative way of life as his followers (10:41-45), from their understanding that God's reign is already among them (1:15), and from their anticipation of Jesus' return to establish God's rule in full (13; 14:62). Jesus' appearance before Pilate is not just important as a scene within the gospel's plot. The presentation of Pilate, the Roman governor who executes Jesus, also functions to address Christians living in this difficult imperial context where conflict with Roman authorities, as well as with imperial values and structures, is a real but unpredictable danger.

Jesus Meets Pilate: 15:1-15

Mark's scene of Jesus' condemnation by Pilate begins as the Jerusalem elite, the chief priests, elders, and scribes centered on the Temple, hand Jesus over to Pilate (15:1). The verse connects the Pilate scene with the preceding gospel narrative. Pilate will complete a process that has involved Jesus' conflict with the Jerusalem elite throughout the gospel, his betrayal by Judas (14:10-11), his arrest (14:43-50), and his condemnation by a

council or Sanhedrin of the Jerusalem elite (14:53-65). But the verse also introduces the scene with Pilate by emphasizing crucial political dynamics and imperial perspectives that shape the whole scene.

1. The first dynamic involves the power structure in which Jesus' trial takes place. The key players up to now have been Pilate's allies, the Jerusalem elite that forms the council that hands Jesus over to Pilate. This council is presided over by the high or chief priest Joseph Caiaphas, who was appointed by Pilate's predecessor and remained chief priest throughout Pilate's rule (14:53). Along with Caiaphas, the council comprises "all the chief priests, the elders, and the scribes," groups that include both the dominant religious groups, the Pharisees and Sadducees. These people are Jerusalem's leaders, the powerful, the wealthy, the educated. Though tensions frequently existed between them and Rome's representatives, they were fundamentally allies of Rome and its representative, Pilate. As we saw in Chapter Three, this alliance is profoundly committed to maintaining the hierarchical social structure and their own positions of power, status, and wealth based on upholding Temple practices and religious traditions. Religion, politics, economic well-being, and social status are intricately connected. When they hand Jesus over to Pilate they do so as Pilate's allies, committed to maintaining this structure by removing a disruptive opponent. In this first verse these Jerusalem leaders do all the action. They are the subjects of the verbs. They act as if they are in control. Jesus is the object, passive, acted upon, initiating nothing, subject to their power. Or so it seems!

2. The second reality concerns the longstanding conflict between Jesus and this elite alliance. Throughout the gospel Jesus has challenged their legitimacy to rule and the social vision they enact. His challenge to their socio-political structure was not with violence, but with words and practices that point to a different social structure. Jesus offered a third way between violent opposition and passive compliance.

From the beginning of the gospel members of this alliance are angered by Jesus' claim to be God's special representative or agent in pronouncements of forgiveness (2:1-12), by his association with lowlife friends (2:13-17), and by his very different way of honoring the Sabbath and total disregard for their control of it (2:23-28; 3:1-6). These actions challenge their claim to exercise power as God's representatives and their right to determine societal practices. By the beginning of ch. 3 they are planning his death (3:2-6).

The cycle of animosity increases. Jesus condemns their ally, Rome, when he uses the name "Legion" to identify destructive demons (5:1-20). "Legion" designates the basic unit in Rome's military and so allies the devil with Rome's military muscle. He suggests that this central means of

enforcing Rome's will belongs to the devil. Jesus also denounces the Jerusalem elite for holding onto traditions that reinforce an unjust social order. For instance, they approve the removal of support for elderly people by encouraging gifts to the Temple, and justify this callous action (from which they benefit!) as God's will (7:9-13). In turn, they demand proof of his legitimacy (8:11-13). Three times he predicts that they will kill him but God will raise him (8:31; 9:31; 10:33-34), an announcement that clearly declares God is not on their side!

Worse, Jesus attacks their support of the hierarchical social structure and abuse of power (10:42-45). Instead of domination, his followers are to live lives of service that seek the good of others, not themselves. He condemns the Temple, the center of their power. Quoting the words of the prophet Jeremiah against the Temple's injustices (Jeremiah 7), Jesus declares that they have turned what should be a place of encountering God into a money-making "den of robbers" (11:15-17). It is a scathing condemnation of their Temple-based economy that robs the poor (most of the people) through taxes and tithes and unjustly maintains the social hierarchy.

At the heart of the conflict between Jesus and the Jerusalem elite, then, is a vision of how society should be organized. Central to their struggle—and to Jesus' death—are claims about what a just society that manifests God's will looks like. Jesus declares that their maintenance of a hierarchical society that benefits only the elite (themselves and their Roman allies) is unjust and contrary to God's merciful and life-giving purposes. Not surprisingly, the Jerusalem elite fears that Jesus' ideas might become popular! So to control the message and to maintain their status, power, and wealth, they attack the messenger by renewing their efforts to kill him (11:18).

Again they question his legitimacy as God's representative, but Jesus turns the question back on them (11:27-33). Jesus announces judgment on them (12:1-11, 38-40), and they on him (12:12). After more verbal sparring Jesus predicts the Temple's downfall (13:2). Their renewed determination to kill him (14:1-2) is aided by Judas' willingness to betray him (14:10-11). They arrest him and conduct a trial in which his opposition to the Temple, and its role in maintaining an unjust society, plays a prominent role (14:57-58).

So too does Jesus' identity. They ask him if he is "the Christ" or Messiah (the Hebrew term), God's anointed representative (14:61). There were in the first century diverse expectations of what a Messiah or Christ might be and do.[4] Jesus answers positively (14:62a), but goes on immediately to define his future role and to convict himself (14:63). Quoting the book of

---

[4] Marinus de Jonge, "Messiah," *Anchor Bible Dictionary* (New York: Doubleday, 1992) 4:777–88.

Daniel (7:13) and the royal Psalm 110:1, and addressing the assembled leaders directly ("you"), he says:

> "I am; and 'you will see the Son of Man seated at the right hand of the power,' and 'coming with the clouds of heaven.'"

This is a staggering and very subversive claim that ensures Jesus' execution. His references to Daniel and Psalms evoke scenes of God's power and rule in judgment. Jesus points to a future time and claims that he will share God's power and rule. That future time is "the last day" when he will enact God's judgment. His words declare the end of the whole hierarchical and imperial system over which they preside and from which they benefit! God will destroy it. That is, in his trial he dares to judge the Jerusalem elite who now sit in judgment on him. He pronounces God's judgment on the elite, its system, and its ally, Rome. In this high-stakes, life-and-death struggle the prisoner claims that he will wield vast power over his judges! Jesus declares that the judgment they pronounce on him is not final but is subject to God's more powerful purposes. God will vindicate him and condemn them.

His declaration, predictably, meets with howls of outrage. Such a claim by a human to share in the very power, reign, and judgment of God is, in their view, outright blasphemy, a mocking of God's exalted position. He deserves death (14:64).

But in a world in which political and religious power are intertwined this blasphemy is not only a religious matter. It is also political. Jesus' claim about his future role and about God's future purposes leaves no place for the Jerusalem elite and its allies! Jesus and God's kingdom bypass the chief priests appointed by Rome to maintain their own and Rome's interests! God's future kingdom means the end of their system and its benefits! His blasphemy is religious *and* political. In political language, announcing in God's name one's own role (blasphemy) in bringing about the end of the empire is treasonous. Blasphemy is treason!

Naturally it is the patriotic duty of the Jerusalem elite to "hand over" Jesus to its ally Pilate for execution as a blasphemous "treasoner" and a treasonous blasphemer. Such threats to the status quo cannot go unpunished. Jesus is bound because he is now a condemned prisoner. As we saw in Chapter Three, Pilate is the only one in Judea with the power to execute this sentence. He uses it to protect the elite's privileged way of life.

3. A third perspective emerges in 15:1 with the very important verb "handing over." This verb has at least four levels of meaning. Its use is especially significant in putting a spin on the scene with Pilate that relativizes his claims to power.

(1) Jesus has used this verb three times previously to predict this very act of having him put to death (9:31, translated as "betrayed"; 10:33 [2x]). Even though the Jerusalem leaders and Pilate seem to have all the power and are acting to control Jesus, Jesus' use of this verb to predict their actions suggests that he knows much more about what is happening and is in control.

(2) The verb has also been used as early as 3:19 to identify Judas Iscariot as the disciple who "betrays" Jesus, the one who hands Jesus over (14:10, 11, 44). Judas' action makes it possible for the Jerusalem elite to kill him (14:10-11, 43-50). Jesus predicts Judas' act, reinforcing the sense that Jesus is in control (14:18, 21, 41-42). The translation of this verb as "betray" conveys a negative verdict on Judas' action.

(3) Jesus uses the same verb to describe the arrest or "handing over" of his followers to councils, synagogues, and governors (13:9, 11), including by members of the same household (13:12). What happens to Jesus in this scene concerns his followers also.

(4) Biblical traditions use this verb to describe God's actions and control of human circumstances. In Num 21:34 and Deut 2:24, for example, it expresses God's control of international affairs and military actions as God establishes the people in the promised land. The verb denotes the accomplishment of God's purposes. That is, Pilate and his allies think they are in control as they act to preserve a world ordered according to their purposes. But the verb discloses, to those who know, that God's just purposes, despite all appearances to the contrary, are being worked out in the condemnation, crucifixion, and resurrection of Jesus.

4. Fourth, while Pilate is named in 15:1, no information is given about him. There is no sidebar explaining that he is the Roman governor and outlining his power. The author assumes we know this identity and his role. We are expected to know the sort of information I outlined in Chapter Three, and to be able to pick up any further information from the scene itself.

Pilate Questions Jesus: 15:2-5

Pilate asks Jesus two questions. Presumably the "handing over" included some form of briefing for Pilate. Jesus' statements to the council that they would soon see him execute the very power, rule, and judgment

of God on their world (14:62) have been very appropriately translated into kingship language for Pilate. Pilate understands Jesus' identity and threat. Blasphemy is treason. Jesus claims to exercise a sovereignty independent of Rome. So Pilate, the "rightful" ruler, takes the initiative, asserts control, and asks Jesus, "Are you the king of the Jews?"

The question is a dangerous one for both Pilate and Jesus. As far as Pilate is concerned, there is of course only one king or ruler. The same noun is used for the Roman emperor (Josephus, *Jewish War* 3.351; 4.596; 5.58 [Titus]; 5.563; 1 Pet 2:13, 17). Rome could legitimize puppet kings that were loyal and subservient to Rome such as King Herod ("King of the Jews," *Jewish Antiquities* 16.311) who ruled Judea-Galilee until 4 B.C.E. But to claim the title without sanction was rebellion. Pilate's task as governor was to maintain Roman control and rule against any possible threat.

The title is a dangerous one for Jesus. Other figures in Judea and Galilee claimed to be kings in the first century as they seek sovereignty independent of Rome. Josephus names several (Judas son of Ezekias, Simon, Athronges: *Jewish Antiquities* 17.271-85; *Jewish War* 2.57-65), and generalizes about the rest, "anyone might make himself a king . . ." (*Jewish Antiquities* 17.285). About the time Mark's gospel was written, Menachem (*Jewish War* 2.433-48) and Simon bar Giora continued the tradition in rebelling against Rome (*Jewish War* 4.503-44, 556-84). These kings met a common fate; Rome executed them (*Jewish War* 7.153-55 for Simon's execution). Certainly Jesus did not employ the same means of opposition with violent attacks on the elite and their property. But like them, Jesus had followers. And like them, Jesus claimed to exercise sovereignty that was not permitted by Rome nor exercised on Rome's behalf or for Rome's benefit.

Throughout the gospel Jesus proclaims God's reign or empire, "the kingdom of God" (1:15; 4:11, 26, 30). It is present in his ministry as well as in his future return (9:1; 14:25, 62). God's reign or empire does not favor the rich and powerful or their social hierarchy and domination (10:42-45), but embraces marginal nobodies (10:14-16, 23-25). Jesus condemns Judea's rulers for not exhibiting God's just rule in their actions (12:1-11). He views Rome's empire as Satan's agent (5:1-20) that resists God's kingdom. And God's kingdom, active through Jesus, provides things that Rome's empire cannot, such as healing, food, and an alternative community marked by service rather than domination (10:42-45). Jesus' claim that he would return manifesting God's reign means certain judgment on Rome's empire and its way of life (14:62). Jesus also accepted the title Son of David (10:47-48; 11:10). This title places him in the line of kings to whom God had promised an eternal reign that embodies God's just will (2 Samuel 7). While Jesus did not employ violent opposition, his words

and practices were very political in opposing Rome's order and offering God's alternative kingdom.

Jesus' strange answer to Pilate's question, "You say so" (15:2), perhaps echoes these ambiguities. He is king in that he represents God's reign present in part now but not yet in full until he will judge all things and establish God's empire. That future judgment is bad news for Rome. For those with ears to hear, he is a definite threat to Rome.

But he is not a king in the sense of these other figures noted above. His resistance to Rome's order is not violent, at least not in the present. He does not use force to attack the powerful and their property. But attack he does as he verbally condemns Rome and the Jerusalem leaders for their unjust society, and as he advocates and forms an alternative way of life marked by mercy and service that represents God's kingdom. Jesus is guilty as charged.

Accusation and Silence: 15:3-5

The Jerusalem elite accuses Jesus of many things (15:3). Their accusations are not specified, thereby keeping the focus on Jesus' identity as king. Jesus does not respond to the accusations, prompting Pilate's second question. Pilate, amazed that Jesus is not fighting back or defending himself, asks Jesus why he is silent. But still Jesus does not answer (15:4-5). Why not? What does his silence represent? This is a little detail with great significance for the scene!

In part Jesus has nothing further to say to those who have refused to listen to him previously and who now wish to silence him permanently. Jesus' words have been subversive precisely because he has exposed the injustices of the present social order and dared to imagine a different sort of world. His silence evidences his disdain for this corrupt system as it protects its own interests. The empire always strikes back.

Further, the biblical writings, shaped by centuries of living under the control of numerous imperial powers, attest the same dynamic. To confront the power group, even nonviolently, brings inevitable retaliation. Moses challenged Pharaoh to "let my people go" from Egyptian slavery and had to flee for his life (Exodus 14). The prophet Elijah challenged King Ahaz and Queen Jezebel and they tried to kill him (1 Kings 19:1-3). Previously, Mark's gospel narrated the grisly conflict between King Herod Antipas and John the Baptist in which John challenges Herod's lifestyle and Herod has John beheaded (Mark 6:14-29). This is the way of the imperial world. The deck is stacked against Jesus.

His silence evokes another biblical image, the silent, suffering "servant of the Lord." This image comes from the book of Isaiah. Babylon defeated

Israel, destroyed the Jerusalem Temple, and exiled its leading citizens to Babylon in 587 B.C.E. In the midst of this terrible tragedy Isaiah 40–55 predicts that God will save the people from exile and return them home.

Isaiah images the people as the "servant of the Lord." Though the language is singular ("the servant," "he"), this figure probably represents at least in part the people, Israel (Isa 49:3), defeated by the imperial power Babylon in 587 B.C.E. and taken away into exile in Babylon "by a perversion of justice" (Isa 53:8). But the servant also has a mission to Israel and the nations (Isa 49:5-6), suggesting that it also represents a particular group (or person). The servant, Israel or a group within the people, is commissioned to manifest God's justice (Isa 42:1) and salvation (Isa 49:6) in the midst of the injustice and captivity of exile in Babylon.

They/the servant suffer(s) greatly in this situation:

> He was despised and rejected by others;
> A man of suffering and acquainted with infirmity. (Isa 53:3)

But the servant, Israel or a group within it, does not strike back. The servant remains faithful to God's purposes and to its mission of God's salvation and justice. But it does not carry out this mission with military violence and domination as nations like Babylon do. Instead the servant absorbs the imperial violence without retaliation:

> He was oppressed, and he was afflicted
> Yet he did not open his mouth;
> Like a lamb that is led to the slaughter,
> And like a sheep that before its shearers is silent,
> So he did not open his mouth. (Isa 53:7)

Surprisingly, through this suffering God's purposes are carried out. Israel is freed from exile in 539 when Persia defeats Babylon. The servant's suffering is on behalf of others and has benefits for them because it breaks the cycle of imperial violence and points to a different way of being:

> But he was wounded for our transgressions,
> crushed for our iniquities;
> upon him was the punishment that made us whole,
> and by his bruises we are healed. (Isa 53:5)

Isaiah's suffering servant, who heals others in carrying out God's just purposes of salvation, depicts one of the ways that God works in the

world.[5] Members of the early Christian movement found in this image from Isaiah an important way of understanding Jesus' death. They understood Jesus to suffer silently on behalf of and for the benefit of others. He remains faithful to his mission from God and does not resort to violence and domination. Through his suffering (and subsequent resurrection), Jesus shows that imperial violence does not have the final word even though it so often seems to control the world. In Jesus' resurrection God will reveal that the worst that Pilate and empires like his can do—put opponents to death—does not thwart God's purposes for a just world.[6]

Jesus' silence evokes this important tradition from Isaiah. It links two situations of imperial rule in which the rulers (Babylon, Rome) seem to have all the power over their suffering subjects. But Isaiah's suffering servant participates in Babylon's downfall. In evoking Isaiah's vision of triumph through suffering, along with the historical circumstances of Babylon's downfall and the exiles' return, Jesus' silence anticipates Rome's downfall!

Any such significance for Jesus' silence is of course completely lost on Pilate. He is amazed at Jesus' silence, lack of defense, and lack of fight (15:5). But that is the point. He thinks he has all the power. He thinks that by executing this king of the Jews he removes this threat. But this little detail of Jesus' silence that evokes Isaiah's suffering servant frames Pilate in the perspective of God's purposes for a just world. In God's kingdom Pilate has no place and power at all! At the very moment Pilate's power is on display in condemning Jesus, the narrative is revealing, for those with eyes to see, Pilate's vulnerability. It is also anticipating his demise along with the imperial system he represents.

Passover and Barabbas: 15:6-7

Pilate's very brief exchange with Jesus is finished. The narrator interrupts the story to tell the audience two pieces of information crucial for understanding what subsequently will happen between Pilate and the crowd in vv. 8-15.

---

[5] Two further links between Mark's narrative about Pilate and Isaiah's suffering servant should be noted. The verb "handing over" in 15:1 appears in Isa 53:12, and the verb "wonder/amaze" appears in Isa 52:15.

[6] Jewish expectations of resurrection first emerged in contexts of imperial struggles, especially with the Seleucid ruler Antiochus IV Epiphanes in the 160s B.C.E. See Dan 12:1-3; 2 Maccabees 7.

The first piece of information concerns one of Pilate's practices, that of releasing a prisoner at the festival of Passover (15:6). There is no other evidence for this practice, but since governors controlled the administration of "justice" they could release prisoners if it suited them.[7] Such a release would show Pilate to be a benign and generous ruler! It also befits Passover since this festival celebrated God's freeing of Israelites from slavery in Egypt (Exodus 12–15). This central festival set forth Israel's identity as God's chosen people redeemed or freed by God from slavery. It depicted God's powerful covenantal loyalty to save the people from whatever opposed God's purposes, including tyrant rulers. And it called the people to trust God and live faithfully.

But there is the irony. It was impossible to celebrate Passover without being very aware that Israel was in another slavery, now to Rome. The Passover story stirred hopes that God would be faithful in delivering the people again. Pilate is sitting on a powder keg! The practice of releasing a prisoner was a typical imperial gesture aimed to defuse a dangerous situation. It was sufficiently generous to encourage the subject people to be appreciative, to make them more indebted to Roman power, and to mask that brutal power as benign and generous. The governor hoped to appease resentment and defuse expectations. But it was also carefully controlled— one prisoner, not two!, for which the crowd subserviently had to ask/beg— to uphold Roman power.

By linking Jesus' death to Passover (emphasized in 14:1, 12, 14, 16) the narrative again suggests Rome's demise. Just as Egypt was defeated by God's purposes, so will Rome be. God will raise Jesus from death, and he will return in power to judge Rome's world represented by Pilate and the Jerusalem elite (14:62).

The second piece of information concerns a prisoner, Barabbas. He is introduced "with the rebels who had committed murder during the insurrection" (15:7). It is not clear which insurrection is in mind. Nor is it clear precisely what Barabbas' crime is (Mark's Greek is a little loose in v. 7!). But there is no doubt that Barabbas is associated with a group that poses a violent threat to Pilate's rule. Josephus uses the same word "rebel" to describe those who attack Roman troops in the 66–70 war (*Jewish War* 6.157). The narrative does not say whether Barabbas has been convicted and sentenced yet, but his association with rebellion and murder suggests the death penalty is inevitable.

---

[7] For example, the governor Albinus releases prisoners (Josephus, *Jewish Antiquities* 20.215).

The Crowds, Pilate, and Jesus: 15:8-15

With these two pieces of information in place, the story continues in v. 8. A new group enters the scene, the crowd (15:8). Crowds in Galilee have been ready recipients of Jesus' healing (3:9-10) and teaching (4:1), and have often been amazed or astounded at him (5:20; 7:37). In Jerusalem they hear his teaching (11:18; 12:37). But Mark shows them also to support the Temple economically and maintain the elite's power and wealth (12:41). In 14:43 a crowd "with swords and clubs" join in Jesus' arrest.

How *this* crowd in 15:8 will relate to Jesus is not clear. They take the initiative in asking for a prisoner's release.[8] Pilate does not offer to continue this custom. But his responsiveness to their asking[9] masks the tight control he maintains. The crowd, though, does not immediately ask for Jesus or intercede specifically on his behalf.

First Question (15:9)

In v. 9 Pilate retakes the initiative by asking the crowd about Jesus. More accurately, he asks them, "Do you wish/want me to release for you the King of the Jews?" The question is very shrewd. He gives them, momentarily, the role of judge. Second, he uses the question to gauge levels of support for Jesus. He does not ask for their advice ("what should I do"), but for their explicit wishes. And he frames the question in a very personal way—"do *you* want" and "for *you*." But he maintains control. They can express their wishes, but it is very clear that he, Pilate, will do the releasing. His question puts them in a subservient role in that they have to ask him for something that only he has the power to do. And he makes it sound as though they will benefit from his action, "for you." His power over them is disguised as benign and beneficial but is exposed by the narrative for what it is.

Most importantly, Pilate's choice of title for Jesus, "King of the Jews," astutely guides the subsequent exchange and determines its outcome. By using this title Pilate shrewdly presents the question as a test of loyalty to Rome and the emperor. The title reminds the crowd of Pilate's power as

[8] The Greek text says they "come up" to Pilate, a reference either to the raised platform in front of the *praetorium* where he dispenses decisions or to the *praetorium*'s possible location in a fortress on Jerusalem's western hill. Raymond E. Brown, *The Death of the Messiah* (New York: Doubleday, 1994) 706–10. Some have suggested unconvincingly that the crowd has some sort of formal role in the proceedings. Brown, *Death* 720–22.

[9] The verb "ask" is used nine times in Mark. Four of those uses are in 6:22-25 in which Herodias asks King Herod Agrippa for the head of John the Baptist. The verb subtly recalls another scene in which an opponent of corrupt rule loses his life.

Rome's representative and their status as a subjugated people. The crowd of course knows, and is reminded by the governor's presence and question, that there is only one "King of the Jews," the emperor in Rome. It knows that the death penalty follows for those who claim the title illegitimately. And it knows what happens to those who follow, support, and associate with such rebels! Given this context, no one in the crowd is likely to shout for Jesus' release, in the very presence of the governor! To do so would be to sign one's own death warrant! Pilate has astutely reminded them of his control, challenged them to express loyalty to Rome, and stacked the deck to make sure it happens!

In asking the carefully-phrased question Pilate is shrewdly assessing the situation. He knows Jesus claims to be "King of the Jews." That is a capital offense. But Pilate does not know how much support Jesus has. Nor did the Jerusalem leaders bring any of Jesus' followers for trial. So Pilate has to do some polling to find out what level of support Jesus has. In asking "do you wish me to release for you the King of the Jews?" he is not being indecisive or weak. He is not reluctant to condemn an innocent man. Jesus is guilty. He will die. But to execute someone's king—even a pretender—may well have socially disruptive fallout! It could spark revolts that get out of hand. Pilate is doing damage control. To maintain his control he needs to find out how many others think Jesus is king.

Explanation

Verse 10 recalls that Pilate knows the perspective of his allies, Jerusalem's elite. They see Jesus as a threat, as does Pilate. The verse gives us a momentary glimpse inside Pilate's head. Gospels usually present characters by external factors, their actions and words. Audiences construct the character from these clues. Rarely do the gospels describe a character's inner world, thoughts, and emotions. Pilate knows the Jerusalem elite's motivation for handing Jesus over. It was "out of jealousy or envy." This is not surprising. Jesus has been popular with the crowds and has attacked the leaders and their societal vision and leadership (Mark 1:22; 11:18; 12:12). The leaders recognize the threat! They fear Jesus and want him removed (14:1-2).

What is the significance of Pilate's statement about their motivation? Is it a good, neutral, or bad thing that they have handed Jesus over for this reason? Is Pilate discrediting or dismissing them for acting out of jealousy and envy? Or is he observing that they acted in this way because Jesus threatens their (and his) interests and taking it very seriously?

The latter option seems more likely. It is unlikely, given imperial realities, that Pilate is discrediting or dismissing them for this motivation. They

are, as we saw above and in Chapter Three, his allies. He needs them to secure his own rule, just as they need him to maintain their power. Jesus has not denied being "King of the Jews," a claim that clearly threatens their interests and Pilate's. He deserves the death penalty. His allies have discovered this threat, so Pilate must take it very seriously. There is some basis, a reason, for their jealousy. They have handed Jesus over, as Pilate recognizes, because he poses a real threat to their society. Pilate has to discern how extensive is this threat in handling Jesus' execution. How much support from the crowds does Jesus have?

The Answer (15:11)

Like most questions in a poll, Herod's question to the crowd in v. 9 is weighted, as we have seen, to produce the answer he wants. By making it a test of loyalty to Rome's rule Pilate ensures that no one will support Jesus. Pilate can execute this royal pretender after engineering a display of no support. He can execute Jesus without social unrest. As Pilate's ally, the Jerusalem elite shares exactly the same goals. It manipulates the crowd (whom Jesus earlier in 6:34 viewed as "sheep without a shepherd")[10] to accomplish its will by calling for Barabbas rather than Jesus. This release, described as being "for them," maintains the delusion that Pilate exercises benign rule for their benefit.

It is not clear why the elite chooses Barabbas from among the rebels. He is not identified as a leader or crowd favorite. But conveniently, he offers an alternative to Jesus. The option is not, though, between a rebel (Barabbas) and an innocent man (Jesus). Both men are guilty of different sorts of opposition. The absence of violence does not make Jesus nonpolitical, innocent, or harmless! The choice is between one who used violence and murder (Barabbas), and one who is a nonviolent agent of God's kingdom with a different social vision, an alternative way of living, and the anticipation of his future participation in God's judgment that will establish God's just kingdom in full (14:62).

The demand for Barabbas is good for Pilate. He can appear benign in releasing one rebel (but not the rest). To release any rebel is a risk for Pilate, but he calculates that the benefits outweigh the risk. He backs himself to control the threat of violence. His question about the "King of the Jews" has effectively stifled any cries for Jesus.

---

[10] The image of shepherd was common for rulers. Jesus again denies that the Jerusalem elite is legitimate! For further material on shepherds see Chapter Five, "Matthew's Pilate."

A Second Question (15:12-13)

Pilate checks out the situation with a further round of polling. His question in v. 12, "Then what do you want me to do with the man you call the King of the Jews?" develops his first question in v. 9 in two ways. First, he removes the option of release. It was never a real option anyway, since he names Jesus "King of the Jews" and manipulates their response. But Pilate learned from it that there will not be public unrest when he executes the "King of the Jews." Again the use of the title displays his power over a subjugated people.

This second question is a follow-up to increase their support for his action. Like his first question, it sets up a very clear response. The crowd knows that only one thing happens to a royal pretender. With the question, Pilate ensures that the crowd calls for Jesus' execution. Skillfully, with the leaders' support, he manipulates them to demand what he was going to do anyway. His question secures their compliance.

To secure this outcome he modifies his question in a second way by adding the words "the man you call" before "King of the Jews."

> Verse 9: "Do you wish/want me *to release* for you the King of the Jews?"
>
> Verse 12: "Then what do you want me to do with *the man you call* the King of the Jews?"

This addition of "you call" sharpens the issues of loyalty and ownership. On the surface it seems that he will execute their supposed king because they demand it. Pilate appears responsive, benevolent, and benign, acting "for them." But the narrative has exposed what is really happening. He will execute Jesus as a threat to the privileged status and interests of the elite, both the Jerusalem leaders and Pilate himself. He will act for himself and his allies. But with his questions he has managed to secure the crowd's loyalty, assent, and support while disguising his own interests!

Set up skillfully by Pilate, the crowd predictably calls for Jesus' crucifixion (15:13). That they would call for the execution of one of their own by the occupying force witnesses both to the skill with which Pilate has engineered the scene and to the fear that Rome instilled in its subjects. Rome employed crucifixion as a means of execution to remove those who threatened its rule and the social order that benefited the elite at the expense of the rest. It was used for Roman citizens only if they were guilty of treason. Otherwise it was reserved for "less worthy," lower-status people like provincials, violent criminals, rebels, slaves. Symbolizing social rejec-

tion, it was a cruel and painful way to die, marked by shame and humiliation. Carried out in public, it was intended to deter behavior that challenged and contested Rome's order.

A Third Question

Pilate responds with a third question, "What evil has he done?" (15:14). Often this question is interpreted as indicating that Pilate knows Jesus is innocent and not deserving of the death penalty, so he tries a last-ditch effort to get Jesus off! Often it is seen as showing Pilate's weakness in not remaining firm to his (noble) conviction that Jesus is innocent (Verdict 2 in Chapter One).

But such views make no sense of the imperial dynamics of the scene. Jesus is guilty as a treasonous/blasphemous rebel. He is as good as dead when the Jerusalem elite hand him over to their ally Pilate the governor (15:1). He is dead when he does not contest Pilate's question about being "King of the Jews" (15:2).

Rather, Pilate's question should be read in the context of his two previous ones. He continues to solicit statements of loyalty to Rome. He continues to secure support for his execution of Jesus. His question about Jesus' evil offers the crowd an opportunity to name rebellion against Rome as Jesus' evil. Jesus was an illegitimate king. To have them name this reality would further secure their loyalty and compliance. The answer would function as a reminder to the crowd and a warning about such actions at the very moment when Pilate was taking the risk of releasing the rebel Barabbas. Pilate's message is clear: I am releasing a rebel, but don't dare join him! Pilate gives with one hand and takes away with the other.

The sequence of questions and answers goes like this:

Pilate's Question:	Do you want me to release Jesus? (15:9)
Crowd's Answer:	No. Release Barabbas (15:10-11)
Pilate's Question:	What shall I do with Jesus? (15:12)
Crowd's Answer:	Crucify him! (15:13)
Pilate's Question:	What evil has he done? (15:14a)
***Desired* Answer:**	He said he was King of the Jews. He is a rebel against Rome's rule.

Of course, the third question does not elicit this exact response. But the crowd's response is comparable as it shouts again for Jesus' crucifixion

(15:14b). So Pilate releases Barabbas to a crowd that has just recognized what happens to rebels and their followers! That is reassuring news for Pilate the governor. The use of the same verb "release" as in Pilate's first question about Jesus (15:9) underlines that Pilate's release of Barabbas means his rejection and condemnation of Jesus. Pilate flogs Jesus and "hands him over" for crucifixion (15:15).

Again, at the very moment when Pilate seems to exhibit great power in protecting the elite's and Rome's interests in condemning Jesus, the narrative undercuts or qualifies the image. As we noted in looking at v. 1, the verb "handing over" has multiple dimensions, including Jesus' prediction that this would happen (9:31; 10:33), as well as the sense that God's purposes are being accomplished. Likewise Jesus had predicted in 10:34 that he would be flogged (though a different verb is used) and this has now happened. Pilate thinks he is in control, but the narrative points beyond Pilate's efforts to maintain his system to God's purposes represented by Jesus. Jesus has previously announced that God's purposes for a just world will mean the future establishment of God's empire or kingdom when he returns in power to judge Rome's world (14:62). That return will mean Rome's demise. His "handing over," then, involves God's much greater purposes, about which Pilate has no clue at all.

Conclusion

Mark presents a Pilate who has both power and skill. He is not weak or reluctant to use either in maintaining Roman interests against a threat like Jesus. He does not think Jesus is innocent. Working with his allies, the Jerusalem elite, he skillfully and astutely manipulates the crowd to express their loyalty to the emperor as well as their compliance with his plan to execute Jesus the king. Jesus is just another case needing a decision. Pilate, the skillful governor, dispatches this royal pretender efficiently and without social unrest.

But throughout the scene, as I have noted, the narrative subtly points to God's larger purposes that frame and interpret Pilate's actions. Pilate imagines that as Rome's representative he is in control. But he has no idea of God's larger purposes that will mean the downfall of the very empire and way of life he represents and defends.

The scene makes clear to Mark's Christian audience in Rome that Roman power is not benign or beneficial, but dangerous and contrary to God's purposes. Conflict is inevitable, though not constant or predictable. They are urged to be faithful to Jesus even if it means death, knowing that God's kingdom will eventually be victorious.

CHAPTER FIVE
Matthew's Pilate

The gospel of Matthew probably uses Mark's gospel as one of its sources.[1] All but 55 verses of Mark's gospel appear in Matthew, and there are significant similarities in the order and wording of the scenes common to both. But Matthew's gospel, with 28 chapters, is nearly twice as long as Mark (16 chapters). The gospel's author recycles and reshapes Mark's story by adding new material and editing or redacting material from Mark.[2] We might expect, then, both some significant similarities as well as some important differences in Matthew's presentation of Pilate.

> **Matthew 27:1** When morning came, all the chief priests and the elders of the people conferred together against Jesus in order to bring about his death. **2** They bound him, led him away, and handed him over to Pilate the governor.
>
> **3** When Judas, his betrayer, saw that Jesus was condemned . . .
>
> **11** Now Jesus stood before the governor; and the governor asked him, "Are you the King of the Jews?" Jesus said, "You say so." **12** But when he was accused by the chief priests and elders he did not answer. **13** Then Pilate said to him, "Do you not hear how many accusations they make against you?" **14** But he gave him no answer, not even to a single charge, so that the governor was greatly amazed. **15** Now at the festival the governor was accustomed to release a prisoner for the crowd, anyone whom they wanted. **16** At that time they had a notorious prisoner, called Jesus Barabbas. **17** So after they had gathered,

---

[1] As with Mark's gospel, we do not know who the gospel's author, commonly called Matthew, is.

[2] See Warren Carter, *Matthew: Storyteller, Interpreter, Evangelist* (Peabody, Mass.: Hendrickson, 1996) 1–115.

Pilate said to them, "Whom do you want me to release for you, Jesus Barabbas or Jesus who is called the Messiah?" **18** For he realized that it was out of jealousy that they had handed him over. **19** While he was sitting on the judgment seat, his wife sent word to him, "Have nothing to do with that innocent man, for today I have suffered a great deal because of a dream about him." **20** Now the chief priests and the elders persuaded the crowds to ask for Barabbas and to have Jesus killed. **21** The governor again said to them, "Which of the two do you want me to release for you?" And they said, "Barabbas." **22** Pilate said to them, "Then what should I do with Jesus who is called the Messiah?" All of them said, "Let him be crucified!" **23** Then he asked, "Why, what evil has he done?" But they shouted all the more, "Let him be crucified!" **24** So when Pilate saw that he could do nothing, but rather that a riot was beginning, he took some water and washed his hands before the crowd, saying, "I am innocent of this man's blood." **25** Then the people as a whole answered, "His blood be on us and on our children!" **26** So he released Barabbas for them; and after flogging Jesus, he handed him over to be crucified.

Many have seen Matthew's Pilate as weak and indecisive. He is unable, so the usual reading goes, to act on his conviction that Jesus is innocent, and he is unable to withstand the manipulative pressures of the Jewish leaders and crowds. He is forced into a religious, non-political Jewish dispute and, politically neutral, he condemns Jesus to die so as to avoid trouble. Matthew attributes the responsibility for Jesus' death to the Jews. The scene culminates, so it is argued, with the self-cursing of the Jewish people (27:25) as they reject God's Messiah and are rejected by God.[3] This view has fed a very longstanding anti-Jewish stance among Christian readers.

I do not find this reading of Matthew's scene convincing. As with Mark's presentation, I will argue that this reading overlooks important and pervasive imperial realities that the scene assumes but does not spell out. Pilate participates in the scene as Rome's governor. Far from being neutral or weak, he is skillful and astute in applying the death penalty to protect Rome's interests. As far as the Roman and Jerusalem elite is concerned, Jesus is guilty of treason. But as with Mark, Matthew's narrative exposes the self-interested nature of Pilate's justice and shows it to be all washed up.[4]

---

[3] Helen Bond, *Pontius Pilate in History and Interpretation*. MSSNTS 100 (Cambridge: Cambridge University Press, 1998) 120–37 argues this view.

[4] Warren Carter, *Matthew and Empire* (Harrisburg, Pa.: Trinity Press International, 2001) Chapter 9.

Matthew's Audience

Since Matthew's gospel has used Mark, Matthew must have been written after 70 C.E. This conclusion is confirmed by a reference to Rome's defeat of Jerusalem in 70 C.E. that is added to a parable. The parable is an allegory about the Jerusalem elite's rejection of Jesus. In it a king (God) invites the elite (Jerusalem leaders) to a wedding feast for his son (Jesus), but they kill the messenger-slaves.

> The king was enraged. He sent his troops, destroyed those murderers, and burned their city. (Matt 22:7)

This verse is not in Luke's version of the parable (Luke 14:15-24; the parable is not in Mark). And the verse seems out of place in Matthew's parable. It interrupts the sequence from v. 6 to v. 8. Burning the city is an extreme reaction to a rejected wedding invitation, and the smoking ruins of the city provide an unlikely context for a wedding feast. Moreover, burning cities was a common tactic of victorious armies. Josephus describes at length Rome's burning of Jerusalem in 70 C.E. (*Jewish War* 6.249-408).

Matthew's gospel, then, was written after 70 C.E. It was also written before 100 C.E., since this gospel seems to be known by two writings from around that time (Ignatius' letters and the *Didache*). Within the period 70–100 C.E., several factors point to the decade of the 80s. One involves the necessary time for Mark's gospel, one of Matthew's sources, to circulate and become well known. A second factor involves time for a dispute to develop between Matthew's audience (followers of Jesus) and a synagogue community of which they have been a part. There are increased hostile references to synagogues in Matthew (e. g., 6:1-6) and intensified negative references to Jewish leaders including Pharisees, priests, and scribes (ch. 23).[5] This conflict was present in Mark, but it is increased significantly in Matthew. What has happened to cause this increased animosity?

Many scholars think that conflict within the synagogue community has developed in the post-70 period as Jewish people, faced with the destruction of the Temple in Jerusalem, have to reconstruct their religious life, observance, and thinking. The gospel suggests that claims about Jesus' identity and roles were central to this conflict. Jewish followers of Jesus claimed he was the agent of God's salvation (1:21; 26:28), manifested God's presence (1:23; 18:20; 28:20), and revealed God's will (chs. 5–7;

---

[5] For details see Carter, *Matthew* [1996] 55–102.

10; 13; 18; 24–25). But other members of the synagogue rejected these claims.

As a result Matthew's audience, mostly Jews but also some Gentiles, seems to have departed from the synagogue. The gospel helps this audience define its identity and way of life as a separate community. The conflict seems to have been intense, costly, and bitter, with no winners. It left Matthew's audience feeling rejected and displaced, with considerable animosity between the two groups.

Where did this community live? We do not know for certain, but several factors point to the city of Antioch in Syria as a real possibility. The earliest citations of Matthew appear in documents probably written in Antioch. A strange reference to Syria that looks like a home-town touch is added at 4:24. Peter plays an especially prominent part in the gospel, and other material, especially Gal 2:11-14, recognizes his prominent role in Antioch.

If Matthew's audience does live in Antioch, two further observations are important. Antioch was a big city, probably the third largest in the Roman empire after Rome and Alexandria. The city was crowded, with great extremes of wealth and poverty, numerous ethnic groups, and diverse religious observances. One of the challenges for Matthew's group was to work out how to live in this society now that it was no longer part of the synagogue.[6]

Second, Antioch was the capital city of the province of Syria. It was the administrative center of Roman imperial rule. The governor of Syria resided there and was visible as he moved around the city with his entourage. Three to four legions, over twenty thousand troops, were stationed in this city of about 150,000 people. Buildings, temples, festivals, statues, coins, and taxes proclaimed Roman sovereignty. Roman troops assembled at Antioch to march south against Jerusalem in the 66–70 C.E. war. There were outbreaks of violence against Jews in Antioch in this time. Titus, the victorious commander and future emperor, visited Antioch in 71. To be a follower of Jesus, one whom Rome had crucified, one who proclaimed the kingdom or empire of God, was difficult in this context that paraded Roman control and power. To experience and look for the kingdom or empire of God meant vulnerability and challenge. The story of Jesus' trial before Pilate warns this audience of likely collisions with the values and structures of the Roman-controlled world. It encourages them to be faithful and brave in similar circumstances.

---

[6] For details see Warren Carter, *Matthew and the Margins* (Maryknoll, N.Y.: Orbis, 2000) 17–49.

Pilate and Jesus: The Introduction (27:1-2)

Pilate first appears in 27:1-2.[7] The alliance of Jerusalem leaders, the chief priests and elders, hands the condemned Jesus over to him (27:2). Pilate will complete the process of execution narrated in ch. 26: namely Jesus' betrayal by Judas (26:14-16, 20-25), his arrest (26:47-56), and his interrogation by the Jerusalem leaders (26:57-68).

Jesus has been in conflict with these leaders throughout Matthew. The Jerusalem leaders first appear as allies of the powerful King Herod at Jesus' birth (ch. 2). Hearing reports that a "king of the Jews" has been born, King Herod is worried and takes steps to guard his threatened throne. He summons his allies, the chief priests and scribes, and demands information about where a Messiah might be born. They inform him that one Messiah tradition identifies Bethlehem, the city of David (2:3-6).[8] In providing this information they assist Herod's terror, endangering Jesus' life and abetting the death of all males under two years old in that area (2:16-18). Clearly they are supporters of current practices and social structures.

Once Jesus' public ministry begins in 4:17 with his declaration that God's kingdom or empire is at hand, the conflict increases. Jesus criticizes the leaders' practices and denies their place in God's purposes (5:20; 6:1-18). He pronounces God's forgiveness (which they regard as blasphemy or dishonoring God, 9:3-8), offensively associates with low-status people (9:9-13), heals the sick and exorcizes demons (9:32-33), declares the people to be without legitimate leaders (9:36), and honors the Sabbath differently (12:1-8, 9-14). The leaders decide he is an agent of the devil, not of God (9:34; 12:24), and decide to kill him (12:14).

Subsequently Jesus accuses them of disregarding God's will. He threatens them with God's judgment because they falsely claim to represent God (15:3-7, 12-14). They demand evidence to support Jesus' claims, but he refuses (16:1-4) and warns his disciples against their teaching (16:5-12; 19:3-12).

In ch. 21 the conflict intensifies as Jesus goes to Jerusalem, their base. Citing the words of Jeremiah 7, Jesus attacks and condemns the center of their power, the Temple. They have made a place of encounter with God into a business that sustains their elite hierarchical way of life at the expense of the people (21:12-17). Again they challenge his legitimacy, but he turns the tables on them and in a series of three parables announces God's

---

[7] Pilate is mentioned or appears in 27:1-2, 11-26, 57-65; 28:11-15. I will focus on 27:1-2, 11-26, but will refer to the other scenes as necessary.

[8] In some traditions such as 1 Enoch 46–48 the Messiah is not born, but is a heavenly judge called the "Son of Man."

judgment on them (21:23–22:14). The last parable refers to Rome's destruction of the Jerusalem Temple in 70 C.E. (22:7). They determine to arrest him (21:45-46) and engage in a series of verbal sparring matches to try to trap him (22:15-45). But he silences them and they withdraw from any further exchanges (22:34, 46). In a harsh and uncompromising chapter (ch. 23), Jesus condemns their failure as leaders to represent God's will:

> You have neglected the weightier matters of the law: justice and mercy and faith. (Matt 23:23)

Then, in chs. 24–25, Jesus announces the end of their Temple (24:2) and the end of the world as they and Rome structure it. He will return in judgment to establish God's reign over all (24:27-31; 25:31-46). Their response to the one who claims to exercise God's judgment is to arrest him (26:1-5) with Judas' help (26:47-56). When they interrogate Jesus he reasserts his claim to participate in God's purposes and reign (26:57-68). By referring to himself as the "Son of Man" (as he has done previously in 17:22, for example), he declares that he will return to establish God's kingdom, an event that will mean their judgment and demise:

> But I tell you, from now on you will see the Son of Man seated at the right hand of Power and coming on the clouds of heaven. (Matt 26:64)

They judge that Jesus' claim to such an elevated role dishonors God, and of course it threatens their leadership and society under Rome's rule. He commits both blasphemy and treason. So they condemn him to die (26:66) and hand him over to Pilate the governor for execution (27:1-2).

Attention to four realities of imperial societies that I described in Chapter Three clarifies the dynamics of Jesus' "handing over." I will briefly recall information about priestly political power, about Rome's alliances with local elites, about the legal system's protection of elite privileges and bias against lower-status provincials, and about the tasks and power of Roman governors.

1. Priests and Political Power

Legally Jesus' transfer to Pilate is necessary because only the Roman governor has the power to employ the death penalty (Josephus, *Jewish War* 2.117). Restricting the power of execution to Pilate enables him to defend Roman interests, ensures his control over legal decisions, coerces compliance, and keeps the local elite dependent on him. But as we saw in Chapter

Three, it would be inaccurate to think that in this scene Jesus is being transferred from the hateful, vengeful religious officials to the secular power of the weak and disinterested Pilate.

Aristocratic imperial societies simply do not work like that. So-called "religious" officials are not a separated or isolated group. They are not exclusively concerned with religious matters. They are, rather, part of the retainer class within the ruling elite.[9] Their interests are not narrowly religious. They are the nation's leaders. Political, economic, social, and religious power is intertwined. Their teaching about the Temple and their religious practices like tithing and taxes maintain the social hierarchy and power, while ensuring their own wealth at the expense of the rest. Jesus' teaching and actions threaten their wealth, power, and social status. They will remove him.

Nor is Pilate's power, secured with military muscle, only political. With taxes and tribute, it is also economic and social in maintaining the current hierarchical and vertical social structure. And all of this is expressed through and legitimated with religious affirmations and practices. Pilate represents a system and empire that Jupiter and the gods have decreed. Rome rules at their behest and expresses their blessings and will through its rule.

2. Rome and Alliances with Local Elites

We also saw in Chapter Three that part of Rome's strategy for control over its empire was to secure the cooperation of local elites such as the Jerusalem leadership.[10] Rome did not have sufficient troops to coerce compliance across its vast empire. Cooperation between Rome and local elites, built on their common interest in maintaining the status quo, was crucial. But while the Jerusalem leaders were allies of Rome, it was not an alliance of equals. Rome's control of local elites was crucial in order to protect Rome's interests. Always there was the threat of punitive action that could remove the economic wealth, political power, and social status of local elites that did not comply.

[9] Gerhard E. Lenski, *Power and Privilege: A Theory of Social Stratification* (New York: McGraw-Hill, 1966) 256–66; John Kautsky, *The Politics of Aristocratic Empires* (Chapel Hill: University of North Carolina Press, 1982) 81–83, 161–66; Anthony J. Saldarini, *Pharisees, Scribes, and Sadducees in Palestinian Society* (Wilmington, Del.: Michael Glazier, 1988) 35–49.

[10] Peter Brunt, "The Romanization of the Local Ruling Classes," *Roman Imperial Themes* (Oxford: Clarendon, 1990) 272; Peter Garnsey, *Social Status and Legal Privilege in the Roman Empire* (Oxford: Clarendon Press, 1970) 77–79.

Rome's control of the Jerusalem elite is exhibited in the governor's appointment of the chief priests. Caiaphas was chief priest throughout Pilate's administration (Matt 26:57), at Pilate's pleasure. Caiaphas understood that keeping the boss happy, upholding Rome's interests, was crucial for his grip on power. Given that he remained in power throughout Pilate's rule, Caiaphas was skilled at doing so. Some forty or so years later in 66 C.E., when lower-ranked priests refused to offer the daily sacrifices "for Caesar and the Roman people," Josephus notes (*Jewish War* 2.410-11; 197; cf. 2.321-23, 336, 342) that the chief priests and the "most notable Pharisees" assembled with "the powerful citizens" to pressure the priests to stop their defiance. They also quickly send delegations to the governor, Florus, exonerating themselves from blame and expressing loyalty to Rome (*Jewish War* 2.418).

3. Roman Provincial Justice

These two factors, the multifaceted power of the Jerusalem leaders and their alliance with Rome, have a crucial impact on this scene involving Pilate and Jesus. They shape how "justice" works in this Roman world. The elite administers justice to protect its own interests. The scene does not play the "wicked" Jewish leaders determined to kill Jesus off against the "good guy" Pilate who is reluctant to do anything. There are no checks and balances whereby the "secular" branch guards against excesses by the "religious" branch. Instead there are aristocratic alliances and bias against lower-status provincials.

It is most unlikely, then, that Matthew's Pilate will resist the decision of the local leaders to kill Jesus. They are going to make sure he understands that his interests are being served in putting Jesus to death. He knows that their cooperation is vital in maintaining his power, wealth, and social status, so he will keep them happy. A system administered by the Roman governor and his allies, the local elite, means a stacked deck against a low-status provincial like Jesus. Jesus' "handing over" in 27:2, with the Jerusalem leaders wanting his death (26:66), means he is as good as dead!

The next scene in the narrative reinforces the audience's knowledge that Jesus' death is inevitable under Rome's system of justice. As soon as Jesus is handed over to Pilate, the narrative about his trial stops for eight verses (27:2). Instead of immediately developing the interaction between Pilate and Jesus, the narrative shifts attention to Judas, who had previously handed Jesus over to the Jerusalem elite (27:3-10). The interruption and the juxtaposition of scenes provide commentary on the handing over.

This next scene begins, "When Judas, his betrayer, saw that Jesus was condemned . . ." (27:3). The verb "handed over" in 27:2 has been replaced by a new verb, "condemned." The two verbs are synonyms, with "condemned" interpreting the meaning of "handing over." The verb "condemned" has been previously linked with Jesus' "death" in 20:18 ("they will condemn him to death"). And the death sentence is what the Jerusalem leaders have already announced for Jesus (26:66). Jesus' handing over to Pilate is his condemnation to die.

But also important is Judas' response. Having observed Jesus' "handing over" or "condemnation," Judas concludes that it is all over for Jesus. Judas, who seems to have changed his mind about Jesus, is so sure of the outcome for Jesus, so certain that Jesus' death is now utterly inevitable, that he returns the money and kills himself—before Pilate has even interrogated Jesus (27:3-10)! Judas' action attests the inevitability of Jesus' death.

The juxtaposition of the two incidents enables Judas' action to interpret the previous one. Jesus' handing over is not a neutral or mere procedural act. The language of condemnation and Judas' action provide commentary on the significance of what is happening. Jesus' death is inevitable in this judicial system when one part of the elite hands a low-status, powerless, and poor provincial over to another part of the elite. Throughout the scene Roman "justice" is exposed for what it is, an instrument of Roman imperial control, administered by the elite for the elite.

In addition to exposing the bias of Roman justice, the scene's introduction also exposes Rome's limited power. Jesus predicts his death four times before chs. 26–27 (16:21; 17:22-23; 20:17-19; 26:1-2). In 20:19 and 26:2 he uses the same verb to predict his "handing over" to the Jerusalem elite and to the Romans. It is the inevitable fate of those who challenge the representatives of the imperial order. Their actions are quite predictable.

But in the same statements Jesus predicts that God will raise him to life on the third day. That is, the worst that the elite can do in putting him to death is not the end of him! Their power to coerce and crucify is put in the context of and shown to be subservient to God's powerful and life-giving purposes. Ironically, at the very moment when they think they exhibit the fullness of their power, the gospel narrates its limits. The scene shows that their power is contrary to God's purposes and is judged by God. This is not to minimize Roman power. The power to execute is horrific and intimidating. But it is to recognize that the narrative exposes their legal agenda and qualifies their power by contextualizing it within God's greater purposes.

4. Pilate the Governor

The fourth imperial reality impacting the scene concerns Pilate's identification in 27:2 as "the governor." This commonly used term is important for two reasons. First, it identifies Pilate's position and power as Rome's representative. The narrative assumes that the gospel's audience knows the sort of information about Roman governors that I outlined in Chapter Three. A governor like Pilate

- was appointed by Rome,

- came from the wealthy, powerful, and high-status equestrian ranks,

- embodied tremendous privilege,

- exercised responsibilities for military, fiscal, and judicial control,

- advanced elite Roman interests in an exploitative, oppressive, and largely unaccountable relationship with those he governed,

- was widely known for greedy, self-serving practices, being compared to "blood-sucking flies,"

- was protected from most provincial protest by distance from Rome, the expense of a delegation to Rome, and the threat of subsequent retaliation.

The term "governor" appears seven times in the scene and so keeps Pilate's power and role to the fore (27:11 [twice], 14, 15, 21, 27). In addition to establishing Pilate's powerful role, the term underscores the conflict that is central to this scene. It has appeared twice previously in the gospel, both in contexts of conflict. Jesus is designated a governor or ruler! In 2:3-6, King Herod responds to news of Jesus' birth by demanding to know where the Messiah was to be born. His Jerusalem allies combine Scriptures from Mic 5:1-3 and 2 Sam 5:2 to identify Bethlehem:

> And you, Bethlehem, in the land of Judah, are by no means least
> among the rulers/governors of Judah;
> For from you shall come a ruler
> Who is to shepherd my people Israel. (Matt 2:6)

The word translated "ruler" in the second line is the same word used for Pilate and translated "governor" in 27:2. The term "ruler" in the third line is very similar to it. Jesus, the ruler/governor from Bethlehem, gives Bethlehem prominence among the rulers in Judah.

The verb "shepherd" in the last line underlines his governing task. The image of "shepherd" is commonly used for rulers.[11] Suetonius has the emperor Tiberius respond to a governor who was advocating more "burdensome taxes" for his province that "it was the part of a good shepherd to shear his flock, not skin it" (*Tiberius* 32). The same image appears in Matt 9:36 where Jesus, in a criticism of the ruling elite, regards the people as "harassed and helpless . . . like sheep without a shepherd." The adjectives "harassed and helpless" indicate violent and repressive actions. The people are "beat-up" and crushed by the Roman governor Pilate and the Jerusalem leaders.[12]

The shepherd image as it is used for Israel's leaders in Ezekiel 34 clarifies their misrule. The elite/shepherds feed themselves, but through taxes, tributes, rents, and temple dues deprive the sheep/people of food and clothing. They do not strengthen the weak, heal the sick, bind up the injured, or look for the lost and scattered (Ezek 34:3-6). They do not protect the people, but let them be enslaved, plundered, frightened, starved, and insulted (34:27-29). The leaders are condemned for their imperial style: "With force and harshness you have ruled them" (34:4). God promises a reversal with a Davidic prince and God's saving presence (34:23-24, 30-31). By using the same image Jesus, son of David, transfers its condemnation to the present rulers, both the Jerusalem elite and Pilate, Rome's representative.

Two Governors in Conflict

Describing both Pilate and Jesus as "governor/ruler" emphasizes the fundamental contrast and conflict between the two.

- Pilate represents the Roman emperor and empire. Jesus proclaims and embodies God's kingdom or empire (4:17-25).

- Pilate represents an empire that claims its rule derives from the will of Jupiter and the gods. Jesus claims the anointing of Israel's God and attacks the imperial order as a representative of Satan's false claims (4:8).

- Pilate embodies a domination system of rule over others. Jesus rejects this system as antithetical to God's will and requires the community of his followers to practice an alternative social order marked by service, not domination (20:25-28).

---

[11] Jer 23:1-4; Ezek 34:5-6; Dio Chrysostom 4.43-44; Dio 56.16.
[12] Carter, *Matthew and the Margins* 230–31.

- Pilate promotes a system that benefits the few at the expense of the many. Jesus, son of David (1:1; 9:27; 15:22; 20:30-31), makes available to anyone the benefits of God's inclusive mercy and transforming power.

- Pilate oversees a system that makes people sick by depriving (taxing) them of adequate food and nutrition and by burdening them with hard work. Jesus manifests God's empire in healing and feeding (4:23-25; 9:35; 14:13-21; 15:32-39).

Jesus' appearance before Pilate is a conflict between two governors or rulers. It continues the confrontation between two empires—Rome's and God's—that has been underway throughout the gospel. Jesus has at all times offered a different vision of the world and contested Rome's claims. Now the empire strikes back. It seems, of course, that Pilate has all the power and secures an easy victory. But Matthew's narrative emphasizes that God's purposes are being accomplished and will ultimately triumph.

However, the conflict is not only between Pilate and Jesus. The term "governor" also appears in 10:17-18. In ch. 10 Jesus instructs his disciples to continue his mission of representing God's kingdom or empire and transforming Rome's world: "cure the sick, raise the dead, cleanse the lepers, cast out demons" (10:7-8). But Jesus warns that the world will not welcome their challenge and alternative way of life.

> Beware of people; for they will deliver you up to councils and flog you in their synagogues, and you will be dragged before governors and kings for my sake. . . . (Matt 10:17-18)

Opposition is certain in the disciples' life of mission, and persecution is inevitable as the two empires collide. There is a fundamental antipathy from governors toward Jesus' followers. But the experience of Jesus' followers imitates Jesus' experience. The sequence of conflict that begins with Jewish councils (10:17) and then moves to governors (10:18), and the use of the same verb, "handing over," in 10:17 as in 27:2, link what is happening with Jesus in chs. 26–27 to the experience of disciples. They, too, will confront governors as they faithfully follow Jesus' instructions.

5. The Name "Jesus"

The opening verse of this Pilate scene employs another means to emphasize the nature of the conflict in the scene. It uses the name "Jesus" in

27:1 in place of pronouns ("he/him"). The scene with Pilate will use Jesus' name another seven times.[13]

The prominent use of Jesus' name recalls Matt 1:21, where the angel instructs Joseph to name the newly conceived baby "Jesus." Then the angel explains the name's meaning:

> She will bear a son, and you are to name him Jesus, for he will save his people from their sins. (Matt 1:21)

Jesus' name encapsulates his mission of salvation. As God's agent, Jesus carries out this mission of salvation in his life (teachings, actions), death, resurrection, and return. But what is salvation? Is it something that happens only to people's souls? Not in Matthew's gospel. Salvation consists of saving the people Israel from their sins. Rome punished those sins, especially the elite's rejection of Jesus and of God's purposes for a just world, in the fall of Jerusalem to Rome in 70 C.E. (22:1-10). Salvation will mean, as it so often does in the biblical traditions shaped by experiences with imperial powers like Egypt, Assyria, Babylon, and the Seleucid Antiochus IV Epiphanes, rescue from those punished sins and from Rome, the agent of God's punishment, who will be punished in turn for rejecting God's purposes. Jesus accomplishes this deliverance finally at his powerful return that establishes God's just and good reign over all things in a new heaven and earth (24:27-31, 35; 26:64).[14] The repeated use of the name "Jesus" in 27:11-26 recalls his salvific mission. In this confrontation between Jesus and Pilate, God's purposes are being enacted, purposes that will lead to Rome's demise and the establishment of God's just heaven and earth.[15]

Pilate of course knows nothing of this. He thinks he is in control and preserving Rome's interests. But again the narrative shows his power to be limited within God's much greater purposes that will ultimately destroy Pilate's world.

Jesus and Pilate: Establishing Jesus' Guilt (27:11-14)

After the account of Judas' suicide (27:3-10), the Pilate-Jesus scene continues. Pilate takes control, as he will throughout, and asks Jesus: "Are you the King of the Jews?" The "handing over" presumes a briefing. Jesus' claim to manifest God's triumphant reign, asserted before the Jerusalem council (26:64), implies a claim to kingship. To claim kingship without

---

[13] Matthew 27:11 (2x), 17, 20, 22, 26, 27; only three times in Mark 15:1, 5, 15.
[14] For detailed support see Carter, *Matthew and Empire* 75–90.
[15] Ibid., Chapter 5, especially 86–88.

Rome's sanction is, in their view, blasphemy against God and treason against Rome's empire.

Jesus seems to accept the title "the King of the Jews" in replying: "You have said so." The narrative emphasizes four more times that Jesus does not contest this title. In 27:12 Jesus "made no answer" to their further charges. Pilate questions his silence (27:13). The narrative records it (27:14, "he gave him no answer") and underlines it ("not even to a single charge"). If Roman law presumed that the lack of a defense meant "guilty as charged,"[16] Jesus has admitted his "guilt." He is King of the Jews.

But what is the significance of the title? What is Pilate asking Jesus, and what does Jesus confess to with his answer and silence? In the account of Jesus' birth, the magi from the east referred to Jesus by this title (2:2). Whatever else it means, it means trouble! King Herod (2:1), Rome's puppet king who dutifully acknowledged Rome as "masters of the world" (Josephus, *Jewish Antiquities* 15.387), was himself called "King of the Jews" (*Jewish Antiquities* 16.311). Knowing that the Messiah was to be born in Bethlehem, where King David, to whom an eternal line of kings was promised (2 Samuel 7), had been anointed (1 Samuel 16), Herod employs violence to remove any possible threat (2:16-18).

The title "king" was used for Rome's rulers or emperors.[17] Various "rebels" claimed the title in the first century, but Rome had no patience with their royal pretensions and disregard for Rome's sovereignty. Simon is beheaded (Josephus, *Jewish Antiquities* 17.273-76), Athronges is captured (*Jewish Antiquities* 17.278-85), Menachem is killed (though not by Rome, *Jewish War* 2.433-48), and Simon, leader of the longest and most successful of the revolts (*Jewish War* 4.510), is ritually executed in Rome during Vespasian's triumph (*Jewish War* 7.153-55). A claim to be king was regarded as a rejection of Rome's rule. In asking Jesus if he is "King of the Jews," Pilate asks Jesus: "Are you the head of the resistance?"[18] The title charges Jesus with sedition against the empire and Caesar.

Pilate's question is on target, and Jesus' answer is correct. Throughout, Jesus has proclaimed God's kingdom or empire present already in his words (4:17-25) and actions (12:28), but yet to be established in full over all things (24:27-31; 25:31-46; 26:64). God's kingdom is not like Rome's empire, which Pilate represents, nor is Jesus' kingship the same as Caesar's or those of the executed claimants. As a king:

---

[16] A. N. Sherwin-White, *Roman Society and Roman Law in the New Testament* (Oxford: Clarendon Press, 1963) 25–26.

[17] Josephus designates Roman emperors as kings with the same word in *Jewish War* 3.351; 4.596; 5.563; (Titus) *Jewish War* 5.58; see also Appian, *Civil Wars* 2.86 (Hadrian).

[18] Sherwin-White, *Roman Society* 24.

- Jesus rejects imperial staples such as violence (5:38-42; 26:52) and domination (20:25-28).

- He rejects the exploitative and oppressive ways of kings (6:29)[19] and the hoarding of wealth (6:24-34).

- He rejects triumphant celebrations of domination through military subjugation (21:1-11).[20]

- Rather, he prefers the way of meekness (21:5), service (20:28), and prayer for God's alternative empire marked by sufficient bread and forgiveness of debt (6:9-13).

The empire and kingship that his words and actions have attested differ significantly from Rome's. He has offered a clear alternative and challenge to Rome's political authority and to its hierarchical social structure that benefits the elite. But however he defines it, he is a king, and that claim threatens the elite.

Throughout Pilate's two questions and the Jerusalem leaders' further accusations, Jesus remains silent. His silence evidences several possible important dimensions:

- His dismissal of the power group that has consistently refused to listen to him and now wants to put him to death. Their conflict came to a head at the end of ch. 21 as they sought to arrest him (21:46), and at the end of ch. 22 when "from that day no one dared to ask him any more questions" (22:46). In turn, Jesus announces a series of seven woes against the Jerusalem elite (23:13-36).[21]

- Awareness from the biblical tradition that the powerful ruling elite always retaliate against those who challenge it. The narratives of King Herod's attempts to kill Jesus and slaughter of the children of Bethlehem (Matthew 2), and of Herod Antipas' beheading of John the Baptist (Matt 14:1-12) demonstrate their violent modes of operation. In predicting his own death (16:21; 17:22; 20:17-20), Jesus recognizes that the empire always strikes back.

- Consistency with his own teaching. Jesus has taught previously that to try to save his life would be to lose it; but to lose it in crucifixion is to save it because it opens the way for him as Son of Man to return "in his empire" (16:25-28; 24:27-31; 26:64). Jesus denies Pilate

---

[19] Carter, *Matthew and the Margins* 178.
[20] Ibid. 413–18.
[21] For discussion of this troubling chapter see Carter, *Matthew and the Margins* 449–65.

and his imperial system the power to intimidate him into conformity and submission, but he maintains the challenge of his commission.

- Evocation of the tradition of the suffering servant from Isaiah, a tradition that Matthew has explicitly employed on two previous occasions to interpret Jesus' actions (8:17; 12:18-21). Here, like the servant Israel in Babylonian exile, Jesus absorbs imperial violence (this time from Rome, not Babylon) for the benefit of others, trusting that God's purposes of overcoming their violence and establishing a just world will be accomplished. (See the discussion in Chapter Four on Mark 15:4-5.)

Pilate's response to Jesus' confession and silence misses all of this. In a rare glimpse into a character's inner world the audience learns that Pilate "was greatly amazed" (27:14). Pilate is amazed not because he thinks Jesus is "not guilty" or not a threat, as some mistakenly claim. Jesus' confession in word and silence has removed any doubt of his guilt (27:12-13). Pilate wonders because Jesus has readily acknowledged that he is a threat to Rome. Strangely, Pilate has not been able to intimidate Jesus into trying to save his life!

The narrative's echoes of the biblical tradition, especially of the suffering servant, again contextualize Pilate's assertion of power. These echoes point to God's larger purposes at work, to which Pilate is ironically and unwittingly subject, in which he has no place, and to which he is resistant.

Two Short Explanations (27:15-16)

Pilate's brief exchange with Jesus is finished. Pilate is now clear that Jesus is guilty of treason. He deserves the death penalty. Jesus is as good as dead. The rest of the scene shows Pilate the politician astutely and skillfully minimizing any social and political fallout from executing a figure who claims to be king of a subjugated people. To prepare for Pilate's skillful management of the crowds, the narrative provides the gospel's audience with two pieces of information that are crucial for understanding what will happen subsequently between Pilate and the crowd in vv. 8-15.

The first piece of information concerns Pilate's practice of releasing a prisoner at the festival of Passover (27:15).[22] The second concerns a "notorious" prisoner, Barabbas (27:16). Nothing further is said about his crime, though the adjective also carries the sense of "prominent" or "outstanding." It would be reasonable to assume that Barabbas is well known for his unspecified crime. In the subsequent scene he is the elite's choice to be re-

---

[22] See p. 68 above.

leased. This preference is not explained, but it may reflect a crime not as serious, and therefore not as threatening to the elite's interests, as Jesus' claim to be king—or they may think that Barabbas' threat can be more readily managed and contained than Jesus'.

Pilate Polls the Crowds (27:16-26)

After these two pieces of information are supplied, the narrative of Pilate's skillful control of the crowd in building an alliance with it, in pretending to respond to its wishes, and in securing its assent to this king's execution commences with a vague "so after they had gathered." It is not until v. 20 that the "they" is clearly identified as crowds who have gathered to watch the governor administer "justice" on the elevated "judgment seat" in Jerusalem (27:19) outside the praetorium or governor's headquarters (27:27). Previously crowds in Galilee have responded with interest and appreciation for Jesus' ministry (4:25; 7:28; 9:8, 33) though often without conviction about its significance (12:23; 14:23). In Jerusalem crowds welcomed Jesus to the city as a prophet (21:8-11) and marveled at his teaching (22:33). But other crowds supported Judas in Jesus' arrest (26:47, 55).

A Choice (27:17)

Pilate initiates the choice of a prisoner to be released and specifies the candidates, "Jesus Barabbas or Jesus who is called the Messiah/Christ?" (27:17). No reason is given for the choice of Barabbas. But given Jesus' confessed identity as king, and the elite's manipulation of the crowd, perhaps Barabbas' crime is less serious. The two men are linked by the same name. They may also be linked by their disruption of Rome's order. Whatever the details of Barabbas' crime, his "notorious" reputation suggests he poses some unspecified (violent?) threat to Roman order, just as Jesus does.

However, they are separated by their motivations for opposition. Pilate unwittingly and without consent attests to Jesus' purposes by referring to him as "Jesus, the one called Messiah." The gospel's audience knows this claim about Jesus' identity and role from the beginning of the gospel (1:1). It has heard Jesus accept this role (11:2-6; 16:16) and declare it to be revealed by God (16:17). There was no monolithic or widespread expectation for a Messiah in first-century Judaism.[23] At root the term means "anointed" or commissioned. Numerous people were anointed or commissioned to perform various God-given roles: prophets (1 Kings 19:16),

---

[23] See Marinus de Jonge, "Messiah," *ABD* 4:777–88, for an excellent discussion of the texts.

priests (Leviticus 4), kings (Ps 2:2), a Gentile ruler, the Persian Cyrus, to deliver Israel from Babylonian control (Isa 44:28–45:1), a ruler to overcome Rome (*PssSol* 17; 4 Ezra 11–12). To use the term "Messiah" (or its Greek equivalent "Christ") is to claim that God has commissioned or anointed or chosen Jesus.

But it is also to pose a question: what has God anointed or commissioned Jesus to do? The gospel narrative shows that Jesus is commissioned to save from sins (1:21), to manifest God's presence (1:23) and rule (2:6; 4:17). Most recently Jesus has talked of his identity as "Messiah" as the returning Son of Man who will manifest God's rule and judgment over the world, including Rome's empire and its allies, the Jerusalem elite (26:63-64). "Messiah" signifies Jesus' commission to a role that is not good news for Rome and its allies. He is commissioned to end their world with the assertion of God's rule. The title "Messiah," then, is a synonym for "King of the Jews" (27:11).

This is how the title was used in the scene depicting King Herod's violent response to Jesus' birth (2:1-6, especially vv. 2 and 4; also 1:17), and it is how Pilate uses it. Both titles denote Jesus' claims to manifest God's rule. That claim has both religious and political dimensions. Pilate's use of "Messiah" does not mean an emphasis on Jesus' religious rather than political role. The two are interconnected. For Pilate the title "Messiah" as a synonym for "King of the Jews" expresses Jesus' treason of claiming kingly power without Rome's approval. And Pilate is right. He correctly understands that the term denotes opposition to Rome's rule, and so Jesus must be eliminated. In doing so, Pilate represents the empire's fundamental opposition to God's purposes, for which there can only be judgment. Pilate and Jesus stand in confrontational opposition to each other as representatives of vastly different systems of structuring human society.

Pilate invites the crowd to secure the release of either Barabbas or Jesus (27:17). Pilate seems confident that his power will not be threatened by their choice. And he seems confident in his ability to gain the crowds' compliance. His use of the synonym "Messiah" for "King of the Jews" is astute. It turns the question into a test of their loyalty and stacks the deck against Jesus. Whatever Barabbas has done, it is not as serious as claiming to be king. The crowd knows what happens to those who claim kingdoms without Rome's sanction and who announce Rome's downfall. They also know what happens to loyal followers of such people. No one is going to call for Jesus' release in the presence of the governor! They will express their loyalty to the governor and Rome while protecting their own necks. Pilate's question has skillfully determined the answer he will get. They will express support for the elite's plan.

Moreover, he reminds them of his control in saying that he will do the releasing ("I will release"). But he emphasizes that the benefit is theirs. The release is "for you." Pilate emphasizes the "for you" nature of Roman justice in order to appear benign and concerned for his subjects and responsive to their wishes so as to minimize opposition. But the narrative reveals his claim to be an outright lie. Jesus is crucified because he threatens the elite. Pilate will skillfully continue to conceal this reality over the next few verses as he continues to secure this alliance with the crowd.

Pilate's Motivation (27:18)

Before the crowd responds, two things happen. Verse 18 provides an explanation ("for") for the choice Pilate offers and for his bias against Jesus. With a rare glimpse inside a character's head, it explains that Pilate knows the perspective of his allies, the Jerusalem elite. They see Jesus as a threat. They have handed Jesus over "out of jealousy or envy." This is not surprising. Jesus has been popular with the crowds and has attacked the leaders and their societal vision and leadership (Matt 4:23-25; 7:28-29; 21:8-11, 46; 22:33). The leaders are clearly not pleased with such a threat! That there is no comparable claim for Barabbas again suggests the lesser nature of his crime.

Pilate does not discredit or dismiss them for acting out of jealousy and envy. He realizes that his allies are threatened, so the source of the threat must be removed. Pilate and the Jerusalem elite need each other to secure their power. Pilate knows they have not been mistaken in their perception of the danger Jesus poses. He has himself heard Jesus acknowledge that he is King of the Jews. Pilate takes their jealousy seriously. But in order to handle Jesus' execution with minimal fallout he must discern the extent of the threat Jesus poses. How much support from the crowds does this king have?

Mrs. Pilate's Message (27:19)

The second thing that delays the crowd's response to Pilate's selection of two prisoners for possible release (27:17) is a message from Mrs. Pilate about Jesus. The message informs Pilate, seated on the judgment bench outside his headquarters, about her dream in which she has "suffered much." She advises him to have "nothing to do with that righteous man." She does not describe Jesus as "innocent." The word "righteous" has been used sixteen times previously in the gospel and not once has it been, or should it be, translated as "innocent" (1:19; 5:45; 9:13; 20:4). The translation "innocent" makes no sense here anyway. Pilate has known since vv. 11-14 that Jesus is guilty and deserves to die for treason.

What does Mrs. Pilate mean in declaring Jesus to be righteous? Fundamental to this word is the notion of faithfulness in which people act consistently to their commitments and obligations. It is used, for example, in the Bible to speak of God being faithful to the promises and covenant God has made. Because God is faithful, God acts powerfully to overcome what resists God's purposes (Ps 98:1-3; Isa 51:6, "salvation"). It also describes individuals who act faithfully to their relational or societal obligations (Gen 18:19; Tamar in Gen 38:26, spoken by Judah).

Mrs. Pilate's declaration, then, about "that faithful man" reminds Pilate that her dream about Jesus has shown that Jesus acts consistently or faithfully to his commitments. No wonder she has suffered much! Jesus' faithfulness will mean the end of her world! Her dream seems to have revealed Jesus being faithful to God's saving purposes, and that is clearly bad news for Rome and Pilate! Pilate should have nothing to do with this dangerous threat. What does that mean? It cannot mean a simple dismissal of Jesus. Pilate knows from vv. 11-14 that Jesus is a threat to Rome. Mrs. Pilate's statement, then, must function as encouragement to Pilate to remove Jesus quickly.

There is an irony in her use of the word "faithful." That word reminds the gospel's audience, as this death-sentence scene approaches its culmination, that his imminent crucifixion results from his being faithful to his God-given commission as "Jesus," "King of the Jews," and "Messiah/ Christ." He enacts God's justice (3:15) and kingdom (4:17). He is rejected because of his threat to the empire, in anticipation of his participation in God's final vindication (26:64).

Further, dreams have been a means of accomplishing God's purposes in ch. 2. There both the magi and Joseph receive dreams that enable God's purposes for Jesus to be carried out (2:12, 13, 19, 22). Here Mrs. Pilate's dream achieves the same purpose in urging Pilate to execute Jesus.

The two events in vv. 18-19 underline the perspective of the elite in removing Jesus as a threat. But they also judge them in God's perspective. The elite regard Jesus as a threat and as trouble that must be removed. In doing so they think to assert their control over the world. But the narrative puts that control in the context of God's purposes to establish God's just rule that Jesus righteously enacts.

The Crowd's Responses (27:20-22)

In v. 20 the crowd, (mis)led by the Jerusalem elite, calls for Barabbas' release and Jesus' death. The verse attests the Jerusalem leaders' involvement with Pilate in manipulating the crowd into accomplishing the elite's

will. The crowd passes Pilate's loyalty test. Its opposition to Jesus supports the elite's agenda, demonstrates compliance, and indicates little risk of social unrest in crucifying Jesus. Presumably the elite targets Jesus because this self-confessed king poses a greater risk to their society. Barabbas' release is a more manageable risk.

Pilate tests the intensity of their support by repeating his question and choice between Jesus and Barabbas (27:21). He gets the same answer, a call for Barabbas' release. Their repeated answer is encouraging for Pilate. It suggests that he can crucify this kingly pretender Jesus without fearing social disturbances. His strategy to release a prisoner, his choice of these . particular men, his choice of words that bias the crowd against Jesus, the opportunity for the crowd to express a preference, his reminder to them that the power to release is his, evidence his skill in (1) eliciting the crowd's support for the elite's choice while (2) disguising it as the people's will.

His third question removes the option of release for Jesus. "What should I do with Jesus called the Messiah?" (27:22). The repeated use of "Messiah" reminds the crowd of Jesus' threat. There is only one thing to do with such a pretender as far as the elite is concerned. And it is clearly the elite's will that is being done here, as references to their intent to kill Jesus in 26:66; 27:1, 20 attest. So the deceived and intimidated crowd dutifully and supportively calls for the crucifixion of one of their countrymen.

But Jesus' previous predictions of his own death (16:21; 17:22-23; 20:17-19; 26:1-2) and Pilate's ironic use of the significant names/titles "Jesus" and "Christ" remind the gospel's audience again that it is the elite that remains deluded. It thinks it is in control. But its rejection of Jesus is a rejection of God's purposes, for which it will reap the consequences when God's purposes are finally accomplished.

Fourth Question (27:23)

Pilate's fourth question in v. 23 guards against social unrest by seeking the crowd's further support for his action of crucifying an occupied people's kingly pretender. The question "Why, what evil has he done?" does not mean that Pilate thinks Jesus is innocent or that he does not have a clue about what is happening. He knows Jesus is guilty (27:11-14), and his skillful control of the crowd has been evident throughout (27:15-23). This fourth question continues Pilate's strategy throughout the scene. It offers the crowd the opportunity to parrot back to him Jesus' crime, that Jesus the king claimed sovereignty without Rome's support and against Rome. Such an answer would demonstrate beyond any doubt their compliance with and understanding of Jesus' execution as an appropriate action that they support.

But instead they offer Pilate the next best thing, a repeated and stronger cry for Jesus' crucifixion. Pilate and the Jerusalem elite have been so successful in managing the crowds that a riot in support of, not against the governor's action of crucifying Jesus is about to break out (27:24b). The crowd's fourth response in v. 23 confirms their previous three (vv. 20, 21, 22) but adds nothing new. So "when Pilate saw that he was benefiting nothing" (27:24a, my translation), his questioning stops. The strength of the cry and the demand for urgent action may explain why none of Jesus' followers is hunted down and crucified with him. Pilate decides that Jesus, while dangerous, does not have extensive popular support. True to his word, Pilate releases Barabbas "for them," flogs Jesus, and hands him over to be crucified (27:26). This has been a good five-minute piece of work for Pilate.

This reading takes account of imperial realities and identifies the progression of the scene. In vv. 11-14 Pilate establishes Jesus' guilt as a threat to Roman interests. In vv. 15-23 he is presented as a ruthless and politically astute governor, securing the crowd's support for the elite's plan to execute Jesus while fostering the impression that he is responsive to their wishes and thereby disguising the elite's manipulation. He can execute Jesus knowing there will be little social unrest. In fact, there will be more if he does not!

Pilate's Handwashing (27:24b)

Pilate takes some water and washes his hands before the crowd. His cry, "I am innocent of this man's blood," is not a testimony to Jesus' innocence as is often argued. The statement claims Pilate's innocence, not Jesus'.[24] Nor is it the cry of a defeated and frustrated governor who has not been able to free this innocent man. Pilate knows Jesus should be condemned. Rather it is a triumphant cry, accompanied by a final gesture of handwashing that celebrates—and judges—Pilate's governing skill.

His handwashing and declaration of innocence acknowledge what he and his allies have accomplished in this scene. They have successfully identified a threat to their power, decided on Jesus' execution, and manipulated the crowd not only into not supporting Jesus but also into actively (al-

[24] The similarity between Pilate's statement in 27:24 and Judas' statement to "the chief priests and elders" in 27:4 should be noted. Judas' statement functions to reinforce the complicity of the Jerusalem elite in Jesus' death as they dismiss Judas' confession with a hasty "What is that to us?" Pilate's similar language allies him with the Jerusalem leaders against Jesus.

most riotously) advocating that he be executed, precisely what the elite had already decided to do. With his questions and the Jerusalem elite's work among the crowd Pilate has astutely turned the crowd into advocates of the elite's will! He can now carry out the execution of the people's kingly pretender as *their* will and with *their* support. He can mask his use of Roman justice to protect the elite's threatened interests under the guise of his "for you" approach. With his handwashing and declaration of innocence Pilate places *onto the people the responsibility for what he as governor in alliance with the Jerusalem elite has done.* This is a masterful piece of work.

The proof of the effectiveness of Pilate's work—and the final tragedy of the scene—comes in 27:25 as the people accept the responsibility that Pilate dumps on them.[25] The people shout, "His blood be on us and on our children!" Such is the extent of the ruling elite's control over the people in this imperial situation. Such is the extent to which the crowd has "owned" the elite's agenda. They are puppets prompted by, and in this instance permitted by, their masters to declare themselves in control of this situation in doing the elite's will.

But Matthew's narrative does not join in the celebration; rather, it exposes the self-serving workings of Roman justice administered by and for the elite. Jesus is not crucified because the people demand it. Jesus is crucified because the elite engineer it and disguise their work. The scene displays the how (elite alliances, crowd manipulation, information spin), the who (the Jerusalem elite, the Roman governor), the why (Jesus' challenge), and the outcome. While Pilate's handwashing foregrounds the people's demand for Jesus' execution and backgrounds the elite's involvement, the narrative does precisely the opposite. It narrates—and thereby unmasks—the elite's commitments, initiatives, and strategies.

The narrative exposes the cynicism of Roman justice. It rips away the masks. It shows the self-serving nature of Roman administration that masquerades behind claims of benefiting the people and responding to their demands—demands orchestrated by the elite! Public benefit, the public good, is shown to mean nothing other than maintaining the elite's privilege and benefit while deceiving the people. Pilate's "for you" justice (27:17, 21) is nothing of the sort. It is a lie because it misrepresents the oppressive imperial relationship as one of public benefit. The handwashing and pronouncement of his own innocence are part of the same deception. There is no doubt that by Rome's rules Jesus deserves to die. But this scene, in the

---

[25] For discussion of the numerous issues raised by 27:25 (not addressed here) see Carter, *Matthew and the Margins* 528–29, and the literature cited there.

context of the gospel story, raises profound questions about the nature of those rules and in the handwashing scene delivers the verdict that Roman justice is all washed up.

Matthew's narrative, then, is not deceived. We are reading a piece of literature very subversive in its exposure of and opposition to Roman control. The narrative casts its judgment. Rome's ultimate power in coercing compliance, the taking of life, is shown, in Matthew's next chapter, as another hoax. Rome cannot keep Jesus dead! The final references to Pilate show him trying in vain to seal Jesus' tomb against God's resurrecting power. But soldiers and stones (27:62-66), lies and political spin, imperial propaganda and bribe money—a veritable catalogue of elite manipulative strategies—cannot do it (28:11-15). Ironically, the death that Pilate brings about will mean his own death and that of his imperial system. The risen Jesus who shares "all authority in heaven and earth" (28:18) with God, not with Rome, will return, and Rome's empire will end as God's empire is established in full (24:27-31; 26:64). That will be the final exposure of the powerlessness of Pilate, the powerful Roman governor.

Conclusion

In Matthew's presentation Pilate has enormous power, considerable political skill, and much self-confidence. As the governor, he is the center of the action, either the focus of other people's actions and words or initiating events and conversations. The Jerusalem leaders bring Jesus to him (27:2). The leaders talk to him in accusing Jesus (27:12). Jesus stands before him (27:11). Pilate initiates addresses to Jesus twice (27:11, 13). He has power to release a prisoner at Passover (27:15). He knows the Jerusalem elite's thinking (27:18). Four times he addresses the subservient crowd, astutely manipulating them to do the elite's will without any risk to elite interests (27:17, 21, 22, 23). They speak to him and ask for a prisoner's release (27:20-21). His wife sends a report of her dream to him (27:19). He washes his hands (27:24), releases Barabbas and hands Jesus over for crucifixion (27:26). He has power of life and death. By contrast, Jesus and Barabbas are totally dependent on him, being done to rather than doing. Pilate is very sure of his power in offering to release a prisoner. Throughout the scene he carefully and astutely accomplishes the elite's agenda of removing Jesus and protecting the elite's interests.

Pilate occupies the center, yet his power has limits. He cannot intimidate Jesus (27:14), and the crowds' support for Jesus' crucifixion almost gets out of hand (27:24). And he cannot keep Jesus dead. God's purposes are, ultimately, more powerful and just.

Matthew's audience lives in the imperial world exposed by the narrative. They cannot underestimate its danger and power. They are to live faithfully, performing the acts and practices that embody God's empire, sustained by the community of disciples, anticipating Jesus' coming. But they must not be intimidated by Rome's power either, even though they too walk the way of the cross, in which to give one's life is a real option.

CHAPTER SIX

Luke's Pilate

Even though Luke's gospel probably uses Mark as a source, Luke's presentation of Pilate differs significantly from Mark's. Luke's scene involving Pilate and Jesus is a very difficult one and, as we will see, it has provoked much debate.

The scene divides into four subscenes:

23:1-5   The Jerusalem elite accuses Jesus; Pilate instantly dismisses the charges.

23:6-12   Pilate sends Jesus to Herod who also finds no charge against him.

23:13-16   Pilate decides there is no basis for executing Jesus.

23:18-25   Pilate eventually condemns Jesus.

Luke 23:1 Then the assembly rose as a body and brought Jesus before Pilate. **2** They began to accuse him, saying, "We found this man perverting our nation, forbidding us to pay taxes to the emperor, and saying that he himself is the Messiah, a king." **3** Then Pilate asked him, "Are you the king of the Jews?" He answered, "You say so." **4** Then Pilate said to the chief priests and the crowds, "I find no basis for an accusation against this man."

5 But they were insistent and said, "He stirs up the people by teaching throughout all Judea, from Galilee where he began even to this place." **6** When Pilate heard this, he asked whether the man was a Galilean. **7** And when he learned that he was under Herod's jurisdiction, he sent him off to Herod, who was himself in Jerusalem at that time. **8** When Herod saw Jesus, he was very glad, for he had been wanting to see him for a long time, because he had heard about him and was hoping to see him perform some sign. **9** He questioned him at some length, but

Jesus gave him no answer. **10** The chief priests and the scribes stood by, vehemently accusing him. **11** Even Herod with his soldiers treated him with contempt and mocked him; then he put an elegant robe on him, and sent him back to Pilate. **12** That same day Herod and Pilate became friends with each other; before this they had been enemies.

13 Pilate then called together the chief priests, the leaders, and the people, **14** and said to them, "You brought me this man as one who was perverting the people; and here I have examined him in your presence and have not found this man guilty of any of your charges against him. **15** Neither has Herod, for he sent him back to us. Indeed, he has done nothing to deserve death. **16** I will therefore have him flogged and release him."

[. . .]

18 Then they all shouted out together, "Away with this fellow! Release Barabbas for us!" **19** (This was a man who had been put in prison for an insurrection that had taken place in the city, and for murder.) **20** Pilate, wanting to release Jesus, addressed them again; **21** but they kept shouting, "Crucify, crucify him!" **22** A third time he said to them, "Why, what evil has he done? I have found in him no ground for the sentence of death; I will therefore have him flogged and then release him." **23** But they kept urgently demanding with loud shouts that he should be crucified; and their voices prevailed. **24** So Pilate gave his verdict that their demand should be granted. **25** He released the man they asked for, the one who had been put in prison for insurrection and murder, and he handed Jesus over as they wished.

What sort of figure is Luke's Pilate? The most common reading of this scene between Jesus and Pilate, a reading with which I do not agree, says Pilate is weak and spineless (see Verdict 2 on Pilate in Chapter One above). As early as v. 4 Pilate declares there is no basis for the charges against Jesus. He repeats this conclusion and wants to release Jesus in vv. 13-16, 20, and 22. But, so this view goes, though his intentions are noble, he is unable to stand up to the pressure exerted by the Jerusalem leaders and crowds to crucify Jesus. Pilate capitulates to their demands and executes Jesus.

Why would Luke present Pilate in this way? What circumstances among Luke's audience would such a presentation address? Those who read the scene this way make several suggestions.

Explaining Christianity to the Empire

One explanation proposes that Luke wants to show officials of the Roman empire (such as "Theophilus," addressed in 1:1-4) that Jesus and his

followers pose no threat to the empire. Even the Roman governor, Pontius Pilate, knew Jesus was innocent, so the argument goes. It was the Jewish leaders who forced him to execute Jesus.[1]

But it seems doubtful that Luke was writing for nonbelievers. Theophilus' identity remains something of a mystery. But his name means in Greek "one who loves God," representing precisely what Jesus' followers are to do (Luke 10:27). That suggests he is a believer or, at least, represents believers. This likelihood is supported by the verb "instructed" in 1:4 that elsewhere describes instruction about God's purposes (Acts 18:25). Most probably Theophilus has previously received such instruction. Nor is there any evidence for extensive persecution that would account for the need to assure Roman officials of Christianity's harmlessness. And Luke's gospel includes some details that could be understood as quite threatening to the empire: Jesus is a king (Luke 19:38); there was a "zealot" (committed to the violent overthrow of Rome) among Jesus' followers (Simon, Luke 6:15); Jesus commands his followers to take swords (22:35-38). Why weren't these potentially harmful aspects omitted?

Explaining the Empire to Christians

A second explanation reverses this first one. Instead of Luke justifying the Christians to the Roman empire, perhaps Luke was justifying the empire to Christians. This second explanation suggests that Luke wants to show members of the Christian community (or communities) that the Roman empire poses no danger to them. Certainly Pilate the Roman governor crucified Jesus, but, so this theory goes, Luke wants to assure his readers that Pilate did so only because he had his arm twisted by the Jewish leaders, and that governors are not hostile to Christians.[2] Either way, Pilate is part of a presentation that is supposed to show that the church and the empire pose no threat to each other, that one can be a follower of Jesus and loyal to the empire at the same time.[3] It is possible for church and state to cooperate with each other.

---

[1] For a summary and discussion of this view see Paul W. Walaskay, *'And so we came to Rome:' The Political Perspective of St Luke.* MSSNTS 49 (Cambridge: Cambridge University Press, 1983) 1–37.

[2] This is Walaskay's view.

[3] So Philip Francis Esler, *Community and Gospel in Luke-Acts.* MSSNTS 57 (Cambridge: Cambridge University Press, 1987) 201–23. Helen Bond (*Pontius Pilate in History and Interpretation.* MSSNTS 100 [Cambridge: Cambridge University Press, 1998] 138–62) follows Esler.

This second explanation is not convincing either. Whether one views Luke's Pilate as weak, or pressured, or capricious, he is definitely not harmless. The fact remains that Luke shows Pilate condemning Jesus to death. If a *weak* governor can do that, if governors can be pressured into such capricious actions, how frightening is that for Jesus' disciples! Any follower of Jesus could be subject to the same whims of gubernatorial weakness at any time! And if weak governors do that, what will strong, determined governors do? The scene with Pilate hardly offers a reassuring display of the empire's lack of threat! Nor does it show benign cooperation between Jesus and Pilate! Pilate executes Jesus.

Further, as I have already shown in the previous chapters, the phrase "weak governor" is an oxymoron. Roman governors like Pilate were not weak. They represented the most powerful empire on planet earth. Pilate personifies that enormous military, legal, economic, religious, social, and political power over Judea. Luke introduces him in the company of the emperor to emphasize his role as the emperor's representative or agent (3:1-2). And twice previously Luke has shown Pilate to be very capable and willing to use severe power (Luke 13:1; 20:20).

Nor can we think about this scene as though religious and political matters are unrelated to each other. In Chapter Three I pointed out that in the Roman world these areas, often separated in our world, were not regarded as separate spheres. Rome's political power was understood to originate with and be sanctioned by Jupiter. Rome manifested the will and blessings of the gods. Jesus may talk much about God's reign or empire in the gospel, but that does not make him an exclusively "religious" figure. God's reign has important political, social, and economic implications that challenge the way Rome organizes the world. Jesus does not pose a military threat and does not advocate violence, but that does not mean he is harmless.

However we think about Luke's presentation, we cannot ignore the socio-historical realities of Roman imperial power and the narrative context of Luke's presentation.

Another Way of Thinking About Luke's Pilate

I will argue that Luke's Pilate is not weak and spineless, but rather is arrogant in his displays of power.[4] He is arrogant in his facile dismissal of the "nobody" Jesus as posing no threat to Rome, and arrogant in his un-

---

[4] My analysis has some affinity with that of Joel B. Green, *The Gospel of Luke*. NICNT (Grand Rapids: Eerdmans, 1997) 797–813.

willingness to listen to the complaints of his allies, the Jerusalem elite, against Jesus. He arrogantly dismisses the apparently harmless Jesus by sending him to Herod. When Herod returns Jesus, Pilate proposes a quick release for Jesus, but the Jerusalem elite will not give up on their demand for Jesus' crucifixion. Pilate finally consents because Jesus is not worth a rift with his allies. His action has little to do with whether he thinks Jesus is innocent.

The scene exhibits what is at the heart of Pilate's arrogance. His arrogance blinds him to what is really happening. Jesus poses a significant threat and is guilty as charged. The Jerusalem elite perceives his threat and extensive popular support, and so wants to kill him as a threat to their control over society. But neither of these elite allies can perceive and accept what the gospel audience knows, that God's reign is being manifested in Jesus. Jesus does not pose the sort of threat that empires fear and know, namely a military or violent threat. Rather his is a very different kind of threat, a social and ideological or theological threat. In the midst of Roman power he proclaims and enacts another kingdom or empire. God's reign claims people's allegiance, shapes their lives in unusual ways, and anticipates Rome's downfall. But Pilate's arrogance prevents him from understanding who Jesus is or seeing the danger that exists right under his nose. Pilate belongs with the group of "many prophets and kings" who could not see or hear what the blessed disciples of Jesus are able to see and hear, namely the reign of God manifested in Jesus in their midst (10:23-24).

Luke's gospel is written to provide "security" or "certainty"[5] that God is doing the saving work that God promised to do (1:3-4). The need for such security or certainty arises from doubts about God's action. Even with Jesus' death, resurrection, and ascension (Luke 24), the world has not changed significantly. Rome's power seems solidly in place. There has not been a major confrontation with Rome (cf. Acts 1:6). Can God accomplish and complete God's purposes for a just world? Is imperial control too strong? Are things unchangeable? Why isn't God's reign so much more evident? Will Jesus return to finish the job?

The gospel addresses these doubts by assuring its audience that God is at work in Jesus' life. But more importantly, it wants the audience to understand *how* and *where* God is at work, and *what* God's reign looks like. God works among the apparently insignificant, the nobodies, creating an alternative allegiance, community, and set of practices. God's reign and its means of operation are not conventional imperial fare and are often invisible to the elite. God's reign effects not violent resistance, but a social

---

[5] The NRSV translates the term "truth" in 1:4.

and theological alternative to Rome's empire. It forms a new and different society in the midst of Rome's hierarchical and exploitative system, in anticipation of its full establishment and Rome's demise at Jesus' return. Pilate portrays Rome's control, which is so arrogant and self-serving that it cannot recognize God's unconventional challenge in Jesus.

The scene with Pilate reassures Luke's audience by affirming that it, unlike Pilate, has correctly discerned Jesus' identity and commission to manifest God's reign. The scene continues the emphasis on God's reign at work in unusual ways in their midst, and challenges the audience to be faithful in its commitments and in living its distinct way of life that manifests God's reign, whatever the risk.

God's Reign: Jesus Threatens Rome

The scene with Pilate must be understood not only in relation to the socio-political realities of Roman imperial power (Chapter Three above) but also in the context of what precedes it in Luke's gospel. So before looking specifically at the Pilate scene I will analyze Luke's presentation of Jesus' ministry, paying particular attention to dimensions that prepare for the scene with Pilate.

Luke's gospel shows that God's purposes enacted by Jesus pose a threat to the Roman empire, a threat that the Jerusalem elite discerns but Pilate does not. What God is doing in Jesus, however invisible it might be to many, is not harmless. It challenges Rome's interests and power at every point, with different commitments and visions of human society. The gospel's opening chapters sound this theme from the outset. As is typical of what literary critics have called "the primacy effect," important emphases located in the opening chapters of the gospel shape our understanding of the whole of Luke's story.

MARY

In chapter 1 Mary learns from the angel that she will have a baby (Luke 1:26-38). There is nothing to indicate that Mary has great wealth, status, power, or family connections. She is one of the "nobodies" of the empire, but though she is unnoticed by the elite, God has a special task for her. The angel tells her about Jesus' mission or job description:

> **Luke 1:32** "He will be great, and will be called the Son of the Most High, and the Lord God will give to him the throne of his ancestor David. **33** He will reign over the house of Jacob forever, and of his kingdom there will be no end."

The angel's announcement identifies Jesus (who is not yet born!) as God's son in the line of David and promises that he will rule forever. That link with David is enormously important because it connects Jesus to the line of Israel's kings. These kings were regarded as God's sons or agents who were to represent God's just reign in their own reign (see Psalms 2; 72). But also God promised King David that his line would last forever, that God's reign would be established forever (2 Samuel 7). Moreover, God's reign would extend beyond Israel to the Gentiles or the nations. They would come to Jerusalem and submit to Israel's God as their God and live according to God's just purposes and will (Isa 2:1-4).

By linking Jesus to King David the angel shows that God is being faithful to God's purposes. Like kings before him, Jesus will manifest God's reign, but now it will last forever and all the nations of the earth, including Rome, will submit to it! The angel does not say how Jesus will carry out this task, but it is a difficult and threatening one. Jesus must carry it out in a world ruled by "eternal Rome," whose power will last forever (or so it claims). Jesus, commissioned by God, will inevitably challenge Rome, commissioned by Jupiter to rule the world and to submit to no other (see Chapter Three above).

What do God's purposes of salvation look like? Mary celebrates God's work in the conception of Jesus with a song known as the "Magnificat" (1:46-55). In this song Mary, a young pregnant girl from an inconsequential family and town, a "nobody" as far as the elite is concerned, proclaims nothing other than the total overthrow of the powerful and rich, those who rule Rome's empire! She announces that God, being faithful to God's promises to Abraham, will destroy the present order based on hierarchy, greed, exploitation, domination, and unequal access to resources (see Chapter Three above). Through Jesus, God is mercifully creating a very different world in which the "nobodies," the hungry and the poor, the exploited victims of Rome's system, know God's blessing and access to life-sustaining resources.

Luke 1:46 And Mary said, "My soul magnifies the Lord, **47** and my spirit rejoices in God my Savior, **48** for he has looked with favor on the lowliness of his servant. Surely, from now on all generations will call me blessed; **49** for the Mighty One has done great things for me, and holy is his name. **50** His mercy is for those who fear him from generation to generation. **51** He has shown strength with his arm; he has scattered the proud in the thoughts of their hearts. **52** He has brought down the powerful from their thrones, and lifted up the lowly; **53** he has filled the hungry with good things, and sent the rich away

empty. **54** He has helped his servant Israel, in remembrance of his mercy, **55** according to the promise he made to our ancestors, to Abraham and to his descendants forever."

ZECHARIAH

Zechariah, the father of John the Baptist, who also figures prominently in Luke 1, emphasizes similar points. In a famous hymn known as the "Benedictus" (1:67-80) he celebrates God's faithful action that will save or "redeem" Israel from powers like Rome that rule in ways contrary to God's purposes. In so acting, God is being faithful to God's promises to David and to Abraham and to God's covenant with Israel. In addition to promising David that God's reign would be established forever, God promised Abraham that "all the nations of the earth" would be blessed through him (Gen 12:1-3). This promise also contrasts with Rome's world in that the Roman empire favors only the few, the wealthy powerful elite, at the expense of the rest. But God has promised to rescue people from a rule that is contrary to God's purpose to bless *all* people. Zechariah announces that God's promises are being fulfilled in Jesus:

> **Luke 1:68** "Blessed be the Lord God of Israel, for he has looked favorably on his people and redeemed them. **69** He has raised up a mighty savior for us in the house of his servant David, **70** as he spoke through the mouth of his holy prophets from of old, **71** that we would be saved from our enemies and from the hand of all who hate us. **72** Thus he has shown the mercy promised to our ancestors, and has remembered his holy covenant, **73** the oath that he swore to our ancestor Abraham, to grant us **74** that we, being rescued from the hands of our enemies, might serve him without fear, **75** in holiness and righteousness before him all our days. . . ."

JESUS' BIRTH

The same challenge and visions of an alternative world continue in chapter 2. Jesus' birth happens while a census takes place (2:1). Caesar Augustus decrees the census as a means of registering people in order to tax them. The census asserts Rome's power, secures the elite's wealth, and subjugates the people to Rome's control. It is a tried and tested means of maintaining imperial power, of supervision, and of surveillance.

But while the Roman emperor and his officials think they are ordering and controlling their world for their own benefit, God is quietly at work,

undetected by and invisible to the ruling elite. God and Rome are not co-operating in the census as is usually claimed;[6] God is undermining Roman power. God, who is not subject to the census and Roman power, is, in the very midst of this instrument of Roman control, bringing about the birth of God's son, the agent of God's purposes and reign. Hidden from imperial view, God is subverting the domination that Rome works so hard to impose!

SHEPHERDS

An angel announces Jesus' birth (2:8-14). The angel's audience comprises not the powerful and important, but shepherds, people of very low social status, insignificant and unimportant, near the bottom of the empire's social hierarchy. They hear of what God is doing, while the elite have no clue about what is happening in "their" world. The angel, God's messenger ("of the Lord," 2:9), emphasizes that God is acting faithfully to God's promises. The birth happens in "the city of David" (2:11), a name for Bethlehem that underlines God's faithfulness to the promise to David of establishing God's reign that will last forever (2 Sam 7:13-14) and will be marked by justice (Psalm 72). Bethlehem was a small town. In this apparently unimportant place, not the main city Jerusalem, the center of the elite's power, God is at work.

The angel describes Jesus as "Savior," "Christ/Messiah" (anointed one), and "Lord" (2:11). The titles express key aspects of Jesus' identity. He carries out God's saving work. Mary describes God as her Savior in 1:47. Zechariah celebrated God's salvation active in Jesus in 1:69, 71, 77. Zechariah proclaims that God saves the people "from our enemies and from the hand of all who hate us," an apt description of Rome's oppressive rule (1:71). As "Christ/Messiah" Jesus is anointed or commissioned by God to "reign over the house of Jacob forever, and of his kingdom there will be no end" (1:33). As "Lord" he manifests God's purposes.

But in announcing Jesus' birth the angel uses language that is widely associated with the Roman emperor. Both "savior" and "Lord" identify emperors such as Augustus, Tiberius, and Vespasian. The new emperor Vespasian is hailed as "savior" as he travels to Rome after the defeat of Jerusalem in 70 (Josephus, *Jewish War* 7.71). But the angel refers to Jesus, not the emperor, in such terms.

---

[6] Bond (*Pontius Pilate* 140) thinks the census shows "the politics of Rome working hand in hand with God's divine purpose for salvation;" also Walaskay, *Political Perspective* 25–28.

Good News

In vv. 10-11 the angel describes Jesus' birth as "good news." This term also refers to the "good news" of the Roman emperor's birthday, the end of wars, the benefits he supposedly conveys to "all people," his accession to power, his victory over rivals.[7] Again the language sets up a collision between the emperors and God's action in Jesus. Jesus' birth is not the same kind of "good news." In fact, the good news seems to be that God saves people from the oppressive rule of empires like Rome's! It is bad news for Rome. How so? The term "good news" is used in the Hebrew Scriptures to proclaim God's salvation from enemies (Pss 40:9-11, "glad news;" 68:11-14, "tidings") and from empires that tyrannize God's people (Isa 40:9-11, "good tidings;" 52:7, "good news"). In the case of Isaiah the references are to the good news of God saving the people who were forced into exile by Babylon. God will free them and they will return home. Now the good news concerns God saving people from Rome.

Peace

And God's action brings "peace" on the earth (2:14). This claim also directly contests Rome's claims that Rome had brought peace to the earth (*Pax Romana,* Roman peace). This was a shorthand term for subjugation to Rome's rule, accomplished through military might, enacted in economic measures like taxes and tributes, embodied in hierarchical social structures, established as the political order, and legitimated by the gods such as Jupiter as their "gift" through their agents, Rome's emperor and his troops. But the angel directly contradicts Rome's propaganda. The angel claims that

- God, not Jupiter, effects peace;
- God works not through the emperor, but through Jesus;
- God's peace-making work centers not in Rome but in a backwater town amidst very common folks;
- And in the biblical tradition peace refers to God's just order marked not by Rome's exploitation and military domination but by wholeness, protection, and benefit for all (see Psalm 72).

These passages indicate that all is not well between God's purposes and Rome. The two are in conflict, not cooperation. God does not validate

---

[7] Green (*Gospel of Luke* 133) provides texts for Augustus; for Vespasian see Josephus, *Jewish War* 4.618, 656.

Rome or turn a blind eye to how Rome structures and rules the world. God's action in the birth of Jesus, involving insignificant people in insignificant places, contests Rome's claims, challenges its world, and condemns its injustice. And God's "forever" kingdom, manifested in Jesus, remains invisible to Rome's empire.

JESUS: DOING GOD'S WORK

God's way of working, its invisibility to the imperial order, and the opposition it provokes are not just evident in Jesus' conception and birth.[8] Luke begins the account of Jesus' public ministry at 4:18 with a citation from Isa 61:1-2a. The citation expresses what Jesus is anointed or "christed" to do in his ministry.

> **Luke 4:18** "The Spirit of the Lord is upon me, because he has anointed me to bring good news to the poor. He has sent me to proclaim release to the captives and recovery of sight to the blind, to let the oppressed go free, **19** to proclaim the year of the Lord's favor."

Israel's traditions concerning "the year of release" or the Jubilee year influence this citation from Isaiah 61. The words translated as "release" and "go free" indicate that Jesus' transforming agenda is shaped by these traditions in Leviticus 25. According to this chapter, every fifty years slaves are to be freed, land returned to its original clan owners, and loans canceled. These Jubilee-year traditions envisioned a more equitable society, and provided a mechanism to correct social injustices and protect against massive inequalities. In this context Jesus' announcement of good news for the poor means a different economic system that provides access to adequate resources and participation in a society that accords all its members dignity and equal inclusion. Such a system would remove numerous diseases like blindness, associated with poor nutrition and inadequate food supply. Jesus' ministry is one of social, economic, and political transformation.

Jesus' agenda is to enact these traditions. But to adopt such an agenda is to challenge every aspect of Roman imperial society. To return land to its original clan owners would require the Roman elite to give up a huge source of income that was foundational to its power, wealth, and status. To free slaves was to surrender an enormous source of free labor and to abandon an institution that intimidated and humiliated opponents. To cancel

---

[8] Richard J. Cassidy, *Jesus, Politics and Society: A Study of Luke's Gospel* (Maryknoll, N.Y.: Orbis, 1978) 20–62, 77–86.

loans was to give up a vast source of wealth, not only from repayments but also from those who because of high interest rates, the demands of extended households, and poor soil and/or weather conditions defaulted on payments and surrendered their property. To envision any of this is to challenge Roman power, to contest Rome's hierarchical organization of society for the benefit of the elite, and to threaten Roman political control, even if Rome remains unaware of the challenge.

Luke's presentation of Jesus does not show Jesus carrying out this agenda by launching a military attack on the Romans or resorting to a direct, violent confrontation. But neither does he throw his hands up in the air or shrug his shoulders and mutter, "You've got to be dreaming!" Rather, his strategy is to do what God commissioned him to do: to proclaim God's reign or kingdom or empire in words (4:43, where the term "must" expresses God's will), to enact it in healings among the poor (7:22-23), and to form an alternative community of followers that lives a distinctive way of life shaped by God's reign (6:12-16; 12:31) and that prays for (11:2-4) and eagerly awaits the final establishment of God's kingdom and just purposes (18:1-8).

An Alternative Community

This community of Jesus' followers adopts practices of social and economic interaction that are counter to the practices of the dominant elite. It opposes the accumulation of wealth (12:15-21) and obsessing about or serving wealth (12:22-32; 16:13; 18:24-25). Jesus denounces the wealthy whose abundance means that others go without (6:24-25). The community of disciples lends without expecting repayment (6:30, 34-35), helps the poor (16:19-31), and gives up possessions for the benefit of others (14:33; 18:18-23, 26-30; 19:1-10). Comprising mainly the poor, it welcomes and includes other poor people rather than despising and excluding them as the empire's elite does. The inclusion of and assistance to their fellow poor is offered without looking for any reciprocal benefit, the normal expectation in the Roman world (14:12-24). Women as well as men play active roles (8:1-3; 10:38-42).

Jesus' community adopts different patterns of social interaction. Its meals do not reinforce and reflect conventional patterns of social hierarchy and reciprocity of benefit but an alternative and more egalitarian pattern of inclusion (14:7-14). His community renounces the seeking of status (9:46-48; 14:7-11) and the use of power to dominate others (22:24-27). Unlike "the kings of the Gentiles (who) lord it over them" (22:25), the community of Jesus' disciples chooses humility and service in seeking the good of the

other (17:7-10; 22:27). It engages violence not with retaliation or passivity but by nonviolent resistance that refuses to be intimidated, that displays a different way of being, and that creatively maintains human dignity in the face of attacks (6:27-31).

This commitment to God's empire, along with the practices and way of life that result, contrasts with the commitments of the elite. Humility and service have little part in the dominating and arrogant ways of "the kings of the Gentiles," the Roman emperors (22:24-27)! Jesus teaches that taxes should be paid to the emperor but that supreme loyalty belongs to God (20:20-26). That means that what the empire does is to be evaluated in relation to God's purposes. As we have seen, Jesus' concern for a different socio-economic order indicates that Rome resists, not submits to, God's purposes.

CONFLICT AND OPPOSITION

Jesus' proclamation of God's reign and establishment of a community with alternative socio-economic practices mean inevitable conflict with the elite. The last thing a small ruling elite wants is someone bold enough to declare that society does not have to be organized this way. The elite comprises various powerful groups allied by their common commitment to maintaining the status quo.

As retainers, the Jerusalem chief priests are allies of Rome's rulers. They are first introduced in 3:1-2, where the chief priests Annas and Caiaphas are associated with the emperor Tiberius, the governor Pilate, and Rome's puppet king Herod Antipas. This introduction attests their alliance with Rome and complicity in Rome's system, a complicity confirmed by the chief priests' active and dominant role in the efforts to put Jesus to death in chapters 22–23.

The Pharisees are described negatively as "lovers of money" (16:14), and Jesus condemns them for this commitment to money because it is not in line with God's purposes: "What is prized by human beings is an abomination in the sight of God" (16:15). He also condemns them for their love of status and neglect of "justice and the love of God" (11:42-43). For upholding the hierarchical status quo and not recognizing God's reign manifested by Jesus (17:20), the gospel declares that they reject God's purposes (7:30).

Likewise scribes, the educated group that maintains the status quo with its interpretations and applications of laws, are often associated with the power groups. They are allied with the Pharisees (5:17-26; 6:1-11; 15:2) and with the chief priests (19:47; 20:1). In addition to their guilt by

association, Jesus shames them publicly and specifically condemns them for their love of status in the hierarchical society that upholds wealth and power, rather than justice and inclusion (20:45-47).

Jesus' teaching challenges and condemns the societal vision and structure maintained by these allied elite groups for their own benefit and at the expense of the rest. Within their hierarchical and exploited society, the alternative social and economic practices of Jesus' followers point to a more just society. Ever-present crowds gather to hear him and admire his authoritative teaching and displays of power.[9] Their support for Jesus is as threatening to the ruling elite as his alternative social vision. Jesus conflicts with these leadership groups over matters of social structure,[10] and his teaching causes disruption to households (12:49-53).

Jesus announces that prophets who confront the elite's power become its victims (13:31-33). As he travels to Jerusalem, the elite's center and power base, he recalls that Jerusalem has not often welcomed God's prophets and messengers (13:33-35). Various alliances of these power groups, the chief priests, scribes, and elders, plan to kill Jesus and so remove this threat to their way of life. He predicts their violent response (9:22). They try to trap him (11:53). He predicts Rome's destruction of Jerusalem in 70 C.E., the center of their power, as a consequence of their "not recogniz(ing) the time of your visitation from God" (19:44). The pronouncement declares they have no place in God's purposes.

JESUS' ARREST

The final trigger for Jesus' arrest is his attack on the Jerusalem Temple, which these groups administer (19:45-48). He condemns it by quoting the prophet Jeremiah's words against a corrupt temple. Citing Jeremiah 7, he calls their Temple a "den of robbers." They are more intent on taking money from the people to maintain their own wealth, power, and status than on fostering encounter with God. They respond with a renewed commitment to kill him, though the people's receptiveness to his message makes it difficult to accomplish (19:47-48). Further conflicts over his and their authority (20:1-2) and further condemnations of their misrule and rejection of God's alternative (20:9-18) fuel efforts to arrest and kill him

---

[9] For the ubiquitous crowds and Jesus' ministry see 4:42; 5:1, 15; 6:17-19; 8:4, 40; 9:11, 37; 11:14, 29; 12:1, 54; 13:17; 14:25; 19:3.

[10] Previous disagreements with the scribes and Pharisees have involved his claims to manifest God's forgiveness (5:17-26), the use of the Sabbath (6:1-11), and the company he keeps (5:30; 15:2). These issues involve visions of how society is structured, where God's blessing is encountered in society, and who is included in God's blessing.

(20:19; 22:2). He announces judgment on Jerusalem and predicts that the city, the elite's power base, will fall to Gentile (Roman) armies and its inhabitants will be exiled, just as in the defeat of 587 B.C.E. by Babylon (21:20-24). With Judas' help, they arrest him (22:47-54).

The elders, chief priests, and scribes interrogate Jesus, asking him if he is the Messiah (22:67). It is a question about his identity and commissioning. Does Jesus have authority to speak and act as he does? Does he have any right to claim to manifest the kingdom or reign of God? Jesus refuses to answer these questions, but he does predict that he "will be seated at the right hand of the power of God" (22:69). This prediction confirms what he has claimed throughout. He will participate in the final, full, victorious establishment of God's reign, just as he has manifested it in part in his ministry. They repeat their question by asking if he is Son of God, God's agent who manifests God's kingly rule (22:70). Jesus rightly does not dispute the title, first used of him by the angel in 1:32 ("Son of the most High"), nor the role of king that it implies. But they refuse to accept his claim. With Jesus' confession to be the agent of God's reign, the Jerusalem elite, with a crowd of supporters (23:4), takes Jesus before Pilate.

Jesus and Pilate

This overview of Jesus' ministry, its claims and conflicts, establishes the context for Pilate's involvement. It is only when Jesus comes to Jerusalem for Passover (22:1) that Jesus and Pilate meet. We are not told why Pilate leaves his official residence in Caesarea to be in Jerusalem. Perhaps he is on his regular tour of his province to hear cases and deliver judgments on provincials like Jesus. Jesus would simply be one more case on the docket. Perhaps Pilate is in Jerusalem to maintain order during Passover.

It is not, though, the first reference to Pilate in the narrative. He has appeared three times previously.[11]

> 1. Pilate is first mentioned in 3:1-2 in a list of the ruling elite. Pilate appears second on the list and is described as "governor of Judea." The gospel's audience is assumed to know what governors do in the Roman empire, the sorts of tasks I outlined in Chapter Three. But there is no doubt about Pilate's importance and power. He is listed after the emperor, Tiberius, who appointed him to be governor of Judea, and whose interests, authority, and will Pilate represents. And he is listed before the chief priests Annas and Caiaphas, leaders

---

[11] Pilate also receives brief mentions in 23:52 and in Acts 3:13; 4:27; 13:28.

of his allies, the Jerusalem elite. These are the people who think they run the world. But v. 2 offers a surprise. Precisely in the midst of such daunting power structures, but not through them, "the word of God came to John son of Zechariah in the wilderness."

2. Pilate is mentioned a second time in 13:1. In a brief reference, he is reported to have mixed the blood of some Galileans with their sacrifices! No details are given here or elsewhere about this slaughter of people while they are in worship. But the scene, though brief, reveals several important things about Pilate. Nothing seems to be sacred for him, not even worship. He arrogantly asserts his deadly authority even in a sacred place without fear of reprisal. He is willing to use his power to take life if it serves his purposes. And, anticipating Jesus' death, we know that this will not be the last blood he spills.

3. A brief third reference to Pilate as governor follows in 20:20c. The Jerusalem elite, the scribes and chief priests (20:19), respond negatively to Jesus' parable of the vineyard that condemns their leadership and exposes their involvement in his death (20:9-18). So rather than be warned of God's judgment by the parable, they confirm Jesus' depiction of them and seek again to arrest him and hand him over to the governor. Pilate is not named, but the governor is presented as their ally and agent. They are sure of his support and action in helping them to remove Jesus since he has the power to execute. His interests are their interests. Pilate and the Jerusalem elite are on the same side.

Accusations and a Quick Dismissal (23:2-5)

In taking Jesus to Pilate, the Jerusalem elite repeatedly accuse Jesus of "perverting" or leading astray the people. Four references emphasize their role as Jesus' accusers:

CHARGE	VERSE
This man perverts/misleads our nation	23:2
He stirs up the people by teaching . . .	23:5
The chief priests and the scribes stood by, vehemently accusing him.	23:10
You brought this man as one who was perverting the people	23:14

Ruling elites often charge opponents with leading the people astray. The oppressive Pharaoh of Egypt accuses Moses of "perverting" or misleading the people when Moses challenges the Pharaoh to release the people from slavery (Exod 5:4). And the wicked king of Israel, Ahab, accuses the prophet Elijah of perverting or leading the people astray after Elijah opposes the king's execution of the prophets and advocacy of the worship of Baal (1 Kings 18:17-18). "Perverting the people" seems to mean resisting the status quo! Powerful opponents of God's just purposes accuse God's representatives of perverting the people when that representative challenges their practices and demands a more just society. Ironically, Jesus has already denounced the people and society led by the Jerusalem elite as "perverse" (9:41).

In bringing this charge the Jerusalem elite denies Jesus' claim that he is authorized by God to reveal God's will and reign in his words and actions (4:43). In so doing they reveal their own resistance to God's purposes. They are of course right to accuse Jesus. As we have seen, Jesus has offered a very different socio-economic and political vision. He has challenged the status quo from which they benefit and which they defend. He has tried to lead the people away from the elite's unjust social structure and control, away from business as usual. He has enacted the reign of God, proclaimed an alternative commitment, and shaped a different communal way of life. He is guilty of "perverting" their world. He is not violent, but he is very dangerous.[12]

They offer Pilate two examples of Jesus' "perverting" work (23:2). The first, appropriately, concerns his opposition to Rome's taxes. In 20:20-26 Jesus did not forbid paying taxes, but he did put loyalty to God above loyalty to the emperor. The effect of such a ranking is to deny taxes their significance in the imperial system as an expression of submission to Rome's rule!

Second, they accuse him of saying "he himself is the Messiah, a king" (Luke 23:2). Again they are correct.[13] From his conception Jesus is linked with the line of David, the representative of God's "forever" reign. Jesus begins his public ministry by declaring he is God's anointed or "christed" one (4:18). "Christ," meaning "anointed one," is the Greek form of the Hebrew "Messiah." Throughout his ministry he has announced God's reign

---

[12] Scholars often claim that this charge is false because Jesus describes the nation as being perverse already in 9:41. But this claim is not convincing since in 9:41 Jesus is describing their rejection of him, whereas the ruling elite in 23:2 identifies his attempts to change the status quo as constituting his "perverting the people."

[13] Bond (*Pontius Pilate* 145–46) is typical of many in trying, unconvincingly, to argue that Jesus is innocent of these charges.

in accord with his divine commission (4:43). And when he entered Jerusalem he refused to reject the disciples' acclaim that he was ". . . the king that comes in the name of the Lord!" (19:38-40). Jesus did not deny the charge in 22:67 and in 22:69 declared himself to share in God's reign.

KING JESUS

Pilate, having heard the charges, asks Jesus if he is "king of the Jews" (23:3). To claim to be a king is a capital offense. The title "king" was used for Rome's rulers or emperors.[14] Other rulers could be Rome's puppet kings, such as King Herod who dutifully acknowledged Rome as "masters of the world" (Josephus, *Jewish Antiquities* 15.387) and was called "King of the Jews" (*Jewish Antiquities* 16.311). But to claim the role and title of king without Rome's sanction was to challenge and reject Rome's authority and to bring death on oneself. Various "rebels" had done so in the first century, but Rome had no patience with their royal pretensions and disregard for Rome's sovereignty. (For a list of such rebels and the sources of our knowledge about them, see above, Chapter Five, at Matt 27:11-14.) In asking Jesus if he is "king of the Jews," Pilate asks Jesus, "Are you the head of the resistance?"[15] The title charges Jesus with sedition against the empire and Caesar. And Pilate's question is right on target. Jesus does oppose Rome's rule, though not with the violence employed by these other figures. Jesus' response does not contest the title: "you say so."

In this context Pilate's declaration in v. 4, "I find no basis for an accusation against this man," is very surprising. The first shocking aspect is that Pilate's declaration is instant. Pilate has just heard the uncontested accusations, but he has not heard from any witnesses or carried out his own investigation. His verdict is too quick. The second shock concerns Pilate's dismissal of Jesus' accusers. These are Pilate's allies in Jerusalem who have been monitoring Jesus' ministry. Together, Pilate and these Jerusalem leaders have a great investment in maintaining society as it is and swiftly removing any challengers. They need each other to protect their common interests. Pilate should take their accusations very seriously. Instead he ignores them. The third surprise involves the context of Pilate's declaration. It follows immediately on Jesus' reply to the charges, which Jesus does not contest.

---

[14] Josephus designates Roman emperors as kings with the same word in *Jewish War* 3.351; 4.596; 5.563; (Titus), *Jewish War* 5.58; see also Appian, *Civil Wars* 2.86 (Hadrian).

[15] A. N. Sherwin-White, *Roman Society and Roman Law in the New Testament* (Oxford: Clarendon Press, 1963) 24.

What are we to conclude about Pilate's instant verdict? Is the man stupid? Does he not hear well? Did he not hear what Jesus just acknowledged? Does he regard it as impossible that Jesus poses any threat? And why does he ignore his allies so blatantly? He is certainly not weak. And we know from Chapter Three that he probably has some ability for this vital role as Rome's representative who defends and maintains Rome's interests and rule.

Rather, cocooned in the trappings of Roman power, Pilate seems arrogant. He quickly dismisses his allies, the Jerusalem elite, without taking their reports seriously. And he as quickly dismisses this low-status provincial called Jesus who is charged with being a king. Jesus lacks the trappings of the type of kingship Pilate understands: no royal attire, no army, no wealth, no territory—so he is probably no threat. He cannot be a king worthy of Pilate's attention. Pilate seems blind to any danger being posed to Roman rule. Violent resistance is a clearly defined means of opposition, but visions of an alternative order from a low-status preacher don't seem very dangerous. The Jerusalem elite have seen the threat Jesus poses but Rome's representative cannot discern God's purposes at work.

In rendering such an instant verdict without any investigation Pilate also appears capricious. He does not appear to take the administration of Roman justice seriously. This is not a flattering picture of either the governor or his justice.

Not satisfied with Pilate's hasty dismissal, the Jerusalem elite, the chief priests and scribes (22:66), renew their charges against Jesus (23:5). They charge Jesus with stirring up the people, a charge synonymous with perverting the order the elite establishes (see 23:2). They describe the geographical extent of Jesus' teaching, "throughout all Judea, from Galilee where he began even to this place" (23:5), Jerusalem and the Temple. The gospel has attested Jesus' frequent teaching (4:15, 31; 5:3, 17), including in the Temple (20:1; 21:37). The geographical reference emphasizes the extent of Jesus' influence, and hence of the danger he poses as the agent of God's reign. He is a threat to all Pilate's territory, even to its center Jerusalem. But Pilate is deaf to any danger Jesus might pose, and certainly cannot discern God at work in Jesus.

Pilate, Jesus and Herod Antipas (23:6-12)

The only thing Pilate hears is a reference to Galilee (23:6). This information prompts him to dispense with Jesus by sending him to Herod Antipas, tetrarch or ruler of Galilee, who happens also to be in Jerusalem

(23:7). Pilate's arrogance toward both the elite and Jesus means he will not be bothered with Jesus.

Herod Antipas, the son of Herod "the Great," became ruler of Galilee in 4 B.C.E. after his father's death, with the emperor Augustus' blessing. He reigned until 39 C.E., when the emperor Gaius Caligula deposed him under suspicion of disloyalty to Rome. In handing Jesus over to Herod, Pilate sends Jesus to another representative of Roman rule. Herod was named with the emperor Tiberius and governor Pilate in 3:1. He is clearly identified with the powerful opponents of God's purposes.

That is indeed how Herod appears through the gospel narrative. Verses 8-9 indicate that while this is the first meeting between Herod and Jesus, it is not the first time Herod, ruler of Galilee, had heard of Jesus. Herod beheaded John the Baptist (3:18-20; 9:7-9). He hears about Jesus' ministry and miracles and is "perplexed" about what is happening. One explanation offered to him is that John has been raised from the dead. Not surprisingly it is reported that Herod wants to kill Jesus (13:31). Now he wants to see Jesus perform some sign (23:8). But demanding signs from Jesus while evading his identity as the agent of God's reign has been condemned in 11:16, 29-32 with promises of judgment. To demand signs is what "this evil generation" does (11:29-30), a generation that rejects Jesus as God's agent (17:25). Herod is immediately identified as an opponent of Jesus and of God's purposes.

Jesus does not cooperate with this opponent (23:9). Despite lengthy questioning from Herod, Jesus does not answer him. Herod has had every chance to understand Jesus' identity from John and from Jesus' Galilean ministry but is distracted by miracles. Instead, Jesus assumes the posture of the silent suffering servant of Isaiah 53. He absorbs rather than retaliates to the domination and violence as he awaits God's salvation (see the comments on Mark 15:4-5 and Matthew 27:13-14 in Chapters Four and Five).

By contrast, the Jerusalem leaders are very vocal (23:10). They have accompanied Jesus to Herod and with renewed vigor press their accusations. Not having persuaded Pilate, they try to persuade his fellow representative of Roman power. But their "vehement" charges, Herod's lengthy questioning, and Jesus' silence do not produce the formal condemnation they seek. Instead, Herod demeans himself by joining with his soldiers to mock and humiliate Jesus as a royal pretender.

Their contempt is expressed in part by making Jesus wear a "bright shining garment" or an "elegant" robe. A "real" king, according to their cultural values, parades his power and the wealth he has gained from his subjects. But Jesus has already disputed this definition of kingship by renouncing dominating power (22:24-27) and by distancing himself from

"those who put on fine clothing and live in luxury . . . in royal palaces" (7:25). The kingship he represents benefits the poor.

Yet there is an irony in clothing Jesus in this way. Such "bright shining" clothing is associated with heavenly beings. Jesus wears "dazzling white" garments in his transfiguration (9:29). And a heavenly messenger or angel wears them in appearing to Cornelius in Acts 10:30. Though Herod cannot see it, such clothing is appropriate to Jesus. It anticipates Jesus' heavenly glory, when he will be seated at God's right hand and share in God's power and rule, just as he told the Jerusalem elite when they condemned him (22:69)! Herod openly mocks and rejects God's agent.

Herod returns Jesus to Pilate (23:11). The effect of this excursion to Herod is to cement the alliance of Pilate and Herod (23:12). In what way? As Rome's representatives, they are united in their failure to recognize Jesus' identity as the agent of God's reign, and in their failure to recognize his great threat to their system. Herod is like Pilate, an arrogant ruler who cannot discern what God is doing in the midst of his political rule (10:24; see also Acts 4:26-28).

Pilate's Decision (23:13-16)

Pilate assembles the Jerusalem elite and the people to announce his verdict (23:13). Verse 13 specifically mentions the presence of the chief priests and ruling elite to underscore their continuing efforts to procure Jesus' death. Their determined and continual opposition to God's agent extends to the Jerusalem crowd, whom they mislead to oppose Jesus.

Pilate sums up the action to date, his own cursory encounter with Jesus (23:1-5) as well as Herod's meeting (23:6-12). Pilate's own summary casts further judgment on his arrogant dismissal of Jesus and capricious handling of Roman "justice." To claim that he has "examined" Jesus (23:14) is far too grand a description for his instant, uninformed rejection of the elite's repeated charges and of Jesus' admission (23:2-5). Likewise, to suggest that Herod has reached an informed conclusion severely misrepresents the scene of 23:9-11, which is marked by accusation, silence, and mocking! Pilate, arrogant in his presumption of Roman control, is unable to recognize what is happening under his nose. Even though Jesus has (nonviolently) challenged the very legitimacy of Pilate's system and proclaimed an alternative kingdom, Pilate does not think this "wannabe" king poses any danger. So Pilate proposes a quick dismissal of Jesus' case by flogging and releasing him (23:16).

Why does Pilate propose to flog Jesus if he thinks Jesus is innocent? Jesus had earlier predicted in 18:33 that the "Gentiles" would whip him, so

Pilate is acting true to form. Flogging was one of several punishments such as exile, torture, laboring in the mines, fines, and imprisonment that a governor might impose if he were not sentencing the accused to death.[16] Flogging was typically reserved for low-status individuals and for slaves. Carried out with rods or whips (the latter often used for slaves), it was regarded as degrading and humiliating. Corporal punishment was generally not used for higher-status offenders. Punishment was less about "justice" than it was about keeping people in their place. The punishment had to fit not so much the crime as the social status of the person. Flogging was administered with varying degrees of intensity, with that preceding crucifixion being the most severe. The Greek word used here suggests Pilate proposes to sentence Jesus to a "light" whipping.[17] Imposing this humiliating sentence expresses Pilate's disdain for the low-status Jesus while accomplishing Jesus' dismissal.

Pilate Condemns Jesus (23:18-25)

The focus shifts from the issue of Jesus' guilt (Pilate cannot see what the Jerusalem elite sees) to Pilate's action to maintain the alliances that are crucial for his ongoing rule.[18] His quick dismissal of Jesus does not work. The elite and the gathered crowd instantly reject Pilate's decision (23:18). The elite protests Pilate's arrogant refusal to take their charges and their alliance of power seriously. While crowds have often welcomed Jesus' ministry, some crowds have resisted it (4:22-30). The Jerusalem crowd's solidarity with the elite emphasizes the latter's control over this assembled group.

The Jerusalem elite offers an alternative, double course of action (23:18). First, they call for Jesus' removal ("Away with this fellow!"), a demand for Jesus' death that Pilate rejected in v. 15. Second, they call for the release of Barabbas. Unlike the other gospels' reference to the custom of releasing a prisoner at Passover, Luke's gospel (without v. 17 in its earliest form) offers no reason for their call to Pilate to release anybody, let alone Barabbas. Pilate, though, does not question the demand.

---

[16] Peter Garnsey, *Social Status and Legal Privilege in the Roman Empire* (Oxford: Clarendon Press, 1970) 103–52, especially 136–41.

[17] Sherwin-White (*Roman Society* 24–27) notes three intensities of beatings and suggests Pilate intends the lightest or "disciplinary" beating for Jesus.

[18] Verse 17 is omitted from many early manuscripts, and appears in some later manuscripts in different places, both here and after v. 19. These factors indicate it was a later addition to the text. See Bruce Metzger, *A Textual Commentary on the Greek New Testament* (London: United Bible Society, 1971) 179–80.

Barabbas has not been mentioned previously, but v. 19 elaborates his crime. He has been involved in an insurrection and is a murderer. Whatever the incident, Barabbas has violently challenged Roman control and order. While many interpreters see a contrast between Barabbas and Jesus, the contrast does not consist of the guilt of Barabbas and the innocence of Jesus. Both men pose danger to the Roman system. The difference lies in their means of opposition. While Barabbas employs violence, Jesus proclaims and enacts an alternative reign, community, and set of practices within it. Pilate is attuned to the former threat but is blind to the latter.

The narrative offers no reason for the Jerusalem elite's surprising support of Barabbas, the murdering insurrectionist. Perhaps they think they can "control" him once they have procured his release. But their vociferous support for a violent opponent of Rome's rule and against Pilate's choice cannot be encouraging for their ally, Rome's governor, Pilate.

But despite and in the face of the Jerusalem elite's resistance, for a second time Pilate arrogantly advocates Jesus' release (23:20). It is a contest of wills and Pilate is, after all, the governor. As far as he is concerned, he should prevail. But the Jerusalem elite will not allow its concern to be dismissed so quickly and lightly. It responds even more directly by calling for Jesus' crucifixion, the penalty for treason against the empire (23:21). The Jerusalem elite sees and rejects the challenge of Jesus' ministry, but Pilate remains blind to it and firm in his resolve. In words that largely repeat his verdict of vv. 14-16, Pilate declares for the third time his inability to see any threat in Jesus' words and actions. The verb "find" contrasts Pilate and the Jerusalem elite. Whereas the Jerusalem elite "find" Jesus to be perverting the nation (23:2), Pilate's arrogance means he can "find" no such thing (23:4, 14, 22).

The leaders' and crowd's response to Pilate's restatement of his decision is even more intense as they "urgently demand with loud shouts" that Jesus be crucified (23:23). Ironically, they who accused Jesus of "stirring up" the people (23:5) stir themselves up in opposition to God's purposes and in defense of Rome's threatened system. They out-pilate Pilate in their vigilance to ward off any danger to the current socio-economic system sanctioned by Rome.

After three attempts to release Jesus, Pilate sees he is not prevailing. "Their voices prevailed" (23:23b). For Pilate, the "wannabe" king Jesus is not worth a rift with his Jerusalem allies whose support he needs if his rule is to maintain the elite's and Rome's interests. So, without understanding their passion for Jesus' death, he consents to their demand. The narrative shows Roman "justice" to be nothing other than the accomplishment of the elite's will (loudly voiced by the controlled crowd). "So Pilate gave his verdict that their demand should be granted" (23:24).

Despite his arrogance, when push comes to shove it is in Pilate's interests to maintain the support of the Jerusalem elite. In condemning Jesus he acts *for* them and *for* himself rather than *against* Jesus, though Jesus of course bears the brunt of that action as Pilate sacrifices him for his own political interests. Pilate acts to keep this alliance and power in place rather than to counter a threat from Jesus (that he cannot see). He can see Barabbas' threat. He is attuned to violence. And he is confident that Roman power can handle one violent insurrectionist, so he releases Barabbas and crucifies Jesus.

Verse 25 continues to emphasize Pilate's arrogant blindness to the threat Jesus poses. His action against Jesus stems *only* from the demands of his allies, not from anything he understands Jesus to have done. So the verse begins, "He released the man *they asked for*," and ends, "he handed Jesus over *as they wished*."

Conclusion

Luke's scene with Pilate differs significantly from those of Mark and Matthew. In contrast to those scenes, Luke's Pilate cannot discern any threat from Jesus. He repeatedly asserts this conclusion, offers it as a verdict, and proposes a course of action based on it (Jesus' whipping and release). Herod, tetrarch of Galilee, reinforces Pilate's verdict. But the Jerusalem elite repeatedly accuses Jesus. It calls for Barabbas' release. Because Pilate thinks Jesus poses no threat he does not have to poll the crowd to see what reactions there will be to Jesus' crucifixion. Their ardent advocacy of it already expresses great support. Accordingly Luke does not present Pilate so much as the very politically astute and effective manager of Jesus' crucifixion that Mark and Matthew present him to be. Rather, he appears as a very arrogant representative of Rome's rule, dismissive of his allies, impervious to the threat that "the king of the Jews" poses to his rule and imperial system, and protective of his own interests. It is to ensure the continuing support of the Jerusalem elite that he acts against Jesus.

This presentation serves the gospel's purpose of offering its audience "certainty" or "security" concerning God's purposes (1:4). Unlike Pilate, the gospel's audience has rightly discerned Jesus' identity and God-given commission to manifest God's reign. But the unfinished nature of God's work raises doubts about the effectiveness of what God is doing. Can God accomplish God's purposes? Another cause of doubts is the unusual, non-violent way in which God is at work. The massive transformation of the world has not eventuated.

The gospel counters these doubts by narrating Jesus' identity and commission as the agent of God's reign. It has demonstrated Jesus' faithful carrying out of this commission in his words and action. It provides assurance that God's distinctive reign is doing its transformative, challenging, unfinished work in the midst of Rome's world even without a violent struggle, even by means of someone the empire's representatives, Pilate and Herod, consider to be a harmless nobody. As followers of Jesus, the audience is to continue Jesus' mission, faithfully enduring hardship, conflict, and doubt, and confidently trusting God to complete God's purposes.

CHAPTER SEVEN

John's Pilate

John's scene with Pilate is the longest of the four in the gospels. As with the other gospels, many interpreters have decided that Pilate is weak in not standing up for his conviction that Jesus is innocent and in capitulating to pressure from the Jerusalem elite to crucify Jesus.

I suggest that this is not an adequate reading. John's Pilate emerges as a powerful but mean governor who efficiently takes care of Roman interests. Pilate participates in Jesus' arrest and then taunts his Jerusalem allies, reminding them four times of their subjugated status and dependence on his power. They in turn will remind him of his duty to enforce Roman interests. But while Pilate tries to assert his superiority, he allies himself with them in rejecting Jesus, whom God has sent. In not "seeing" Jesus' identity and his God-given commission to reveal God's kingship or sovereignty Pilate, along with the empire he represents, belongs to "the world." Pilate thinks he asserts Rome's sovereignty and declares judgment on Jesus, but in effect Pilate is shown to be subject to God's sovereignty and to bring God's judgment on himself and the empire.

John 18:28 Then they took Jesus from Caiaphas to Pilate's headquarters. It was early in the morning. They themselves did not enter the headquarters, so as to avoid ritual defilement and to be able to eat the Passover. **29** So Pilate went out to them and said, "What accusation do you bring against this man?" **30** They answered, "If this man were not a criminal, we would not have handed him over to you." **31** Pilate said to them, "Take him yourselves and judge him according to your law." The Jews replied, "We are not permitted to put anyone to death." **32** (This was to fulfill what Jesus had said when he indicated the kind of death he was to die.)

33 Then Pilate entered the headquarters again, summoned Jesus, and asked him, "Are you the King of the Jews?" **34** Jesus answered, "Do you ask this on your own, or did others tell you about me?" **35** Pilate replied, "I am not a Jew, am I? Your own nation and the chief priests have handed you over to me. What have you done?" **36** Jesus answered, "My kingdom is not from this world. If my kingdom were from this world, my followers would be fighting to keep me from being handed over to the Jews. But as it is, my kingdom is not from here." **37** Pilate asked him, "So you are a king?" Jesus answered, "You say that I am a king. For this I was born, and for this I came into the world, to testify to the truth. Everyone who belongs to the truth listens to my voice." **38** Pilate asked him, "What is truth?"

After he had said this, he went out to the Jews again and told them, "I find no case against him. **39** But you have a custom that I release someone for you at the Passover. Do you want me to release for you the King of the Jews?" **40** They shouted in reply, "Not this man, but Barabbas!" Now Barabbas was a bandit.

19:1 Then Pilate took Jesus and had him flogged. **2** And the soldiers wove a crown of thorns and put it on his head, and they dressed him in a purple robe. **3** They kept coming up to him, saying, "Hail, King of the Jews!" and striking him on the face.

4 Pilate went out again and said to them, "Look, I am bringing him out to you to let you know that I find no case against him." **5** So Jesus came out, wearing the crown of thorns and the purple robe. Pilate said to them, "Here is the man!" **6** When the chief priests and the police saw him, they shouted, "Crucify him! Crucify him!" Pilate said to them, "Take him yourselves and crucify him; I find no case against him." **7** The Jews answered him, "We have a law, and according to that law he ought to die because he has claimed to be the Son of God."

8 Now when Pilate heard this, he was more afraid than ever. **9** He entered his headquarters again and asked Jesus, "Where are you from?" But Jesus gave him no answer. **10** Pilate therefore said to him, "Do you refuse to speak to me? Do you not know that I have power to release you, and power to crucify you?" **11** Jesus answered him, "You would have no power over me unless it had been given you from above; therefore the one who handed me over to you is guilty of a greater sin."

12 From then on Pilate tried to release him, but the Jews cried out, "If you release this man, you are no friend of the emperor. Everyone who claims to be a king sets himself against the emperor."

13 When Pilate heard these words, he brought Jesus outside and sat on the judge's bench at a place called The Stone Pavement, or in Hebrew

Gabbatha. **14** Now it was the day of Preparation for the Passover; and it was about noon. He said to the Jews, "Here is your King!" **15** They cried out, "Away with him! Away with him! Crucify him!" Pilate asked them, "Shall I crucify your King?" The chief priests answered, "We have no king but the emperor."

16 Then he handed him over to them to be crucified.

So they took Jesus; **17** and carrying the cross by himself, he went out to what is called The Place of the Skull, which in Hebrew is called Golgotha. **18** There they crucified him, and with him two others, one on either side, with Jesus between them. **19** Pilate also had an inscription written and put on the cross. It read, "Jesus of Nazareth, the King of the Jews." **20** Many of the Jews read this inscription, because the place where Jesus was crucified was near the city; and it was written in Hebrew, in Latin, and in Greek.

21 Then the chief priests of the Jews said to Pilate, "Do not write, 'The King of the Jews,' but, 'This man said, I am King of the Jews.'" **22** Pilate answered, "What I have written I have written."

John's Audience

Traditionally, John's gospel has been associated with Ephesus, though this location is by no means certain.[1] Several factors point to the decades of the 80s–90s C.E. as its most likely date, and to considerable strife and pain as the fundamental experience of the gospel's audience.

- The latest date for its writing is provided by a papyrus copy of John 18 ($\mathfrak{P}$52) found in Egypt that probably dates to the 120s or 130s C.E.

- John 11:48 refers to the Romans coming to destroy the holy place (the Jerusalem Temple) and nation, probably a reference to Rome's destruction of Jerusalem in 70 C.E.

- The absence of Sadducees and scribes from the gospel may reflect the post-70 situation in which the Pharisees were dominant.

- Three texts (9:22; 12:42; 16:2) claim a separation of Jesus' followers from the synagogue to which they have belonged. The separation results from disputes over Jesus' identity in which his followers assert that he reveals God's will, saving presence, and purposes. This

---

[1] For good discussions of John see Robert Kysar, *John, the Maverick Gospel* (rev. ed. Louisville: Westminster John Knox, 1993); Sharon Ringe, *Wisdom's Friends: Community and Christology in the Fourth Gospel* (Louisville: Westminster John Knox, 1999); Gail R. O'Day, "The Gospel of John," *The New Interpreter's Bible* (Nashville: Abingdon, 1995) 9:491–865.

dispute most readily belongs in the post-70 situation in which various Jewish groups wrestled with questions about knowing God's will, atonement, presence, and purposes after the Temple's destruction. John's community seems to have argued forcefully that commitment to Jesus, God's revelation, was the only way ahead. This claim seems to have been rejected by other Jewish groups, notably those in their synagogue committed to Abraham (8:33) and Moses (9:28). The separation seems to have been bitter and painful for both sides.

• Jesus attacks the Temple in 2:13-22 and presents himself as an alternative temple where God's presence, will, and saving work are revealed and encountered (2:19-22). Such a claim also makes sense after Rome's tragic destruction of the Jerusalem Temple in 70 C.E.

The gospel, then, was probably written in the 80s or 90s C.E. Its audience seems to have experienced a bewildering and painful separation from a synagogue community to which it has belonged. This audience lives in a world in which Roman power has been asserted over Jerusalem with devastating effect, not only in terms of physical damage but also by profoundly impacting the very institutions and practices of late-first-century Judaism. The gospel helps this small, struggling, and hurting community of followers of Jesus make sense of its place in this world in relation to the synagogue and its Jewish tradition, in relation to Rome and its empire, and in relation to God's purposes. The Pilate scene recognizes Rome's rule but emphasizes that its representatives like Pilate cannot "see" God's purposes. In this difficult context Jesus' followers must continually renew their loyalty to Jesus and not to Rome. The scene fosters their discipleship by undercutting Pilate's power in the much greater context of God's sovereignty.

John's Story of Jesus

John's story divides into four major sections, with the Pilate scene in the fourth section:

CHAPTERS	FOCUS
1:1-18	The Prologue
1:19–12:50	Jesus' Public Ministry
13–17	Jesus' Retreat with his Disciples: The Farewell Discourse
18–21	Jesus' Death and Resurrection

The Prologue (1:1-18)

The short but very important Prologue or Introduction provides the audience with key perspectives for understanding the gospel. The eighteen verses focus on Jesus:

- his identity as God's Word or communication or revelation (1:1, 14);
- his origin from the beginning in intimate relationship with God (1:1-3);
- his role as the source of life and light (1:4-5);
- John the Baptist's witness to him (1:6-8, 15);
- his rejection by many in Israel (1:10-11);
- his positive reception by some who believe and receive power to share his relationship with God (1:12-13);
- his mission in becoming flesh, which reveals God's saving power and gracious presence ("glory") among humans (1:14-18).

Jesus' Public Ministry (1:19–12:50)

The narrative of Jesus' ministry expands these themes as Jesus encounters a range of characters:

- Nicodemus, the wealthy, powerful, high-status Jerusalem leader (ch. 3);
- the unnamed Samaritan woman at the well (ch. 4);
- the paralyzed man by the pool of Bethzatha in Jerusalem (ch. 5);
- the man born blind (ch. 9);
- Lazarus, Mary, and Martha (ch. 11).

In an intriguing story Jesus, the light of the world, the revealer of God's salvation (9:5), restores sight to a blind man, but, typically, the story and language operate on several levels. The blind man's literal sight is miraculously restored at 9:6-7. The rest of the chapter focuses on the attempts of various groups—the man himself, his neighbors, his parents, Jesus' opponents—to understand who Jesus is and what he has done. Progressively the healed man comes to "see" Jesus' identity. At v. 11 the healed man describes Jesus as "the man called Jesus." At v. 17 he calls Jesus "a prophet." At v. 33 he declares Jesus is "from God." At vv. 35-38 he confesses him as "Son of Man" and "Lord." It is precisely this insight that Pilate will lack.

The man develops these insights as Jesus' opponents hassle and pressure him. The stronger their opposition and declarations that Jesus is a sinner, the more vociferous and insightful the man's confessions become (9:24-34). The man pays a price for his confession. He is driven out of the synagogue for recognizing Jesus as God's anointed or commissioned one ("the Christ," 9:22, 34-35). Jesus' opponents cannot "see" this identity (9:39-41). Scholars have suggested that the chapter narrates the "history" of John's audience, both its growing understanding of Jesus' identity and its resultant rift with the synagogue over claims about Jesus.

Throughout the encounters that comprise his public ministry Jesus claims to be God's son or agent, commissioned by God to reveal God's purposes (5:19-30). He comes from God and is sent by God (3:16; 6:38, 41; 7:28-29; 8:23). He does God's will (5:30). His words and actions are God's words and actions (3:34; 5:36; 7:16). Not to honor Jesus is not to honor God (5:23). Jesus bestows God's gifts: healing (4:46-54; 5:1-18; 9:1-41; 11:1-44), abundant wine and food (2:1-11; 6:1-14), salvation (4:22, 42), and "eternal life," life in intimate relationship with God not interrupted by sin and death (3:36; 5:24; 6:40-51). He effects judgment as people respond to him. Those who believe in him experience salvation; those who reject him condemn themselves (3:16-21, 31-36; 5:19-30). Responding to Jesus reveals people's origin and identity: Either they too come from God, from above, born of the spirit, belonging to the light and truth (3:3-9, 17-21; 6:47) or they come from below, of the devil, born of flesh, belonging to falseness and darkness (8:39-47).

This dualism of belonging to Jesus and experiencing God's salvation or belonging to the devil and experiencing condemnation is typical of John's gospel (8:42-44). A number of pairs and images express it:

Belonging to God	Belonging to the Devil	Examples
Light	Darkness	8:12
Life	Death	3:16; 5:24
Truth	Lies/Falseness	8:44-46
Spirit	Flesh	3:6
From Above	From Below	3:3-7; 8:23
Sight	Blindness	8:12; 9:39-41
Believe	Not believe, Disobey	3:18, 36
Save	Condemn	3:15-18
Not from this world	The World	8:23; 17:14, 16

The dualism has multiple levels. In addition to revealing people's origins (either "from God" or "from the devil"), it identifies people's destiny in the judgment. Those who believe encounter God's salvation. Those who do not, experience condemnation. The division is also social. God's salvation defines a distinctive and separate community (John's audience) that has an ethical task of living lives faithful to God's purposes.

Conflict and Opposition

Such claims inevitably cause great tension and conflict. Who is Jesus to claim that he speaks for and reveals God? John's gospel's answer is that he is sent from God as God's son or commissioned agent ("Christ/Messiah") to reveal God's purposes (20:30-31). Those who accept this claim become disciples (1:35-51), but others find it totally unacceptable.

"The Jews"

Jesus' main opponents are the Jerusalem elite, retainers or allies of Rome. They are based in the Temple with its tremendous socio-economic and religious power. They attempt to control Jewish society so as to order it according to their interests (see Chapter Three). This ruling elite is identified throughout the gospel as "the Jews" or the Judeans: so in 1:19 "the Jews sent priests and Levites (Temple functionaries) from Jerusalem" to investigate John the Baptist's testimony about Jesus (1:19, 24, "from the Pharisees."). Chapter 2 confirms their identity. When Jesus attacks the Temple, condemning its priests and officials and talking about its destruction (2:19), the Temple officials are twice called "the Jews" (2:18, 20). In 3:1 Nicodemus, "a Pharisee . . . [and] leader of the Jews," engages Jesus about his teaching and its origin but cannot understand what Jesus says.

These opponents are identified over seventy times as "the Jews" (though the term has some neutral or even positive uses, 2:13; 11:31). It is a term that we have to be very careful to understand clearly. In the church's history its incorrect understanding has led to dreadful attitudes and horrendous actions against Jews, with hateful and tragic consequences.

The term "the Jews" does not refer to all Jews. It does not even refer to an ethnic group! Jesus is, ethnically, a Jew, but he is not included in "the Jews." Some ethnic Jews believe in Jesus (1:35-51, disciples), but they are also distinct from "the Jews." Also distinct from "the Jews" at times are people who are ethnically Jewish! The following scene in chapter 7 distinguishes "the Jews" who in 7:1 want to kill Jesus from the crowds:

7:11 The Jews were looking for him at the festival and saying, "Where is he?" **12** And there was considerable complaining about him among the crowds. While some were saying, "He is a good man," others were saying, "No, he is deceiving the crowd." **13** Yet no one would speak openly about him for fear of the Jews.

Clearly "the Jews," Jesus, and the crowds are distinct groups. And "the Jews" are the powerful figures, the movers and shakers who intimidate the crowds into silence. Subsequently "the Jews" are explicitly identified as "the chief priests and Pharisees" (7:15, 32, 45). The term "the Jews" does not, then, refer to an ethnic group in John's gospel. Rather, it is a specialized term referring to the powerful, high-status, wealthy Jerusalem elite (the chief priests and Pharisees) who reject Jesus.

Why Do They Oppose Jesus?

- *Jesus threatens their power over and vision of society.* He attacks their exploitative use of the Temple, their base (2:13-22). He contests their teaching and practices with a different social vision. Like them he honors the Sabbath, but observes it differently in giving life rather than resting (5:1-18; ch. 9, especially 9:14). His healings and feedings (ch. 6) anticipate the time when God's just purposes ensure that everyone, not just the powerful and wealthy, enjoys wholeness and abundance. Interested crowds threaten the leaders' control (2:23; 4:39, 45; 6:15; 12:19).

- *Jesus denies the legitimacy of their leadership.* He describes his own mission and origin with the image of "good shepherd" (10:11, 14). As we saw in discussing Matthew (p. 85 above), "shepherd" is a traditional image for rulers and leaders. It is also an image for God (Psalm 23). Jesus labels all others, including the chief priests, Pharisees, and their Roman allies, as "hired hands" or "bandits" who abandon, threaten, and do not care for the sheep (10:1, 8, 12). In chapter 8 Jesus declares outright that God is not their father (8:41-42). They come from the devil (8:44)!

- *Jesus claims to be the supreme revealer of God.* He emphasizes his own origin from God and his identity as God's son or agent. Only he has seen God (6:46). Quoting a phrase that God uses to reveal Godself and salvation to Moses (Exod 3:14) and to the exiles in Babylon (Isa 41:4; 45:18), Jesus declares himself to be "I am" (6:20; 8:23-24, 28, often translated "I am he" or "It is I"). He is the functional equivalent of God, who reveals God's salvation and life:

6:35, I am the bread of life.

6:51, I am the living bread that comes down from heaven.

8:12; 9:5, I am the light of the world.

10:7, 9, I am the gate for the sheep.

10:11, 14, I am the good shepherd.

11:25, I am the resurrection and the life.

The Jerusalem elite regard such claims about Jesus' origin ("from heaven"), identity (the functional equivalent of God), and mission (to reveal God) as utterly unacceptable. It is blasphemy, dishonoring to God, for a human to claim such things (10:33, 36), and a major challenge to their positions of power. As followers of Abraham (8:39-40) and Moses (9:28), they represent God's will. Jesus deserves only one fate, so they plot to kill him (5:16; 7:1, 25, 30, 32, 44; 8:40; 10:31, 39).

The World

"The world" is the technical term with which John's gospel describes this opposition. God has created (1:10) and loves (3:16) the world, the realm of people. It is good. But what God has made and loved refuses to recognize God as its creator and to live in a loving, trusting way accountable to God. This is the hierarchical, unjust society that the ruling elite has established for its own benefit. This "world" sees itself as a self-sufficient realm over which God has no claim. Jesus' mission among people (in the world) reveals God's loving, life-giving claim, and confronts this unbelief, blindness, and rejection of God. His task is to help "the world" find its true identity again (3:16-17), to save it from such a way of life (4:42). But rejection prevails. The world "hates" Jesus (7:7; also 15:18-23):

> He (Jesus) was in the world, and the world came into being through him; yet the world did not know him. (John 1:10)

Jesus exposes "the world" for what it is, the realm that rejects God even after Jesus offers it another chance (12:31). The powerful elite's rejection of Jesus shows that they belong not to God (as Jesus does, 8:23), but to "the world," the realm of rejection. Judgment results (3:18-21; 12:44-50).

The Devil

The world comprises humans who reject God's revelation in Jesus. These humans are agents of the devil, the world's ruler and God's supreme opponent (12:31). Not surprisingly, John's gospel especially identifies the

ruling elite as the devil's agents. Jesus accuses them of belonging to the devil and doing the devil's work (8:39-44). The word "ruler," used for the devil in 12:31, is used in 3:1 for Nicodemus, a "ruler of the Jews." The same word refers to the Jerusalem elite in 7:26, 48 and 12:42! This elite is, in turn, allied with Pilate, Rome's representative, who is also identified in 14:30 as "the ruler of the world." The whole ruling group and empire comprise the devil's agents, the opponents of God's purposes, as "the world" that rejects Jesus, the revealer of God's just purposes. John's Pilate belongs to and represents "the world."

But there is good news for the gospel's audience. Jesus claims to overcome "the ruler of the world" (12:31), both the devil and his agents like Pilate. God's greater power raises Jesus from the dead (chs. 20–21). They cannot keep God's agent dead.

By chapter 12 Jesus' public ministry is completed. While some have believed, rejection has prevailed. The "world" does not "see" Jesus' origin, identity, and mission (12:40, 44-46). The opposition has been intense and will result in Jesus' death. But that death is no surprise or defeat. Because his "hour" has not come, no one has been able to arrest or kill him (7:30; 8:20). He willingly lays down his life; no one takes it from him (10:15-18). God's purposes are being accomplished even though it seems the powerful elite is having its way.

Chapters 13–17

With his public ministry completed and his death imminent, Jesus gathers his disciples for instruction. He will return to God through his death, resurrection, and ascension (13:1-3; 16:28). But though he will be absent, he assures the disciples that he will return for them and take them finally to live in intimate relationship with himself and God (14:3). In the meantime, in his absence, they must live faithfully.

Repeated themes outline characteristics of the "meantime" life of his community of disciples:

- This community is marked by service of one another, not domination and self-interest (13:12-17), and by unity in God's purposes (ch. 17);

- This community's members must love one another, reflecting the loving relationship between God and Jesus in which the community participates (13:34-35; 15:9-13);

- This community does Jesus' teaching (14:12-15, 23-24);

- This community knows God's presence through the Holy Spirit (Paraclete), who will help and guide them in God's purposes (14:16-17; 15:26; 16:7-15);

- This community abides in Jesus to obey and live fruitfully (15:1-11);

- This community lives in tension and conflict with "the world" (unbelievers, 15:18–16:4; 16:33);

- This community anticipates Jesus' return to take believers to God (14:1-4, 19; 16:16-24);

- This mission community witnesses to God's purposes in the "world" (17:14-18).

The "retreat" or "farewell speech" ends with Jesus praying for the disciples that they live in union with God and with each other (ch. 17).

Chapters 18–21: Death, Resurrection, Ascension

The movement from Jesus' lofty prayer in chapter 17 to his betrayal by Judas and arrest by Roman and Temple troops in chapter 18 (18:1-14) is abrupt and harsh. His betrayal and arrest result from an alliance of a false disciple (into whom Satan or the devil has entered, 13:2, 27), the Jerusalem elite, and Rome. This alliance is the "world" at work, the rejecting "world" marked by hate and to which Jesus does not belong, but to which Jesus and his disciples have a mission (17:14-18). Once arrested (18:1-14), Jesus is denied by Peter (18:15-18, 25-27) and taken to the chief priest Caiaphas and his father-in-law Annas (18:19-24). They question Jesus "about his disciples and his teaching" to assess the extent of his threat (18:19). Jesus defends the openness and correctness of his teaching. He has not spoken wrongly or blasphemously (18:23). But without a formal confession or sentence, they hand him over to Pilate (18:28).

Jesus' Trial before Pilate (18:28–19:16a)

Changes in participants and location identify the seven subsections of this long scene.[2] Pilate moves between the inside of the *praetorium* or governor's headquarters where he interacts with Jesus, and outside where the

---

[2] My reading has some affinity with David Rensberger, *Johannine Faith and Liberating Community* (Philadelphia: Westminster, 1988) 91–106; Helen Bond, *Pontius Pilate in History and Interpretation.* MSSNTS 100 (Cambridge: Cambridge University Press, 1998) 175–93.

Jerusalem elite, especially the high priests and leading Pharisees (18:3), gather. This latter group is identified six times as "the Jews" (18:31, 36, 38; 19:7, 12, 14) to underline their opposition to Jesus (see discussion above).

No.	SECTION	LOCATION	PARTICIPANTS	MOVEMENT
1	18:28-32	Outside	Pilate and "the Jews"	Pilate went out, 18:29
2	18:33-38a	Inside	Pilate and Jesus	Pilate entered the headquarters, 18:33
3	18:38b-40	Outside	Pilate and "the Jews"	Pilate went out, 18:38b
4	19:1-3	Inside	Jesus and the Soldiers	Pilate took Jesus, 19:1
5	19:4-7	Outside	Pilate, Jesus, and "the Jews"	Pilate went out again, 19:4
6	19:8-12	Inside	Pilate, Jesus, and "the Jews"	Pilate entered the headquarters, 19:9
7	19:13-16	Outside	Pilate, Jesus, and "the Jews"	Pilate brought Jesus out, 19:13

In each scene Pilate is the key figure. The narrative follows his movements. He initiates conversations with "the Jews" (18:29, 38b; 19:4, 14) and with Jesus (18:33; 19:9). Even the whipping scene (4) begins with ascribing that action to Pilate. Literally it says, "Pilate took Jesus and whipped him" (19:1), though his soldiers probably did the task. The NRSV appropriately translates, "Pilate had him whipped."

Scene One: The "Jews" Hand Jesus Over (18:28-32)

Verse 28 carries the action forward from Jesus' brief appearance before the chief priest Caiaphas (18:19-24). Representatives of the Jerusalem elite, the chief priests and leading Pharisees (18:3), take Jesus to Pilate. Their motive, to have Jesus put to death, will be clearly identified in v. 31. The physical setting is Pilate's *praetorium,* the headquarters for Rome's occupation of this foreign nation. The display of power is intimidating. The previous scene has shown Peter cowed by "the world's" opposition into denying his loyalty to Jesus (18:25-27). But Jesus will not be intimidated. He will announce judgment on this misdirected power.

The scene has a second setting, in time. Jesus' trial takes place immediately prior to Passover (the day of preparation, 19:14). As I have noted in relation to the other gospels, this festival celebrates the deliverance of God's people from slavery in Egypt (Exodus 13–16). The repeated references to Passover (18:28, 39; 19:14) underline an important irony. In one sense, nothing like another liberation from oppressive ruling power seems to be happening with Jesus. The elite is efficiently securing its control by removing a potential troublemaker. But the Passover references provide one of several signs that the elite's power is being undermined, not secured, through the scene. By association, Jesus' death is an act of liberation from "the world" opposed to God's purposes (1:10; 16:33), a world represented by the political, social, and religious elite. His resurrection will show how limited the elite's power is. They do not control the world, even though they think they do. Their opposition cannot prevent God's purposes from being accomplished now and being completed at Jesus' return.

They bring Jesus to Pilate "early in the morning," at the time when morning light overcomes night's darkness (18:28). The image of light has depicted Jesus' revelation of God's salvation in the darkness of a sinful world (1:5-9; 3:17-21; 8:12; 9:5). Jesus' death reveals God's salvation in and from a sinful world committed to rejecting God's purposes.

The Jerusalem elite do not enter the Gentile Pilate's headquarters, so as to avoid becoming impure before the Passover. The verse does not explain how this defilement might happen, but clearly the elite take the Passover celebration very seriously. The irony, of course, is that they do not find their involvement in the execution of an opponent, God's agent and revealer of God's salvation, to be impure!

Pilate respects their religious scruples and goes out from his headquarters to meet them (18:29). No title or explanation identifies Pilate's role, though his association with the *praetorium* or governor's headquarters serves as a reminder. The gospel's audience is assumed to be familiar with a governor's power and duties as representative of Rome's interests (Chapter Three above).

- The emperor in Rome appointed governors of Judea; Pilate took office in 26 C.E.

- The appointment provided an opportunity for getting rich by exploiting the locals through taxation and commandeering goods.

- The position was essentially unaccountable; locals could protest to Rome (as happened to Pilate in 36 C.E.), but there were obstacles: the governor's permission, expense, and the governor's allies in Rome.

- The governor was responsible for "justice," taxation, public building, and public order (commanding troops).

- Roman propaganda touted Roman justice as a gift to the world. This narrative exposes Roman justice as interested in defending the elite's benefits against any challengers. Roman justice was biased toward the elite. A low-status provincial and royal claimant has no chance against the elite.

- Governors ruled in alliance with local elites. The Jerusalem high-priestly families do not just provide *religious* officials. They are socio-political leaders and allies of Rome. The governor appointed the chief priest. Caiaphas was chief priest from 18–36 C.E., through all of Pilate's reign, so he knew how to keep Pilate happy. Jesus' condemnation seems to be a foregone conclusion because of this alliance.

- Only the Roman governor could execute.

Outside his headquarters Pilate takes charge by inquiring about the accusation against Jesus (18:29). The Jerusalem elite expresses surprise, even offense, at having to justify his arrest. With some animosity, they refer to Jesus as a "criminal" (literally as "one who does evil")[3] without specifying his wrongdoing. They describe their transfer of Jesus to Pilate as "handing over." This verb on each of its eight previous appearances has described Judas "betraying" Jesus (6:64, 71; 12:4; 13:2, 11, 21; 18:2, 5). Jesus has predicted Judas' action (6:64, 71; 13:11, 21). The choice of verb not only recalls this alliance but also shows that Jesus is not surprised or defeated by these actions. Despite appearances and claims to the contrary, Jesus is in control!

The elite's evasive and offended tone and impatient animosity toward Pilate (which continue through the scene) may stem from its previous discussions with him about Jesus. Both Roman soldiers and police from the Jerusalem Temple arrested Jesus (18:3, 12) in a display of "the world's" or the ruling elite's alliance against him.[4] These Roman troops could not

---

[3] Ironically, the same image is used in 3:19-21 to describe the world of darkness and evil over which the elite rules and to which Jesus has a mission. That world resists the light and so judges itself. In charging Jesus they want to remove the one who judges them.

[4] Several factors identify these soldiers as troops from the Roman army. (1) The term translated as "detachment of soldiers" in 18:3 denotes a cohort, a unit in the Roman army. Being one tenth of a legion, a cohort comprised about 600 soldiers. (2) Elsewhere in the New Testament this term clearly denotes Roman soldiers (Matt 27:27; Acts 10:1). (3) Verse 12 identifies their commander or "officer" with a term that translates the Latin words *tribunus militum*, the commander of a cohort. See BAGD, 761, 881. Do six hundred soldiers turn up

have been deployed without Pilate's command. It seems, then, that at a previous meeting or meetings Pilate heard the Jerusalem elite's concern about Jesus as a major threat to the society over which he as governor and they as the Jerusalem elite rule (cf. 11:45-48). The presence of Roman troops at Jesus' arrest expresses Pilate's consent to remove Jesus. His inquiry about a charge *after* Jesus' arrest seems out of place and surprises them.

But Pilate does not like their offended and hostile tone. They might be allies, but they shouldn't use that tone with the boss! So he puts them in their place by telling them to deal with Jesus themselves (18:31a). Of course they cannot, because only the Roman governor has the power to execute. His comment makes clear their common and already established commitment to execute Jesus.

His remark also recalls their status as subjects of Rome and humiliates them. They concede that they are powerless to remove Jesus without Pilate's assistance (18:31b). The exchange reestablishes his supremacy and their dependence within the alliance. It also confirms Jesus' previous predictions (3:14; 12:32) that he would die by crucifixion (a Roman form of execution), and not, for example, by stoning (18:32). The ruling elite thinks it is in control, but Jesus' prediction is another reminder that God's agenda is being worked out.

Two factors, then, establish that Jesus' death is certain at the outset of the scene. The involvement of Pilate's troops and Temple police in Jesus' arrest attests their common commitment to remove Jesus. The elite's impatient response to Pilate's question about a charge assumes such an agreement. Pilate has already signed off on it, as his next question to Jesus also indicates.

Scene Two: Pilate meets Jesus (18:33-38a)

Having put the Jerusalem leaders in their place, Pilate goes inside his headquarters and authoritatively summons Jesus. He asks, "Are you King of the Jews?" (18:33), a question that presumably utilizes knowledge gained from his previous discussions with the Jerusalem elite before Jesus' arrest. This is a political charge of insurrection in Rome's imperial world. As we have seen, Josephus mentions a series of figures who, claiming to be kings, led revolts that were harshly crushed. Pilate's question is in essence, "Are you leader of a revolt?"

---

to arrest Jesus? If that seems unlikely, the language indicates both a display of force and Roman involvement. The Temple police had tried to arrest Jesus, unsuccessfully, in 7:32, 45. They succeed on this occasion because it is Jesus' "hour" to die (12:23, 27; 13:1). He is in control.

Jesus has been addressed as king previously (1:49; 6:15; 12:13, 15), and the title recurs through the trial (18:33, 37, 39; 19:3, 12, 14, 15; also 19:19, 21). The issue concerns power and sovereignty, as well as *how* that sovereignty is expressed. While Jesus' kingship does not present a military threat to Rome, it is nevertheless a very political challenge to the way Rome and Jerusalem order the world. His kingship participates in the completion of God's purposes, the establishment of God's reign/empire (3:3, 5). That means the end of Rome's unjust order.

Jesus, the interrogated, becomes the interrogator (18:34). In response to Pilate's question, he questions Pilate about the source of his knowledge. Jesus' question draws attention to Pilate's alliance with the Jerusalem leaders. Pilate feigns ignorance of and tries to hide the alliance, but the narrative has already uncovered it (18:35). Pilate responds with a somewhat derisive question, "Am I a Jew?" that is formulated in Greek in a way that makes inevitable the answer "No, of course not!" But while Pilate uses the term to highlight an ethnic difference between himself and the Jerusalem elite, the gospel has used the term to identify all those with power who reject Jesus. Pilate's actions show his complete alliance with that group.

Jesus responds to Pilate's questions about being king of the Jews (18:33) and about his actions (18:35) not with silence as in the other gospels, but with a statement about the origin and nature of his reign (18:36). Twice Jesus asserts that his "kingdom/ kingship is not from this world." That is, it does not originate in what is hostile and hateful toward God, as does the reign of Pilate, "ruler of this world" (though created and loved by God: 1:10; 3:16; 15:18-19; 14:30). Rather, Jesus' reign is from God (3:31; 8:23, 42; 16:28). It reveals God's claim on and sovereignty over human structures and lives. It is a mistake to say that Jesus' kingship is not political. While it is not violent or limited to one nation, it is very political in that it claims to establish God's rule over all things, including Pilate's empire. Pilate, though, cannot "see" or accept such kingship.[5]

The sign that Jesus' reign or kingdom is not "from the world" is the lack of armed resistance from his "followers." Jesus identifies violence or military domination as the defining characteristic of worldly (hostile to God) empires like Pilate's. The absence of violence and force marks Jesus' reign. Jesus refers to his "followers" with exactly the same word that denotes the "police" sent from the chief priests to arrest Jesus (18:3, 12, 18, 22; 19:6). The same term contrasts Jesus' kingship from God, from above, marked by love, service, and believing, with Pilate's empire based on coer-

---

[5] Andrew T. Lincoln, *Truth on Trial: The Lawsuit Motif in John's Gospel* (Peabody, Mass.: Hendrickson, 2000) 123–38, especially 127.

cive power and domination. Such is the "world," dominated by Roman imperial power and its allies, that rejects Jesus.

Pilate asks again "so you are a king?" (18:37). The question moves from the issue of the type of kingship and its origin (the exchange in 18:36) to the related issue of Jesus' identity. The question elicits the repeated confirmation that Pilate has been looking for. Jesus agrees to the title.

But Jesus also defines his kingship. The mission or purpose of his reign is to "testify to the truth" in "the world." The word "truth" is a key term in the gospel and needs careful definition. Previously Jesus has described himself as "truth":

- You will know the truth and the truth will set you free (John 8:32);

- I am the way, the truth and the life (John 14:6).

What does John mean by this term?

The term "truth" often means "faithfulness" or "loyalty" in the biblical tradition. It then denotes being faithful to one's commitments and obligations. So in Gen 24:49 Abraham's servant, charged with procuring a wife for Isaac, appeals to Rebekah's father Bethuel and brother Laban to deal "loyally and truly" with Abraham in arranging the marriage. The opposite of such truthfulness or faithfulness is falseness, wickedness, and injustice when humans do not carry out their commitments (see Isa 59:9-15). The same term "truth" or "true," often translated "faithfulness" (so Exod 32:10; 34:6), is often applied to God. God acts "truthfully" or "in truth" or "truly" when God is faithful to God's covenant promises to show loving kindness and to save God's people. God's "truthfulness" means that God acts powerfully and faithfully to save the people from their enemies (see Pss 40:10-12; 108, especially v. 4).

By declaring that his mission is to witness to "the truth," Jesus tells Pilate that he witnesses to God's faithfulness in saving the people. He witnesses to God acting faithfully to God's own commitments to save. When Jesus declares that he is "the truth" (14:6), he claims to reveal God's faithful, saving action. When he declares that the truth shall set "you" free he claims that God's saving actions, manifested in him, will free people from everything that resists and rejects God's purposes (8:32). Jesus comes from above (8:23), from heaven (3:13), where he has heard (8:26) and seen (5:19) the Father, so that he can reveal God's "truth," God acting powerfully and faithfully to save the world (3:16-17).

Jesus further explains to Pilate that the mark of "belonging to the truth," of participating in and trusting oneself to God's saving work and reign, is listening to Jesus' voice (18:37b). To listen to Jesus is to accept

and understand his revelation of God's truthful or faithful saving purposes, to believe and do his commandments (10:3-5, 16). To listen to Jesus shows that one is "from God;" not to listen shows that one is not from God (8:47), and that one is Jesus' opponent (10:20).

Pilate is not listening. Jesus' words about his kingdom and about "truth" (God's faithful, saving action) give Pilate the opportunity to decide that Jesus speaks "truthfully" or faithfully about God's work. But Pilate cannot "see" any of it. Pilate has already decided against Jesus in allying with the Jerusalem elite to arrest and kill Jesus. He rejects the second chance Jesus gives him. Though he asks Jesus "What is truth?" he does not wait for an answer (18:38a).

Pilate's unwillingness to listen to Jesus' answer reveals Pilate's continued opposition, his blindness. He does not participate in God's saving work (18:47). He reveals that he does not "see" Jesus' identity, origin, and mission. Jesus' words place him in a crisis of decision, and he condemns himself and the imperial system he represents by rejecting Jesus and God's saving purposes. He belongs to the unseeing world (12:40).

Scene Three: Pilate and "the Jews" (18:38b-40)

Pilate leaves Jesus and returns to his allies. His declaration that "I find no case against him" and his offer to release Jesus according to the Passover custom are strange after his previous consent to arrest Jesus and after Jesus has twice not disputed being king! This context shows how blind Pilate is to Jesus' identity. But it also suggests that Pilate is not making serious suggestions.[6] Rather, having heard the Jerusalem elite admit that they depend on him to remove Jesus (18:31), Pilate taunts them, provoking another expression of their subservience to and dependence on him.

In a display of submission to the Roman governor, the Jerusalem elite in effect beg for Jesus' death by rejecting his release (18:40). They request instead the release of Barabbas, the "bandit." The Jewish writer Josephus identifies "bandits" as political guerillas and insurrectionists or "revolutionary fighters." Such figures emerge from oppressive agrarian socioeconomic circumstances to exploit lapses in control. They often employ violence in attacking members of the ruling elite and their property and in establishing alternative realms of sovereignty.[7] In John 10:8, Jesus used the

---

[6] Also Rensberger, *Johannine Faith* 93; Bond, *Pontius Pilate* 181; Lincoln, *Truth on Trial* 129.

[7] Richard A. Horsley with John S. Hanson, *Bandits, Prophets, and Messiahs: Popular Movements at the Time of Jesus* (San Francisco: Harper & Row, 1985) 48–87; Brent Shaw, "Bandits in the Roman Empire," *Past and Present* 102 (1984) 3–52.

same word "bandits" to identify leaders who harm God's people (the sheep) by not heeding God's/Jesus' voice.

There are several ironies in their choice. In preferring Barabbas (no reason is given), they reject Jesus as one who comes from God and reveals God's life and kingship. In choosing Barabbas they hold an impromptu referendum on preferred means of opposition to the Roman empire, either violence against it or its demise at Jesus' return. They opt for violence, a form of resistance that Rome has shown it can overcome! Ironically, in 11:48 the Jerusalem leaders feared that Jesus' nonviolent but disruptive teaching and actions would provoke Rome's action against them, yet now they call for the release of a violent revolutionary! The gospel ridicules them, exposing their contradictions and lack of integrity. Violence, though, is not God's way. The followers of Jesus live an alternative existence committed to service, not domination (13:12-20), awaiting the completion of God's purposes and the end of all forces of sin and death, including Rome.

Scene Four: Pilate has Jesus Whipped (19:13)

Pilate responds to their appeal not to release Jesus by having him flogged. Such flogging is degrading and usually preceded crucifixion. Some argue that this act is intended to placate the Jerusalem leaders, but it is hard to imagine that whipping Jesus and releasing him would satisfy people who wanted him dead! Rather, Pilate's action is consistent with his previous agreement to remove Jesus. He is preparing to put Jesus to death. Yet while Pilate honors his agreement with the Jerusalem elite, he continues to reinforce their inferiority. The flogging brutally demonstrates the futility of any aspirations for independence from Rome. The whipping asserts Pilate's control, their status as subjects, and his intolerance for any resistance to Rome. It is an act of imperial violence and intimidation.

Pilate's torture of Jesus is not only physical. Pilate's soldiers mock Jesus with a fake coronation or investiture as king. "Crown" and "robe" are traditional symbols of ruling power, domination, and wealth (1 Macc 8:14; 10:20; 2 Macc 4:38), precisely the opposite of the servant community Jesus establishes (John 13:12-17). The crown and robe imitate the laurel wreath and purple robe worn by the emperor (also identified as "king"). In this conflict between Rome's emperor and king/emperor Jesus there is no doubt in anyone's mind as to the winner. A leader of the Jewish revolt against Rome in 70 C.E., Simon son of Gioras, surrendered to Rome in a purple cloak and was executed in Vespasian's triumph in Rome. But amidst this display of Roman power and intimidation there is an irony. In calling Jesus "king" these Gentiles speak more truly than they know.

Scene 5: Pilate and "the Jews" (19:4-7)

Pilate parades Jesus outside before the Jerusalem elite (19:4-5). The repetition of the details of Jesus' kingly attire in 19:5 emphasizes the conflict over sovereignty and rule that pervades the scene. Jesus demonstrates what happens to Jews who claim kingship without Rome's consent. Pilate's repeated comment that he finds no case against Jesus again can hardly be serious, given his involvement in Jesus' arrest, previous humiliations of the elite, and the whipping of Jesus. Rather, Pilate continues to display his power and his blindness about Jesus, to mock the subjugated political situation of the Jewish leaders by humiliating and bullying this kingly pretender, and to reinforce their dependence on him.

Pilate's dramatic announcement "Behold the man" is a disdainful taunt (this pathetic specimen is *your* king!). But ironically, the taunt is a poor choice of words that undercuts Roman claims. The term "man" invokes the title "Son of Man" from earlier in the gospel. In 1:51 this title "Son of Man" identifies Jesus as the revealer of God's purposes. In 5:27-28 Jesus is the eschatological judge, in the tradition of Daniel 7, who exercises God's judgment over all (including the ruling powers now condemning him to death). "Son of Man" is also used in association with Jesus' "lifting up," a phrase the gospel uses to describe his crucifixion, resurrection, and ascension to God. His death is the means of his return to God, of giving life to many, and anticipates his triumphant return to earth (3:14; 8:28; 12:23, 32-34). That is, Pilate's parody is exposed in the very words he chooses. The one whom he mocks is none other than the eschatological judge, the revealer of God's saving purposes. Pilate cannot see it. He condemns himself in his own words.

Pilate's taunt again forces the Jerusalem leaders, "the chief priests and the police," to recognize Pilate's superior power and their own dependence on him. Dutifully they shout (beg?) for Jesus' crucifixion (19:6). This is the first specific reference to the means of putting Jesus to death (18:31). The narrative assumes its audience knows about crucifixion. The Jewish writer Josephus described this death penalty as the "most pitiable of deaths" (*Jewish War* 7.203).

- Crucifixion was a distinctively Roman form of execution.

- It was reserved by Rome for non-citizens, foreigners, those of little status (like slaves), those who posed a political or social threat, violent criminals, the non-elite. Roman citizens who committed treason (and so were not worthy to be citizens) could be crucified.

- Crucifixion removed those who were not welcome in Roman-controlled society. It divided the acceptable from the unacceptable,

the vulnerable from the powerful, the non-cooperative from the compliant. It was a symbol of shame, humiliation, pain, and social rejection.

- Crucifixion meant a painful death. Crucified people could take days to die and sometimes died from being mauled by wild beasts and birds while on the cross.

- Crucifixion was used as a deterrent and social control. There were no special crucifixion places out of public sight. Crucifixions were very public and visible, often near scenes of crimes or busy roads and gathering places. The message for passersby was clear.

- Flogging and carrying one's cross beam were part of the pre-crucifixion torture and social humiliation.

Pilate continues to mock the elite with his flip response, "Take him yourself and crucify him" (19:6). He knows they have no such power (18:31), and the involvement of his troops in Jesus' arrest indicates his consent to use this power (18:3, 12). He has the power of life and death; allies of Rome have only what Rome allows. Ironically, in calling for Jesus' crucifixion the leaders demand that Jesus be lifted up, the very means by which he said he will draw all people to himself (12:32-34).

New Tactics: In the face of the governor's taunts and inaction, the Jerusalem elite change tactics. They remind Pilate, who already knows about Jesus' kingship, of another aspect of Jesus' offensiveness. Jesus has claimed to be Son of God, God's agent (5:17-20; 10:30-39), and according to Lev 24:16 he should die for such blasphemy or dishonoring of God. This would seem to be a good tactic for four reasons.

1. Pilate has respected their religious commitments and practices. He has not forced them to enter his headquarters before Passover, but three times has gone outside to them (18:28, 29, 38b; 19:4).

2. Their request expresses dependence on Pilate. They have previously tried to stone Jesus without success (8:59; 10:31), so now they ask for Pilate's help to carry out the sentence.

3. While Pilate has cruelly and repeatedly reminded them of their dependence on him, their request, phrased in terms of their traditions, reminds Pilate that this is a partnership. He needs to act on their behalf to ensure their cooperation. The narrative demonstrates a typical expedient, imperial, power-sharing arrangement among the elite!

4. The language of "Son of God" was common kingship language, and was applied to various emperors, so they return the emphasis to Jesus' threat as a "King of the Jews" not sanctioned by Rome (18:33, 37).

The opponents' charge that Jesus made himself son of God has been the focus of two previous disputes (5:18; 10:33). The titles "Son" and "son of God" have been common through the gospel. They derive from the Hebrew Scriptures, where they describe people in close relationship with God who are agents of God's purposes: kings in the line of David who represent God's rule forever (Ps 2:2, 6, 7; 2 Sam 7:13-14), the people Israel (Hos 11:1), the wise person (Wisdom 2). The term denotes Jesus' identity and mission as God's agent or commissioned representative sent by God, from heaven, to manifest God's purposes. In calling for Jesus' crucifixion the elite rejects any such claim and so rejects God's purposes. The gospel's audience recognizes an irony in that it knows that Jesus did not make himself anything; he is God's son from the beginning (1:1-3, 18).

Scene Six: Pilate and Jesus (19:8-12)

The change of tactic gets Pilate's attention, but it is not clear why he becomes "very afraid." As a Roman he knows that gods could be sons of other gods (Hermes was son of Zeus). Humans with exceptional abilities or actions were called divine, and emperors were called sons of gods. Does he fear that Jesus is some sort of extraordinary religious being who might have some power over him? Does he especially associate this title with his previous questions to Jesus about being king of the Jews? Has he heard the leaders' description as an accusation that his inaction shows he is not taking the situation seriously enough? Or does he fear because their (unintended) proclamation of Jesus' identity again, ironically, puts him in a crisis that requires a momentous decision and response to Jesus' claims?

Whatever the reason for his fear, Pilate returns to ask Jesus the gospel's most important question, "where are you from?" (19:9). The gospel began by showing that Jesus comes from God (1:1-18), and throughout its length various characters have wrestled with the issue of his origin (3:34; 6:33, 41-2; 7:25-29: 16:27-28). To know Jesus' origin is to know his authority and legitimacy. To accept that Jesus is from God is to know one's own identity and allegiance (8:39-47). But Jesus does not answer. He had answered Pilate's question in 18:36-37 about the origin of his kingship from God, but Pilate wasn't listening. Like the suffering servant of Isa 53:7, Jesus adopts the classic pose of the powerless (who accomplish God's redeeming purposes!) before the "powerful."

Pilate interprets Jesus' silence as defiance. He will be answered. Impatiently, he tries to intimidate Jesus. He asserts complete power over Jesus by boasting that he has power to release or to crucify (19:10). Basic to this claim again is the issue of sovereignty. Pilate thinks that his will is being done, that the interests of Roman power are being furthered. The matter is very political; death threats by the state are always political. Pilate uses the death sentence to coerce compliance in his society.

Jesus is not intimidated, but Pilate does at least get Jesus to talk. His response, though, is probably not what Pilate wanted to hear. Jesus puts Pilate's claims and power into perspective by contextualizing them in God's purposes (19:11). Jesus recognizes that Pilate has power to kill him. But Jesus also claims that that power is given to Pilate "from above," from God to accomplish God's purpose (4:34). Jesus lays down his life (10:17-18). His crucifixion lies within God's purposes. It is not Pilate's or Rome's victory.

This theological interpretation of historical events, specifically the claim that earthly rulers carry out God's will even without recognizing it, is common in the Scriptures. Babylon defeats Jerusalem without knowing that it thereby enacts God's punishment (2 Kings 24:1-7). Cyrus the Persian ruler defeats Babylon in 539 B.C.E. and lets the Judean exiles return home, without knowing he accomplishes God's purposes of salvation (Isa 44:28; 45:1). This theological perspective undermines the claims of empires and rulers like Pilate to have absolute power by setting them in the context of God's greater, though often unseen, purposes. While Pilate can and will put Jesus to death, his goal of controlling a threat to the empire's world will not be accomplished. Rather, God's purposes will be furthered, purposes that are not good news for Rome!

But this theological perspective does not exonerate Pilate from responsibility. Jesus identifies Pilate's action as "sin." In John's gospel sin consists primarily of not believing Jesus' revelation about God (8:24). Pilate does not recognize Jesus as God's agent. But as of this moment in the story Pilate has not yet handed Jesus over for crucifixion. Judas has done so (6:64; 18:2, 5), as has the Jewish leadership (18:30, 35-36). As of this moment their sin is greater. But Pilate is about to join them (19:16).

Pilate responds to Jesus' words by trying, for the first time, to release him (19:12). What motivates this attempt is not stated, but it has to be understood in relation to his previous commitment to arrest Jesus and, in whipping him, to crucify him. He has no intention of releasing Jesus, but continues to taunt the Jerusalem leaders with reminders of their subservient status. Each time his taunts bring forth expressions of dependency as they plead with the governor to act according to their wishes (see 18:31-32, 39-40; 19:4-6)

The same pattern is evident here. The Jerusalem leaders respond with another display of subservience and loyalty to Rome. They remind Pilate of his responsibilities and spell out Jesus' threat to Pilate in very personal terms. To release Jesus, one who claims to be King of the Jews and the agent of God's purposes as God's son, is to betray Rome's interests. Pilate would fail to do his job of upholding the "peace" of the empire and the power of the emperor. He would not be the emperor's friend or reliable servant, a trustworthy client deserving the emperor's patronage, if he were to release someone who has committed treason in claiming kingship without out Rome's consent. Their statement succinctly summarizes Jesus' threat: He asserts a sovereignty that challenges Rome's. The ruling alliance, both Rome and Jerusalem, cannot tolerate this assertion.

Scene Seven:
Pilate Pronounces Sentence (19:13-16a)

Now Pilate acts. They have explained Jesus' claim to be son of God (19:5) in political and personal terms. Jesus is a king who threatens Caesar's interests, which Pilate is supposed to be upholding. Pilate chooses to be a friend of the emperor rather than a friend of Jesus (15:14-15). So for the second time he brings Jesus out and sits on the judge's bench, the raised platform outside his headquarters. Verse 14 notes the time, emphasizing the Passover context first mentioned in the scene's opening verse (18:28). Pilate condemns Jesus, thinking that he asserts control but without "seeing" that he rejects and enables God's work of effecting another liberation from imperial control.

Pilate maintains the focus on the issue of sovereignty and allegiance by identifying Jesus as "your King." He again taunts the Jerusalem leaders with a reminder of their subjugation and a warning of what happens to those who resist Roman control. The elite (John, unlike the other gospels, mentions no crowd) distances itself from Jesus by shouting again for his crucifixion (19:15). The shout rejects God's agent and embraces Rome's sovereignty. Pilate further secures their loyalty by asking again if he should crucify "your king." Again they reject any identification with Jesus by choosing Rome: "We have no king but the emperor."

Pilate has gained an amazing declaration! With these words the Jerusalem leaders repudiate their centuries-old covenant with God as Israel's king (1 Sam 8:7; Pss 47:2; 93:1). God's kingship was manifested in the Davidic king (2 Sam 7:11-16), who as God's son represented God's rule (Pss 2:7; 72:1). The Jerusalem leaders are supposed to represent and foster this covenant with God as king among the people! But with these words

they abandon their heritage and calling. They renounce the biblical traditions and aspirations that looked for God's just and life-giving reign to be established over God's creation and over all empires (like Rome's) that resist God's purposes (Isa 2:1-4). Their cry is a complete vote of support for the way things are. They who in 8:33 claimed never to have been slaves of anyone enslave themselves to Rome and recognize the emperor's, not God's, rule. But in a sense none of this is a surprise. The narrative of their cry simply reveals their "true" commitments, which have been operative throughout the story as they reject Jesus, God's anointed agent!

Having drawn from them this amazing statement of loyalty to Rome and renunciation of their heritage, Pilate hands Jesus over to be crucified (19:16). The use of the same verb ("hands over") to describe the actions of Judas (18:2, 5), the Jerusalem elite (18:30, 35), and now Pilate (19:16) allies them as "the world" in opposition to and rejection of God's purposes, and in support of the world over which they presently rule.

Pilate's Last Appearance (19:19-22)

Pilate appears once more, two verses later. Jesus is being crucified according to Pilate's command (19:17-18). Pilate insists on a notice for Jesus' cross that reads "Jesus of Nazareth, King of the Jews" (19:21). The notice is written in three languages so that everyone can understand it. Jesus is Pilate's visual aid, a poster boy for the futility of rebelling against Roman rule. Jesus' crucifixion comprises another aspect of Pilate's campaign to intimidate coercion and to silence Jewish aspirations for independence.

Pilate's allies, the Jerusalem elite, predictably resent the humiliation contained in Pilate's wording. They try to distance themselves from it. They ask Pilate to qualify his notice by adding the words, "This man said, 'I am the king of the Jews.'" Pilate refuses. He remains the tough and efficient Roman governor who mocks and subjugates his Jewish allies and who does not "see" God's purposes at work.

But again the narrative undermines his claims. While Pilate intends that his notice will intimidate and coerce compliance, ironically it proclaims Jesus' identity as the king who represents God's reign and identifies the cross as a place of coronation! In Jesus' resurrection God's reign will be seen to be more powerful than Rome's empire that is unable to keep Jesus dead. And in Jesus' return God's reign will have the final word at Rome's expense. Pilate's notice anticipates such realities. At the very moment of Pilate's apparent triumph the narrative ironically sets his actions in a larger context of God's purposes that Pilate cannot see, and in which he will not do well.

But his Jerusalem allies fare no better. In fact, they share Pilate's dilemma. Their amendment to Pilate's proclamation, the addition of the words "This man said, 'I am . . .'" does the same thing. This change would highlight the words "I am," words that Jesus has used to emphasize his identity as God's revealer. As much as Pilate wants to assert superiority over his Jerusalem allies, the narrative allies them closely as futile and unseeing opponents of God's purposes. Even in declaring their supposed triumph and Jesus' defeat, they end up together proclaiming Jesus' identity and God-given mission. Unknowingly they further God's purposes that will destroy their power and pretensions.

Conclusion

John's Pilate is an efficient and powerful governor who in crucifying Jesus protects Rome's interests against this threat. He walks a fine line between working with his Jerusalem allies to remove Jesus (even showing some respect for their religious customs) and repeatedly taunting them about their defeated status and keeping them in their subservient place as a people dependent on him. At the close of the scene he skillfully elicits an amazing declaration of their loyalty to Rome. Pilate also clearly chooses loyalty to the emperor (who gave him this job) rather than openness to God's purposes that he cannot see. But throughout, the scene employs considerable irony to offer glimpses into God's larger purposes about which Pilate has no clue and that will eventually mean the demise of the very system Pilate represents so efficiently.

For John's audience the scene demonstrates that the Roman empire is not committed to God's purposes. Rather, the empire is part of "the world." It cannot see what God is doing, and resists it by defending its own interests. John's audience is always faced with a choice of loyalties, between King Jesus and Rome's emperor. But that choice is not just an individual, private, and personal one. It has profound sociopolitical implications. The audience cannot give up on "the world" and retreat from it, but carries out its mission precisely in and to the world (17:18; 20:21). That mission does not mean violence against, nor does it mean peaceful coexistence with the empire. Rather it means telling the "truth," lovingly proclaiming God's saving purposes (18:37). The scene warns the gospel's audience that often this mission will not be well received, that the empire will strike back. But conflict, even death, is not defeat. Even in the midst of displays of apparently untouchable Roman power God's purposes for a different order, one marked by God's just and abundant reign, are being worked out.

CONCLUSION

We have engaged each of the four gospels to delineate their portraits of Pilate. Some similarities are evident, but so too are some significant differences. We have especially paid attention to the impact of Roman imperial realities on these scenes. Our conclusions challenge the conventional portrait of Pilate, the weak governor who thinks Jesus is not guilty but does not have enough strength of character to reject the Jewish demands for Jesus' execution.

Mark's Pilate is a powerful and skillful governor who efficiently represents and protects Roman interests. Early in the scene he establishes that Jesus is guilty of treason in claiming to be king. Through his astute use of his alliance with the Jerusalem leaders and some very carefully worded questions he manages to execute one who claims to be an occupied people's king with the people's support! Not only are there no riots against his action, but he manages to elicit the people's support for removing one who (nonviolently) challenges the empire. In contemporary terms, he is an astute pollster and manipulator of public opinion. But Mark's scene subtly frames Pilate's actions in the larger context of God's purposes that will, finally, mean the downfall of Pilate and his empire.

Matthew's Pilate is presented in quite similar terms. He is astute, powerful, and efficient in furthering the elite's interests. Matthew's narrative emphasizes Pilate's central role in the action, the inevitability of Jesus' condemnation because of the elite alliances, and Pilate's arrogant and dramatic celebration of his accomplishment in having the people claim responsibility for Jesus' death. Throughout, the scene exposes the self-interested nature of Roman justice by focusing on Pilate's misleading "for you" claims as he manipulates the people into doing the elite's will of killing Jesus. Matthew's scene also frames his actions in the context of God's purposes, about which Pilate has no clue.

Of the four portraits only Luke's Pilate does not find Jesus either guilty or a threat. He seems arrogantly uninterested in Jesus and tries to avoid dealing with him by sending him to Herod. He is dismissive of his

allies, the Jerusalem elite, and their concern over Jesus' threat, and he is dismissive of Jesus, finally crucifying him under pressure. Pilate emerges as an arrogant representative of Rome's power. He remains completely oblivious to God's transforming, challenging, nonviolent, unfinished reign at work in the midst of his empire.

John's Pilate is also an efficient and powerful governor who protects the elite's interests in removing Jesus. As the involvement of Roman troops in Jesus' arrest suggests, Pilate has already decided on Jesus' fate. He confirms quickly that Jesus does treasonously claim to be a king. Thereafter Pilate continually frustrates and humiliates his allies with reminders of their subjugated status and dependence on him as they beg him to crucify Jesus. By the end of the scene he cleverly gains from them an amazing repudiation of their covenantal heritage and an astounding confession of their undivided loyalty to Rome. John's narrative casts its theological verdict on Pilate. He belongs to the world that rejects God. He cannot "see" what God is doing.

Pilate on Trial

In reading these trial scenes and their diverse portraits of Pilate, it is hard not to reverse the roles and put Pilate on trial. We have noticed the consistent irony that while Pilate casts judgment on Jesus he also judges himself. Jesus, so the narratives claim, will share with God in judging and ruling the world, including Pilate. That is an unenviable position for Pilate to be in, and one that is hardly an even contest. How might Pilate give account of himself? What defense strategies might he employ?

1. I Was Only Doing My Job

He could plead that he was only doing his job. He was only following orders, playing it by the book, implementing company policy, looking out for the boss's bottom line, representing the firm, doing what he was paid the big bucks to do, being a loyal employee, supporting the system, doing what he ought to have done. And so he was. As governor he was obligated to protect and further Roman elite interests. That means removing perceived troublemakers. And as we have seen, he was very good at it: manipulating crowds and leaders into wonderful affirmations of loyalty, cooperating with as well as intimidating his local allies.

Pilate has a point. The nation, the corporation, the firm, the revolutionary cause can swallow up the individual in displays of allegiance. In a

sense Pilate can be seen as a classic model of one whose personhood is overwhelmed by his commitment to a larger system. There is always a price to be paid for committing oneself to such a system. And Pilate, at least as the gospel narratives present him, seems very willing to pay.

If Pilate argued his defense in this way, his attempt to avoid responsibility poses some big and crucial questions. Should the orders be followed? Was the policy just? Should it be implemented? Is the bottom line always the final consideration? Was the nation/firm worth representing, the system/cause worth supporting? Had Pilate considered the merits of the empire to which he had pledged loyalty? Is a system that exploits and oppresses the majority for the benefit of a few ever worth one's life, then or now? What sort of system is it that requires its representatives not to thoughtfully evaluate its demands? Is it worth one's loyalties?

The intriguing part is that such questions are also very modern. In questioning Pilate we question ourselves. Of course the Roman empire has gone (something Pilate could not have imagined, though Jesus did!). But if empires are about extending power and influence over territory, resources, and human lives, empires are very much part of our contemporary scene. They come in different shapes and sizes: the nation state, the capitalist system, oppressive regimes, multinationals, "the firm," religious groups, educational institutions, personal circles. . . . Pilate's issues become questions for us about our loyalties and commitments, about the values and worth, the impact and consequences, the benefits and harm of what we represent, defend, advocate. These questions confront anyone in contemporary political, business, and religious life who is brave enough—and honest enough—to ask and answer them.

2. I Was the Wrong Person in the Wrong Place at the Wrong Time

As a second possible defense Pilate could plead that fate simply stacked the deck against him. He just happened to be governor of Judea at this time. He was fated, cursed if you like, to play a part. It was hopeless to resist. He was caught up in great impersonal forces that were beyond his control. He played his allotted part in a great cosmic drama. Fate made him do it and he should not be held responsible.

Pilate has a point. Empires and the forcible occupation of a people's land put in motion forces that are bigger than any one person, beyond any one person's control. So does any system of political power, economic activity, and religious organization. But Pilate actively participated in this system. Gubernatorial appointments don't just happen. They are sought, lobbied, networked. People can choose not to seek the wealth, glory, power

that usually come on the backs of others, then and now. Pilate did not so choose. Whatever the larger forces, he is responsible for his decisions and participation.

3. I Did the Best I Could

Or third, Pilate could plead that knowing the right thing to do in any situation is desperately difficult. In making those decisions one can only turn to one's upbringing, experience, training, community, job. Pilate arguably weighed the factors and made what appeared to be the best decision in the circumstances.

Pilate has a point. Human societies and lives are always complex and we have to make difficult decisions constantly. Knowing the right thing to do or say is often a challenge. But in arguing this defense Pilate seems oblivious to the unsatisfactory basis for his decision. Certainly he made his decision according to his upbringing, experiences, and position. But such a context is a closed circuit, and very dangerous because it is so limited. Pilate (as far as we can tell) was brought up as one of the elite; his experiences were those of the privileged few; his position was designed to protect the elite's interests! Pilate shows little interest in listening to or considering the situation of a low-status person like Jesus. That is, his perspective was narrow and privileged, not tested by any genuine openness to other perspectives, other values, other commitments. Because of his upbringing and experience he has little clue about how most of his subjects live, and even less desire to find out.

To put it another way, his understanding of the "common social good" was to maintain and protect the privileges that elite people like himself enjoyed, literally at the expense of the rest. The prisoner Jesus offered him a vastly different experience and vision of the "common social good." Jesus offered him a much less hierarchical and much more inclusive society marked by service, not domination. But Pilate found him to be too challenging to Roman interests and power. Pilate protects a seriously deficient view of the "common good" that was neither "common" (since most people did not benefit from it) nor "good" (since it inflicted considerable suffering and hardship on most of the population). Discerning the good and the bad is a vital human skill in which Pilate seems sadly deficient.

4. God Trapped Me But God Couldn't Have Done It Without Me

Fourth, Pilate could play the "blame" card. He could plead entrapment. He could claim that he was an unknowing and unwilling pawn in

God's purposes that, according to the gospel narratives, are being worked out in Jesus' death. In raising Jesus from the dead, God exposes the limits of Rome's power and the ultimate emptiness of its intimidating threats because it cannot keep Jesus dead. Jesus overcomes the worst that the sinful, rejecting empire can produce, for the benefit of millions of believers.

As we have seen, Pilate has no clue about these divine purposes. Yet he could plead that he plays an indispensable part in them. God could not have carried out this saving work without Pilate! What would have happened if Pilate had not handed Jesus over to be crucified? Was Pilate, then, merely a puppet with God pulling the strings? Was his free will violated? Did he have no control over what he was doing? Perhaps Pilate ought to be thanked for what he did! Perhaps he should be hailed as a saint, rather than tried as a villain as some in the church's history have concluded (see Chapter One). God couldn't have done it without him!

Again Pilate has a point. According to the gospel narratives God was at work in Jesus' death. They make this claim with twenty-twenty hindsight, some forty to fifty years later. But how was Pilate to know this? How was he supposed to discern God at work in this kingly pretender from Galilee? How was he to know for sure? How does anyone know what God is doing (if anything), when, where, and how? Are skepticism and faith opposite ends of a spectrum or two sides of the same coin?

But blaming God will not relieve Pilate of his own responsibility. There is no doubt that discerning whether God exists and what God might be about are big challenges for anyone at any time, and not everyone shares the gospel writers' confidence about these issues. But Pilate had opportunity to find out from his accused prisoner what God was doing, and he did not even take his opportunity. Pilate asks very few questions of Jesus, spends little energy or time in investigating him, does not listen to him, and reaches a hasty, self-interested conclusion. Pilate chose to conduct himself and make his decisions without reference to God and without any effort in investigating the issues. In fact, he chose to represent a system that opposed God's purposes for human society in which all have access to the resources they need to sustain life. God did not turn him into a robot, but worked in and around Pilate's decisions.

5. The Jews Made Me Do It

Fifth, instead of (as well as?) blaming God, he could blame his allies, the Jerusalem elite. These leaders made him do it. They twisted his arm. They manipulated the crowd to call for Jesus' crucifixion and backed Pilate into a corner. What option did he have if he was to save face?

Does Pilate have a point? Only if we ignore basic realities of his imperial situation! As I have argued in Chapters Four through Seven, this line of reasoning has often provided Pilate with an escape hatch. The Christian tradition has often (very regrettably and tragically) employed this "blame-the-Jews" approach to relieve Pilate of all responsibility.

But it is not so easy. First, the Jerusalem leaders are his allies. He appoints the chief priests. Their interests are his interests. If they find someone to be threatening their interests, that person threatens Pilate's interests also. Second, Pilate as governor is not weak. No one twists his arm. He has military, political, economic, and religious sanctions to accomplish whatever he wants. Pilate could have resisted his allies if he chose. But while he mocks and humiliates them (especially in Luke and John), he does not go against them. He cannot afford to. He has too much to lose. Instead he works with them. Third, Pilate oversaw a judicial system that was biased against low-status defendants in every way. This system was set up as an instrument of the elite's control over society. Pilate happily participated in and administered this system. He had power to resist it. But he didn't. He used it to further his own interests in removing Jesus. This time Pilate does not have a point.

6. I Did Nothing Wrong

Finally, Pilate could proudly refuse to take any responsibility, just as numerous other leaders in history have done.[1] He could refuse to second-guess himself. He could deny any wrongdoing. He could assert that he acted as he should have done in the circumstances and that he would do exactly the same thing again. He represented the emperor's interests as faithfully as possible, as he was supposed to do. One's nation deserves loyalty and unquestioning duty ahead of all else, and if someone like Jesus has

[1] Two recent examples: Slobodan Milosevic, the former President of Yugoslavia, has been charged before the United Nations' War Crimes Tribunal with crimes against humanity stemming from atrocities (including murder, deportation, and prosecution of people on political, racial, and ethnic grounds) committed against ethnic Albanians in Kosovo in 1999. He is reported to have declared in a television interview, "I am proud for everything I did in defending my country and my people. All my decisions are legitimate and legal . . ." (CNN, August 24, 2001; July 3, 2001). George H. W. Bush, while campaigning to be elected President of the United States, responded to the shooting down of an Iranian airliner on July 3, 1988 by the U.S.S. *Vincennes* with the loss of 290 civilian passengers by saying, "I will never apologize for the United States. I don't care what the facts are" (cited in L. H. Lapham, "The American Rome: On the Theory of Virtuous Empire," *Harper's Magazine* 303, no. 1815 (August 2001) 31–38, especially 35–36.

a problem with that he deserves to be executed. The end justifies the means. Pilate did a patriotic thing in faithfully removing a subversive enemy and there is nothing for which he has to answer.

Pilate has a point. It is precisely such unquestioning loyalty, the love that asks no questions, that numerous political, economic, and religious systems have cultivated and rewarded. The most feared thing for such systems is to do what Jesus did, namely to utter that highly dangerous observation, "It does not have to be this way." Pilate knew the danger of that thought, and in at least three of the gospel narratives (the exception being Luke), he actively ensured Jesus' death.

But there is an irony here. Pilate's defense in this option is that he acted appropriately, faithfully, loyally. As we saw in the last chapter, those are crucial dimensions of what John's gospel calls "truth." Pilate was interested enough to ask "what is truth?" but unfortunately not interested enough to wait for the answer. Pilate's question raised an important issue: loyalty to what? For John truth is about living faithfully to God's purposes for a just world. That was not Pilate's truth. Pilate's truth or loyalty or faithfulness was to an empire that in its very structures established, protected, maintained, and advocated injustice to the huge detriment of most of its subjects. Loyalty can be very commendable, but the key question concerns the object of loyalty. What is our truth?

Pilate: A Verdict?

Pilate has often provoked people's curiosity precisely because all of us experience similar dilemmas and issues. Is doing one's duty always the best thing? Do we have an option? How do we decide on the "best thing?" What is the balance, if any, between our own interests and those of others? How do we know what is "worthy" of our loyalty? What do our lives represent? What or who are we committed to and how worthwhile are our commitments? What impact, positive and negative, do they have on others? How do we know and encounter God's purposes in the midst of daily life? How do we live in tune with those purposes? What happens if we don't?

Pilate's actions as presented in the four gospel portraits raise these sorts of questions. The verdict we offer on any of these portraits is likely to say as much about ourselves as about Pontius Pilate, Roman Governor.

BIBLIOGRAPHY OF
CLASSICAL WORKS CITED

Aristides. "Roman Oration." In J. H. Oliver, "The Ruling Power: A Study of the Roman Empire in the Second Century After Christ Through the Roman Oration of Aelius Aristides," *Transactions of the American Philosophical Society* 43/4 (1953) 895–907, 982–91.

Cicero. "Pro Fonteio." In *Cicero*. 28 vols. Vol. 24. Translated by N. H. Watts. Loeb Classical Library. Cambridge, Mass.: Harvard University Press, 1931.

_____. "The Letters to His Brother Quintus." In *Cicero*. 28 vols. Vol. 28. Translated by W. Glynn Williams, M.A. Loeb Classical Library. Cambridge, Mass.: Harvard University Press, 1953.

"Didache." In *Apostolic Fathers*. 2 vols. Vol. 2. Loeb Classical Library. Cambridge, Mass.: Harvard University Press, 1913.

Hermas. "The Shepherd of Hermas." In *Apostolic Fathers*. 2 vols. Vol. 2. Translated by Kirsopp Lake. Loeb Classical Library. Cambridge, Mass.: Harvard University Press, 1913.

Josephus. "The Life Against Apion," "The Jewish War," and "Jewish Antiquities." *Josephus*. 9 vols. Translated by H. St. J. Thackeray, M. A., Ralph Marcus, and Louis H. Feldman. Loeb Classical Library. Cambridge, Mass.: Harvard University Press, 1926–1963.

Juvenal. "Satire VIII." In *Juvenal*. Translated by G. G. Ramsay. Loeb Classical Library. Cambridge, Mass.: Harvard University Press, 1918.

Philo. "In Flaccum." In *Philo*. 10 vols. Vol. 9. Translated by F. H. Colson. Loeb Classical Library. Cambridge, Mass.: Harvard University Press, 1941.

_____. "Embassy to Gaius." In *Philo*. 10 vols. Vol. 10. Translated by F. H. Colson. Loeb Classical Library. Cambridge, Mass.: Harvard University Press, 1962.

Pliny. "The Letters of Pliny." In *Pliny*. 10 vols. Vol. 2. Translated by Betty Radice. Loeb Classical Library. Cambridge, Mass.: Harvard University Press, 1969.

Plutarch. "Brutus." In *Lives*. 11 vols. Vol. 6. Translated by Bernadotte Perrin. Loeb Classical Library. Cambridge, Mass.: Harvard University Press, 1918.

_____. "How to Tell a Flatterer From a Friend." In *Moralia*. 16 vols. Vol.1. Translated by Frank Cole Babbitt. Loeb Classical Library. Cambridge, Mass.: Harvard University Press, 1927.

_____. "Virtue and Vice." In *Moralia*. 16 vols. Vol. 2. Translated by Frank Cole Babbitt. Loeb Classical Library. Cambridge, Mass.: Harvard University Press, 1928.

_____. "Philosophers and Men in Power." In *Moralia*. 16 vols. Vol. 10. Translated by Harold North Fowler. Loeb Classical Library. Cambridge, Mass.: Harvard University Press, 1936.

_____. "Precepts of Statecraft." In *Moralia*. 16 vols. Vol. 10. Translated by Harold North Fowler. Loeb Classical Library. Cambridge, Mass.: Harvard University Press, 1936.

Seneca. "On Mercy." In *Moral Essays*. 3 vols. Vol. 1. Translated by John Basore. Loeb Classical Library. Cambridge, Mass.: Harvard University Press, 1928.

Suetonius. "The Deified Vespasian." In *Suetonius*. 2 vols. Vol. 2. Translated by J. C. Rolfe. Loeb Classical Library. Cambridge, Mass.: Harvard University Press, 1913–14.

Tacitus. "Agricola." In *Tacitus*. 5 vols. Vol. 1. Translated by M. Hutton. Loeb Classical Library. Cambridge, Mass.: Harvard University Press, 1914.

Tacitus. "The Annals." In *Tacitus*. 5 vols. Vols. 1-5. Translated by John Jackson and Clifford Moore. Loeb Classical Library. Cambridge, Mass.: Harvard University Press, 1925–37.

Tertullian. "Apologeticus" and "De Spectaculis." In *Tertullian*. Translated by T. R. Glover. Loeb Classical Library. Cambridge, Mass.: Harvard University Press, 1931.

Virgil. "Aeneid." In *Virgil*. 2 vols. Vols. 1-2. Translated by H. Rushton Fairclough. Loeb Classical Library. Cambridge, Mass.: Harvard University Press, 1916–18.